DAVID FELLMAN
Vilas Professor of Political Science
University of Wisconsin
ADVISORY EDITOR TO DODD, MEAD & COMPANY

THE SOVIET POLITY

Government and Politics in the U.S.S.R.

Sue Swanson
11-13-73

THE SOVIET POLITY

Government and Politics in the U.S.S.R.

JOHN S. RESHETAR, JR.
UNIVERSITY OF WASHINGTON

Dodd, Mead & Company
NEW YORK 1972 TORONTO

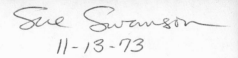

LIBRARY OF CONGRESS CATALOG CARD NUMBER: 76-143293
ISBN: 0-396-06315-2

THIRD PRINTING

PRINTED IN THE UNITED STATES OF AMERICA

PREFACE

THE purpose of this volume is to provide a reasonably thorough but relatively brief general exposition and discussion of Soviet politics. I have sought to provide an essentially eclectic approach to the subject, emphasizing institutional structures, functional analysis, the nature of the Soviet leadership, the principal components of Soviet political life, and the definition of the major problems confronting the Soviet polity. I have also sought to convey something of its ethos and have endeavored to deal with the question of the Soviet political culture. An effort has been made to enable the reader to relate the Soviet polity to other political systems—especially in Chapter 10, where a number of relevant models are analyzed and compared.

Where possible and relevant I have attempted to treat the Soviet polity in terms of problems and issues that are comparable to those confronted by other political systems. However, I have eschewed the direct imposition of a single mode of analysis, or of conceptual schema or a set of research categories that are derived essentially from the study of certain Western political systems. Although there is now a vast fund of knowledge regarding Soviet politics, there remain serious lacunae of the kind that do not burden the student of American politics, who is with unfailing regularity inundated by ever-increasing bodies of new empirical data, the results of survey research, efforts at theory-building, and the never-ending revelations of innumerable participants and observers. Unfortunately there are certain significant closed aspects of the Soviet polity, and some sources of data are denied the investigator. Two examples will suffice. Important, indeed vital, sources of personal testimony are lacking; honest memoirs by Molotov, Mikoyan, and Bulganin would provide invaluable data but are not to be had as yet. Field research in the Soviet Union by Western political scientists is severely circumscribed and can be conducted only on innocuous subjects and in the face of numerous obstacles.

It is always easier to raise questions than it is to provide acceptable answers. I have undertaken to deal with certain controversial aspects of the Soviet polity that have not received adequate attention. Thus I have dealt with certain aspects of Russian political experience that some might ignore or minimize, and in doing so I have advanced certain hypotheses. However, my purpose has been neither to denigrate nor to justify the Soviet polity but only to attempt to explain it.

In matters of transliteration I have generally followed Library of Congress usage except for certain minor modifications. I have employed commonly accepted spellings of certain Russian proper names in English (Trotsky, Berdyaev), and I have usually employed "x" in lieu of "ks" in names. I have sought to avoid anglicizing plural forms of Russian names and have usually employed the Russian plural form instead.

During the more than two decades that I have concerned myself with the study of Soviet political phenomena I have benefited from the counsel, research, and example of far more colleagues than can be acknowledged in a brief preface. To some extent my debt is recognized in the citation of various works. In particular, I wish to thank certain of my colleagues in the Russian and East European Studies Program at the University of Washington for advice on several matters and Professor John A. Armstrong of the University of Wisconsin for his counsel. I am grateful to Mr. William Oman and to Professors David Fellman and William Livingston for their encouragement, patience, and advice, and to the editorial staff of the College Department of Dodd, Mead & Company for their aid. My wife deciphered my handwriting and typed the original draft of the manuscript and, most important, she patiently bore with the many inevitable inconveniences inflicted upon our household as a result of this enterprise. However, I alone am responsible for all sins of omission and commission, and for any errors of fact or judgment that may be found in the pages that follow.

JOHN S. RESHETAR, JR.

CONTENTS

THE SOVIET POLITY

Government and Politics in the U.S.S.R.

CHAPTER 1

THE U.S.S.R.: A MULTINATIONAL EMPIRE

There are compelling reasons for studying the political system of the Union of Soviet Socialist Republics. The world's third most populous country, the Soviet Union emerged from World War II as a great power. When it subsequently acquired a nuclear-weapons and missile capability and embarked upon space exploration, it acquired still greater importance. For political scientists the Soviet Union is also significant as the prototype of the twentieth-century totalitarian regime. As the first and oldest polity of this type the Soviet regime's future development is a matter of great interest. Furthermore, as a type of industrial system and as an urbanized society the Soviet Union offers an area of investigation for all the social sciences. Its efforts to provide a developmental model for Asian, African, and Latin American peoples also make the study of Soviet domestic politics and Russian political behavior relevant. The twentieth century has been confronted with the challenge of communism both as a doctrine and as a political system. Since the Soviet Union is the world's oldest communist regime, the study of Soviet political practice is essential to an understanding of what communism is and what it has to offer its adherents and subjects.

However, for a broader and more profound understanding of the contemporary Soviet Union it is necessary to be cognizant of its origins and of the nature and development of the Russian Empire from which it emerged. It is all too simple—and erroneous—to treat the Soviet polity as a homogeneous and fixed entity when, in fact, it is the result of a protracted process of development that involved the "gathering together" of diverse lands and peoples. In order to appreciate the complex composition and substance of the Soviet polity, it is important to view it initially with reference both to its precursor and its ethnic composition.

1. THE SOVIET UNION: SUCCESSOR TO THE RUSSIAN EMPIRE

The uninformed frequently equate the entire Soviet Union exclusively with Russia and incorrectly identify Soviet citizenship with being "Russian." In fact, the Russians constitute but a bare majority of the U.S.S.R. population. Prior to World War I the Russians had only a plurality of 43 percent of the population of the Russian Empire. The millions of non-Russians who have retained their sense of national identity despite Russian rule represent a broad variety of cultures, languages, and distinctive historical development which will be treated later. However, as the most numerous and dominant nationality in the Soviet Union, the Russians have always attracted greater attention.

The term "Russian" has at times been used indiscriminately (and incorrectly) to refer to all persons under Russian rule. Strictly defined, the term refers to the most numerous of the Slavic peoples, who began to emerge as an identifiable entity in the northern part of Eastern Europe in the period between the ninth and eleventh centuries. The Russians originated as an offshoot of the earlier Eastern Slavic population which had come to inhabit much of the central forested part of Eastern Europe, mingling with the indigenous Finnish population and acquiring other ethnic admixtures as well. The Eastern Slavs were originally divided into a number of different tribes to which the term "Russian" can hardly be applied. The term *Rus'* (probably of Scandinavian or Varangian origin), applied to the territory of the Eastern Slavs, was originally used in a territorial rather than an ethnic sense. Indeed, in the basic chronicle, *The Tale of Bygone Years* (*Povest' vremennykh let*), there is no reference to a Russian language (but in the entry under the year 1037 it is stated that translations were made from Greek into "Slavic writing"). The early Eastern Slavs did not constitute a homogeneous entity, let alone something that can be termed "Russian." Nor did they possess a single political jurisdiction. The chronicles make it clear that the Eastern Slavic tribes and the various principalities were often in conflict.

There was no political unity in *Rus'*, despite the existence of a single dynasty of Varangian origin (the successors of Rurik or Hrörekr); the various princes frequently engaged in fratricidal conflict. In 1169 Andrei Bogoliubsky, prince of Vladimir-Suzdal, sacked Kiev, the original seat of the Rurik dynasty and source of culture, thus demonstrating the lack of unity. As the tribes abandoned paganism the sole unity that *Rus'* acquired was based on a single Orthodox Christian ecclesiastical jurisdiction (the Kiev metropolitanate), usually headed by a Byzantine Greek.

Growth of the Russian Empire. Russia as a distinctive ethnic and political entity can be said to have developed in the area of the Vladimir-Suzdal principality, in which Muscovy (first referred to in the chronicles in 1147) emerged as the cradle of the Russian state and nation. The phenomenal growth of the Russian Empire from a territory of 15,000 square miles in the fifteenth century to a vast domain 570 times its original size four centuries later, furthermore, had its origins in the emergence and rise of the principality of Muscovy. Indeed, the Russian historian Vasilii O. Kliuchevsky has stated that Muscovy in the time of Ivan Kalita (1328–40) hardly extended over 500 square miles.[1] This process of expansion began with the acquisition by Muscovy of other Russian principalities as a result of the advantageous position which it had enjoyed during the latter part of the so-called Tatar yoke. Novgorod, whose unique political system is discussed in the following chapter, was annexed by Muscovy in 1478 after having lost its northern and eastern colonies. Tver was seized in 1485, Viatka in 1489, Pskov in 1510, Smolensk in 1514, and Riazan in 1517. Ivan IV ("the Terrible") not only annexed other ethnically Russian territories, but in 1552 also commenced the process of seizing non-Russian territory in conquering Kazan, capital of the Volga Tatars. By 1554 Russian rule was established at the mouth of the Volga at Astrakhan and access to the Caspian Sea obtained.

[1] V. O. Kliuchevsky, *Kratkoe posobie po russkoi istorii*, 5th ed. (Moscow, 1906), p. 67.

The stage was now set for the great eastward push across the Urals through Siberia to the Pacific Ocean. By the late 1580's Western Siberia had been conquered to the Ob' and Irtysh rivers, largely as the result of the activities of Yermak Timofeievich, an energetic adventurer in the employ of the Stroganovs, a wealthy landowning and commercial family. Expansionism in Siberia persisted—the Sea of Okhotsk reached in 1638—and by the end of the seventeenth century the Russians had discovered the Kamchatka Peninsula.

Russian expansionism was to persist across the North Pacific and the Bering Sea, as well as in Eastern Europe during the seventeenth and eighteenth centuries. Eastern Ukraine (east of the Dnieper River) was acquired in 1654 and Kiev in 1667. Unable to gain much territory in southern Ukraine at the expense of the Ottoman Empire, Peter I concentrated his expansionist efforts on the Baltic coast and challenged Sweden's supremacy in that area by building a navy. The process of successfully breaking through to the Baltic, attempted in vain by Ivan the Terrible during a quarter century of conflict against Sweden and Poland, commenced in 1701–04 with the seizure of Ingria (the area southwest of what is today Leningrad), along with the cities of Narva and Tartu. This acquisition enabled Peter to begin to build his new "western" capital on the marshlands at the mouth of the Neva River. By 1710 the Finnish city of Vyborg (Viipuri) and all of Karelia were annexed; Estonia and Livonia were also taken along with the city of Riga. By carrying the war into Swedish waters and raiding the Swedish mainland (the first Russian naval victory was won in 1714), Peter was able to compel Sweden to recognize his Baltic territorial gains in the Treaty of Nystad (1721), which concluded more than two decades of intermittent but bitter warfare (the "Great Northern War"). Russia could now claim to be a European power, and her coarse and willful ruler proclaimed himself "the Great" and emperor as well.

Apparently unsatiated with warfare and having his appetite for more non-Russian territory whetted by the Nystad settlement, Peter turned to the Caspian Sea to wage war against Persia. Taking advantage of internal turmoil in Persia, he obtained the western and southern shores of the Caspian (including Baku) in 1722; after his death the coastal area was returned to Persia but the western shore of the Caspian was reannexed by Alexander I. The Ottoman Empire had prevented Peter from breaching the Caucasus.

The growth of the Russian Empire during Catherine's reign (1762–96) resulted from two wars against Turkey (1770–74 and 1787–92) and the three successive partitions of the Polish State. By the Treaty of Kuchuk-Kainardji (1774) Catherine gained most of the northern shore of the Black Sea; and the Crimean Tatar Khanate was removed from Ottoman Turkish suzerainty and became nominally independent (which independence was terminated by Russian annexation in 1783). The second Russo-Turkish war ended with Turkey's recognition of Catherine's annexation of the Crimea, and Russia also acquired a new frontier along the lower reaches of the Dniester River. Imperial Russia now became a Black Sea power, building a naval base at Sevastopol and founding the new port city of Odessa in 1794. The partitioning of the Polish State (1772, 1793, and 1795) enabled Catherine to gain Lithuania, part of Latvia, Belorussia, and a large part of Western Ukraine.

As a result of the Napoleonic Wars, Alexander I changed sides —joining Napoleon in 1807—and took Finland from Sweden, making it a Russian Grand Duchy in 1809. Bessarabia was obtained from the Ottoman Empire in 1812. By being on the winning side against Napoleon in 1815, Russia acquired "Congress Poland," along with Warsaw.

The eighteenth century witnessed a Russian push across the North Pacific and the establishment of "Russian America"[2]; by the 1760's, the Russians had established themselves as fur traders in the Aleutian Islands and in the southern coastal part of Alaska. The ruthless individual traders (who mistreated the natives in the search for sea otter pelts) soon formed companies; and in 1799 the Russian American Company, a semigovernmental firm, was granted a hunting and commercial monopoly extending southward from Alaska to 55° N. The company was authorized to maintain

[2] See Frank A. Golder, *Russian Expansion on the Pacific, 1641–1850* (1914; reprinted Gloucester, Mass.: Peter Smith, 1960).

armed forces and to claim lands south of 55° N as Russian possessions.[3]

In 1812 the Russian American Company established Fort Ross on the California coast seventy miles north of San Francisco in order to provide a base for hunting sea otter and to serve as a source of food supply for the Russians in Alaska. Spain, in possession of San Francisco, protested the Russian settlement and demanded its abandonment, and the Mexicans also protested the Russian presence when they replaced the Spaniards. As more Americans arrived in California, the Russians abandoned Fort Ross in 1841.

The sale of Alaska and the Aleutian Islands was considered by the Russians as early as 1853, but the American Civil War caused its postponement until 1867. The Russian decision to sell to the United States for $7,200,000 was prompted by a number of factors. The land was remote from Russia, and the Crimean War (1853–56) had revealed Russian military weakness and an inability to defend an overseas empire. The Polish revolt of 1863 demonstrated the weakness of Russia's fleet when it had to seek refuge in New York and San Francisco because of the possibility of an international crisis resulting from Russia's suppression of the revolt.[4] Alaska had become an economic liability and was requiring an annual government subsidy of 200,000 rubles; the fur resource had become seriously depleted. The decision to sell to the United States was also due, in part, to Russian antipathy toward Great Britain. Russia's commitments in North America had apparently exceeded her capabilities and a retreat was in order.[5]

[3] In 1810 Russia attempted to claim the Pacific Coast as far south as the Columbia River, despite the fact that it had been claimed by Lewis and Clark in 1804; and in September, 1821, she attempted to claim the American coast to 51° N. See Samuel Flagg Bemis, *John Quincy Adams and the Foundations of American Foreign Policy* (New York: Alfred A. Knopf, 1950), pp. 173–74. For a general account of the Russian occupation of Alaska's southern coastal area see Stuart R. Tompkins, *Alaska, Promyshlennik and Sourdough* (Norman, Okla.: University of Oklahoma Press, 1945); also see Clarence A. Manning, *Russian Influence on Early America* (New York: Library Publishers, 1953).

[4] Many Americans misinterpreted this act as "proof" of Russian friendship for the Union cause. See Frank A. Golder, "The Russian Fleet and the Civil War," *American Historical Review*, XX (July, 1915), 801–812.

[5] A clumsy effort by a representative of the Russian American Company to annex Hawaii in 1815–17 ended in failure due to the tsarist government's un-

Despite the retreat in North America, the claim to a larger Russian empire was pressed in Asia and in the Caucasus. By 1801 much of Georgia was reduced to the status of a Russian province. The hardy freedom-loving Moslem peoples of the Caucasus fought Russian encroachment for a quarter-century under the leadership of Shamil, but by 1859 Russian rule was established in the Eastern Caucasus. By 1864 the Russians were in control of the Western Caucasus, but only after resettling large numbers of Circassians and permitting 200,000 to immigrate to Turkey.

A renewed campaign to conquer Turkestan came in the wake of Russia's defeat in the Crimean War. Tashkent was taken in 1865, and when Samarkand was captured in 1868, the Emir of Bukhara became a vassal of the tsar. In 1873 the Khiva Khanate was conquered by General Kaufmann and the khan also became a Russian vassal. The Kokand Khanate, which had become a vassal state in 1866, was abolished in 1876 following suppression of a revolt and was annexed as a Russian province. In January, 1881, the taking of the fortress of Geok Tepe was followed by a massacre of Turkmens. The Russian annexation of Turkestan was completed with the acquisition of Kushka from Afghanistan in 1885 and the recognition of the Pamir area as a Russian possession in 1895.

In the Far East, Northern Sakhalin was occupied in 1853, and in 1875 Japan ceded Southern Sakhalin to Russia in return for the Kurile Islands.[6] The Amur Region and the territory east of the Ussuri River, which Russia had recognized as being Chinese in the Treaty of Nerchinsk (1689), were seized from a weakened China in 1858. Recognition of this conquest by local Chinese authorities in the Treaty of Aigun (1858) was confirmed by the hard-pressed Chinese government in the Treaty of Peking (1860). The city of Vladivostok ("Ruler of the Orient") was founded in 1860 at the southern extremity of this territory annexed from China. It was only the Rus-

---

willingness to support it. See Klaus Mehnert, *The Russians in Hawaii, 1804–1819* (Honolulu: University of Hawaii Occasional Papers No. 38, 1939) and Richard A. Pierce, *Russia's Hawaiian Adventure, 1815–1817* (Berkeley: University of California Press, 1965).

[6] Japan regained Southern Sakhalin in 1905, following the Russo-Japanese War, but the Soviet Union seized the entire island as well as the Kurile Islands in 1945 after declaring war on Japan.

so-Japanese War of 1904–05 that halted the Russian advance and prevented Russia from obtaining control of Southern Manchuria and Korea.

The Soviet regime regained most of this vast empire of the tsars; although Poland, Finland, Estonia, Latvia, Lithuania, and Bessarabia went their separate ways as a result of the Russian revolution of 1917. However, in September, 1939, the Soviet Union annexed Western Ukraine and Western Belorussia, which had been part of the Polish State created in 1919. In 1940 the three Baltic States lost their independence and became soviet republics; Bessarabia was also retaken by Moscow after having been under Rumanian rule. The Ukrainian territory of Northern Bukovina, which had never been under Russian rule, was also annexed in 1940. The Carpatho-Ukraine was taken from Czechoslovakia in June, 1945. World War II resulted in the annexation by the U.S.S.R. of an additional non-Russian population of at least 22 million. In addition, the war enabled the Soviet Union to seize the Karelian isthmus from Finland, along with the city of Vyborg as well as the Petsamo (Pechenga) region—the loss of which deprived Finland of access to the Barents Sea. In 1945 Russia also acquired the northern half of East Prussia, including the German city of Koenigsberg (renamed Kaliningrad).

Motive Factors in Russian Expansionism. The record of Russian expansionism is significant because of its continuity over more than four centuries and its relentless nature in spite of having suffered certain setbacks. It is unique also, in that the Russians have been able to retain their multinational empire, contiguous with their own ethnic territories, while the overseas empires of the European powers, in contrast, have been liquidated with the granting of independence to the colonies. No single factor can explain the phenomenon of Russian expansionism, but it undoubtedly was facilitated by Muscovy's absolutist political order.

Another factor was the relative weakness of the conquered peoples. Thus, the Russian acquisition of Siberia was effected by relatively small forces which had firearms, while the vanquished were armed with bows and arrows. In Europe the extent of Russia's acquisitions depended upon the international balance of power: Sweden, Poland, Lithuania, the Livonian (Teutonic)

Knights, and Denmark had been able to prevent Ivan the Terrible from acquiring an outlet to the Baltic, but Peter I succeeded in this endeavor as a result of a shift in the balance of power to Muscovy's advantage. Furthermore, weak neighbors, incapable of defending themselves, invited aggression. Poland's internal weakness led to intervention and to her partition, for example, as some Poles, members of the ruling class, could always be found to look to Russia for support and would do its bidding in the shortsighted hope of promoting their own interests. The weakness of the Ottoman Empire and of China also invited Russian expansion.

The search for security has been cited as an important cause of Russian expansionism—with Muscovy reacting to Tatar, Polish, Lithuanian, and Swedish neighbors and protecting itself against a supposedly hostile non-Russian world. The difficulty in explaining the entire process in terms of this single cause lies in the fact that Russia frequently annexed peoples who constituted no threat to her security. In addition, it should be pointed out that the search for security knows no limits and can be used to justify any aggression because each new acquisition usually requires another aggression if it, too, is to be in turn made "secure." Indeed, it might be contended that the very vastness of Russia's empire complicated its defense and simultaneously promoted new acquisitions.

A geopolitical interpretation of Russian expansionism stresses the lack of natural barriers confronting Muscovy and the relative ease and rapidity with which the eastward movement was accomplished. However, geographical determinism does not explain very well the fact that the Russian eastward movement, beginning in the fifteenth and sixteenth centuries, was a dramatic reversal of the earlier centuries-long westward movement of alien populations which had been emerging from Asia to invade and populate parts of Europe in successive waves. If the plains and lack of natural frontiers left Russia open to foreign incursions, they also facilitated Russian expansionism once the necessary power base arose in the form of the autocratic Muscovite State.

It has also been contended that the Russians had an inexorable compulsion to reach the sea.[7] This provocative thesis is based on a

[7] See Robert J. Kerner, *The Urge to the Sea, The Course of Russian History* (Berkeley and Los Angeles: University of California Press, 1942).

geographical determinism which holds that in the Russian expansion rivers were followed to their mouths and, with the use of numerous portages and the construction of forts, provided trade routes. A similar point of view has endeavored to justify Russian expansionism in terms of a desire for warm water ports.

However, to argue that the Russian urge to colonial expansion resulted primarily from a desire to reach the sea is to oversimplify. This explanation appears to be applicable only in the drive to reach the Baltic and in Catherine's wars against Turkey. Prior to the eighteenth century Russia had neither a navy nor a naval tradition, and Peter had to hire foreigners in order to establish a fleet. The bulk of Russian expansionism occurred long before Russia undertook to become a maritime power. Indeed, the Russians had reached the Kola Peninsula and the ice-free open sea as early as the thirteenth century but did not develop maritime interests until much later; they did not bother to build a port at Murmansk until they were compelled to do so in 1915 as a result of the Central Powers' blockade of the Baltic and Black seaports. The port of Arkhangelsk, closed two-thirds of the year by ice, had been founded in 1584 at the request of Dutch traders and was Russia's great port during the seventeenth century, serving her modest foreign commercial needs very adequately. The eastward expansion across Siberia cannot be explained either in terms of a desire to reach the sea; Yermak did not have this as his motive when he pushed across the Urals in search of personal gain. The original Russian acquisition of Eastern Ukraine cannot be explained in terms of a need for ports. Russian expansion into the Caucasus and the acquisition of Poland and of Turkestan cannot be explained in terms of a need to reach the sea.[8]

More important as a motive—especially for eastward expansion—was the quest for furs, gold, and commercial routes to the Orient. The quest for gold and a route to India motivated Peter I in sending an ill-fated expedition to Turkestan in 1715–17. Furs were

[8] For a refutation of the thesis that Russian expansionism can be explained by Russia's need for access to the seas see John A. Morrison, "Russia and Warm Water; A Fallacious Generalization and Its Consequences," *United States Naval Institute Proceedings,* LXXVIII (November, 1952), 1169–79.

also a motive in the Russian attempt to establish an overseas empire in North America. Tribute in the form of furs (*iasak*) was frequently imposed by the Russians upon subjugated peoples; in fact, furs constituted the most important single Russian export in the seventeenth century although Russia was not a significant participant in world trade at that time.[9] The lure of rapidly acquired wealth in the fur trade and the rate of depletion drove Russian traders, hunters, and trappers from the Urals to the Pacific within eighty years.

However, Russian expansionism was not in all instances due to official policy. When strong monarchs like Ivan III, Ivan IV, Peter I, and Catherine II reigned, expansion was the order of the day. Yet the beginning of the conquest of Siberia occurred as a result of the activity of the brigand Yermak; originally frowned upon by Ivan IV as a risky enterprise, it was viewed approvingly once its relative ease and its lucrative aspects became apparent. Another Russian who initiated expansionist policy was Nikolai Murav'ev, the governor general of Eastern Siberia, who moved forces into the Amur region without waiting for official approval. The Russian military, probing into Turkestan in the nineteenth century, exceeded its orders on occasion and accelerated the process of empire-building in its desire for decorations and promotions. Indeed, over the centuries Muscovite absolutism and serfdom provided a host of rough and ready pioneers who preferred flight to the established order and who were prepared to risk their lives on some distant new frontier.

If empires have frequently grown as a result of a combination of governmental policy, individual daring, the quest for adventure, and the desire for personal gain and glory, they have not been lacking in pretense and rationalization. Thus, the Russians could claim that they had fulfilled a "civilizing mission" in bringing the Orthodox faith to the Aleuts, in introducing domestic animals into Alaska, and in "pacifying" the nomads of Turkestan. Russian concern over the fate of the Orthodox Christians of the Balkans also provided a convenient pretext for an anti-Turkish policy which

[9] See Raymond H. Fisher, *The Russian Fur Trade, 1550–1700* (Berkeley and Los Angeles: University of California Press, 1943).

served the interests of Russian expansionism. The preoccupation with acquiring Constantinople, dating back at least to the eighteenth century, reflected a Russian tendency to adopt a messianic role.[10]

2. THE NON-RUSSIAN NATIONALITIES

Although the diverse non-Russian peoples have often been termed "national minorities" and their territories "Russian provinces" or "borderlands," most of them constitute a substantial majority of the population of their own territories.[11] The presence of numerous smaller ethnic groups, many of whom are in the Russian Republic, makes it possible to discuss here only the more numerous non-Russian peoples.

The *Ukrainians* are the second most numerous Slavic people and also the second most numerous nationality in the Soviet Union. Possessing a distinctive language with a rich melodious quality and a substantial literary tradition, the Ukrainians inhabit a republic which has Kiev (*Kyiv* in Ukrainian) as its capital. Historically, they trace their origins to the Kiev *Rus'* of the ninth-thirteenth cen-

[10] In 1782 Catherine II proposed, without success, to the Austrian emperor Joseph II that the Turks be driven out of the Balkans and that a Greek Empire (including Bulgaria, Macedonia, and Albania) be established with Constantine, her grandson, on the throne. The Russian preoccupation with the Straits and Constantinople began to bear fruit in the secret agreements of February–March, 1915, negotiated by the tsarist foreign minister, S. D. Sazonov, under which Britain and France conditionally agreed to transfer the Straits, along with adjacent territories and the Turkish capital, to Russia. Not satisfied, the Russians in April, 1916, claimed all of Eastern Turkey (Erzerum, Trabzon, Van, Bitlis) and much of Kurdistan as well. Russia also obtained "complete freedom" in delimiting its western frontier, which would have enabled it to annex Western Ukraine. The Russian Provisional Government, despite its democratic pretensions, did not renounce these claims in 1917; if Russia was unable to obtain the spoils of World War I it was, in large part, due to Lenin's destruction of the Provisional Government. See Iu. V. Kliuchnikov and Andrei Sabanin, eds., *Mezhdunarodnaia politika noveishego vremeni v dogovorakh, notakh i deklaratsiiakh* (Moscow: NKID, 1926), Part II, pp. 25–27, 38–39, 69. Also see Sergei D. Sazonov, *Vospominaniia* (Paris, 1927), pp. 292–322.

[11] Major exceptions are the Kazakhs and the Kirghiz (who are minorities in their own republics) and the Jews, who do not possess their own republic but are dispersed over various parts of the Soviet Union.

turies. The Kiev State was followed by the Galician-Volynian State in Western Ukraine in the thirteenth century but was ultimately absorbed into the Lithuanian State, which flourished in the fourteenth and fifteenth centuries; the Western Ukraine was annexed by the Polish State. The Union of Poland and Lithuania in 1569 then brought almost all Ukrainians under Polish rule. During this lengthy period, the Ukrainians had no contact with the Russians.

As a result of the presence of Tatars in the Crimea, it became necessary—in a significant development—to defend the southern Ukrainian frontier. This responsibility was fulfilled in the sixteenth and seventeenth centuries by the Zaporozhian *Kozaks* of Eastern Ukraine who bore arms, in addition to engaging in agriculture, and over whom the Polish government could not usually exercise authority. The term *Kozak* (cossack) is of Turkic origin and refers to a guardian, a free and independent man; it was not, as is sometimes assumed, an exclusively Russian term—although Cossacks (*kazaks,* in Russian) in Russian service to the east of Ukraine performed a similar function.

The Ukrainian *kozaks,* who possessed their own administration and elected their commander (*hetman*), revolted against Polish rule in 1648 under the leadership of Hetman Bohdan Khmelnytsky. Finding it difficult to defend their independence in the face of Polish and Crimean Tatar opposition, the Ukrainian *kozaks* turned to the tsar of Muscovy for aid. They concluded with Muscovy the Treaty of Pereiaslav, which they thought to be an alliance and which the tsar regarded as an act of submission. In this way Eastern Ukraine came under Russian rule, during the eighteenth century losing its rights under the treaty (including the right to have diplomatic relations and impose tariffs), as well as its separate military establishment; the hetmanate was abolished in 1764 by Catherine II, who also introduced serfdom.

The attempt of Hetman Ivan Mazepa in 1709 to ally with Sweden and regain Ukrainian independence failed, and the partitioning of the Polish State brought many more Ukrainians under Russian rule. The Western Ukrainians in Galicia, who were of the Catholic faith (as distinct from the Orthodox Eastern

Ukrainians) but who employed the Slavonic rite, exchanged Polish for Austrian rule in 1772. Bukovina came under Austrian rule in 1775.

Despite these vicissitudes, a nationalist movement grew among the Ukrainians. When the Russian government endeavored to destroy Ukrainian nationalism during the second half of the nineteenth century, the movement found more favorable conditions in the Ukrainian lands under Austrian rule. Despite oppressive conditions of Russian rule during this period, Eastern Ukraine developed a national literature and produced the greatest Ukrainian poet, Taras Shevchenko (1814–61)—a prophet of national liberation—and Professor Mykhailo Hrushevsky (1866–1934), the nation's most prominent historian. With the collapse of the Russian Empire in 1917, the Ukrainians finally proclaimed their independence (the anticommunist Ukrainian People's Republic led by Symon Petliura), but lost it to the superior military forces of the Soviet regime after three years of bitter struggle. While the national movement won a victory of sorts in the establishment of the Ukrainian Soviet Socialist Republic, severe repressions against the Ukrainian intelligentsia and peasantry followed in the 1930's. World War II led to the unification of almost all Ukrainian territories as a result of Soviet annexations. In its level of industry, agriculture, and population, the Ukrainian S.S.R. surpasses most other European countries; Ukraine is also a charter member of the United Nations and holds membership in a number of international bodies.

The *Belorussians* or *White Ruthenians* are not Russians despite the similarity in name, since they are known as *Belarusy* while the Russians are *russkie*. Their homeland lies between Russia and Poland, and their language is distinct from those of their Slavic neighbors. The economy is agricultural to a significant degree, but includes such industries as textiles and lumber; other industries are based largely on imports from other parts of the Soviet Union.

Historically, the *Belarusy* are descended from such early Slavic tribes as the Western Krivichi, Dregovichi, and Radimichi. Later the Polotsk Principality in Belorussia was an important center in the ancient *Rus'*. Between the fourteenth and eighteenth centuries the *Belarusy* were united with the Lithuanians in the Great Lithuanian Principality and, as a result of the union of Lithuania and Poland, were later included (along with the Ukrainians) in this unique East European multinational state. The partitioning of the Polish State (which was far larger in size than ethnic Poland) brought the *Belarusy* under the rule of Imperial Russia. Catholic influences were suppressed by the tsarist regime as part of the effort to russify the *Belarusy*. Although World War I and the Russian Revolution enabled the *Belarusy* to proclaim their independence, their country was partitioned in 1921—Poland receiving the western part and the eastern part becoming the Belorussian S.S.R., with Minsk as the capital. Poland's military defeat in 1939 led to the Soviet annexation of Western Belorussia. Although the national consciousness of the *Belarusy* has not been equal to that of their neighbors, this sturdy people has remained attached to its homeland.

The *Turkic* (or *Turco-Tatar*) *peoples* in the Soviet Union are related to the Osmanli Turks of Turkey. The area populated by Turkic peoples extends from Iakutia in the Lena river basin in Siberia to the Mediterranean. Although differing racially, the Turkic peoples are closely related linguistically, despite the existence of various idioms. Another unifying factor has been their Moslem faith, the overwhelming majority being of the Sunni branch. The Turkic settlement of Central Asia began as early as the sixth century; and the Arab conquest of Samarkand in 712 led to the removal of Chinese influence and to the introduction of Islam. The rise of the Mongols in the thirteenth century meant the subjugation of the various Turkic peoples and their inclusion in the Mongol Empire. Although various Turkic tribes were in contact with the Eastern Slavs since the earliest times, the Tatars are the Turkic people who have left the most recent mark upon European Russia. Their subjugation by the Russians began in the sixteenth century, and the process of acquiring Turkic peoples for the Russian Empire was not completed until the latter half of the nineteenth century with the conquest of Turkestan in Central Asia.

The *Uzbeks,* who inhabit the south central part of Turkestan bordering on Afghanistan, are the most numerous of the Soviet

Turkic peoples. Uzbekistan, with its capital at Tashkent, is the leading Soviet cotton-producing center and also has an impressive industrial establishment specializing in textiles, chemicals, and metallurgy. The ancient capitals of Bukhara and Samarkand are also located in Uzbekistan. The *Kirghiz* live to the east of the Uzbeks, bordering on Sinkiang or Chinese Turkestan. Traditionally the Kirghiz were nomadic horsemen who tended their herds in mountain pastures. In 1916 they participated in a revolt of the Turkestanis against the tsarist regime's efforts to conscript native manpower for labor (after requisitioning flocks and imposing heavy taxes); the Kirghiz suffered heavy losses in the repression which followed. The revolt, which began among the Uzbeks, led tens of thousands of Kirghiz to flee across the border into China to escape punishment.

The *Kazakhs*,[12] a formerly nomadic Turkic people, have inhabited the plains to the north of Kirghizia and Uzbekistan, and many of them experienced the same fate in the suppression of the 1916 revolt. The Kazakhs have been reduced to a minority in their own republic as a result of a great influx of Russians and Ukrainians connected with the development of agriculture, mining, and industry and intensified after 1955 by Moscow's decision to cultivate the vast, dry virgin lands of the Kazakhs.

To the west of Uzbekistan live the *Turkmens*, whose land—which lies north of Iran and Afghanistan and borders on the southeastern shores of the Caspian Sea—is largely desert. The bulk of the population lives in the foothills near the Iranian frontier, where the capital of Ashkhabad is located. The *Azerbaidjanis* inhabit the western shores of the Caspian Sea. Unlike the other Turkic peoples, who are Sunni Moslems, the Azerbaidjanis are Shi-ite and partly Sunni Moslems. Although both Persians and Anatolian Turks had an interest in Azerbaidjan prior to its annexation by the Russians early in the nineteenth century, the Azerbaidjanis were able to reestablish their independence in May, 1918, only to lose it two years later as the result of a Russian communist invasion. Petroleum at Baku (Azerbaidjan's capital), cotton, rice, tea, fruits,

[12] Not to be confused with the Russian term (of Turkic origin), *kazak* (cossack).

fisheries, and caviar have figured prominently in the Azerbaidjan economy.

The *Tatars* constitute another Turkic group.[13] The *Volga Tatars* live along the middle reaches of that river and to the east of it and include the Kazan Tatars (descended from the Kazan Khanate). The *Siberian Tatars* are found in Western Siberia north of Kazakhstan in the Tiumen', Tobolsk, and Tara regions and near Tomsk. The *Crimean Tatars*, who lived in the Crimea from the thirteenth century until World War II, were forcibly resettled because of their opposition to the Soviet regime. The *Bashkirs* number nearly one million and live on the southern slopes of the Urals and on the adjacent steppe. The *Chuvash* are related to the Turkic peoples linguistically, although they are mostly Christian rather than Moslem and have been subjected to russification; their homeland lies to the southeast of the great bend in the Volga River, and their capital is at Cheboksary. Other Turkic people are the *Iakuts* (also Christianized), the *Kara-kalpaks* (who live in northwestern Uzbekistan), the *Tuvinians* (of the Mongolian border area), the *Karachais* and *Balkarians* of the Northern Caucasus, and the *Gagauzy* (a Christianized Turkic minority living in Bessarabia).

The *Tadjiks* are a Persian people who are often associated with Turkestan because they inhabit its southeastern corner on the Afghan frontier and are Moslems. The Tadjiks live in a land of high peaks in the Pamirs, and in addition to mining they engage in agriculture and animal husbandry in the valleys. Their capital, Diushambe, was named Stalinabad from 1929 to 1961.

The *Armenians* in the Soviet Union are the heirs of an old Christian culture which was flourishing and had a written alphabet long before the development of the Russian nation. When Christianity was introduced in A.D. 303, Armenia became the world's first Christian state; later it developed a unique national church which has

[13] The term "Tatar" originally was a popular and imprecise name used for the Mongols by the Chinese, Moslems, and Europeans. Certain Turkic peoples acquired the name when they were subjugated by the (non-Turkic) Mongols and became allied with them in military campaigns. The army of the Golden Horde, which subjugated much of Russia in the mid-thirteenth century, had a Mongol nucleus but was composed largely of Turkic warriors. The Horde's Slavic subjects called both the Mongols and the Turkic invaders "Tatars."

its center at Etchmiadzin. Situated to the north of Iran and Turkey, Armenia was long exposed to Persian and Turkish influences. The arrival of Russian military forces in the area south of the Caucasus Mountains and the Russian acquisition of Armenian territory from Persia in 1828 (Treaty of Turkmanchai) caused the Armenians to seek Russian protection against their non-Christian neighbors and to become pawns in Russia's efforts to defeat the Ottoman Empire. The collapse of the Russian Empire enabled the Armenians, who had been under Russian rule, to proclaim their independence in May, 1918, under the leadership of the Dashnak Party; Soviet Russia invaded Armenia in November, 1920, and established a small Armenian Soviet Republic with its capital at Yerevan. However, many Soviet Armenians live outside the boundaries of Armenia, mostly in neighboring Azerbaidjan and Georgia.

The *Georgians*, whose country on the eastern shores of the Black Sea south of the Caucasus is more correctly known as *Sa-kartvel-o* in Georgian (*Gruzia* in Russian), possess an ancient and unique language and culture far older than that of the Russians. Converted to Orthodox Christianity by Saint Nina in the fourth century, the Georgians—like the Armenians—were subjected to numerous foreign incursions, often accompanied by pillaging and devastation. However, the ancient capital of Mtskheta (with its extant great cathedral, Sveti Tskhoveli, behind fortress walls) remained a bastion of Georgian culture as did Tbilisi, the capital since the fifth century. In the late twelfth and early thirteenth centuries, during the reign of Queen Tamara, Georgia experienced a cultural flowering personified by the poet, Shota Rustaveli. The hostility of Turkey and Persia caused the Georgians to seek Russian protection at the end of the eighteenth century, which led to annexation in 1801. In May, 1918, Georgia seceded from Russia; and its independence was recognized by Moscow in a treaty of May 7, 1920. However, in February, 1921, Soviet Russia invaded Georgia and established a Georgian Soviet Republic, after defeating the Social Democratic government which had proclaimed the country's independence. One of the reasons for the Soviet invasion was Georgia's rich manganese deposits at Chiatura, as well as its tea, citrus fruits, viticulture, and fine wineries. Georgia is a colorful land whose people are proud of their heritage and have a high degree of national consciousness.

The *Lithuanians* are the most numerous of the three Soviet Baltic peoples. Like the Estonians and Latvians, they belong neither to the Slavic nor to the Germanic worlds, but constitute a separate ethnic entity. Lithuanian is an old Indo-European language related to ancient Sanskrit and is of great interest to philologists. The Lithuanians have been predominantly Roman Catholic since 1386 when their king, Jogaila, married the Polish Queen Jadwiga and a union of the two countries resulted.

The *Latvians* speak a language which is related to Lithuanian (although subjected to Germanic and Russian lexical influence). German influence among the Latvians was very considerable as a result of their having been under the rule of the Teutonic Order, a body of military crusaders sent ostensibly to convert the Baltic peoples to Christianity in the twelfth century but which established a harsh system of rule and cruelly exploited the native Latvians. Riga, the capital, early emerged as the commercial, ecclesiastical, and political center. The presence of German rulers caused the Latvians to embrace Lutheranism early in the sixteenth century, although Latgallia remained Catholic. By 1561 the Order was secularized and the descendants of the knights became powerful landowning laymen ("Baltic Barons"). The attempt of Muscovy's Ivan the Terrible to break through to the Baltic in the second half of the sixteenth century and the developing conflict between Muscovy and the Polish-Lithuanian State led to the establishment of Polish suzerainty over most of Latvia. This was followed in the seventeenth century by Swedish rule, which ended in 1721 when the Russian Empire annexed Latvia.

The *Estonians* speak a Finno-Ugrian language and are related to their neighbors, the Finns.[14] They are of the Lutheran faith. Estonia's history has paralleled that of Latvia—with seven centuries of foreign rule by Danes, German crusading knights and nobles, Poles (in southern Estonia), Swedes, and Russians. The rule of the

[14] Other Finno-Ugrian peoples in the Soviet Union include the Udmurts, Mordvinians, and Mari—each of whom has an autonomous republic in the area of the great bend in the Volga River east of Moscow.

Swedish Vasa kings was the most enlightening, in relative terms, and led to the founding of the University of Tartu in 1632. Imperial Russian rule left intact the privileged position of the German nobles and even enhanced it—as in Latvia—and also brought attempts at russification. Estonia, Latvia, and Lithuania enjoyed two decades of political independence between the two world wars, only to be annexed by the Soviet Union in 1940 and reduced to the status of soviet republics.

The *Jews* were originally regarded with suspicion and hostility by the Muscovite State, which excluded them from permanent residence. The Jewish population under Russian rule was acquired as a result of the partitions of the Polish State. Most of this population had originally left the German lands and Bohemia during the twelfth and thirteenth centuries and settled in Poland, Lithuania, Ukraine, and Belorussia. The Jews played an important role in the development of commerce and industry in the areas under Polish rule. Annexation by Russia meant that almost all Jews were confined to the Pale of Settlement in Ukraine and Belorussia, and experienced various forms of official discrimination. Although the Soviet regime initially provided many opportunities for Jews, their involvement in the system was subsequently circumscribed. The Soviet Jewish population suffered severe losses as a result of German occupation policies.

The Soviet *Moldavians* are actually Rumanians, most of whom live in Bessarabia, which lies between Ukraine and Rumania. They differ from the Rumanians principally in having been compelled to use the Slavic Cyrillic alphabet rather than the Latin alphabet in their language. Prior to 1812 Bessarabia was part of the greater Moldavian Principality (now Eastern Rumania) under Ottoman Turkish suzerainty. From 1812 to 1917 Bessarabia was part of the Russian Empire, and from 1918 to 1940 it was included in Rumania. The Soviet Union seized Bessarabia from Rumania in June, 1940. Soviet Moldavia's capital is at Kishinev (Chisinau) and its population has been traditionally Orthodox Christian.

Other peoples who live in the U.S.S.R. include the Germans, Poles, Bulgars, Koreans, Greeks, Hungarians, Gypsies, and Kurds; they do not have their own politico-administrative units as they are dispersed over various parts of the Soviet Union. Finally, as pointed out before, most of the principal peoples of the Soviet Union have separate union republics, which together with the Russian S.F.S.R. constitute the U.S.S.R.

3. FORMATION OF THE SOVIET UNION

With the formal proclamation of the Russian Socialist Federated Soviet Republic in July, 1918, at the time its first constitution was adopted,[15] the Soviet Union had as its nucleus the world's first communist regime established in Russia. The Russian communist regime—in an effort to distinguish itself from Imperial Russia—had already promulgated a "Declaration of the Rights of the Peoples of Russia" on November 2 (15), 1917.[16] This document, signed by Lenin and Stalin, promised the non-Russian nationalities complete equality and sovereignty and the right of self-determination, including the right to secede and establish independent states.[17] The non-Russian nationalities accepted this document at face value and proceeded to secede from the defunct Russian Empire and its Soviet successor state. Thus, the Soviet regime granted recognition to the anticommunist Ukrainian People's Republic on December 4 (17), 1917, and to independent Finland's new government on December 18 (31), 1917.[18] However, in each case the Russian communists endeavored (with the aid of such non-Russian communist support as they could find) to overthrow these regimes and replace them with communist regimes. Finland succeeded in preserving

[15] Following the seizure of power by the communists in central Russia in November, 1917, the regime was first known as that of the Russian Soviet Republic or as the Republic of Soviets of Workers, Soldiers, and Peasants Deputies. With the adoption of the 1936 Constitution the words "socialist" and "soviet" were transposed to read Russian Soviet Federated Socialist Republic.

[16] The use of two dates for events occurring prior to February 1 (14), 1918, is due to the fact that Russia until that time adhered to the Julian calendar, which in the twentieth century was thirteen days behind the Gregorian calendar. The Russian Orthodox Church has continued to observe the Julian calendar, but the Gregorian calendar has replaced it in all aspects of public life.

[17] *Istoriia Sovetskoi Konstitutsii, sbornik dokumentov, 1917–1957* (Moscow: Akademiia Nauk SSSR, 1957), pp. 19–20.

[18] *Ibid.*, pp. 32–33, 36. Also see David L. Zlatopol'skii, *Gosudarstvennoe ustroistvo SSSR* (Moscow: Gosiurizdat, 1960), p. 80.

her independence from Russia (proclaimed after 108 years of Russian rule), while Ukraine, Belorussia, Georgia, Armenia, Azerbaidjan, and Turkestan were invaded by Moscow's forces and had Soviet rule imposed upon them by 1920–21.

However, the fiction of independent Soviet republics had to be preserved. By 1921 the Russian, Ukrainian, and Belorussian Soviet republics had entered into treaty relationships which governed military and economic affairs. In foreign affairs there was nominal independence, reflected in the participation of the Ukrainian S.S.R. along with the Russian S.F.S.R. in the negotiation of the Treaty of Riga with Poland (March 18, 1921). However, on February 22, 1922, the non-Russian Soviet republics as well as the so-called Far Eastern Republic signed a protocol in Moscow which authorized the Russian S.F.S.R. to represent them at the Genoa Conference.[19] This act presaged the formal absorption of these republics into the Soviet Union.

With the liquidation of the Far Eastern Republic in November, 1922, and its annexation by the Russian S.F.S.R., the stage was set.[20] The Union of Soviet Socialist Republics was formally established on December 30, 1922, with four constituent parts (union republics): the Russian S.F.S.R., the Ukrainian S.S.R., the Belorussian S.S.R., and the Transcaucasian Socialist Federated Soviet Republic (consisting of Armenia, Azerbaidjan, and Georgia). The Russian S.F.S.R. in 1923 included much of Turkestan; but the remainder of that region was organized as two "soviet people's republics," Khorezm and Bukhara, populated largely by Uzbeks. In October, 1924, two new union republics were created—the Uzbek and Turkmen—and all of Turkestan was divided into separate so-called national states. In December, 1929, the number of union republics increased to seven when the Tadjik Autonomous S.S.R. was elevated in status (largely in the hope of enabling Moscow to influ-

[19] Zlatopol'skii, *ibid.*, pp. 91–92.

[20] The Far Eastern Republic was formally established in April, 1920, exercising authority over Eastern Siberia and the Maritime Region; its capital was at Chita. It served as a convenient communist-controlled Russian buffer state between the Russian S.F.S.R. and the part of Siberia occupied by the Japanese, as well as a means of misleading world opinion and of bringing about an end to Japanese military intervention.

ence developments in neighboring Afghanistan). The adoption of the 1936 Constitution saw the number of union republics increase to eleven as a result of the dissolution of the Transcaucasian Federation and the transformation of the Kazakh and Kirghiz autonomous republics into union republics. World War II added four more union republics to the U.S.S.R. with the annexation of Estonia, Latvia, Lithuania, and Bessarabia (Moldavian S.S.R.).[21]

The establishment of the Soviet Union as a nominal federation of national republics, one which has grown in size, resulted from a number of causes. The Soviet Union was a means of replacing the Russian Empire under a new name, with an apparently different form of multinational structure harnessed to the objectives of communist political action. In view of the fact that communist regimes were established in the non-Russian lands largely as a result of the preponderance of Russian arms, it followed that these regimes had no choice but to accept full union with Soviet Russia. Since the non-Russian communist parties were treated as subordinate units of the Russian Communist Party, it was logical that centralism in Party structure and rule by a single party should be accompanied by governmental centralism, in lieu of the earlier treaty relationships between the republics. The subjugated status of the non-Russian Communist parties became evident when they were denied membership in the Third Communist International (Comintern), founded by Moscow in March, 1919.

If the Soviet Union is primarily a Russian creation ruled from Russia's traditional capital, its politics cannot be understood apart from the Russian political heritage. This heritage has influenced the fate of both Russians and non-Russians in the Soviet Union and will also condition to a considerable degree their future development. Study of the Russian political tradition, discussed in Chapter

[21] Between 1940 and June, 1956—as a result of the existence of the Karelo-Finnish S.S.R.—there were sixteen union republics. This republic, located between the White Sea and Lake Ladoga and inhabited largely by Russians, became a union republic in March, 1940, following the Soviet war against Finland, and included depopulated territory seized from that country. The decision taken in 1956 to reduce this republic to its former status as the Karelian Autonomous S.S.R. (and to eliminate the reference to a Finnish population) was due, in part, to the small number of Finns living in the Soviet Union. See Zlatopol'skii, *op. cit.* (above, n. 18), pp. 106, 111–112.

2, is thus an essential aspect of any investigation of the Soviet political system.

Before proceeding to a consideration of the major components of the Soviet polity, it is essential to examine certain aspects of the physical and social environment within which the polity functions. To this end it is important to consider at least briefly the country's geographical and climatic features, certain essential facts regarding its economy, the nature of its communications media, and the principal social strata of its population.

4. THE LAND AND CLIMATE

The vastness of the Soviet Union, with its 8.6 million square miles of territory, makes it the world's largest area under a single political regime. From the Baltic Sea to the Bering Sea and the North Pacific, this one-sixth of the earth's landmass extends a distance of more than 6,000 miles over 150 degrees of longitude. Thus when it is noon on the Soviet-Polish frontier, it is 11:00 p.m. in the easternmost extremities of this far-flung modern empire. From north to south, exclusive of the bleak Soviet island possessions in the Arctic, it extends, in varying width, from 1,800 to 2,600 miles.

Although the Soviet landmass is more than twice the size of the United States, a simple comparison based on area is misleading. A demographic map of the Soviet Union makes it clear that large parts of the country are not very conducive to protracted habitation for sizable populations. In certain areas, such as the Ukrainian and Moldavian Soviet Republics, the density of population approaches that of parts of Western Europe; but the U.S.S.R. as a whole has an average population density of only one-ninth of Western Europe's. Thus, there is a large area of high concentration of population in the western and southwestern parts of the Soviet Union, while to the east there is a long, thin, sparsely settled belt extending along the Trans-Siberian Railway to the Maritime Region north of Vladivostok.

Zones. Although the U.S.S.R. (with its population of more than 242,000,000 in 1970) is the world's third most populous country, it has a relatively small population for such an enormous area. This is due to the quality of Soviet territory and to climatic conditions.

The land is divided into a series of zones based on soil, vegetation, fauna, topography, and climate. In the Far North the *tundra zone*, constituting nearly 15 percent of the U.S.S.R., extends from the Murmansk area in the northwest across to the northern part of the Kamchatka Peninsula. It is treeless and supports only mosses, lichens, and berries; in winter it is a frozen wasteland and in the brief, pale summer surface-thawing creates marshy conditions in which gnats and mosquitoes abound. The *forest zone* is the world's largest and covers 52.5 percent of Soviet territory. It extends in a broad belt from Finland and the Baltic Sea across the entire central portion of the European U.S.S.R. and Siberia. Coniferous forests cover the northern part of this zone and most of Siberia (the *taiga*); in the southern part mixed deciduous and coniferous forests predominate.

The forest zone gradually gives way to the *steppe zone*, covering approximately 17 percent of the U.S.S.R. and extending from the Ukrainian Republic in the west to the Altai Mountains, which border on the Mongolian People's Republic. The treeless steppe includes the rich black earth (*chernozem*) area with its soil of high humus content. The arable part of the Soviet Union is limited largely to this belt, in which the quality of the soil and dependability of rainfall decline as one moves eastward. To the south of the steppe zone lie the *semidesert* and *desert zones*, which comprise approximately 13 percent of Soviet territory and extend from the northern and eastern shores of the Caspian Sea to the valleys and high mountains of Soviet Central Asia (Turkestan), where China, Afghanistan, and Iran border on the U.S.S.R. Irrigation has made possible the cultivation of parts of these zones having better soils. The Amur and Ussuri areas in the Soviet Maritime Region east of Manchuria, and the eastern part of Kamchatka, constitute a special maritime zone with cold winters and cool, moist summers. Two small *subtropical zones* extend over two percent of the country. These include the southern tip of the Crimean Peninsula, the eastern coast of the Black Sea, and the area south of the Caucasus Mountains. These areas are exceptional in that they obtain rather heavy rainfall and enjoy a mild climate because of their sheltered location between mountain ranges and the sea.

In marked contrast to the subtropical zones is the 43 percent of

Soviet territory which is affected by permafrost. This special zone, which includes the entire tundra zone and most of the Siberian forest zone, extends far south of the Arctic Circle and is distinguished by the failure of the subsoil to thaw during the brief summer. In the Soviet Far North the subsoil is perpetually frozen to depths of several hundred feet. Although the depth of the permafrost diminishes as one moves southward in Siberia, it creates difficulties in construction and agriculture.

Most of the Soviet Union is a vast plain extending from Poland and the Baltic Sea to the Yenisei River in Central Siberia. This plain is interrupted by the Ural Mountains, which are old and rounded and form a low barrier between European Russia and Siberia. The average altitude of the great East European plain is 600 feet. Beyond the Urals lies the West Siberian Plain, which is centered on the Ob' river basin. Much of this vast western Siberian region consists of forested lowlands having poor drainage because the Ob' River has a very slight gradient, sluggishly descending only 295 feet in the 1,860 miles between Novosibirsk and its mouth. East of the West Siberian Plain—between the Yenisei and Lena rivers—lies the Central Siberian Plateau, the altitude of which varies from 1,300 to 1,900 feet. Eastern Siberia beyond the Lena River is mountainous and includes such ranges as the Verkhoiansk, Cherskii, Kolyma, and Anadyrskii (or Chukotsk) Mountains, which reach heights of from 6,000 to 9,750 feet. In southeastern Siberia the Iablonovyi, Stanovoi, and Dzhugdzhur ranges extend from the area east of Lake Baikal to the Sea of Okhotsk. The mountainous nature of Eastern Siberia also manifests itself in the rugged topography of the Maritime Region, Sakhalin, and Kamchatka.

Much of the southern frontier of the Soviet Union lies within mountainous areas bordering on the Mongolian Peoples Republic, Communist China, Afghanistan, Iran, and Turkey. This chain of frontier mountain ranges commences in the area west of Irkutsk and Lake Baikal with the Saian Range and continues in the Tannu Ula and Altai ranges in the area east of Semipalatinsk. The highest mountain ranges in the Soviet Union are the Tien Shan and Pamir ranges, which lie in the Kirghiz and Tadjik Soviet Republics. The highest peak, Mount Communism—formerly Mount Stalin—(24,-

590 feet) is in the Pamirs. Farther to the west lie the Caucasus Mountains between the Caspian and Black Seas. The main range of the Caucasus includes Mount Elbrus (18,470 feet), Europe's highest peak.

Climate. The absence of mountain ranges on the Soviet Union's northern frontier, comparable to those in the south, exposes the great Eurasian Soviet landmass to the frigid climate of the Arctic. Another factor which causes the Soviet Union to have a severe, extremely continental climate is its distance from oceans, other than the Arctic, which would have a moderating effect—warming the land in winter and cooling it in summer. Thus the climate is for the most part harsh and intemperate and is characterized over much of the area by extremes of heat in the short summer and cold in the long winter. In Leningrad the mean temperature in January is 15° F and in July it is 64° F. In Iakutsk in Eastern Siberia the mean temperature in January is −46° F, while in July it is 66° F. Snow remains on the ground in most of Siberia for at least seven or eight months of the year, yet the heat of summer is often intense.

Much of the Soviet Union has limited rainfall, receiving well under twenty inches of precipitation annually. The Soviet Union lies in the high northern latitudes and extends northward to a greater degree than does North America, so that a far greater part of Soviet territory lies within the Arctic Circle. Leningrad at 60° N is in the same latitude as Seward, Alaska, while Moscow at 55° N would correspond to Edmonton, Alberta, at 54° N. Murmansk at 69° N lies as far north as the middle range of Baffin Island or northwestern Alaska but has an ice-free port. Correspondingly, the southern parts of the Soviet Union also lie rather far north. The Ukrainian capital of Kiev at 50.5° corresponds to Winnipeg, Manitoba, in latitude while the southernmost point in the Soviet Union at Kushka in Turkmenistan (35° N) is in the latitude of Memphis, Tennessee. Irkutsk and Novosibirsk in Siberia correspond, respectively, to Saskatoon, Saskatchewan, and to the southern shores of Hudson's Bay. Vladivostok, the southernmost port in the Soviet Far East, lies in the latitude of Portsmouth, New Hampshire.

5. INDUSTRY, AGRICULTURE, AND TRANSPORT

Well-endowed with natural resources—all of which are state-owned, as is the entire Soviet industrial establishment—the Soviet Union emerged after World War II as the world's second industrial power. This feat was accomplished as a result of governmental direction of the economy by means of heavy taxation and human deprivation, controls over allocation of labor, and the skewed and forced development of heavy industry (production of the means of production) at the expense of light industry (consumer goods). Thus between 1940 and 1970 steel production rose from 18.3 million to 116 million metric tons. Coal production, including lignite, doubled between 1951 and 1970, reaching a level of 610 million metric tons. Soviet production of electricity during the 1951–70 period rose from 117 to 740 billion kilowatt hours. Petroleum output increased phenomenally from 47 to 345 million metric tons between 1951 and 1970 as a result of the exploitation of new fields located between the Volga River and the Ural Mountains.

Much of this economic growth was facilitated by the development of a new economic heartland in the Urals, southwestern Siberia, and Kazakhstan. The iron ore of Magnitogorsk in the Urals and of Kustanai in Kazakhstan, as well as the coal of the Kuznetsk Basin (in Kemerovo province) and of Karaganda in Kazakhstan have provided the basis for the development of this inner region. Furthermore, mammoth hydroelectric installations have been constructed at great cost on the Angara River at Bratsk and on the Yenisei River at Krasnoiarsk, although the Soviet Union must still rely primarily on thermal generation of electric power. The development of a formidable industrial establishment has thus enabled the Soviet Union to make great strides in the manufacture of machine tools, a key sector in any modern economy.

However, the spectacular successes of Soviet industry have not been matched in agriculture. This has been due in large part to natural conditions, such as limited rainfall in the areas of better (chernozem and chestnut) soils, the limited growing season due to the Soviet Union's location in northern latitudes, and the need to use costly fertilizers in the areas of poor podsolic soils. The amount of arable land, therefore, is limited in spite of the vast territory. Extensive rather than intensive agriculture has been the rule—the tendency being to bring marginal land under cultivation instead of increasing crop yields.

In view of the fact that approximately one-third of the Soviet labor force is committed to it, Soviet agriculture has been an expensive undertaking. This is a rather wasteful disposition of the labor force for a country with such a high level of industrial development. Another distinctive characteristic of Soviet agriculture has been its organization in terms of gigantic (and often inefficient) farms. Three-quarters of Soviet agricultural land is cultivated by the collective farms (*kolkhozy*), which are cooperatives in theory, with the state holding ultimate title to the land. One-quarter of Soviet agricultural land is held by state-owned farms (*sovkhozy*), on which the laborers are paid a fixed wage in contrast to the less certain collective farm method of basing members' income on the individual member's labor contribution and on the farm's earnings.

In spite of the resources and large amounts of manpower committed to agriculture, the Soviet Union has had only moderate success in adequately feeding its growing population. It has had difficulty in developing livestock and dairy industries of sufficient quality because of fodder shortages and poor animal husbandry. The need to close the protein gap in the Soviet diet and to compensate for the livestock shortage has led to Moscow's building large modern deep-sea fishing fleets which operate in waters remote from the Soviet Union.

The establishment of large Soviet fishing and whaling fleets has accompanied the Soviet Union's emergence as a maritime power possessing an impressive merchant marine—much of it constructed abroad. This development has occurred in spite of the fact that most of the Soviet ports are icebound for several months of each year. Exceptions include the ports of Murmansk on the Barents Sea; Poti, Batumi, Sukhumi, and Novorossiisk on the Black Sea; and Liepaja and Ventspils (in Latvia), Klaipeda (in Lithuania), and Kaliningrad (Koenigsberg) on the Baltic Sea.

River transport has been limited not only by the fact that Soviet rivers are frozen two or more months of the year in the south and six months in the north, but also by the location and direction of flow. The principal rivers flow in a northerly or southerly direction, while the country's great longitudinal extent creates a demand for transport which the rivers cannot fulfill. Thus European Russia and Siberia are not linked by a network of waterways except for the Arctic maritime link provided by the Northern Sea Route. However, this waterway can be traveled only during the short summer navigation season and often requires the use of icebreakers.[22] In the European part of the U.S.S.R. navigable rivers and a system of canals link the White and Baltic Seas with the Black and Caspian Seas. Yet river transport, though increasing in tonnage over the years, has declined relative to rail transport.

The state-owned railways remain the prime mode of transport and have been carrying the greater part of Soviet freight. The density of railroad trackage corresponds generally to the population pattern. Soviet railroads cover enormous distances, and are largely single-track, although there are lengthy electrified lines. The widely dispersed location of Soviet natural resources, industrial establishments, and markets has resulted in high transportation costs and in high traffic density. There is no hard-surfaced all-weather network of highways linking the various parts of the Soviet Union. As a result, the trucking of freight is limited to short hauls and is confined largely to urban areas.

The absence of a modern highway system and the vastness of the Soviet Union have necessitated the development of an extensive network of airways. In addition, the Soviet civil air fleet has military significance, as well as usefulness in cartography, in crop-dusting, and in aerial reconnaissance—as, for example, in guiding vessels through the pack ice on the Northern Sea Route. Soviet interest in transpolar flight was demonstrated as early as 1937, when two nonstop flights were made from Moscow to Vancouver, Washington, and San Jacinto, California, in single-motor aircraft.

[22] On the Northern Sea Route see Constantine Krypton, *The Northern Sea Route and the Economy of the Soviet North* (New York: Frederick A. Praeger, 1956).

Governmental direction and a willingness to ignore the cost factor in selected cases enabled the Soviet Union to inaugurate the first successful international jet civilian passenger service in August, 1956, with the Tupolev-104. If the state-owned Soviet air carrier Aeroflot, enjoying a monopoly, was slower than the competitive airlines of the United States in effecting the vast conversion from piston-driven to jet aircraft, it has not lagged in the development of the supersonic transport.

6. COMMUNICATIONS MEDIA

The most significant fact concerning Soviet communications media is that they are official organs either of the Soviet government or the Communist Party of the Soviet Union or one of its subordinate units or of public organizations directly controlled by the Party. The fact that all printing plants, radio and television stations, news agencies, newsprint suppliers, and cinema studios are government-owned testifies to the subordination of the media to political ends. The dissemination of Soviet newspapers and magazines is centralized in *Soiuzpechat'* (the Chief Administration for the Dissemination of the Press), a department in the Ministry of Communications which collects subscriptions and operates newsstands.

The content of the Soviet news media is effectively controlled by TASS (Telegraphic Agency of the Soviet Union), which is an official governmental body attached to the U.S.S.R. Council of Ministers. TASS often issues important announcements on behalf of the Soviet government. It provides the bulk of articles of more than local significance which appear in the local party and government press organs subscribing to the TASS service. TASS sends Soviet correspondents on foreign assignments and selects the news despatches from foreign media—usually those which confirm the stereotypes of the non-Soviet world.

The *Novosti* (News) Press Agency (APN) was established in 1961 to provide news and feature articles, commentaries, and photographs about Soviet life primarily for dissemination in foreign countries; it also publishes books, brochures, magazines, and a variety of visual materials in foreign languages. The *Novosti* Agency claims to be "commercial" and unofficial. Finally there are, in addition to TASS, subordinate official news agencies for the non-Russian union republics such as RATAU for Ukraine, BELTA for Belorussia, GRUZTAG for Georgia, UZTAG for Uzbekistan, and others. However, these republic news agencies do not deal directly with non-Soviet news agencies and have no foreign correspondents.[23]

The Soviet journalistic profession is under direct Communist Party control in that much of its membership is in the Party and is subject to its discipline. Nor does the Party hesitate to replace those editors with whose performance it is dissatisfied. State Committees for the Press and for Television and Radio Broadcasting are responsible for supervising the media under the watchful eye of the Party apparatus. Another means of control is through the Union of Journalists of the U.S.S.R.—founded in November, 1959, to give a special status to the writers of the press, periodicals, radio and television, and to enable the Party to mobilize and utilize their talents more effectively.

The leading Soviet newspaper is *Pravda,* official organ of the Communist Party of the Soviet Union, founded by V. I. Lenin in 1912. *Pravda,* which means "truth," is appropriately named if one bears in mind that it truthfully reflects the current line of the Soviet Communist Party. *Pravda's* importance lies in the fact that it gives the cue to Party members and to other Soviet media, and also prints in full Party decrees and key speeches. The official organ of the Soviet government is *Izvestiia* (The News).

Other Soviet newspapers with large circulations include *Komsomol'skaia Pravda,* official organ of the Central Committee of the League of Communist Youth, and *Trud* (Labor), official organ of the Central Council of Trade unions—as well as the *Literaturnaia Gazeta* (Literary Gazette), published by the Union of Writers. Other newspapers are published for teachers, children, sportsmen, medical workers, farmers, military personnel, civil defense workers,

[23] For a thorough study of Soviet journalism see Mark W. Hopkins, *Mass Media in the Soviet Union* (New York: Pegasus, 1970). Also see Theodore E. Kruglak, *The Two Faces of TASS* (Minneapolis, Minn.: University of Minnesota Press, 1962).

and "cultural workers." In all more than 8,000 newspapers are published in the Soviet Union, ranging from *Pravda* and more than 20 other press organs of an all-Union nature through approximately 140 union republic newspapers in various languages down to small collective farm and factory organs.[24]

Soviet newspapers have been limited in size to four or six pages per issue and have relatively little foreign news. Though containing little advertising, there is no dearth of exhortatory and remonstrative articles, especially in the fields of economic affairs and ideology. The Soviet press frequently fails to publish accounts of events which are regarded as newsworthy in many other countries. Much of the Soviet press is characterized by an official optimism, and news stories are often didactic in tone. Feature articles, essays, editorials, and commentary tend to overshadow news reporting. There is no open debate in the Soviet press on Party policies or on the military or foreign policy, although journalists do seek to expose local instances of maladministration and serious social problems—often with prompting in the form of letters to the editor. During the 1960's, the Soviet press tended to become more competitive, making an effort to be less dull and to heed readers' interests and preferences to a greater degree. The periodical press also acquired greater acceptance and academic journals could even sponsor printed discussions. Yet what is published still is printed always with a purpose—not merely to inform or entertain. The objectives of communist journalism were stated succinctly by Lenin as early as May, 1901, in an editorial published in *Iskra* (no. 4): "A newspaper is not only a collective propagandist and a collective agitator; it is also a collective organizer."[25] This statement, frequently quoted in Soviet journalistic circles, is equally applicable to Soviet radio and television, which also seek to indoctrinate and mobilize the population.

The Soviet radio network is distinctive in that nearly 40 percent of the receivers are simple wired speakers connected to a closed circuit over which a broadcast is retransmitted from a conventional

[24] *Yezhegodnik Bol'shoi Sovetskoi Entsiklopedii, 1969* (Moscow, 1969), p. 101.

[25] V. I. Lenin, *Polnoe Sobranie Sochinenii,* 5th ed. (Moscow: Gospolitizdat, 1961), V, 11.

radio receiver. This system has had several advantages from the point of view of the government: it is inexpensive; it prevents the listener from receiving foreign radio broadcasts; it compels the subscriber to the local radio service to listen to the limited program offering or forego use of the service; in public places the loudspeaker cannot be turned off by the listener. However, Soviet citizens may purchase conventional radio receivers and have been doing so in increasing numbers.

All broadcasting and telecasting facilities and programming are controlled by the State Committee for Television and Radio Broadcasting, attached to the U.S.S.R. Council of Ministers, which supervises bodies of the same name in the union republics. Soviet television, though less accessible than that of Western Europe, the United States, and Canada, has developed rapidly. One of its principal shortcomings has been limited programming.

7. SOCIAL STRUCTURE

Communist ideology has required the Soviet leadership to claim that the Soviet Union is in the process of establishing a "classless" society. This assertion is based upon the assumption that exploitation of man by man and the resultant class differences derive solely from precommunist societies and are to be found only in "bourgeois" or "capitalist" countries. However, it is a fact that marked differences exist between the various strata of the Soviet population. While claiming that the entire Soviet population consists of "toilers," the regime has been compelled to recognize the existence in the Soviet Union of two "friendly" classes—the workers and peasants—and a "stratum" in the case of the intelligentsia.[26]

The normal criteria for distinguishing between classes in terms of income differentials (reflected in housing, clothing, and living standards); prestige and the varying degrees of deference accorded certain groups; and the degree of influence and self-expression en-

[26] Iakov N. Umanskii, *Sovetskoe gosudarstvennoe pravo* (Moscow: Gosiurizdat, 1959), p. 95. Cf. V. V. Nikolaev, *Sovetskoe sotsialisticheskoe gosudarstvo* (Moscow: izd-vo "Nauka," 1968), pp. 38 and 359.

joyed by various groups, are all applicable to Soviet society and its class structure. Indeed, among the factors which have led to distinct social stratification is the industrial and urban Soviet economy—which has required an extensive hierarchy, a complex division of labor, and various kinds of technical expertise. The elitist nature of the Communist Party, with its political hierarchy and its use of various incentives in an economy characterized by many scarcities, has also been an important cause of stratification.

The total Soviet population of 242 million in 1970 was 56 percent urban and 44 percent rural (as contrasted with 48 percent urban in 1959). Females outnumbered males in 1970 by 19.1 million and constituted 53.9 percent of the population. However, Soviet data on social classes are hardly revealing because they refer to broad categories which embrace more than one stratum. Such categories as "workers" or "employees" are not homogeneous. A more realistic image of the class structure of the Soviet population requires that it be viewed in terms of the following strata: the Soviet ruling class, the "middle class," the intelligentsia, the urban working class, and the peasantry.

The ruling class cannot be equated with the entire membership of the Communist Party of the Soviet Union, but only with its leading cadres, which in turn must be viewed in terms of gradations of status and degrees of influence. Even all members of the Party's Central Committee are not equal in status and influence, and this pattern persists downward through the hierarchy of Communist Party officialdom. Another definition of the communist ruling class or elite is found in the "new class" concept of the disillusioned Yugoslav communist, Milovan Djilas (a former vice-president of Yugoslavia).[27] According to Djilas, the new class of owner-exploiters consists primarily of certain members of the party and state bureaucracy and is said to be the principal beneficiary of the country's economy. Thus, in spite of the myth that all natural resources and the means of production belong to the "people," the "fruits of the revolution" go to this oligarchy which, says Djilas, enjoys the "right of profit and control" of nationalized en-

[27] Milovan Djilas, *The New Class; An Analysis of the Communist System* (New York: Frederick A. Praeger, 1959).

terprises. The new class, having at its disposal the entire state machine, replaces the former capitalists and employs "socialist ownership" as a disguise for its having arrogated to itself the right to enjoy and dispose of nationalized property as it pleases.[28]

The Soviet "middle class" includes both Party members and non-Party members who serve the regime and benefit from it. It differs from the old petit bourgeoisie in that it is state-created. This stratum includes managerial and technical personnel, accountants, clerks, and persons performing various kinds of semiprofessional or specialized functions which in the West would be termed "white collar" positions. Although it is regarded as part of the Soviet working class, the middle class is frequently distinguished as "salaried" or as "employees" (*sluzhashchie*). This class overlaps with the intelligentsia, which in its broadest and hardly meaningful definition includes all persons who are not engaged in manual labor.[29] However, even if the intelligentsia is defined more precisely to include only professional, scientific, scholarly, educational, artistic, and literary endeavors, it still constitutes an important segment of the population—one that is highly trained and very useful to the government.

The urban working class can be divided into three substrata: the highly skilled workers in special sectors of industry, who are well paid by Soviet standards; the semiskilled and rank-and-file workers possessing medium skills; and the disadvantaged, who are grossly underpaid and who perform simple kinds of operations or menial tasks. The Soviet peasantry is distinguished from the urban working class because much of it is employed in "cooperative collectives" (as the collective farms are regarded in communist theory), although the government insists that both classes have common interests as a result of their presence in a "socialist" society which is "building communism." The Soviet regime has, in fact, sought to liquidate the differences between town and country, seeking in the end to convert collective farm peasants into agricultural laborers devoid of individual plots, livestock, and farm household ani-

[28] *Ibid.*, pp. 27, 35, 39f., 42, 44, 45, 47, 49f., 61f., 81, 82.

[29] *Politicheskii Slovar'*, ed. B. N. Ponomarev, 2d ed. (Moscow: Gospolitizdat, 1958), p. 211.

mals.[30] The income of peasants has varied with the particular collective farm and depends upon many factors, including the quality of farm management, the price paid by the state for agricultural commodities, climatic conditions, and the location of the farm. Thus the peasantry has been viewed by the regime as an indispensable part of the population, potentially dangerous to the extent that it retains the "village capitalist" mentality as reflected in its traditional desire to cultivate land individually.

Smaller but distinct strata or substrata of society are to be found in the secret police and security forces, in the professional military officer corps, and among those working on state farms. Those Soviet citizens who have at one time or other been charged with political (or economic) crimes and whose loyalty has been questioned also constitute a distinct group—but one whose opportunities have been limited.

Finally, however—if one discounts the factors of political unreliability and disadvantaged status resulting from lack of ability or opportunity—there nevertheless is a relatively high degree of mobility in Soviet society. This has been due to the expanding nature of the economy and the resultant demand for persons with skills. Mobility has also resulted from purges and ousters which have created vacancies; one man's misfortune has often been another's opportunity.

[30] Umanskii, *op. cit.* (above, n. 26), p. 96. Also see V. I. Lenin, *Polnoe Sobranie Sochinenii*, 5th ed., *op. cit.* (above, n. 25), XXXIX, 15 and 276–77.

CHAPTER 2

SOVIET POLITICAL CULTURE AND THE RUSSIAN POLITICAL TRADITION

The study of political culture is based on the assumption that peoples are not necessarily alike and that the political ethos varies from one people to another. Each people is regarded as having a distinctive set of political values which determines the form and substance of its political structures. A political culture embodies the "way of life" of a people—its ideals, beliefs, attitudes towards authority and the norms that serve to condition political behavior. It reflects the means by which a country was formed as well as the kinds of expectations its subjects have regarding the role of government and relations between rulers and ruled. Political culture involves the sources of loyalty to and psychological identification with the prevailing system; it determines the degree of commitment to a country's rulers, the trust that they enjoy, and what they can and cannot do. Among its manifestations is the perceptual factor—the particular ways in which those who share a culture perceive what is transpiring both within and beyond it. Thus, a people's self-image and their image of the outside world are of primary concern to the student of political culture.

The study of Soviet political culture is complicated by a number of factors in addition to those that are usually encountered in this area of investigation. It cannot be confined to the "operational code" of the Soviet elite (as derived from Bolshevik Party experience and doctrinal writings, and from the pre-Soviet intelligentsia).

The *modus operandi* of the political elite must instead be distinguished from the mass culture; and this is especially necessary in the case of the U.S.S.R., where the rulers have endeavored to instill in their subjects a set of beliefs different from their own. The ideas and values professed by the Soviet elite are dealt with consequently in the following chapter, while the concern of this chapter is the impact of the Russian political tradition upon Soviet political culture.

In view of the country's vast size and diversity and the common conflict between overt and normative behavior, it would be erroneous to assume that there is a single homogeneous Soviet political culture. Rather, there are various subcultures based on region (as those of Leningrad and the Soviet Far East), on social class, on the rural versus the urban milieu, and on the traditional versus the modern outlook. There are also numerous distinctive non-Russian cultures or subcultures in the various republics. Yet if the Soviet Union is a cultural mosaic of interacting components which has at times experienced extensive fragmentation, it also embodies certain dominant traits that are the central concern of this chapter.

It should be noted at the outset that certain caveats are in order. Although this area of investigation was originally derived from "national character" studies, it should in no sense be regarded as biological (or racist); the subject matter deals, rather, with learned behavior that is transmitted over time through succeeding generations but that is also subject to change. Thus, the presence over time of certain recurring cultural traits or behavioral syndromes does not in itself make them innate or immutable. If there is a danger that this area of study can become a vehicle for prejudice, stereotyped views, sweeping generalizations, and polemics directed against particular cultural traits, there is an equal danger in ignoring the impact upon the Soviet regime of Russian attitudes and traditional political practices. To study Russian (and Soviet) cultural traits, furthermore, does not necessarily imply acceptance of a mystical "Russian soul" nor does it mean adoption of a pessimistic view of the Russians as an incorrigible people.

The investigation of a political culture involves use of a wide variety of data and the astute observations of highly experienced and sophisticated interpreters and students of a people's development.[1] Where possible, mass political culture is studied by means of survey research and public opinion polls. Although these methods have not as yet been applied extensively to Soviet studies, direct observation and oral inquiry of a limited nature have been possible in the Soviet Union since Stalin's death. However, political culture can also be observed "at a distance" by study of historical data, classical literature, folk literature, contemporary fiction, personal documents (including memoirs and life history interviews), proverbs ("collective documents"), and child-rearing methods. As is to be expected, the use of such a variety of data has led to diverse hypotheses dealing with Russian (and Soviet) political culture.

1. THEORIES OF RUSSIAN POLITICAL BEHAVIOR

Attempts to explain the Russian character have ranged from geographic and climatic theories to psycho-cultural and historical ones. For example, the advocates of environmental determinism have emphasized the influence of the harsh Russian climate, the melancholic forests, and the seemingly endless plains.[2] Such speculative hypotheses cannot readily be tested empirically but they do prompt observers to search for underlying explanations of certain behavioral syndromes.

Interpretive Theories. This body of theory is based largely upon personal observation and the study of historic development, linguistic peculiarities, and overt group behavior. Among the most prominent of such observers was the Russian philosopher Nicolas

[1] The relevant literature, methodological problems, and kinds of data are surveyed in Alex Inkeles and D. J. Levinson, "National Character: The Study of Modal Personality and Sociocultural Systems," in Gardner Lindzey, ed., *Handbook of Social Psychology* (Cambridge, Massachusetts: Addison-Wesley, 1954), II, 977–1020; in Arvid Brodersen, "National Character: An Old Problem Re-examined," in James N. Rosenau, ed., *International Politics and Foreign Policy* (New York: Free Press of Glencoe, 1961), pp. 300–308; John S. Reshetar, Jr., *Problems of Analyzing and Predicting Soviet Behavior* (New York: Doubleday, 1955). Also see Alex Inkeles, "National Character and Modern Political Systems," in Francis L. K. Hsu, ed., *Psychological Anthropology, Approaches to Culture and Personality* (Homewood, Ill.: Dorsey Press, 1961), pp. 172–208.

[2] See the Russian historian V. O. Kliuchevsky, *Kurs russkoi istorii* (Moscow: Sotsekgiz, 1937), I, 57–60.

Berdyaev, who described the Russians as a "polarized people to the highest degree, a combination of opposites." He noted that: "One can become enchanted and disenchanted with them; from them one can always expect the unexpected; they are to the highest degree capable of inspiring intense love and intense hatred. This is a people that evokes the uneasiness of the peoples of the West." [3] Berdyaev contended that the Russian character was formed on the basis of two sets of fundamental opposites: "a native, pagan Dionysiac element and ascetic-monastic [Christian] Orthodoxy." He observed in his own people a series of contradictory characteristics:

> despotism, the hypertrophy of the state *and* anarchism, license; cruelty, a disposition to violence *and* kindliness, humanity and tenderness; belief in ritual *and* truth-seeking; individualism, a heightened consciousness of individual personality *and* faceless collectivism; nationalism, self-praise *and* universalism, identification with humanity (*vsechelovechnost'*); eschatological-messianic religiosity *and* outward piety; God-seeking *and* militant atheism; humility *and* impudence; slavery *and* rebellion.[4]

Berdyaev, who possessed one of the most brilliant minds of the twentieth century, cannot be said to have observed Russian behavior impressionistically. He knew Russia and the West well and saw the Russians as a contradictory people characterized by dualisms which had resulted from long historical experience—a conflict between Eastern and Western cultural influences in Russia and the inability of the Russians to identify fully with either. Although the Russian educated classes did endeavor to assimilate Western ideas, Berdyaev could not regard the Russians as a Western people. The Russian variant of Marxism was transformed into Leninism, therefore; and a knowledge of classical Marxism is not of great help in providing one with an understanding of Soviet politics. Berdyaev saw Russian communism as having national roots and regarded Leninism as a Russian phenomenon.[5] Russia's history has been painful and unhappy in Berdyaev's view, involving much suffering.

[3] Nikolai Berdyaev, *Russkaia ideia* (Paris: YMCA Press, 1946), p. 5.

[4] *Ibid.*, pp. 6–7.

[5] The thesis is developed and documented in Nicolas Berdyaev, *The Origin of Russian Communism* (London: Geoffrey Bles, 1948).

The expansive nature of the Russian—as contrasted with Western conciseness—Berdyaev explained in terms of the boundlessness and formlessness of the Russian landscape. He contended that the "Russian people fell a victim to the immensity of its territory." [6] Having acquired the world's largest empire, it had to acquiesce in a despotic regime in order to retain and organize its vast territorial possessions.[7] Ironically, however, this huge empire did not give the Russians the security that they ostensibly sought.

Another interpretive theory—expounded in the early 1950's by the Russian émigré historian of art, Wladimir Weidlé—sees Russia as being an integral part of Europe and desiring to identify with the West.[8] Byzantium, from which Eastern Slavdom received Christianity, is regarded by Weidlé as having been part of Europe. The presence of numerous foreigners in Russia's ruling class (including the dynasty founded by Rurik and the successor House of Romanov after the eighteenth century) is cited as proof for this thesis, along with evidence of Russian cultural and scientific borrowing from the West on a vast scale. The reforms of Peter I are also cited as evidence of Russian desire to be part of the West. According to Weidlé, Marxism was viewed by its Russian adherents as a European phenomenon to be adopted in the name of modernity and progress.

The basic question in assessing Weidlé's thesis is how extensive and profound the desire to identify with the West actually has been in Russian society. In fact, it was the Russian aristocracy that spoke French (Russian was the language of the peasants), vacationed at European spas, and built homes on the Côte d'Azur. If part of the intelligentsia desired to embrace certain European ideas and ways, another part of this class was no less certain in its rejection of Europe. Finally, Weidlé readily concedes that the Rus-

[6] *Ibid.*, p. 9.

[7] This view was held by Empress Catherine II, who, on the basis of Montesquieu's writings, contended that the size of her domain required absolutist rule. Montesquieu had held that large states and despotic rule went hand in hand. See Thornton Anderson. *Russian Political Thought, An Introduction* (Ithaca, N.Y.: Cornell University Press, 1967), p. 139.

[8] See Wladimir Weidlé, *Russia: Absent and Present*, trans. by A. Gordon Smith (New York: Vintage Books, 1961), *passim.* (The English translation was originally published by John Day Company in 1952.)

sian peasantry traditionally could not be absorbed into the nation or made to appreciate the meaning of national unity and pride.[9] He also observes that the Russians failed to produce a unified and stable culture and that their history has not been a "success"; it has lacked continuity and homogeneity and has been repeatedly subjected to upheavals.[10]

It is Weidlé's contention that the Soviet regime has rejected the values of the West and has reduced its ties with Europe. Indeed, he defines the Soviet Union as an "anonymous" Eurasian empire that has broken with Russia's past. Weidlé's interpretation raises many questions and his assertion that the Soviet regime is devoid of much Russian content can be doubted. He defines the Russians as a people endowed with humility and charity but incapable of accepting authority, and he contends that the Russians have succumbed to a "fatal antithesis" that has tragically negated what has allegedly been dearest to them. By failing to seek a compromise between supreme ideals and earthly virtues, the Russian has left himself vulnerable to the very things that he has despised and resisted: hierarchies, command, obedience, injustice, pharisaism, empty rhetoric, and an excess of form.[11] Thus, according to this definition the Russian is the antithesis of most of what he has claimed to profess and to desire. He has fallen victim to harsh rule in an effort to "avoid all rule." Russian history in this view is a series of antinomies resulting from the Russian's apparent inability to achieve self-mastery, overcome his amorphousness, limit his excesses, and pursue modest and attainable goals rather than some "supreme good."

A somewhat different interpretation of the Soviet regime sees it as a reflection of Russia's traditional peasant culture that has been blended with an overlay of modernism. Although Bolshevism was spawned by a segment of the Russian intelligentsia, the Soviet regime and the Communist Party were subsequently taken over by opportunistic Russian peasant types who left the village, became Party members, and made careers for themselves in the large cities,

[9] *Ibid.*, p. 115.
[10] *Ibid.*, pp. 17–18, 26, 47, and 117.
[11] *Ibid.*, pp. 168 and 171–172.

stamping the peasant imprint upon the regime. In this view, expounded by Nicholas Vakar in his *The Taproot of Soviet Society* (1961), the Soviet regime came to embody the triumph of ruthless, hardheaded, and power-conscious rustics, who, under other circumstances, would probably have been *kulaks* (tightfisted, resourceful peasants who acquired wealth initially through usury).

The traditional Russian peasant society promoted conformity through the system of communal landholding and periodic redistribution of the land, and by means of the patriarchal family. The maintenance of paternal authority based on tradition and on physical beating, bred resentment—but it also made acceptance of a political leader more likely. The peasant family was an autocratic order that came close to being a totalitarian dictatorship in microcosm. Peasant life was characterized by hostility and tension resulting from conflict with the father, by quarrels with neighbors, and by the presence of a landlord and of an overbearing officialdom. It existed in cultural isolation and allowed little personal privacy; it was a closed society that provided little room for individualists, although the peasant still retained a certain sense of pride and was suspicious of strangers.

Thus the Russian village—or at least part of it—emerged triumphant when it took over Lenin's party of disaffected intellectuals and effected a second revolution under Stalin. Harsh, covetous, calculating, cunning, and ruthless peasant types and their scions became the new Soviet ruling class. This thesis relegates Marxist-Leninist ideology to a secondary place and will be subject to modification as Soviet society becomes increasingly urban and is modernized and, hopefully, matures. However, the significance of the thesis lies in its view that the communist model for revolution is inevitably subject to the demands of the native culture, even though that culture is itself subject to change.

The Contribution of Historicism. The emergence in the fifteenth century of an autocratically-ruled Russian state based upon Muscovy has prompted the search for its origins in external influences. These have been attributed to two sources: the 240 years of Mongol rule to which the Eastern Slavs were subjected (1240–1480) and the cultural impact of the Byzantine Empire, from which the Slavs received Christianity and other cultural attributes.

The influence of the Mongols upon Russian development has been recognized by prominent Russian historians including Nikolai Karamzin, Paul Miliukov, and the so-called Eurasian School of Russian émigré historians led by Prince N. S. Trubetskoy. The Mongols, leading a large Turco-Tatar force (the two were later referred to as the Golden Horde—from the Turkic *urdu,* "the tent and residence of the khan"), easily succeeded in mastering the steppe and in overrunning and subjugating the Eastern Slavic peoples, who were divided into numerous principalities and could not mount an effective resistance. The Mongols, who were not numerous, not only exacted tribute from their Slavic subjects but exercised a profound impact upon their institutions and statecraft. To the Mongols can be attributed an influence in the system of effective taxation, military organization, census-taking, postal system, and intelligence service.[12] Not least of all, Mongol rule—although it recognized religious toleration and granted churches and clergy exemption from taxes and tribute—taught the Russians submission to secular rulers.

The case for making the Mongols responsible for the introduction of "Oriental despotism" into Russia has been stated most forcefully, and with much erudition, by Professor Karl A. Wittfogel. According to his explanation, Oriental despotism emerged in arid or semiarid regions that required the construction of large-scale water-conservancy works and irrigation facilities; it was also present in humid areas in which aquatic plants, such as rice, were cultivated. The need to erect and maintain such facilities led to the establishment of a "single-centered system," in which the despot and his bureaucracy were able to acquire "total power" based on heavy taxation, corvée labor, service to the state, and terror.[13] Al-

[12] The Russian language was enriched by such Turco-Tartar words as *den'gi* (money), *khalat* (robe), *kreml'* (kremlin), *karakul'* (karakul), and *kazak* (cossack). The state monopoly of alcoholic beverages, retained under the Soviet regime, was originally adopted from Tatar practice.

[13] See Karl A. Wittfogel, *Oriental Despotism, A Comparative Study of Total Power* (New Haven: Yale University Press, 1957).

though private property existed, in such a system its ownership does not entail political power. In this hydraulic-bureaucratic system the population is atomized; it exists in villages that are isolated and offer no effective resistance to the single center, the seat of total power. China, to the study of which Wittfogel devoted much of his academic career, provides the classic model of a self-perpetuating Oriental despotism. However, Wittfogel has also applied the concept of a "hydraulic society" to India, the Near East, and to the Incas. In each case, the state is stronger than society, and both ruler and ruled are alienated and lonely. In contrast, a "multicentered society" is stronger than the state.

Post-Mongol Muscovy and the Russian Empire that emerged from it are viewed by Wittfogel as a "marginal agrarian despotism" based on the Oriental model, although Russia has a rainfall agriculture and did not develop a "hydraulic economy." The Mongols are said to have introduced into Russia methods of despotic rule that they acquired in China.[14] The kind of state which developed in Muscovy was an absolute service state, in which land was distributed and retained conditionally on the basis of service to the ruler (the *pomestie* system). Although Muscovy did not adopt such Oriental institutions as polygamy and political eunuchism, its rulers remained unlimited autocrats until well into the twentieth century. Although pre-Muscovite Russia, by comparison, was not a single-centered society, Imperial Russia, based on the Muscovite model, was an atomized society of isolated villages lacking roads; and the tsarist bureaucracy could not be effectively challenged by other classes.

It is profoundly ironic that the concept of Oriental despotism was developed and actually applied to Imperial Russia by Marx and Engels in the 1850's and that this designation was accepted by such Russian Marxists as Plekhanov and Lenin.[15] Originally Marx and Engels recognized a distinctive "Asiatic mode of production"; and they did not seek to submerge it in their three-stage model for

[14] See the discussion of "Russia and the East" published in the *Slavic Review*, XXII, No. 4 (December, 1963), 627–662.

[15] This is amply documented in Karl A. Wittfogel, "The Marxist View of Russian Society and Revolution," *World Politics*, XII, No. 4 (July, 1960), 487–508. See also Chap. 9 in Wittfogel's *Oriental Despotism*.

explaining Western historical development in terms of slaveholding, feudal, and capitalist periods. Thus Marxism originally denied the notion of unilinear development, so widely held during the nineteenth century. In repeatedly referring to Russia as an "Oriental despotism" and as an "Asiatic" country, Marx and Engels expressed an initial awareness of development as a multilinear phenomenon. Lenin also referred to Russia as "Asiatic" and "savage" and expressed concern that an "Asiatic restoration" might take place despite modernization.[16] The original Marxist-Leninist view of Russia was abandoned by Lenin in 1916 when it became an embarrassing obstacle to the politically expedient notion of unilinear historical development. Under Stalin, the concept of a distinctive Asiatic society was purged from the communist historical and ideological lexicon and was replaced with "feudalism."[17]

The other external influence in Russian development—apart from that of the Mongols (Asiatic society)—was that of Byzantium, which also had several centuries in which to make itself felt. In Wittfogel's view, Byzantium was an Oriental despotism whose influence on the Eastern Slavs was primarily cultural and did not affect political relationships. Yet a case can be made for Byzantine influence on Russian political thought and values. Byzantium provided a model for the Russian ruler both as a defender of religious faith and dogma, and as its propagator; the notion of a state church meant that rulers would be selected on the basis of divine guidance and meant also the general absence of conflict between religious and secular life. Byzantium also served as an example of centralism and of a hierarchic conception of politics. If Byzantium gave the Eastern Slavs and Russians Orthodox Christian religious dogma, liturgical forms, church architecture, and religious art, it

[16] By 1884, in *The Origin of the Family, Private Property and the State,* Engels had abandoned the concept of "Oriental despotism," probably because of its disturbing implications for a movement (Marxism) that wished to establish a dictatorial state and employ despotic means to attain its ends.

[17] In the post-Stalin period, largely due to the impact of Wittfogel's research and the question of China, Soviet writers have been compelled to deal with the problem of the Asiatic mode of production. However, the concepts of a single-centered society and of total power wielded by a state bureaucracy that controls the means of production have had very discomforting implications for those who view the Soviet regime as the embodiment of a new order.

also taught them that Europe (Rome) was heretical. Byzantine influence meant that the Russians were to be cut off from Europe and live in cultural isolation. Russian culture was largely clerical (and monastic) and suffered from a lack of respect for secular learning; the clergy did not usually learn Greek or Latin. Byzantium also provided Russia with a static view of truth, so that orthodoxy extended beyond the religious sphere.

Psycho-Cultural Theories. The body of theory that deals with the relationship between Russian culture and personality attempts to identify and explain modal personality traits. While such traits might not be found in all Russians, their presence is regarded as sufficiently widespread, despite the existence of subgroups, to make possible tentative definition of a modal personality pattern. Personality traits are generally regarded as being derived from child-rearing experiences, from preadult learning, and from the personal experiences of adult individuals with the regime and with political figures. Personality is viewed as a product not only of the social system but of the political culture as well. Thus, various types of data can be used in the search for modal personality traits and their sources.

One of the more controversial psycho-cultural theories is based on the swaddling hypothesis associated with Geoffrey Gorer and Dr. John Rickman, a physician who practiced medicine in Russia from 1911 to 1918; this theory has also been espoused by Dr. Margaret Mead. In an effort to explain the psychology of the Russian national character (in which guilt and group pressure and moral responsibility were all seen as playing a role), Gorer and Rickman concluded that the Russian peasant practice of swaddling infants for all or most of the first year of life provides some possible clues to Russian behavior. According to this practice, still employed in the Soviet Union, the peasant infant is tightly swaddled or wrapped in strips of cloth with its legs straight and its arms at its sides; this involves complete constraint and absence of gratification, alternating with complete freedom and total gratification while the infant is breastfed or bathed and given attention. The swaddled infant can express its emotions only by moving its eyes or by screaming if its mouth is not stuffed with a pacifier. Complete inhibition of movement is followed by its opposite, and the absence of inhibition is then followed by its reimposition when the infant is once again wrapped like a parcel in being swaddled.

The swaddled infant is said to experience "intense and destructive rage" as a result of the complete inhibition of movement. By means of "projection" the infant is said to attribute its own thoughts and wishes to vague figures in its environment and to fear retaliation if it should attempt to gratify its own destructive wishes. However, swaddling makes it impossible for the infant to gratify such destructive wishes and he is spared the retaliation that he allegedly fears. Central to the hypothesis is the notion that hostility is accompanied by a profound and diffused guilt feeling as well as by fear, as a result of this child-rearing practice. Swaddling also allegedly induces in the infant a feeling of "complete loneliness and helplessness" after having exhausted itself both physically and psychologically in expressing rage. Yet the restraint is also seen as preventing gratification of the infant's destructive wishes and as serving to protect the infant from "the fancied perils of retaliation." [18]

Central to the hypothesis is the argument that most Russians manifest a diffuse unconscious feeling of guilt and fear, which originates with the projection of infantile hostility and is subsequently reinforced. In support of this contention, Gorer cites the role of sin and guilt in the Russian Orthodox Church and the relief provided to believers by the ritual of absolution. The importance of enemies and of "dark and sinister forces" is stressed both in traditional Russian folklore and in the Soviet view of historical development ("capitalists," "fascists," "imperialists," "Trotskyites"). Public shaming, used in the traditional peasant community, has been employed by the Soviet regime to induce compliance as has the practice of "criticism and self-criticism." Thus guilt-feeling has been perpetu-

[18] For Gorer's exposition of his hypothesis and its genesis, see Geoffrey Gorer and John Rickman, *The People of Great Russia, a Psychological Study* (New York: Chanticleer Press, 1950), pp. 93–153, 197–226. The hypothesis was not claimed by Gorer to be more than "one of a presumably large number of antecedents" to the development of the Russian character. He conceded that he undoubtedly overemphasized the possible derivatives of the practice of swaddling and stated explicitly that "it is a clue, not a cause of Russian behavior" (p. 198; cf. pp. 128f.).

ated. The alleged presence of a "free-floating unfocused hostility" in the Russian people is said to have been reinforced by the Soviet regime in directing popular hatred toward various countries, class enemies, alleged aggressors, and warmongers.

If "all-pervasive unconscious hostility and guilt" have been attributes of the Russians, then it is understandable that the Russian people have had a tendency to idealize their leadership (whether that of the autocracy or of the Communist Party). Gorer contends that the psychological well-being of the Russians has depended upon their preserving one figure that is supposedly uncontaminated by suspicion, fear, and guilt. Thus, an idealized and strong leadership has been acceptable to Russians to protect them from anarchy and from their own guilt.

The polarity which Berdyaev saw in the Russians was also evident to Gorer as an oscillation syndrome which could have had its prototype in the swaddling experience, with its alternating treatment of constraint followed by gratification. Thus, he too noted sudden switches in Russian behavior: total gratification (orgiastic feasting and drinking) followed by fasting and deprivation; violence changing to gentleness, kindness followed by cruelty, and activity followed by passivity. Similarly, "friends" could suddenly be unmasked as "enemies." Such profound changes of feeling, "swings in mood," and manifestations of instability and inactivity were often evident in the conduct of the Russian intelligentsia and in Russian literature; and—it should be noted—they have been condemned by the communists. The Bolshevik "operational code" as defined by Dr. Nathan Leites, has advocated control of the emotions and feelings and has condemned "emotional incontinence" and passivity.[19]

The apparent tendency to alternate between diametrically opposite extremes has also been attributed to the traditional Russian patriarchal family structure. The alternations of kindness and severity, gentleness and brutality, rebelliousness and resignation have been noted; outbursts of feverish activity and euphoria have alternated with inertia, apathy, and despair; Russian tyranny has bred

[19] See Nathan Leites, *A Study of Bolshevism* (Glencoe, Ill.: The Free Press, 1953), pp. 186–275 and 314–340 *passim.*

demands for absolute liberty and these, in turn, have led to reimposition of harsh rule. It is possible that these traits could be attributed originally to Russian child-rearing practices and to familial relationships. It has been contended that the traditional family structure bred persons (especially males) with such traits as dependence, fear, a sense of guilt, mistrust, power-seeking, duplicity, and emotional instability.[20] Traditionally the male has dominated the female, and submission and fear have characterized the father-child relationship. Children experienced different treatment from the father and the mother: the father tended to demand and receive unquestioning obedience while the mother treated children with warmth and solicitude but also exercised firm and sometimes unpredictable authority. The father-son relationship, one of dominance-submission often characterized by physical beating and abusive treatment, is said to have resulted in much tension and mutual hostility. This, in turn, fostered self-pity; a sense of insecurity, inadequacy, and guilt-feeling; and has produced a personality type that is both domineering and/or servile—depending upon circumstances—and one capable of destructive aggressiveness. Insofar as Russian regimes have been based on arbitrariness and coercion they may be said to have perpetuated and reinforced these traits.

An attempt to identify the traits of the Russian modal personality on the basis of psychological interviewing has provided a degree of confirmation for certain of the statements offered above. Such a survey was undertaken by the British psychiatrist Dr. Henry V. Dicks, who conducted intensive interviews with a group of twenty Russian male defectors, most of whom had served in the Soviet armed forces during World War II. Dr. Dicks observed in his Russians a conflict between oral and anal personality traits characterized by ambivalence and by oscillation in large swings between extremes of behavior. The gratification of oral traits is said to be an important aspect of Russian "need systems." Included

[20] This hypothesis has been advanced in Dinko Tomasic, *The Impact of Russian Culture on Soviet Communism* (Glencoe, Ill.: Free Press, 1953), pp. 77–120. Evidence for this hypothesis can be found in Russian folk literature and proverbs, and in the *Domostroi,* the sixteenth-century code for family life compiled by the priest Sylvester, counselor and confessor to Ivan the Terrible.

here are the Russian preoccupation with food and its acquisition, the fondness for vodka as a means of alleviating tensions, the fondness for talk and singing, and the desire to gratify other impulses quickly and fully. Such outbursts of prodigality, spontaneity, and "manic omnipotence feeling" are succeeded by apathy, hostility, melancholy, and self-depreciation. It is not unusual for feelings of superiority and contempt to alternate with expressions of self-abasement and inferiority.[21]

Dr. Dicks also observed in his respondents a diffuse guilt feeling and a "ruminative self-doubt," as well as a reluctant recognition of a need for an authority that is arbitrary, capable of limiting self-indulgence, and of providing a "coercive moral corset." Authority (*vlast'*) is viewed as something that is to be feared but regarded as necessary; it is expected to be severe and arbitrary, capricious and deprivational, and is resentfully obeyed as well as inwardly resisted, admired, and disliked. The ambivalent attitude toward authority is related to the generally recognized role of the political elite as promoting mastery over the gratification of impulses, mass organization of purposeful activities such as economic growth and achievement of communist goals, and the ability to withstand deprivation. The oral-anal conflict seen in the Russian character means that the subject often recognizes the need for restrictions imposed by those in authority in order to combat anarchic tendencies, depressive apathy, other forms of impulse gratification, paranoid hatred, and self-hatred. Guilt-feeling and doubt are coped with through outbursts of organized effort and by the psychological mechanisms of displacement and projection. However, such anal traits as the acquisition of property, punctuality, orderliness, and discipline have not been congenial to the Russian culture pattern and have had to be instilled in the population by the regime. Thus, the Soviet regime has literally waged war against the Russian modal personality and has also been affected by it.

[21] Henry V. Dicks, "Observations on Contemporary Russian Behavior," *Human Relations*, V, No. 2 (1952), 111–175. Also see Dicks's "Some Notes on the Russian National Character," in Cyril E. Black, ed., *The Transformation of Russian Society* (Cambridge, Mass.: Harvard University Press, 1960), pp. 636–652; and cf. the related papers in the same volume, especially those of Robert C. Tucker ("The Image of Dual Russia"), Frederick C. Barghoorn ("Some Russian Images of the West"), and J. S. Reshetar, Jr. ("Russian Ethnic Values"), as well as the summary and review by Hans Speier.

The Soviet political elite is said to be generally characterized by the presence of anal (and compulsive) personality traits. This is understandable in officials who have risen from humble peasant origins. Anal traits are also related to and lend credence to the viewpoint of Bolshevism as a "reaction formation." In this interpretation Lenin and his fellow Bolsheviks are seen as having reacted in opposition to certain qualities of the Russian intelligentsia that they regarded as harmful.[22] Yet Dicks has contended that the less attractive features of the Soviet regime have been made tolerable by means of "backsliding," and by various forms of oral gratification (including the use of alcohol). Even a harsh and demanding authority can be accepted and tolerated by Russians if it does not become devoid of the paternalistic and human quality and if it does not indulge in *izdevatel'stvo* (mockery and humiliation).

At the same time there is a related Russian tendency to impassiveness reflected in apathy, patience, and endurance, and in a willingness to bear pain and to accept much with fatalism (the *nichevo* syndrome). There is an apparent need in the Russian to see authority as a source of truth and initiative and this helps to induce submissiveness. Adjustment to the regime is facilitated also if it permits a degree of personal autonomy. Submissiveness is made acceptable by the Russian need for affiliation and the desire to confide in someone who is safe and friendly. According to Dicks, there is a need to be loved by the group and to be accepted.

Certain key findings of Dr. Dicks's study were confirmed by a survey based on clinical psychological research conducted by the Harvard Project on the Soviet Social System. This investigation involved the interviewing of 51 former Soviet citizens, nearly all of whom were Russians and most of whom (41) were males. The respondents were also given a battery of psychological tests—as was a matched sample of Americans.[23] The results confirmed Dicks's discovery of a Russian need for affiliation and dependence and a strong desire to interact with other people and to enjoy affection. There is also confirmation of orality as a need and preoccupation

[22] See Leites, *op. cit.* (above, n. 19), pp. 21–22, 148–165, 201–231.

[23] See Alex Inkeles, Eugenia Hanfmann, and Helen Beier, "Modal Personality and Adjustment to the Soviet Socio-Political System." *Human Relations*, XI, No. 1 (1958), 3–22. Reprinted in Alex Inkeles, *Social Change in Soviet Russia* (Cambridge: Harvard University Press, 1968), Chap. 6.

with food and drink, volubility, and singing. By contrast, the American matched sample stressed achievement (not evident in the Russian group) and need for approval, as well as autonomy without being isolated from the group. The Russians were found to manifest "emotional aliveness" and expansiveness and to be very much aware of their impulses, willing to give in to them but also to be highly cognizant of the need to control them. Yet such impulse-control is not seen as emerging from within the person but as resulting from "guidance and pressure exerted by higher authority and by the group."

The Russians were seen as manifesting behavior or viewpoints of a polarized nature and as being concerned with the choices represented by such alternatives. This tends to confirm Dicks's conclusions regarding the contradictoriness and ambivalence of the Russian character. The Harvard clinical study found its Russian subjects to be consciously concerned with conflicts between trust versus mistrust in relation to others, faith versus despair, and activity versus passivity. Russians are seen as desiring leaders to be warm, nurturant, and considerate of their subjects' welfare. Authority is expected to give orders, require obedience, and exercise initiative; it is also expected to employ coercion and other sanctions to "control bad impulses in individuals" and to be stern and demanding. Whether or not a government is properly elected or follows exact legal procedures is not seen as important; a "good" government is one that provides what Dicks termed an "external moral corset" and that is not arbitrary, unjust, and unapproachable. Russians appear to rely less on self-control in curbing emotions and impulses than Americans do. They tend to passively accommodate themselves to difficult situations while also being "capable of great bursts of activity." Relations between ruled and rulers are seen in terms of a "we"–"they" dichotomy that reflects a basic incompatibility between the political elite and its subjects.

Although the psycho-cultural data from which the modal personality traits of the Russians are derived are not as plentiful in a quantitative sense as one would desire, they nonetheless do provide significant hypotheses and tend to confirm some of the interpretive theories and impressionistic observations discussed elsewhere in this chapter. Ultimate confirmation, refutation, or modification of these psycho-cultural hypotheses could only be had if a larger sample of Russians (and subsamples from various strata and non-Russian republics) were to be studied *in the Soviet Union* with the same clinical interview instruments. Such social science field research would not only be very costly but could not be undertaken without the consent of the Soviet regime—an unlikely occurrence.

2. PERSISTENT SYNDROMES

A political culture—which, as has been shown, can be studied in terms of the behavior and character of a people—can also be studied in terms of the relationship and interaction between national cultural traits, and political structures and practices, by viewing the latter in the context of their historical development. A functioning polity can remain the product of a people's political tradition even when a revolutionary regime seeks to remake a system and its people on the basis of a novel creed. Political structures and action reflect attitudes and values; and institutions, once established, can also instill or reinforce certain traits.

Political experience, attitudes, and values are transmitted over generations; and historical experience, in turn, influences attitudes and values. Each political culture can be said to have been shaped by the problems which have confronted the country's rulers and to which solutions have been sought over time. The presence of persistent issues and conflicts, and the preference for one type of solution as against another inevitably have a profound impact upon the political culture. Norms of political conduct, the sources and nature of alienation from the system, and the conditions under which departure from norms is more likely—all must be considered in any attempt at a definition of a people's political culture.

A political culture consists of a set of interrelated traits. While it is possible to find a particular trait in more than one political culture (e.g., Russia, England, and France experienced royal absolutism at particular times), it is the degree to which the trait manifests itself and its intensity over time that are important. Thus, it is the particular combination of traits and their total configuration that are significant and that distinguish one polity from another.

Centralization of Power and the Denial of Autonomy. Probably the most significant fact regarding Russian political culture has been that it spawned an autocratic order and then perpetuated it over a period of four and a half centuries. The advent of Russian autocracy was an outgrowth of the emergence of the principality of Muscovy (Moscow) initially as a modest center in a remote part of the zone of mixed forests during the period of Mongol suzerainty. The princes of Muscovy obtained an advantageous position by pursuing a policy of collaboration with the Mongol rulers and by serving as collectors of tribute from other Russian principalities. They also scored a gain by 1326 in attracting the Metropolitan (Archbishop) of the Orthodox Church to Moscow and causing him to abandon the principality of Vladimir-on-the-Kliaz'ma as his see. Although the hierarch was formally subordinate to the Byzantine Patriarchate at Constantinople, his presence in Muscovy and the close relationship between religious and secular authority gave its princes a decided advantage. Soon they appropriated for themselves the title "of all Rus'" that had hitherto been limited to the ecclesiastical jurisdiction of the Kiev metropolitans. Muscovy's rulers also acquired Mongol-Tatar techniques of statecraft and took the lead in resisting the Golden Horde. With such advantages, it was possible for Muscovy to subjugate neighboring principalities and to become, in turn, the successor to the Golden Horde.

The leading rival of Muscovy was Novgorod (usually referred to in the Chronicles as "Lord Novgorod the Great"), a principality located to the north and west of Muscovy. The significance of Novgorod lay in its older tradition (it antedated Moscow by approximately three centuries), in its role as a great commercial center having ties with the German Hanseatic cities, and in its unique political order. Novgorod developed as a republic ruled largely by the commercial and land-owning class. Although it had princes, they were not hereditary princes and were ultimately compelled to consent to having their powers circumscribed on the basis of a written agreement. Occasionally a prince was ousted. Novgorod had as elected officials the mayor (*posadnik*), the head of its militia, and even its bishop after 1156. Sovereignty reposed in the popular assembly (*veche*), the meetings of which (held in the market place) were often tumultuous; authority was actually exercised by a small number of local magnates.

If Novgorod rather than Muscovy had become the center of Russian political development in the post-Mongol period, it is likely that Russian political culture would have acquired a very different character from that given it by Muscovy. Instead, Novgorod was subjugated by Ivan III and annexed by Muscovy in 1478. The prince of Muscovy had been able to intervene in Novgorod's internal affairs as a result of conflict within the city's population. Following annexation, Ivan III abolished Novgorod's *veche* and removed to Moscow the great bell that had been used to summon the citizens to this popular assembly. Those in Novgorod who resisted Muscovite rule—numbering more than 7,000—were deported, and their homes and lands were given to Muscovites who were sent to replace them. Muscovy was to employ this practice also in subjugating other Russian principalities.[24] The historian Kliuchevsky described the early princes of Muscovy as "shameless plunderers" unhindered by any traditions, lacking any sense of propriety, and guided solely by the desire for self-aggrandizement.[25]

The emergence of absolutist rule in Muscovy occurred in several stages as its rulers extended their domain and claimed more grandiloquent titles and more remote antecedents. In succeeding the rulers of the Golden Horde and also in subsequently claiming the Mongol-Tatar lands, the rulers of Muscovy sought to "legitimize" their self-aggrandizement in various ways. One means was to replace the title of prince (*kniaz'*) with that of *tsar'*, a Russian version of *caesar.* Ivan IV (the Terrible) was the first ruler to be

[24] More than four centuries later the Soviet regime was to adopt a similar practice in some of the non-Russian republics, deporting large numbers of the indigenous population to Russia and introducing Russians in their place, especially in urban centers.

[25] V. O. Kliuchevsky, *Kurs russkoi istorii* (Moscow, 1937), II, 13.

crowned with this title, and he subsequently claimed by conquest the important Mongol-Tatar successor states by proclaiming himself to be "tsar of Kazan" and "tsar of Astrakhan."

The effort to create ties with Byzantium's former rulers and to claim to be the successor to the "Second Rome" had occurred earlier, during the reign of Ivan III—who in 1472 married Sophia Paleologa, a niece of the last Byzantine emperor. Ivan III also assumed the title of *Gosudar'* (sovereign) and was referred to as "autocrat." During the reign of Ivan III there was introduced the so-called cap of Monomakh, which the autocrat placed on his grandson's head. This "crown"—probably of Turkic origin—subsequently became the subject of a legend to the effect that it had been given to Vladimir Monomakh, the Grand Prince of Kiev (1113–25), by the Byzantine Emperor. The absurdity of this claim, in view of the fact that the hat did not even remotely resemble a Byzantine crown, testifies to the penurious nature of Muscovite legitimacy. The effort to embellish the claim continued when the Abbot Philotheus of Pskov early in the sixteenth century asserted Moscow's claim to be the "Third Rome"—the successor to Rome and Byzantium. According to this theory both the western and eastern Roman empires had fallen because of heresy, and the task of preserving true religious faith now fell to the Muscovite tsar. As the sole independent Orthodox Christian ruler, the tsar could claim to possess special virtue and demand unqualified obedience.

Muscovite monarchical authority was enhanced during the half-century reign of Ivan IV (the Terrible) (1533–84), as the power of the aristocratic boyars declined and the tsar's domains increased resulting from foreign acquisitions and domestic confiscation. Ivan's move against his opponents came in January, 1565, after he withdrew from Moscow with a military force; when he was asked to return he stipulated conditions, including the right to arrest those whom he deemed disloyal. He launched a policy of terror, torture, exile, and executions; and by confiscating the estates of his victims, he broke the power of the boyar class. He established a royal reserve of land, the *Oprichnina,* from which he rewarded loyal followers. He also established a royal guard, the members of which were known as *oprichniki;* this 6,000-man force wore black uniforms, rode black horses, and had a dog's head and broom as its emblem, depicting the sweeping out of traitors. The excesses of this royal force and the increased royal prerogative were a marked departure from earlier practice, in which the grand prince relied on the advice of his boyars. Instead, the tsar regarded his domain as his personal estate, and the boyars and others had little choice but to submit or flee.

Among those who fled was Prince Andrei Kurbskii, who sought refuge in Lithuania-Poland in 1564 after serving Ivan IV for many years. Kurbskii—who, like Ivan, was a member of the Riurikide house—exchanged letters with the tsar, and this correspondence figured prominently in Russian political thought. The Prince attempted to reason with Ivan and to persuade him to recognize the value of wise counsel and to avoid "foul parasites and adulators" who told the ruler what he wished to hear. Ivan responded with an unqualified defense of autocracy and rejected the very thought of taking counsel with others, who by definition were his inferiors. The autocrat was responsible only to God and was God's instrument.

Although autocracy experienced a setback during the "Time of Troubles" early in the seventeenth century, after the Riurikide dynasty came to an end, it reasserted itself with the establishment of the Romanov dynasty in 1613. In the middle of the century the Church was again subordinated to the crown, with the failure of the efforts of Patriarch Nikon to claim for the Church superiority or at least coequal status with the state. The autocratic order was also vastly strengthened during the reign of Peter I (the Great) in the first quarter of the eighteenth century. Peter decapitated the Orthodox Church by abolishing the Patriarchate and replacing it with a collegial body, the Holy Synod, headed by a layman. He ignored the Assembly (*Duma*) of Boyars, but he used his enhanced powers to introduce reforms and especially foreign technical skills.

The presence of a strong monarch made possible the extensive utilization and even enhancement of autocratic power. When the monarch was a weak person or a minor, the autocracy functioned through the bureaucracy (rule by arbitrary and uncontrolled officialdom) or—in earlier periods—through the boyars, as during

Ivan the Terrible's childhood or during the "Time of Troubles." Russian monarchs crowned themselves at their coronations as if to demonstrate that their powers were not derived from any human source apart from the autocracy itself. Autocracy remained the basis of the Russian political order until October, 1905, when it was partially modified to allow for a quasi-parliamentary body, the State Duma, to which government ministers were *not* responsible.

It is significant that the Russian word *vlast'* has multiple meaning, being used to express such different terms as "regime," "authority," "dominion," and "power." Thus, the distinction between arbitrary rule based on force and that based on legitimized authority is blurred in this word. Indeed, the blurring may be a semantic reflection of the lack in Russia of adequate countervailing forces to check autocratic power and the absence of effective institutional restraints to prevent its growth. Neither the Church nor the boyars were, in the long run, able to check the autocracy. Although the *Zemskii Sobor* (Assembly of the Land) emerged in the middle of the sixteenth century and included clergy, nobles, and merchants, it did not limit the tsar's prerogatives either. He could hear its advice but did not have to heed it. The fact that the Assembly elected the first Romanov tsar in 1613 did not make the Romanovs limited monarchs. Finally, because it was a purely consultative body and did not meet regularly, the Assembly could not be independent. It did not survive the seventeenth century. The *pomestie* system, which lasted until the eighteenth century (1762), provided for a gentry based on land tenure conditional upon service to the state, and meant that those who enjoyed its benefits were dependent upon the absolute monarch.

The observation of the Russian historian Kliuchevsky that "the state expands, the people grow sickly" reflects the Russian failure —as a result of having nurtured an absolutist polity—to develop a pluralistic or multicentered society. Thus, even the traditional rights of cities assured under the Magdeburg Law to such urban centers as Riga and Tallin—and to Kiev, Poltava, Chernigov, and other Ukrainian cities—were abolished. The failure to develop effective institutional restraints on autocratic power was to have profound consequences.

It is not surprising that the CPSU adapted to its own ends the centralist order of the Russian autocracy. The communist ruling class—which claims a monopoly on truth and political power and claims to be the source of wisdom, justice, and moral good—provides a collectivized modern counterpart to the Russian tsars, who were supposedly all-wise and all-powerful and who ruled on the basis of divine right. The tsars were responsible only to God and to their own conscience, while the communist rulers have claimed to be responsible only to "history," as conveniently understood in terms of their own philosophy.

Resistance, Sectarianism, and Anarchic Tendencies. If the centralist syndrome and the denial of autonomy were the sole dimensions of the Russian political tradition, the task of defining that tradition would be far less complicated. For there is a wealth of evidence indicating that Russians have never submitted totally or permanently to their rulers. The gulf separating rulers from ruled in Russia has been both broad and deep. Rulers have often represented alien forces and have endeavored to impose foreign ways. This applies to the original Rurikide dynasty as well as to the later House of Romanov, which became German after 1762. The imposition of Christianity, the reforms of Peter I, and the modernization introduced by Stalin's regime testify to the presence of rulers who have sought to change traditional ways.

Authority has been distrusted and challenged when the opportunity has presented itself. The *veche,* or popular assembly, in the pluralistic Eastern Slavic society of *Rus'* in the pre-Mongol period, opposed the princes, especially in Kiev and Novgorod. The requirement of unanimity was often satisfied by recourse to violence and under duress, while the emergence of absolutism and serfdom led to the flight of serfs to the frontier areas. It also resulted in the great peasant revolts of Bolotnikov (1606–08), Sten'ka Razin (1670–71), and Emilian Pugachev (1773–74). The burning of manor houses persisted into the twentieth century and the 1917 revolution was accompanied by an outburst of peasant wrath. It is such events that prompted Russia's greatest poet, Pushkin, to refer to Russian rebellion as "senseless and ruthless."

The Russians have a rich tradition of religious sectarianism, despite the earlier presence of a regime dedicated to the propagation of a state religion and the more recent adoption of a polity dedicated to secular salvation, human reformation, and economic and social reorganization. An early sect was that of the "Judaizing heresy," which denied the trinity and the divinity of Christ and refused to venerate icons; early in the sixteenth century it was suppressed. The most profound schism occurred in the mid-seventeenth century and was prompted by a revision of sacred texts and religious practices by Patriarch Nikon, which reforms the dissident Old Ritualists refused to accept. Nikon, with the support of the state, succeeded in imposing the Greek forms in place of the corrupted Russian practices, but at great cost. The Old Ritualists awaited the advent of Antichrist; and when they objected to the reforms of Peter I, saw the tsar as assuming this role. The Old Ritualists divided into two groups, the "Priestists" and the "Priestless"; the former retained a clergy and ultimately reacquired a religious hierarchy and episcopate, while the latter took a separate path, due to the shortage of anti-Nikonian priests. The Priestless also abandoned traditional Orthodox Christian religious ritual because they had believed at the time of the schism's origin that the end of the world was imminent and hence there would be little need for ritual.

Persecuted by the tsarist government, the Priestless Old Believers, their lay readers, and preachers fled from Antichrist (Peter I) and sought refuge in the northern forests and in Siberia, even engaging in acts of mass self-immolation, especially during the regency of Sofiia (1682–89).[26] The Priestless, in time, divided into special sects.

That religious sectarianism was in the Russian tradition is testified to by the emergence of a number of exotic sects. The *Khlysty* (Flagellants) developed at the end of the seventeenth century; various branches developed, with some advocating different forms of abstinence and the abolition of marriage, while others engaged in orgies on the assumption that succumbing to the desires of the

[26] Mussorgsky's opera *Khovanshchina* depicts the faith and sufferings of the Old Ritualists. Religious sectarianism also serves as a theme in Andrei Belyi's novel *The Silver Dove.*

flesh would contribute to its mortification. As a reaction in the latter half of the eighteenth century, there emerged the *Skoptsy* (Emasculates), who at times sought to overcome lust, sin, and temptation by the drastic means of castration. Another sect, the *Dukhobory* ("Spirit Wrestlers"), rejected the notion of private property and refused to pay taxes or recognize political authority. With the aid of the novelist Lev Tolstoy, many immigrated to Canada, where a branch of the sect has at times been a source of difficulty for the authorities in British Columbia because of its anarchist views. One offshoot of the *Dukhobory*, who also regarded themselves as "Spiritual Christians," were the *Molokane* (Milk Drinkers), whose name was derived from their refusal to observe fasting. In the Soviet period the Russian Orthodox Church was itself divided as a result of the emergence of a reform movement, the Living Church, which endeavored to come to terms with the Bolshevik regime. More recently, such groups as the Seventh Day Adventists, Pentecostalists, and Jehovah's Witnesses have also made their appearance in the Soviet Union.

It is highly significant that, in defiance of the established church prior to 1917 and in opposition to the regime's ideology since then,[27] millions of Russians have embraced religious sectarianism. Frequently the religious sectarian fled from political authority in order to get beyond its reach and because he regarded it as being of the devil. However, what might be termed the "sectarian syndrome" has also manifested itself in Russian politics, despite the existence of autocratic regimes, organizational "monolithism," and an official creed or ideology. Indeed, Russian absolutist rule, in its

[27] It is revealing that the Soviet Communist Party, prior to the establishment of the Soviet regime, when it was known as the Bolshevik faction, attempted to utilize the various sectarian movements in its revolutionary struggle against the tsarist regime. The Party's specialist on religious sects, Vladimir D. Bonch-Bruevich, conducted extensive research and published various studies on the sects. The principal works on Russian sectarians are Frederick C. Conybeare, *Russian Dissenters* (Cambridge: Harvard University Press, 1921; New York: Russell & Russell, 1962); Serge Bolshakoff, *Russian Nonconformity* (Philadelphia: Westminster Press, 1950); and Paul Miliukov, *Outlines of Russian Culture*—Part I, *Religion and the Church* (Philadelphia: University of Pennsylvania Press, 1943), Chaps. 3–6. See also Ethel and Stephen P. Dunn, "Religion as an Instrument of Cultural Change: The Problem of the Sects in the Soviet Union," *Slavic Review*, XXIII, No. 3 (September 1964), 459–478.

various manifestations, can be viewed as a reaction to this syndrome, and as a means of restraining the Russian tendency to rebel and to embrace *vol'nost'* (excessive liberty or license). It is significant that much of the Soviet Communist Party's history has consisted of efforts to suppress deviant factions.

It is probably not coincidental that Russians have contributed much to the doctrine of anarchism and that they produced more than one generation of atheistic revolutionaries. Such Russian aristocrats as Mikhail Bakunin, Count Lev Tolstoy, and Prince Peter Kropotkin expounded various kinds of anarchist teachings. Tolstoy's anarchism was nonviolent and religious, and was based on pacifism and the alleged virtues of the rural way of life. Bakunin's was violent and atheistic, dedicated to "creative" destruction and to the establishment of supposedly voluntary communes. Kropotkin's anarchic communism was to be based on the principle of mutual aid and the rejection of both the wage system and the state.

Berdyaev contended that anarchism was principally a Russian creation, and that Russians tend not to like the state and to regard it as something alien to be revolted against or meekly accepted as circumstances dictate or permit.[28] Georgii Fedotov in discussing Russian *buntarstvo* (rebelliousness) noted that Russians have an "organic antipathy to all completeness of form."[29] If these contentions have validity, they help to explain why Russian regimes have often been harsh and repressive and why they have been challenged by alienated and restless subjects. The one reinforced the other by means of mutual reaction and fed its opposite.

The Alienated Intelligentsia. One of the few Russian words absorbed into foreign languages has been "intelligentsia," although the term originally had a very special meaning. It was used to refer to the numerically small but vocal stratum that emerged in the nineteenth century from various classes, consisting of "men of ideas" given to critical thought. Indeed, some of the members of the intelligentsia frequently became so enamored of certain abstract ideas and so committed to their fulfillment that they ceased

[28] Nicolas Berdyaev, *The Russian Idea* (London: Geoffrey Bles, 1947), pp. 142–144.

[29] Georgii P. Fedotov, *Novyi grad, sbornik statei,* ed. by Iu. P. Ivask (New York: izd-vo im. Chekhova, 1952), p. 79.

to be thinking men and, instead, became dedicated fanatics devoted to revolutionary action.[30] Lacking a developed sense of political realism, they frequently pursued grandiose dreams based on a few simple tenets. The intelligentsia was frequently alienated from the Russian state, church, nation, and way of life. Its rootlessness and restless nature prompted it to embrace, variously, German idealist philosophy, philosophical materialism, populism (the "going to the people" movement which the suspicious peasantry rejected), nihilism, scientific rationalism, Slavophilism, and Marxism.

The intelligentsia was frequently melancholic or pessimistic, and given to dreaming, apathy, and helplessness. Yet it could also organize conspiratorial groups in testimony to its alienation from Russian society, its rejection of values, and its determination to remake Russia. The organization of such groups compounded the existing cleavages between rulers and ruled, between the peasantry and the rest of Russian society.

It is significant that prominent members of the intelligentsia should have had to seek refuge abroad: Herzen, Bakunin, Lavrov, Plekhanov, Lenin, Gorky, to name but a few. Such prominent Russians as the Nobel literary prize winner Ivan Bunin, the composers Rakhmaninov and Gretchaninov, as well as the novelist Merezhkovsky, Berdyaev, and the basso Chaliapin, could not accept the Soviet regime and chose exile instead. In continuation of the tradition were the defections of numerous Soviet citizens during and after World War II. The crowning irony was the defection in 1967 of Svetlana Alliluyeva, daughter of the late Soviet dictator Joseph Stalin, who has spoken and written very critically of the regime.

The Soviet regime has created an intelligentsia of specialists—in contrast to the "generalists" who constituted the original Russian intelligentsia—and has endeavored to control it by the discipline imposed on the Communist Party membership. By increasing the size of the intelligentsia and by giving it vital tasks to perform, the Soviet regime has also made that class potentially more significant. Even specialists can pose critical questions, however, and while

[30] For a discussion of the psychological attitudes and "state of mind" of the early Russian intelligentsia, see Vladimir C. Nahirny, "The Russian Intelligentsia: From Men of Ideas to Men of Convictions," *Comparative Studies in Society and History*, IV, No. 4 (July, 1962), 403–435.

some members of the Soviet intelligentsia have joined the "internal emigration" by becoming immersed in their professions, others have persisted in manifesting the restlessness and dedication that characterized their predecessors.

Identity, Appropriation, and the "Search" Syndrome. Both the question of Russian identity and the conflict between indigenous values and foreign ways have figured prominently in the country's development. Russians have long been concerned with the question of their relationship to Europe and with the ways in which their country differs from the West. The great debate between Westerners and the so-called Slavophiles in the nineteenth century reflected this concern. The question persisted in the conflict between the anticapitalist Populists (*Narodniki*), who idealized the Russian peasantry, and the early Russian Marxists, who argued that the country's development on the basis of the European economic model was inevitable. The question of "what is Russia?" and the search for identity in terms of a special role, and a unique mission and way of life, have troubled generations of Russian thinkers as well as rulers.

The problem of identity has been greatly complicated and extended by the superficial attraction to the West experienced during the eighteenth century. The journey of Peter I to Holland and England to learn Western techniques—especially in shipbuilding—his contacts with Germans who lived in a segregated community in Moscow suburbs, and his decree in 1702 ordering the hiring of foreigners had a profound impact on Russian life. His new city of St. Petersburg, moreover, when compared with Moscow, provided a vivid contrast architecturally and culturally between Russia and Europe. Peter's lead was followed to an extent by his successors. Catherine II, who conducted a correspondence with Voltaire, attempted to play the role of the "enlightened despot," but then abandoned the flirtation with Europe as a result of the excesses of the French Revolution. Alexander I also endeavored to play the liberal monarch, granting the Poles a constitution which he would not give his other subjects and subsequently becoming an advocate of monarchical legitimacy.

Some Russians were attracted to Freemasonry, which acquired

a following among members of the Russian gentry during the eighteenth century. The Decembrists, who endeavored to establish a constitutional order by their rebellion in 1825, had been influenced by their contacts with Europe during the Napoleonic Wars and by Freemasonry.

The Russian elite contained many non-Russian elements, in fact, and foreigners frequently contributed to Russian development. Peter I, following his annexation of the Baltic territories, recruited Baltic Germans as trustworthy instruments of reform. Indeed, the Russian ruling family, the House of Romanov, became German after 1762 during the reigns of Catherine II (a minor princess of Anhalt-Zerbst) and her ill-fated husband Peter III (of the House of Holstein-Gottorp, although a grandson of Peter I).

The impressive contribution of foreigners to Russia is evident in many of the leading architectural and historical monuments. Thus, Ivan III had the Italian architect Fioravanti construct the Cathedral of the Dormition (*Uspenskii Sobor*) in the Kremlin (1475–79), and he commissioned two other Italians to erect the Hall of Facets (*Granovitaia palata*). A Venetian architect built the Archangel Cathedral, and another Italian was summoned to build the high Belltower of Ivan the Great. Although Russian architects were erecting smaller structures of distinctive style, only foreigners were entrusted with the building of the imposing structures in Peter I's new capital of St. Petersburg. These included Rastrelli, Rossi, Quarenghi, de la Mothe, von Klenze, de Thomon, Trezzini, Stakenschneider, and many others. Indeed, very few of the principal historical structures of St. Petersburg (Leningrad) were designed and executed by Russians.

The number of foreigners or persons of non-Russian origin who attained positions of great responsibility in public life or prominence in Russian culture is truly remarkable. In Russian literature there are such figures as Pushkin (of African ancestry), Lermontov, Gogol', Blok, Gippius, Korolenko, Kuechelbecker, Del'vig, Fonvizin, Dostoievsky, and Akhmatova. Russia's leading lexicographer, Vladimir Dal', was of Danish origin. The prominent Russian choreographer, Marius Petipa, was French by origin. Explorations undertaken by Russia were usually conducted by foreigners such as

Vitus Bering, I. F. (Adam) Kruzenstern, F. P. Litke, Otto Kotzebue, and Thadeus Bellingshausen.

The presence in modern Russian political life of persons of foreign origin was evident in such figures as Czartoryski, Plehve, and Stürmer, and in the fact that among the tsarist ministers of finance were Witte, Bunge, and Reutern. Russian diplomacy utilized the talents of such non-Russians as A. I. (Heinrich) Ostermann and his son Ivan A. Ostermann (in the eighteenth century), and Count Karl V. Nesselrode, Nikolai Karlovich Giers, Baron F. I. Brunnow, N. Hartwig, Count John Capodistrias, Count N. D. Osten-Saken, O. M. Shtakel'berg, A. F. Benckendorff, and Baron R. R. Rosen.[31]

The willingness of Russians, since the eighteenth century, to adopt those foreign techniques and practices that proved effective, testifies to their abilities as appropriators.[32] The presence in the Russian language of large numbers of English, French, and German loan words as common nouns testifies to the Russian capacity to borrow. Such words as *metro, trolleybus, carousel, sidewalk* (*trottoir*), *overcoat* (*paletot*), *scarf* (*cache-nez*), *greenhouse* (*orangerie*), *mouthpiece* (*mundstück*), *sandwich* (*butterbrot*), *lampshade* (*abat-jour*), and numerous others serve as examples.

By borrowing on an extensive scale and by annexing foreign lands and non-Russian populations, the Russians have inevitably complicated and made more acute the question of their identity.

[31] It was the use of numerous non-Russians that prompted Friedrich Engels to assert, in his essay on "The Foreign Policy of Russian Czarism" (1890), the following rather harsh judgment of Imperial Russia's diplomats: "It is this secret society, recruited originally from foreign adventurers, which has raised the Russian empire to its present plenitude of power. With iron perseverance, eyes set fixedly on the goal, not shrinking from any breach of faith, any treason, any assassination, any servility, distributing bribes lavishly, never overconfident following victory, never discouraged by defeat, over the dead bodies of millions of soldiers and at least one Czar, it is this gang—as talented as it is without conscience—rather than all the Russian armies put together which has extended the Russian boundaries . . . ; it is this gang which has made Russia great, powerful and feared, and has opened up for it the way to world domination." Karl Marx and Friedrich Engels, *The Russian Menace to Europe,* ed. Paul W. Blackstock and Bert F. Hoselitz (Glencoe, Ill.: Free Press, 1952), p. 26.

[32] For a popular but extensively documented treatment of Russian appropriation of Western knowledge and techniques see Werner Keller, *East Minus West=Zero* (New York: G. P. Putnam's Sons, 1962). Although Keller has overstated his thesis—as is evident in the work's unfortunate title—he has provided a mass of evidence regarding Russia's cultural debt.

Appropriation of foreign ways and peoples led to fear of "contamination" and tended to promote the threat of fragmentation of the Russian polity. The diverse, complex, and synthetic nature of Russia's "unity" and the fact that the writing of a Russian history developed only in the eighteenth century—and that with the help of Germans—have prompted concern over the questions "what is Russia?" and "where can the 'true' Russia be found (in which social class)?" There has also been concern over the question of Russia's ultimate goals, her role in history. Self-preoccupation has remained a favorite Russian concern.

"Truth-Seeking" and Maximalism. Russian political thought did not develop under the influence of rationalism but in an environment dominated by modes of thought that can be termed "mystical." Russian philosophy and the role in Russia of superstition and of "dark" and "impure" forces, as well as the obsession with "enemies" and with the sense of mission, testify to this. Thus, "devil" theories have tended to enjoy currency, and Russian political parties have more often than not been doctrinal and sectarian rather than pragmatic and broadly based. Traditionally political power in Russia has been wedded to ideology, a pattern promoting the appeal of the total, ready-made solution and of all-embracing dicta that have tended to rule out the "bourgeois" politics of compromise.

If Berdyaev was correct in describing the Russians as an "apocalyptic people"—one concerned with ends and with the prophetic in life—it is not to be wondered that Marxism, with its facile predictions, held an attraction for some thinking Russians.[33] It is also relevant regarding this attraction that the concept of the *collective* had a precedent in the Russian doctrine of *sobornost'* or religious conciliarism. However, Marxism had appeal not only because it was Western and scientific, but because it was utopian and claimed both to assure social justice and to be of universal application. Class conflict, furthermore, had played an important role in Russian history, while capitalism—because it disrupted the traditional way of life and was disliked both by the landed nobility and the government bureaucracy—had not acquired much popularity.

[33] See Nicolas Berdyaev, *The Russian Idea* (above, n. 28), Chap. 9.

The Russian bourgeoisie was weak, as was the system of private enterprise. The internationalist professions of Marxism attracted support as a reaction to Russian imperialism and to the tsarist regime's mistreatment of the non-Russian nationalities. Finally, Marxism—together with its Russian variant, Leninism—also gave new form to the Russian seeking of purposefulness and commitment to principle (*ideinost'*).

Recurring Problems. Russian governments have functioned in a particular context and have had to confront certain basic problems. For instance, although Russian rulers have promulgated many legal codes, those codes have not been subjected to the kinds of legal restraints associated with constitutional regimes. Spying and exile have traditionally been elevated to the status of established institutions. Coups, depositions, and assassinations have played a significant role in Russian political life. Ivan the Terrible killed his son, and Peter I had his son executed. Catherine II had her husband, Peter III, killed. Catherine's son, Paul I, was assassinated and was succeeded by Alexander I, who apparently knew of the plot. Alexander II and various ministers and officials were assassinated, and Nicholas II and his immediate family as well as the sinister Rasputin were murdered. Attempts were made on Lenin's life and numerous Soviet leaders were purged; Kirov and Trotsky were assassinated. The practice of deposing weaker rulers and of exiling them (or incarcerating them in monasteries in the tsarist period—as Peter I deposed and banished his half-sister, Sofiia, who had served as regent) has persisted in the more recent Soviet period, with the removals of various members of the leadership.

The use of fear and degradation or of swift removal and consignment to oblivion if not to death, have characterized Russian politics all too frequently. The appeal to violence and the use of repression have reflected a tendency to ignore genuine expressions of public opinion. The tendency to rely excessively upon an elite has contributed to the frequent estrangement of Russian regimes from the masses. Thus, the cleavages within Russian society have reflected the uneven race between needed reform that would basically change the system and revolution that would bring its collapse. If Russian rulers have often been reluctant to effect reforms and if reforms, when undertaken, have been nullified or eroded, it is probably in testimony to the persistence of cultural traits. Yet such traits can be modified over time and represent a means of evaluating within-system changes.

CHAPTER 3

THE IDEOLOGICAL HERITAGE

The claim made by communists that they are serious about their convictions and that their actions and policies are motivated by ideological considerations cannot be taken lightly. If on occasion certain ideological tenets have been revised, it should not be concluded from this that the Soviet rulers are mere pragmatists or opportunists. An ideology, in its political meaning, is a set of axioms or a scheme of systematic ideas based upon a particular interpretation of observed phenomena. In the communist case it has also involved a special mode of thinking and method of political analysis, in addition to being a *Weltanschauung* or world outlook (*mirosozertsanie* in Russian)—a system of thought which seeks to explain or rationalize the totality of reality in a convincing manner and also seeks to provide a vision of a vastly improved future designed to influence human behavior. If the ideology frequently has provided a distorted image of reality it is no less significant as a force that has motivated and inspired men.

1. COMMUNISM AS A CREED

The intensity of communist belief cannot be adequately explained if communism is regarded as nothing more than a conventional political or economic theory. Far too many of its attributes are those of a sectarian or quasi-religious movement. While differing from theistic religious movements in rejecting the existence of the supernatural and in preaching a militant atheism, communism promises a species of secular salvation (by which the bulk of mankind is supposedly to be saved from evil) and in its name has demanded and exacted great sacrifices from its followers and subjects. It has required total commitment and surrender to an absolute. It has sought to provide a set of ultimate goals, to give meaning to life, and to inspire men to action; it has also insisted that they accept much on faith. While claiming to be "scientific," it has often conducted itself like a pseudo-church combining a messianic faith with a supposedly rational view of man and the cosmos.

If communism were nothing more than a political or economic theory, it would not claim to explain all historical development and the totality of human experience. It would not be absolutistically claiming to be the sole true philosophy and dismissing all other theories, doctrines, and philosophies as harmful and incorrect. If communism were but a theory, it would be neutral toward religious belief instead of attempting to destroy it and to claim for itself the right to decide all fundamental questions of human existence.

Among the quasi-religious attributes of communism are the reliance upon doctrine, catechism, conversion, and the notion of redemption.[1] The Party membership has in certain respects resembled a secular "priesthood" expected to be dedicated to dogma and to proselytize on its behalf. It has preached a doctrine of human "salvation" in this world based upon the worship of work, economic development, and the supposedly predestined triumph of communist ideology and political rule. It has viewed mankind as having been corrupted by the "original sin" of exploitation (resulting from the ownership of various forms of property), which supposedly brought to an end the "primitive communist" stage of history regarded by communists as characterizing man's natural state. In condemning "exploitation" and private or group ownership of the means of production, communism has based itself on a moral judgment while simultaneously denying that men of antagonistic social classes can be bound by a common morality.

The struggle between communism and its antagonists is viewed as inevitable and the victory of the former is regarded as the

[1] The analogy between communism and religion was first systematically developed by Nicolas Berdyaev in *The Russian Revolution* (1931; republished in 1961 by University of Michigan Press, in Ann Arbor Paperbacks for the Study of Communism and Marxism).

triumph of "good" over "evil." This belief is comparable to the aspect of religious thought known as eschatological—pertaining to the doctrine of final things. Communist leaders have also insisted upon orthodoxy in ideology and have condemned and excommunicated the members of many deviationist movements—the communist counterpart of religious heresies. Communism has its own "scriptural" works in the frequently cited writings of Marx, Engels, and Lenin. The god-substitute of the communist cult is its doctrine of historical inevitability, with the world divided into believers and unbelievers. The Communist Party has employed the hierarchical principle—but without any explicit counterpart of spiritual grace—and has demanded of its members unfailing obedience. It has utilized a probationary period of candidacy for membership similar to the religious novitiate and employs continuing indoctrination. Above all, it has endeavored to explain man's relationship to society and to the entire physical universe.

2. SOCIALISM AND COMMUNISM

The "socialist" label has been adopted by the U.S.S.R. and constitutes part of the country's official name. For communists, socialism is the first stage of communism, but it must be socialism instituted by a ruling Communist Party. Although socialism actually preceded the emergence of communism (the *Communist Manifesto* was published in 1848), communists have insisted that so-called scientific socialism first made its appearance in the writings of modern communism's founder, Karl Marx.[2] The earlier socialist

[2] The term "communist" came into use in 1847 with the founding of an international Communist League in London. The *Communist Manifesto,* drafted largely by Marx with the help of Friedrich Engels, provided the League with a program distinguishing it from the other contemporary socialist movements, which the communists regarded as "conservative or bourgeois." For a general study of the development of modern socialist and communist thought see Edmund Wilson, *To the Finland Station* (New York: Doubleday, 1940; 1953 Anchor Book edition). The most exhaustive study is that of G. D. H. Cole, *History of Socialist Thought,* 5 vols. (London: Macmillan, 1953–60). Also see George Lichtheim, *Marxism, An Historical and Critical Study* (New York: Frederick A. Praeger, 1961); Eduard Bernstein, *Evolutionary Socialism* (New York: Schocken Books, 1961); and Karl R. Popper, *The Open Society and Its Enemies,* 4th ed. (Princeton, N.J.: Princeton University Press; London: Routledge and Kegan, 1962).

theories were dismissed by them as utopian. These included the theories of two Frenchmen, the Comte de Saint-Simon (1760–1825) and Charles Fourier (1772–1837), and of the Englishman Robert Owen (1771–1858), theories which stressed cooperative (group) rather than state ownership. The anarchism expounded by Pierre Joseph Proudhon (1809–65) included establishment of syndicates, or producers cooperatives. Earlier theories include the communism in the consumption of goods which Plato advocated for the ruling class in *The Republic,* as well as the agrarian communism of the Diggers in seventeenth-century England.[3]

If pré-Marxian socialism advocated a more equal distribution of property and cooperative economic enterprises, modern socialism has been a protest against the excesses of pure laissez-faire capitalism. Although communism also protested against an early form of capitalism (no longer existing in industrialized countries), democratic socialism has differed from communism in a number of respects. Socialists are much less doctrinaire than communists and do not attempt to explain the cosmos. Communists usually insist upon complete nationalization or state ownership of the economy; socialists, on the other hand, vary in the degree of state ownership which they advocate but usually favor a mixed economy lying between the two extremes of classical capitalism and the near-total state ownership demanded by Communists. Socialists usually compensate for nationalized property while Communists usually confiscate it. Socialists recognize that state ownership, with government employees managing industry, is not a panacea, as it frequently leads to bureaucracy and waste; they therefore usually limit state ownership to certain public utilities, transportation, communications media, certain natural resources, and medical and social insurance.

In addition to economic policy, socialists and communists differ in their political mores and practices. Democratic socialists achieve their ends by constitutional means, eschewing the violence and coercion which have been standard communist tactics. Democratic socialists respect basic civil liberties and do not suppress other

[3] See Eduard Bernstein, *Cromwell and Communism, Socialism and Democracy in the Great English Revolution* (New York: Schocken Books, 1963).

parties; unlike communists, they are willing to hold free elections and relinquish power if they lose. Genuine socialists will not enter a coalition government with communists because they are convinced that the latter will subvert the coalition. Communists have an elitist conception of their movement while democratic socialists have operated as a conventional political party. In all these ways genuine socialists must be distinguished from communists, who at times freely employ the "socialist" label.

3. BASIC CATEGORIES OF COMMUNIST BELIEF

Communist doctrine is based upon certain broad tenets and basic assumptions which were developed and applied by Karl Marx (1818–83) and Friedrich Engels (1820–95). Both men emerged from a German environment and were influenced by certain movements in German philosophy. Ironically, neither man came from a working-class milieu. Marx was the son of a middle-class Jewish lawyer converted to Christianity; Engels was the son of a textile manufacturer and was himself a successful businessman.

Marx received a doctorate in philosophy from the University of Jena in 1841, but by 1843 had taken refuge in Paris after a brief experience in journalism in Cologne led to the suspension of the newspaper by the authorities. Expelled from France in 1845, he spent three years in Brussels. Upon being expelled from Belgium, Marx returned to Germany during the revolution of 1848, engaged in radical journalism, and was arrested; acquitted when tried for sedition, he went into exile again in 1849. The remaining three decades of his life were spent in London as a political émigré. Isolated from British life, he engaged in journalism, in polemics, and in scholarship.

Marx and his family suffered many privations in England. However, he was able to persist in his activities largely due to Engels' generosity and to two legacies. In addition to the *Manifesto* and newspaper articles, Marx wrote analyses of French politics and his lengthiest work, *Capital.* The first volume of *Capital* appeared in 1867 and attracted only limited attention; the other two volumes appeared after Marx's death and were completed by Engels. While

Marx's ponderous writings dealt principally with economic and political analysis, Engels' more readable works dealt with a variety of historical and philosophical questions.[4] Both men developed their doctrines in response to the abysmal living conditions which characterized urban life during the industrial revolution: the factory system, child labor, unemployment, low wages, and extremes of wealth and poverty.

Marx and Engels claimed that their teachings were scientific and that they had discovered laws which explained the entire historical process. In part, these claims were due to their desire to distinguish themselves from the alleged sentimentalism of utopian and Christian (or ethical) socialism. By claiming to offer a rational analysis of history and by assuming the inevitability of events which would validate their predictions, Marx and Engels sought to endow their system with the guise of scientism. Also, since their system was based upon materialism, it was regarded as being "scientific" by definition because it gave the appearance of dealing with the material world in empirical terms. Unfortunately, however, the distinction between hypothesis and dogmatic assumption or belief became blurred in Marxist thought.

Historical Materialism. This concept is at the very core of communist doctrine. It is based on the assumption that thought, mind, and consciousness are reflections of the objective reality of the material, physical world. The assertion of the primacy of matter over thought is a denial of what communists condemn as the philosophical idealist view, which holds that existence, nature, and matter are a reflection of the spirit or of the Absolute Idea. For communists the mind reflects the material world and is secondary to and dependent upon matter. Matter to communists is the "totality of material things"—the "objective reality" which is perceived by the sense organs and which exists independently of the human mind, consciousness, and perception. This viewpoint tends to limit all experience to the perceptible physical world. It also assumes that the

[4] For detailed accounts of the relationship between Marx and Engels and their thought see Sir Isaiah Berlin, *Karl Marx, His Life and Environment* (London: Oxford University Press, 1948) and Franz Mehring, *Karl Marx* (Ann Arbor: University of Michigan Press, 1962).

totality of reality can be known and that absolute truth is ultimately ascertainable. Since it is only the material world which exists in reality, atheism is an essential element in communist belief.

The emphasis on materialism and atheism in communism resulted largely from the influence upon Marx and Engels of the German philosopher, Ludwig Feuerbach (1804–72), who held that nature exists independently of philosophy and is the source of all knowledge. Feuerbach held that philosophy must be based on the observation of nature and on practical experience, not on ratiocination and abstract ideas; he held man to be little more than a biological entity. Feuerbach's denial of God, expressed in his *Essence of Christianity* (1841), was based on his assumption that religion results from man's unconscious efforts to deify himself and to endow God with qualities which man values. Theology was to be replaced by anthropology, with the latter becoming a secular humanist movement based on love and the achievement of man's supposed potentialities.[5]

Although Feuerbach called himself a "communist," certain aspects of his philosophy have been criticized by communists. Thus Feuerbach advocated a "religion" of love and of humanity; he recognized the power of religious ideas and wished to unite what he regarded as the "positive" aspects of religion with philosophy. In contrast to this, communists have denied the existence of positive features in modern religion. Feuerbach's materialism was philosophical and not historical. He saw men as part of nature but not in relationship to social class, political party, or revolution. He distinguished between various historical epochs on the basis of the criterion of religion and not in terms of the economic system or class structure. Thus, Feuerbach did not apply his philosophical materialism to the study of society. This task was undertaken by Marx and Engels.

Marxists view history as a single process of development conforming to certain laws which, in turn, reflect identifiable social

[5] On Feuerbach and other precursors of Marx and Engels, see Sidney Hook, *From Hegel to Marx* (published originally in 1936; reissued in Ann Arbor Paperbacks for the Study of Communism and Marxism, University of Michigan Press, 1962).

forces. At the bottom of this scheme is the assumption that human relationships and political behavior are determined fundamentally by the ways in which men obtain their livelihood. Thus, politics is seen as a function of the "mode of production" and of the material and social conditions corresponding thereto. Technology, the nature of man's tools, and the uses to which he puts resources are said to determine the mode of production. This, in turn, is said to determine the "relations of production"—or the property (and social) relationships which result from ownership of tools and resources, as well as from the ways in which production and labor are organized and managed. In time, the relations of production conflict with the mode of production. The process was described by Marx in the Preface to his *Contribution to the Critique of Political Economy* (1859), in the following terms:

> In the social production of their means of existence men enter into definite, necessary relations which are independent of their will, productive relationships which correspond to a definite stage of development of their material productive forces. The aggregate of these productive relationships constitutes the economic structure of society, the real basis on which a juridical and political superstructure arises, and to which definite forms of social consciousness correspond. The mode of production of the material means of existence conditions the whole process of social, political and intellectual life. It is not the consciousness of men that determines their existence, but, on the contrary, it is their social existence that determines their consciousness. At a certain stage of their development the material productive forces of society come into contradiction with the existing productive relationships, or, what is but a legal expression for these, with the property relationships within which they had moved before. From forms of development of the productive forces these relationships are transformed into their fetters. Then an epoch of social revolution opens. With the change in the economic foundation the whole vast superstructure is more or less rapidly transformed.[6]

The personal motives of men are irrelevant, for men are held to act as they do because they are seen as the instruments of the socio-economic forces which have produced them.

Base and Superstructure. There are two inseparable parts of an attempt to explain human activity in terms of historical material-

[6] Emile Burns, ed., *Handbook of Marxism* (New York: International Publishers, 1935), pp. 371–372.

ism. The "base" represents the combination of "production relations" which constitutes the economic structure of society corresponding to a particular stage of development. The "superstructure" represents for communists the particular form of social consciousness, political institutions, and legal norms corresponding to the economic base and determined by it. Thus, the superstructure is said to include politics, constitutions, law, religion, morality, political theory, philosophy, the arts, and literature as well as all ideologies. This scheme of analysis holds that ethical judgments and principles of right, liberty, and justice do not exist in the abstract but are tied to the economic system (base), which is the ultimate determinant of history. A philosophy or ideology must be partisan and can only serve as a rationalization of an existing order or as a reflection of "progressive" opposing forces developing in the base.

In theory, communists—especially under Engels' influence—have recognized that the superstructure can exercise some influence upon the base, retarding or accelerating development. Engels, in some of his correspondence in 1890 and in 1894, conceded that noneconomic factors could have a secondary role. In a letter to Heinz Starkenburg, dated January 25, 1894, Engels declared:

> Political, juridical, philosophical, religious, literary, artistic, etc. development is based on economic development. But all these react upon one another and also upon the economic base. It is not that the economic position is the *cause and alone active,* while everything else only has a passive effect. There is, rather, interaction on the basis of the economic necessity, which *ultimately* always asserts itself.[7]

In the end, for communists, it is economic relations which are decisive, and it is economic necessity rather than historical accident or man's free will which determines his fate.

Surplus Value. If economic determinism plays the key role in communist belief, its most essential component is the concept of "surplus value." This economic category is related to commodity production, which is production for exchange rather than for consumption by the producer himself. As a result of economic devel-

[7] Karl Marx and Frederick Engels, *Selected Correspondence, 1846–1895* (New York: International Publishers, 1942), p. 517.

opment and increased division of labor, commodity production becomes characteristic of the entire capitalist economy and ceases to be a mere exchange of goods. Purchase for the purpose of selling at a profit converts money into capital—another form of property with a new and higher value. Money has "grown" into capital—a new value based upon surplus value. Value of this kind exceeds the producer's costs.

The notion that value has its source in labor (the labor theory of value) was first developed by the seventeenth-century political theorist John Locke and later by the classical economists David Ricardo and Adam Smith. This viewpoint was originally based on the assumption that manufacturing by artisans involved no more than the investment of their labor (as they owned their tools), and that therefore the product of their labor did not have to be shared with others. It remained for Marx to take Ricardo's political economy (and that economist's failure to explain profit adequately) and derive from it his theory of surplus value.

Marx contended that capitalist commodity production differs from simple commodity production (exchange of goods) because capitalism treats labor power itself as a commodity. The introduction of steam-driven machinery and the rise of the factory system compelled the formerly self-employed craftsman to become a wage-laborer, as he could not compete with machinery. The capitalist purchased labor power for a specific period of time, paying it only the bare minimum it cost to subsist and reproduce itself (the "iron law of wages"). The surplus results from the difference between the value of the commodities produced by this labor and the value paid to it, and constitutes profit. For Marx the value of a commodity was based exclusively upon the labor embodied in it. The surplus product allegedly produced by labor power alone was not paid for by the capitalist but was appropriated as an unearned increment.

The theory of surplus value assumes incorrectly that the worth of an object is determined by labor alone, while in fact value results from many sources: from the skill of those who perform manual functions or operate machines, from the machines and tools not themselves furnished by the worker, from the capital invested in an enterprise, from land, from the managerial abilities of the entrepreneur. Indeed, how is investment achieved under any system if not by profits and invested savings (whether forced or voluntary)? The theory also ignores the fact that use-value is a variable which changes through time and often cannot be expressed in monetary terms. Thus a priceless painting or piece of sculpture or a classical symphony has a value quite apart from the number of hours the artist or composer devoted to it and whether or not he was adequately compensated. Conversely, as the quality of labor varies, much labor and effort can be expended upon something of little worth. The notion of value, then, is a highly elusive concept which Marx endeavored unsuccessfully to reduce to a simple formula.[8]

Exploitation. Closely related to the concept of surplus value is that of "exploitation," which plays a key role in the communist view of the so-called capitalist order. In the Marxist scheme, "constant capital" is defined as the value of the means of production, such as machinery, tools, and raw materials. "Variable capital" is that expended for labor (wages). The value of commodities produced is equal to constant capital plus variable capital plus surplus value. The "degree of exploitation," finally, is the ratio of surplus value to variable capital. Thus, the owners of the means of production who receive income from rents, interest from investments, and profits from manufactures are accused of exploiting the remaining, nonowning part of society.

Exploitation and the tendency to drive down wages in order to maximize profits (the ratio of surplus value to total capital) are said to be accompanied, under capitalism, by the so-called industrial reserve army of the unemployed. In addition, as competition between capitalists intensifies—with the weaker competitors absorbed by the stronger leading to a concentration of capital (and ultimately monopoly)—the need for new and more expensive machinery increases the value of constant capital and reduces variable capital. With rising costs as a result of the supposed need to increase profits, the rate of profit and of surplus value is said to

[8] For the classic critique of Marx's theory of value, see Eugen von Böhm-Bawerk, *Karl Marx and the Close of His System* (1896), republished with an introduction by Paul M. Sweezy (New York: Augustus M. Kelly, 1949).

actually decline as expensive machinery supplants human labor. The working class is supposedly further impoverished as production costs and output rise, while wages are said to fall. The increased misery of the proletariat, it is alleged, inevitably leads to political crises and proletarian revolution.

The Ruling Class and the State. At the core of communist doctrine lies the notion of a ruling class which in varying form characterizes each stage of historical development. This class owns the means of production and as a result is said to exercise political control in the interest of perpetuating its position of dominance. In accordance with the base-superstructure relationship, ideas, law, ethics, morality, religion, philosophy, and aesthetics are seen exclusively as partisan weapons employed at various stages by slaveowners, landowners, and the industrial bourgeoisie to justify their privileged status. Marx and Engels in *The German Ideology* (1846) gave expression to this thesis in the following terms:

> The ideas of the ruling class are in every epoch the ruling ideas; i.e. the class, which is the ruling material force of society, is at the same time its ruling intellectual force. The class which has the means of material production at its disposal, has control at the same time over the means of mental production, so that thereby, generally speaking, the ideas of those who lack the means of mental production are subject to it.[9]

It follows logically, in the communist view, that the state is nothing more than an instrumentality of a particular ruling class, designed to serve the interests of that class. Thus the *Communist Manifesto* asserts that "the executive of the modern [capitalist] state is but a committee for managing the common affairs of the whole bourgeoisie." It also declares that "political power, properly so called, is merely the organized power of one class for oppressing another."

The Class Struggle. Communist doctrine explains social classes exclusively in terms of their relationship to the means of production, their role in the social organization of labor, and the particular share of social wealth accorded them. Classes are said to have emerged as a result of the division of labor and the introduction of

[9] Karl Marx and Frederick Engels, *The German Ideology, Parts I and III* (New York: International Publishers, 1947), p. 39.

private ownership of the means of production. Each historical epoch is supposedly characterized by a distinctive social structure which reflects the conflict of classes. Irreconcilable class antagonism between "exploited" and "exploiters" is said to result from private ownership of the means of production. The *Communist Manifesto* asserts categorically that:

> The history of all hitherto existing society is the history of class struggles.
>
> Freeman and slave, patrician and plebeian, lord and serf, guild-master and journeyman, in a word, oppressor and oppressed, stood in constant opposition to one another, carried on an uninterrupted, now hidden, now open fight, a fight that each time ended, either in a revolutionary reconstitution of society at large, or in the common ruin of the contending classes. . . .
>
> Our epoch, the epoch of the bourgeoisie, possesses, however, this distinctive feature: it has simplified the class antagonisms. Society as a whole is more and more splitting up into two great hostile camps, into two great classes directly facing each other—bourgeoisie and proletariat.[10]

Although the class struggle is a political struggle, it does not manifest itself with equal intensity at all times. Thus Engels recognized that "there are periods when the warring classes so nearly attain equilibrium that the State power, ostensibly appearing as a mediator, assumes for the moment a certain independence in relation to both."[11] The state, in addition to being the instrument of the ruling class, is a means of holding class antagonisms in check, at least temporarily, so that the conflicting classes "may not consume themselves and society in sterile struggle."[12] Of course, conflict must and will occur but in a form which will supposedly assure historical "progress." The class struggle is regarded as the prime motive force in historical development during the periods characterized by antagonistic class structures.

[10] Emile Burns, *op. cit.* (above, n. 6), pp. 22–23.

[11] Friedrich Engels, *The Origin of the Family, Private Property and the State in ibid.*, p. 330. As examples Engels cited the absolute monarchies of the seventeenth and eighteenth centuries, "which balanced the nobles and burghers against each other," and the First and Second French Empires of the Bonapartes, which "played off the proletariat against the bourgeoisie."

[12] *Ibid.*, p. 328.

Once communists consolidate their rule in a country, such antagonistic relationships between classes supposedly become "friendly" and nonantagonistic. With the alleged liquidation of the exploiters, the class struggle is transferred to the international arena, where it occurs between communist and noncommunist states or, in the Marxist-Leninist terminology, between the "socialist" and "capitalist" systems.

Stages of Historical Development. Communist doctrine endeavors immodestly to explain the entirety of human history in terms of "laws" reflecting philosophical materialism, economic determinism, the class struggle, and the dialectic. For the communist this combination of concepts comprises modern "social science," although it is in fact no more than a philosophy of history. The notion of historical inevitability is based on the assumption that the relations of production and the base determine historical events. Historical periods emerge as a result of socio-economic forces which man cannot resist but which he is "free" to recognize.

All of human history is reduced by communist doctrine to five stages, each of which is characterized by a particular socio-economic structure, base and superstructure, and set of production relations. The *original stage* is defined as a primitive, supposedly communist, society, in which there is said to have been communal ownership of the means of production—simple tools and stone implements. There supposedly were no social classes in this original society. The *second historical stage* is defined as the slaveholding stage, with private rather than common ownership of the means of production (including slaves). The class struggle manifested itself in the antagonism between slave-owners and slaves. The *third stage* is that of feudalism, which supposedly resulted from a different mode of production but which, like the slaveholding stage, involved private ownership of the means of production. The class struggle in the third stage was between landowning nobles and serfs, and between nobles and burghers. The *fourth stage* is that of capitalism, with its large, privately-owned factories and its struggle between owning and exploiting bourgeoisie, and exploited proletariat, resulting from a system of wage labor. The *fifth stage* is that of communism (preceded by a "socialist" transitional stage), with supposedly public or common ownership of the means of production and no class struggle. In stages two, three, and four there are ruling classes, while in the first and fifth stages there are said to be none.

This highly simplified scheme resulted from an effort at historical retrojection, under the influence of the indisputably revolutionary transformation which society had undergone in the nineteenth century as a result of industrialization. Marx and Engels, having witnessed the profound changes caused by these new forces of production, sought to persuade others that a comparable pattern had occurred in previous epochs. In general, Marx dealt with the capitalist system of his day and said little of the slaveholding and feudal societies. The references to primitive communal society in Marx's and Engels' writings are vague.

Marx's and Engels' views regarding the existence of communal property and the absence of a state or social classes among primitive peoples were based on the work of the American ethnologist Lewis Henry Morgan (1818–81), who, ironically, was an upstate New York railroad attorney and a Republican. Marx and Engels were much impressed with Morgan's principal work, *Ancient Society* (1877), which was inspired by his contacts with the Iroquois Indians and was limited largely to the American Indians, Greeks, and Romans. Morgan contended that private property was preceded by primitive communism, in the process of historical development "from savagery through barbarism to civilization." Private property, in Morgan's opinion, arose in an evolutionary process as a result of technological development and new inventions. Although Morgan's views prompted Marx and Engels to greet his work with enthusiasm, Morgan was not a socialist—let alone a communist—and he did not believe in the class struggle as the mover of history. Subsequent research in anthropology has refuted Morgan's contention regarding the existence of primitive communism.[13] However, communists have persisted in their mythology re-

[13] The existence of individual and family-owned hunting territories, fishing locations, and other forms of wealth as well as social castes and slavery among peoples whom Morgan would have regarded as "savages"—had he been acquainted with them—has been adequately documented. See Bernhard J. Stern,

garding a primitive communal society in order to make it appear that they are restoring mankind to a previous "uncorrupted" state which was supposedly enjoyed prior to the advent of private property.

The Dialectic. Where the doctrine of historical materialism has been associated primarily with Marx, the use of the dialectic in Marxism as applied to natural phenomena has been attributed largely to Engels' influence. The dialectic is regarded as the embodiment of the "laws of development" or as the "science of the general laws of motion—both of the external world and of human thought." In its original Greek sense, dialectics refers to the art of disputation by means of which the arguments of one's opponent are exposed and truth is discovered as a result of the clash of opposing arguments. Taken from the philosopher Georg Wilhelm Friedrich Hegel (1770–1831), the dialectic as employed by Marx, Engels, and Lenin was divested of its Hegelian philosophical idealism and combined with historical materialism to form "dialectical materialism"—put simply, a combination of belief in movement with belief in the notion that only matter is real. Hegel saw history as the constant development and enrichment in time of the absolute idea of World Spirit (*Weltgeist*). Development of the "Idea of Spirit" occurred in terms of the Hegelian triad of thesis, antithesis, and synthesis. Thus, a concept was said to inevitably generate its opposite and as a result of the mutual interaction of the two concepts, a new synthesis would emerge. Marx, in the preface to the second edition of *Capital* (1873), asserted that in Hegel the dialectic was "standing on its head" and had to be "turned right side up again, if you would discover the rational kernel within the mystical shell." In reality Marx merely substituted "matter" for Hegel's "idea." Yet the "rational kernel" has endowed communist thought and practice with a highly elusive character.

Basic to the dialectic are the notions of contradiction and conflict, and of a phenomenon being transformed into its opposite.

Lewis Henry Morgan, Social Evolutionist (Chicago: University of Chicago Press, 1931), pp. 179–181. Also see Carl Resek, *Lewis Henry Morgan, American Scholar* (Chicago: University of Chicago Press, 1960).

Among the "laws" of dialectics or the general characteristics of the dialectical method, as interpreted by communists, are the following:

(1) All phenomena and objects are interrelated and interdependent. The dialectical method condemns as "metaphysical" the view which regards phenomena as isolated; for the dialectic only the totality is real.

(2) The dialectic is based upon constant movement and development from the lower to the higher, from the simple to the complex; movement is progressive in an upward cyclical manner. It condemns as "metaphysical" all attempts to view phenomena as static and immutable, and holds that only matter and motion are constant.

(3) The "law" of interpenetration, unity, and strife of opposites holds that every phenomenon or object is not a homogeneous mass but is, instead, a changing unity of contradictory parts. Although the constituent parts of a phenomenon—or of the social order itself—are in conflict, they also constitute a unity of interacting parts which cannot be divorced from each other until protagonist and antagonist have played out their predetermined roles on the stage of history. Development occurs as a result of the struggle of opposites, and the source of movement is internal.

(4) The "law" of the transformation of quantity into quality and vice versa sees development as resulting from gradual, often imperceptible *quantitative* changes which occur in every phenomenon and which lead to abrupt and readily perceptible *qualitative* changes. The new qualitative state is the result of a "leap." A frequently cited example of this formulation is the transformation of water into ice or steam (qualitative change) as a result of changes in temperature (quantitative change). Communists also view political changes in terms of this "law" —quantitative changes resulting from the contradictions which characterize the socio-economic order thus lead to qualitative political changes.

(5) The "law" of the negation of the negation reflects the incessant change which characterizes the dialectic in its pure form. The new qualities which result from quantitative changes are, in turn, subjected to new quantitative changes and are replaced by subsequent qualitative states. Thus development is said to occur in stages, and each new synthesis, which has negated its predecessor as a result of the thesis-antithesis formula, is, in turn, negated by a new synthesis. In this way the negation is itself negated. The historical epochs of Marxism serve as an illustration: the feudal stage was the negation of the slaveholding stage and was itself negated by capitalism which, in turn, was said to be negated by communism. The new supposedly replaces the old in optimistic testimony to inevitable progress.

Dialectical development is based on internal movement, self-generated as a result of the internal contradictions which allegedly result from the struggle of opposites within a unity. Thus the predicted doom of capitalism is seen as resulting from the clash of bourgeoisie and proletariat (thesis and antithesis), which leads to a new synthesis. Proponents of dialectical materialism—that combination of mystical movement and mundane matter—distinguish it from mechanistic materialism or from the so-called vulgar materialism which they reject. Mechanistic materialism is said to diverge from the dialectic in not giving adequate recognition to change, in stressing external rather than internal sources of movement, in recognizing only quantity instead of quality, in denying historical "leaps," and in rejecting the notion of progressive development from the lower to the higher. Vulgar materialism is said to neglect the role of ideas, voluntarism (will), and consciousness.

The dialectic holds that opposites cannot be separated or reconciled: life and death, positive and negative, action and reaction, war and peace, offense and defense, and conflicting classes cannot be understood apart from each other. By this doctrine anything can turn into its opposite, just as friends can become enemies and stability can abruptly be transformed into instability. Since contradiction is the essence of the dialectic, it enables communists to make numerous distinctions. Thus they readily distinguish between the "progressive" or beneficial aspects of slavery or of capitalism (in terms of the development of productive forces), and the evil and oppressive aspects. The *Communist Manifesto* provides eloquent testimony to this dualism: it praises the bourgeoisie and capitalism for promoting the forces of economic development in their time, but denounces each as doomed for the future. When compared with its negation and with that which it negated, the same phenomenon can have two contradictory characteristics at different stages in its development. Capitalism is "progressive" in its earlier stages when compared with feudalism, but ceases to be so as soon as it begets its antithesis. Yet the communists claim that they preserve the "positive" features and achievements of capitalism.

The dialectic is an analytical concept which endows communists with a high degree of flexibility because it thrives on paradox and defies logic. Dialectical materialism claims to furnish ready explanations for all events and to be an accurate reflection of "objective reality." It also enables communists to believe that the course of development is predetermined in their favor as the dialectical dance of history unfolds.

The Ultimate Society. The classics of communism have had little to say regarding the specific nature of communist society except to assert that social classes will cease to exist and the state will "wither away." Such formulas as "an association in which the free development of each is the condition for the free development of all" (*Communist Manifesto*), or "the government of persons is replaced by the administration of things and the direction of the process of production" (Engels' *Anti-Dühring*), or Lenin's "from each according to his ability, to each according to his needs" are hardly helpful signposts on the road to communism. Indeed, it is difficult to escape the conclusion that the future communist society is both mythical and utopian in its avowed egalitarianism.

Commencing with the base-superstructure relationship, communists have believed that a change in the economic base—nationalization of industry plus economic development—will lead to the "expropriation of the expropriators" and pave the way for the new society. This change will also produce a new man, since the suppression of one class by another will ultimately be eliminated—although the majority of the formerly exploited will still need to suppress the minority of former exploiters during a transitional period. In 1917 Lenin expressed this vague and naive hope in this way:

> We are not utopians, and we do not in the least deny the possibility and inevitability of excesses on the part of *individual persons,* nor the need to suppress *such* excesses. But, in the first place, no special machinery, no special apparatus of repression is needed for this; this will be done by the armed people itself, as simply and as readily as any crowd of civilized people, even in modern society, parts a pair of combatants or does not allow a woman to be outraged. And, secondly, we know that the fundamental social cause of excesses . . . is the exploitation of the masses, their want and their poverty. With the removal of this chief cause, excesses will inevitably begin to "*wither away.*" We do not know how quickly and in what succession, but we know that they will wither away. With their withering away, the State will also *wither away.*[14]

By the simple act of making the whole of society "one office and one factory, with equal work and equal pay," it was assumed by Lenin that ultimately all persons will "become accustomed to observe the fundamental rules of social life, and their labor is so productive, that they voluntarily work *according to their ability.*"

For decades communists have been confronted with the task of attempting to define in concrete terms the nature of the future communist society. Yet the 1919 and 1961 Programs of the Communist Party of the Soviet Union were singularly disappointing in their detailing of the communist future.[15]

4. LENINISM

The Russian version of Marxism, known as Leninism, provided twentieth-century communism with many of its distinctive characteristics—the result of Vladimir Ilyich Lenin's efforts to apply the nineteenth-century doctrines of Marx and Engels to Russian conditions. Lenin, a Russian lawyer who reorganized the

[14] V. I. Lenin, *The State and Revolution* (1917) in Burns, *op. cit.* (above, n. 6), p. 747.

[15] For the texts of the 1919 and 1961 Programs, see Leonard Schapiro, ed., and Albert Boiter, assoc. ed., *The U.S.S.R. and the Future* (New York: Frederick A. Praeger, 1963), pp. 255–324.

Marxist movement into the Communist Party, saw the growth of capitalism as inevitable in Russia and saw it also as providing for the triumph of his brand of socialism. He corrected the failure of Marx to address himself to the political form which communist doctrine would assume. Much of Leninism constitutes a blend of practical considerations designed to obtain and retain political power, along with certain theoretical refinements. The principal tenets of Leninism deal with very specific problems.

A Party of Professional Revolutionaries. Lenin's principal contribution, expounded in his *What Is to Be Done?* (1902), lay in his advocacy of a unique type of political party, composed of a limited number of dedicated, disciplined, tested, and trained communists fully conscious of their role. This elite was to be enrolled in a centralized organization, a substantial part of which was to remain conspiratorial in nature. Since it was unwise, in Lenin's view, to rely upon the revolutionary initiative and spontaneity of the proletarian masses, the Party organization was to serve as the vanguard of the working class. That this vanguard was to be mostly of intellectual and bourgeois origin did not trouble Lenin, for he assumed that the conduct of the revolutionary struggle was a task for full-time professionals and not for naive amateurs, however well-intentioned. Thus the Communist Party was to understand the "true interests" of the proletariat far better than the proletariat itself could.

The Need to Seize Power. Lenin's writings abound with admonitions concerning the dangers of settling for economic reforms within the framework of capitalism. In place of trade unionism and reformism Lenin unceasingly advocated the primacy of political struggle directed against the bourgeois state. This preoccupation led to the advocacy of violent seizure of power, combined with appropriate agitational measures and slogans and a ready willingness to capitalize upon any and all issues useful in defeating the "class enemy." While revolutions were said to result from "objective conditions," it was also possible to accelerate the process by means of revolutionary action. Thus, Lenin believed that the "bourgeois epoch" in Imperial Russia—and elsewhere—could be abbreviated and the advent of communism expedited. This reflected the voluntarist element in Lenin's thinking which resulted from the importance given by Marxists to *consciousness*—that is, to thorough and rational knowledge and awareness of the role one is playing. The Communist Party, claiming to be endowed with such consciousness, assumed responsibility both for making the workers class conscious and for promoting the class struggle. Thus the dialectical process of development could be "accelerated" and revolution could occur even in the underdeveloped and semicolonial countries that constituted the "weakest link" in capitalism.

The Dictatorship of the Proletariat. The class struggle was seen as culminating in the "democratic dictatorship of the proletariat" —a contradiction in terms which was inaccurate also because the Party was viewed as its embodiment. To this formula, in practice, the peasantry was added by Lenin—although it was recognized that the peasantry was unstable and contained petit bourgeois elements. The dictatorship was to assure the establishment of socialism and the destruction of the class enemy and all counterrevolutionary forces. Although Marx originally employed this term ("the democratic dictatorship of the proletariat") in his *Critique of the Gotha Program,* it was Lenin who gave it practical expression by equating it with rule by the Communist Party.

Tactical Flexibility. Since circumstances could change, Lenin recognized the need to postpone achievement of goals should that be necessary. Thus, tactical retreats were regarded as proper, as when he decided to sue for peace with the Central Powers in 1918 at any price; in order to revive the economy, to adopt the New Economic Policy in 1921 as a concession to small-scale capitalism; or to abandon the effort to communize Poland in 1920 and instead sign the Treaty of Riga. Such retreats were permissible so long as the basic purpose was kept in mind, and it was known when to abandon a given tactic and turn a retreat into a new offensive. One of Lenin's best treatments of this question is to be found in his *"Left Wing" Communism, An Infantile Disorder* (1920), written for the benefit of European communists to whom he recommended a variety of tactics, including the use of bourgeois parliaments.

***Partiinost'* (Party-Mindedness).** The notion of partisanship in philosophy and in the social sciences—disciplines defined exclusively in terms of their service to the Party and its cause—was derived by Lenin from dialectical materialism. This principle was developed in Lenin's *Materialism and Empirio-Criticism* (1909). For Lenin, man's sense perceptions reflected "objective reality"—as perceived by the Party in terms of its ideology. Perception which did not correspond to this image of reality was therefore to be denounced as "idealist," "subjectivist," "relativist," and the like.

A Theory of Imperialism. Unlike Marx and Engels, Lenin lived to witness World War I—an event which he attempted to explain in terms of historical and dialectical materialism. Ignoring such explanations as the breakdown of the balance of power, nationalism, or the miscalculations of rulers and diplomats caught in a crisis of their own making, Lenin contended (in his *Imperialism, the Highest Stage of Capitalism*) that war resulted from the efforts of a "ripening" capitalism to cope with its internal contradictions and to forestall a revolution. According to Lenin's ideas on war, faced with declining profits and shrinking markets at home, a new kind of finance capitalism characterized by monopoly and a merger of industry and banking was said to export capital abroad to areas possessing raw materials and an abundant, cheap labor supply. The export of capital was followed by colonialism, in the form of annexation of these territories of new investment. Once all colonial territories were annexed, only redivision was possible and this redivision allegedly led to military alliances and wars. The class struggle then entered the international arena in the form of the conflict between exploited colonial nations and the exploiting imperialist powers. The alleged contradictions within capitalism were said to be intensified as a result of the conflict between imperialist powers over colonial spoils. On the basis of these dubious premises and very limited historical evidence, Lenin thus concluded that wars are inevitable so long as capitalism exists.

5. THE STALINIST VARIANT

As dictator of the Soviet Union and leader of world communism from the late 1920's to his death in 1953, Iosif Vissarionovich Stalin claimed only to be Lenin's pupil and the faithful executor of his master's teachings. Yet the one-time theological student and professional revolutionary did enrich the body of Marxist-Leninist thought in his own inimitable way by demonstrating how the ideology could be modified and manipulated.

The doctrine of "socialism in one country" was adopted by Stalin in 1924 in his struggle for power with Lev Trotsky. Stalin contended that the building of socialism in the Soviet Union could be accomplished without the communist revolution in Western Europe which Trotsky was depicted as claiming to be essential to socialism's triumph. However, Stalin did not deny the desirability of communist victories in other countries. It is significant that Stalin was able to buttress his argument with an appropriate quotation from Lenin, who in August, 1915, asserted that: "Uneven economic and political development is an absolute law of capitalism. Hence the victory of socialism is possible first in several or even in one capitalist country, taken singly." [16] Yet Stalin was to reaffirm as late as 1938 in his "Letter to Ivanov" that the victory of socialism in the U.S.S.R. could not be final as "we are living not on an island but 'in a system of states,' a considerable number of which are hostile to the land of socialism and create the danger of intervention and restoration." [17]

It followed logically from this last position that Stalin placed great emphasis upon the doctrine of "capitalist encirclement" of the Soviet Union. He concluded that it would be necessary to launch a program of forced development of heavy industry (production of the means of production rather than of consumer goods) as an essential part of the building of socialism, along with the collectivization of agriculture. These policies led to increased internal tension in the Soviet Union and to Stalin's March 5, 1937, assertion that the remnants of the defeated exploiting classes would become more wrathful and desperate as they grew weaker and as the Soviet regime scored greater successes; this development would intensify the class struggle in spite of the fact that the establishment of socialism in the Soviet Union had been proclaimed.[18] Stalin be-

[16] V. I. Lenin, *Polnoe Sobranie Sochinenii,* 5th ed. (Moscow: Gospolitizdat, 1961), XXVI, 354.

[17] J. V. Stalin, *A Letter to Ivanov* (New York: International Publishers, 1938), pp. 12–13.

[18] Stalin advanced this thesis as early as April, 1929, in his campaign against the Right Deviation and as late as May 4, 1948, in a letter to the Communist Party of Yugoslavia.

lieved firmly that no dying ruling class departs voluntarily from the stage of history. Only a fierce class struggle waged under Lenin's "dictatorship of the proletariat" would destroy the remnants of the old ruling class once and for all. Thus the Soviet state could not be expected to "wither away" under conditions of "capitalist encirclement."

Stalinism came to be associated with blood purges and the adulation of the *vozhd'* (leader), as well as with Russian chauvinism, the supremacy of the Communist Party apparatus, and the subordination of the international communist movement to the interests of Soviet foreign policy. Yet Stalin did introduce certain refinements into communist theory. In 1950 in his *Marxism and Problems of Linguistics* he declared that the superstructure does not merely reflect the base in a passive, neutral manner but is an "exceedingly active force" helping to reshape the base. Stalin exempted language from the superstructure and declared that it had permanent features; it was not dependent upon the base but transcended historical epochs and the class struggle, serving various ruling classes, including the Communist Party, without changing fundamentally. Stalin also asserted that the law of the transformation of quantity into quality did not necessarily involve an abrupt change (an explosion or "leap") in a society not divided into hostile classes—and, of course, the Soviet Union had become such a society by official definition. Basic changes were said to occur in the Soviet Union without "explosions" by means of "revolution from above." However, leaps would still occur under capitalism with its numerous antagonistic contradictions.

These "contradictions" loomed large in Stalin's last theoretical work, *Economic Problems of Socialism in the U.S.S.R.* (1952). There, he asserted that the contradictions between the various capitalist countries were greater and more acute than the contradictions between capitalism and socialism (the communist camp). Thus, while wars *between* capitalist states were still inevitable—as a result of the "struggle for markets" and the desire to "crush competitors"—a capitalist war against the Soviet Union was not very likely. Stalin held out the hope that the "peace movement" which arose in the late 1940's would develop under communist influence into a "struggle for socialism." Yet he also declared that to eliminate the inevitability of war, it would be necessary to abolish "imperialism" (i.e., capitalism).

As a ruler, Stalin did much to advance the cause of communism. In 1952, for instance, he stipulated certain conditions necessary for the achievement of communism. Among these was the disappearance of commodity exchange (by means of purchase and sale) in the collective farms, whose property was to be raised under communism to the level of public property, as "products exchange" replaced "commodity circulation" and money relations. With the achievement of communism, Stalin asserted, the law of value would disappear along with commodity production, and "society's demand for goods" would supposedly regulate production. Commodity production was to disappear once the "essential distinction" between industry and agriculture, between city and country was eliminated and replaced by a single "all-embracing production sector." Although Stalin was vague as to how this was to be accomplished, he did recognize that in the Soviet Union there were contradictions between the "relations of production" (including the peasantry) and the nationalized "forces of production." Such contradictions would have to be eliminated by the abolition of "commodity circulation" (trade based on a money economy) and its replacement by "products exchange," which is essential to the development of a communist society.

Stalin also recognized the need to modify doctrine to fit changing conditions, since a formulation which is correct for one set of circumstances may be incorrect in a different situation. To illustrate this in the 1950 Linguistics Controversy, Stalin referred to the "socialism in one country" formula which, he contended, was rejected by Marx and Engels and accepted by Lenin as a result of differing conditions. Stalin offered the following explanation:

> As is obvious, we have here two different conclusions on the question of the victory of socialism which not only contradict but exclude each other.
>
> Some exegetes and Talmudists, who, without probing into the essence of the matter, quote formally, in isolation from historical conditions, may say that one of these conclusions, being absolutely incorrect, must be dis-

carded, and the other conclusion, being absolutely correct, must be extended to all periods of development. But Marxists must know that the exegetes and Talmudists are mistaken; they must know that both of these conclusions are correct—not categorically so, but each in its time: the conclusion of Marx and Engels for the period of premonopoly capitalism and the conclusion of Lenin for the period of monopoly capitalism.[19]

Stalin concluded the entire discussion with the assertion: "Marxism does not recognize immutable conclusions and formulas obligatory for all epochs and periods. Marxism is the enemy of every kind of dogmatism."[20] Thus, the groundwork was laid for greater ideological flexibility with the accession to office of Stalin's successor, Nikita Sergeievich Khrushchev.

6. THE KHRUSHCHEV VARIANT

Although both Stalin and Khrushchev claimed to be Leninists, Khrushchev in 1956 launched a full-scale campaign against the "cult of personality"—a euphemism employed to refer to certain of Stalin's excesses—and did this in the name of a restoration of Leninism. While not denying the Communist Party's alleged monopoly of truth and wisdom, and its mastery of the "laws of historical development," Khrushchev's denunciation of the "cult of personality" indicated that the dictator who leads the Party need not be adulated or permitted to become a tyrant. The campaign against the "cult of personality" inevitably led to controversy over the correctness of many beliefs and practices which had been taken for granted in Stalin's time but which were now questioned. In addition it evoked the antagonism of those communists who were discomforted by change.

Certain aspects of communist ideology dealing with foreign relations were modified by Khrushchev in February, 1956, when he declared that World War III was "not fatalistically inevitable." Although this declaration was based on Stalin's 1952 pronouncement on contradictions between capitalist states and the communist world, it was followed by Khrushchev's explicit proclamation of

[19] *Bolshevik,* No. 14, 1950, p. 4.
[20] *Ibid.*, p. 6.

the end of the "capitalist encirclement" of the Soviet Union—a key concept in Stalin's thinking. The end of encirclement was said to be due to the emergence of a world socialist system and to the enhanced position of the Soviet Union as a great power. As part of the new Soviet international posture, Khrushchev refurbished the doctrine of "peaceful coexistence." In lieu of a world war waged with nuclear weapons, peaceful coexistence would be based on a relentless economic competition between communism and capitalism, with an intensification of the ideological struggle. Rejecting any notion of a permanent status quo, this doctrine recognized the inevitability and desirability of local "wars of liberation," waged either to destroy alleged remnants of colonialism, or to establish communist regimes or regimes more vulnerable to communist infiltration and subversion. Thus, the two systems were said by Khrushchev to be diametrically opposed and the march of the world to communism was declared to be proof of "*the irrevocable fact that the historic process is irreversible.*" [21]

Khrushchev also reaffirmed the Leninist doctrine of various "roads to socialism," along with the belief that ruling classes do not surrender power voluntarily. However, in 1956 he held out hope for a "parliamentary" road to socialism, along which communists by some unusual means would obtain a majority of the seats in a "bourgeois" parliament—which they would then proceed to save from itself. At the same time, "national communism" was condemned on the grounds that the struggle waged by the various communist parties should be a common one based on a fund of common experience.

Although Khrushchev's claim to be a systematic theoretician could not compare with Stalin's, certain of the latter's doctrines applicable to Soviet internal policy were revised by Khrushchev. The Stalinist dictum regarding the intensification of the class struggle as the class enemy grows weaker was officially repudiated. Stalin's 1952 injunction forbidding the sale of agricultural machinery to collective farms was violated when Khrushchev sold the state-owned machine-tractor stations. In the 1961 Party program the So-

[21] Nikita S. Khrushchev, "On Peaceful Coexistence," *Foreign Affairs*, XXXVIII, No. 1 (October, 1959), 15. Italics in original.

viet Union was declared to be no longer a "dictatorship of the proletariat" but a "state of the whole people"—as a result of the achievement of socialism and the transition to "full-scale construction of communism."

The image of the communism of the future promised by Khrushchev had much in common with Stalin's 1952 pronouncement regarding basic conditions for its establishment: economic abundance, a dramatic rise in real wages, and improved housing. Khrushchev promised the world's highest living standard, but made it conditional upon increased labor productivity and national income, and upon an improved international situation and the future of the arms race. He also insisted that the oft-discussed stateless communist society would be "highly organized" and that the Soviet state would survive intact until the complete victory of communism.

7. EVALUATION OF THE IDEOLOGY'S ASSUMPTIONS

Since historical materialism is an essential element of Marxist-Leninist doctrine, the question of its validity looms large in any evaluation of the ideology. Historical materialism embodies the fallacy inherent in any monistic view of history and is based upon highly selective data. Man's history is far too vast and diverse to be subsumed under a single doctrine or explained by a single theory. How can the entirety of recorded history be reduced arbitrarily to three stages (slaveholding, feudal, and capitalist)? Is it not highly erroneous to base an entire theory of historical development on three cases and then proclaim it to be "scientific"? How can all of history be subordinated to the single principle that human behavior is a function of the mode of production, with everything attributed to man's tools and the way in which man earns his living? Indeed, it can be argued in refutation of the Marxian view that the economic base—the mode of production which supposedly determines the superstructure—is actually determined by the superstructure, for the methods of production are the result of human inventiveness and not vice versa.

Historical materialism is based on the dubious assumption that man is primarily an economic animal. It conveniently ignores the fact that there is also a political man and a religious man. Why should the economic determinant—man's tools and what he eats—be more important than philosophical creeds, ethnic identity, personality, sex, chance or accident? The error of Marxism-Leninism lies in the fact that Marx and Engels devoted their energies and talents to an investigation of their own era—one in which they thought they discerned a certain pattern of inevitable development based on the conflict between the "mode of production" and the "relations of production." Influenced by the technology of the Industrial Revolution and its resultant social dislocations, they posited a historical scheme based upon a particular mode of production by applying the distinctive character of capitalism retrojectively to the stages which preceded it.

Yet one can ask: what "changes in the methods of production and exchange" marked the transition from the slaveholding to the feudal stage? In actual fact the changes in the techniques of agriculture and the crafts employed by ancient slaves and medieval serfs were very slight compared to the changes that characterized the transition from feudalism to capitalism. Thus, one can ask what contradiction resulting from a new mode of production could have led to the fall of the slaveholding society? In reality, two different "relations of production" (slaveholding and feudal) resulted from essentially similar "modes of production." In a similar manner, the allegedly different relations of production which are said to distinguish communism from capitalism are based on industrial techniques and processes common to both systems. Clearly the political and social changes in question cannot be fully explained in terms of economic determinism. In addition, Marx and Engels dealt with ancient and medieval societies superficially, and ignored non-Western societies in general and the "Asiatic" mode of production ("oriental despotism") in particular.

Marxism's obsession with class has led to certain inconsistencies in the ideology. The class concept claims to embrace millions of persons said to be conscious of their class affiliation and possessed of a single will that is capable of determining the outcome of history. Yet in practice it is the Communist Party that is truly class conscious, substituting its own consciousness and will for the ghost class which it claims to represent. Thus, in practice, communist parties have frequently tended to be parties of disaffected intellectuals and bourgeois sympathizers rather than of workers and peasants. The theory of class hardly explains the appearance of Marx and Lenin as leaders of the proletariat, in view of their nonproletarian background. Moreover, class solidarity often fails to materialize, as when a supposedly exploited class refuses to revolt or when some members of the bourgeoisie or proletariat betray the interests of their class and serve its enemies. In basing morality on class interests, furthermore, communism ignores the fact that a moral code usually transcends class lines and can unite supposedly inimical classes. For communist doctrine the morality of the class that is winning is superior to that of the class which is on the way out. By this doctrine what is "moral" is determined by what is successful.

In communist theory, history is the record of class struggle and the future is said to belong to the exploited class. Yet the slaves of ancient society did not overthrow their exploiters and become the ruling class (the feudal lords) of the new epoch. Similarly, it was not the serfs of the feudal epoch who as a class inherited the dominant role in the capitalist epoch as the new bourgeoisie. Thus it is doubtful that the proletariat—supposedly the "gravedigger" of capitalism—will succeed the bourgeoisie as the new postcapitalist ruling class, in accordance with Communist predictions. Indeed, Marxism errs in reducing social relationships to two classes, for society in reality is far more complex. In positing a doctrine of historical inevitability, communism ignores the fundamental fact that predictions are conditional—since man can frequently invalidate them by deliberately changing the conditions which it was erroneously assumed would persist. Thus it must be asked why class war and a communist victory must be regarded as inevitable. Communists, moreover, do not distinguish between their predictions and their actions designed to bring about the events whose occurrence they have predicted. In confusing determinism with voluntarism, they fuse the inevitable with the (to them) desirable. Communism is therefore not a science but a revolutionary reformism whose advocates predict crises and then—thanks to Lenin's influence—do everything in their power to bring them about.

The predictions of communists have often been incorrect. Marx and Engels predicted the progressive impoverishment of the industrial proletariat. In fact, the working class improved its living standard by means of free trade unions, cooperatives, the ballot box, social insurance, the graduated income tax, and other measures which demonstrated that the chain of inevitability can be broken. The middle class was not impoverished and proletarianized as forecast by communists, but flourished and attracted members of the proletariat. Similarly, communism did not take hold in the industrialized countries in which the "contradictions" of capitalism were supposedly most highly developed, but rather in certain agrarian countries whose conditions did not readily fit the Marxist scheme of analysis. Marxists also incorrectly predicted the decline of nationalism as a result of the growing internationalism of trade and communications, and of economic institutions (trusts, cartels) and practices.

If the accuracy of communist prognoses has left something to be desired, the doctrine of dialectical materialism with its emphasis upon contradiction makes these failures palatable. At issue here is not the proposition that man's ideas have been influenced—communists would say determined—by the conditions of material existence, but the blind assumption that historical development occurs exclusively in terms of class conflict in accordance with the rhythmic dissonance of the dialectic. The concept of the dialectic can be a very useful analytical tool since contradiction and conflict characterize many phenomena and the world is not static. However, when this concept is abused and elevated by communists to an all-embracing principle which purports to explain all development in terms of a struggle of opposites *leading to a preordained outcome*, certain questions arise. How can we really be certain of the outcome? Does the dialectic not involve the danger of being a method of analysis by definition, in which the results obtained depend upon the user? Is not proof of this provided by the fact that both Hegel and Marx employed the dialectic with different results and for different purposes? In fact, the dialectic is a process of thought which does not adequately explain the *ultimate* cause and origins of the events it seeks to interpret.

An even greater difficulty arises from the Marxist forced marriage of the dialectic with philosophical and historical materialism, which recognizes only a material world based on sensory perception and assumes that matter is eternal and is its own cause developing by self-movement. Indeed, "matter," as employed by communist philosophers, is never really explained, but is defined as "objective reality" (Lenin) or as the "totality of material things" (Engels). This viewpoint ignores the question of the source of matter; it simply assumes the material world as given and does not inquire into the cause of the order which characterizes the universe. The reliance upon self-movement to explain development dialectically assumes that the causes of change are inherent in everything as a result of internal contradictions and bear no reference to external factors. Thus dialectical causation does not really explain why events develop in a given direction, but when invoked by communists it has provided reassuring confirmation of their conviction that history is developing in their favor along a generally predetermined course.

A fundamental weakness in communist thought is in its treatment of ideology, which it regards as ephemeral and as a rationalization of class interests. Thus ideologies come and go in accordance with the pattern of the class struggle and are simply a part of the superstructure, which is determined by the economic base. However, an inconsistency arises here because of the refusal of Marxists to apply this Marxist concept to the ideology of Marxism. Thus, instead of viewing their own ideology as transitory and relative—like all other ideologies—communists see themselves as the great exception: for the first time in all history man is seen as having discovered absolute truth.

The illogic and the simplistic nature of communist philosophy are evident when one asks why the dialectic, social classes, and the class struggle should cease to be operative (once communists are victorious) if they have been motive forces in all of man's history. Why should the class struggle be replaced by a "classless" society? Why should contradictions be "antagonistic" under capitalism and "nonantagonistic" under a communist regime? Other dubious aspects of communist belief include the assumption that nearly everything can be known, the blind belief in inevitable progress, the utopian nature of professed communist goals, and the willingness to justify the use of any means in the pursuit of these ends. It is ironic but revealing that communists should simultaneously preach the brotherhood of man and class hatred. Indeed, communists have failed to understand that ends are influenced by the means chosen to achieve them. Indeed, the use of base means—so frequently advocated by Lenin and Stalin—served to corrupt noble ends and to debase the entire socialist movement. A basic fallacy in the doctrine has been the a priori assumption that state (communist) ownership of the means of production is the source of moral conduct and will create justice, remake man, and guarantee human happiness.[22] The pursuit of these goals has led to the sacrifice of the individual on the altar of the collectivity in accordance with communism's socio-centric nature. The vaunted humanistic pretensions of communism have often been empty.

8. FACTORS PROMOTING BELIEF

Although the validity of the basic premises and conclusions of communist ideology can be questioned, it does not follow that men will not believe in them. For men all too often observe what they wish to see and ignore what does not correspond to their stereotyped view of "reality." Belief in the ideology has been reinforced by the fact that Soviet communism is embodied in a functioning political system which has achieved successes in rapid industrialization, nuclear weapons, space exploration, and in international politics. The fact that communism made significant political gains after World War II, bringing more than one-third of humanity under the rule of various communist parties, provided "proof" of

[22] One of the errors of Marx and Engels was their apparent inability to distinguish between the evils of a developing industrial economy and early capitalism. By attributing the characteristics of early industrialism to capitalism, they failed to recognize that the fact of ownership itself does not change the character of the industrial system and the hierarchical relationships resulting from it.

the correctness of the ideology for those who wished to accept it.

In the noncommunist world, communists have chosen to single out those events which give them comfort and appear to confirm their prognoses. These have included unrest in the former colonial areas, the competition between capitalist states for markets, the emergence of a number of neutralist countries, and the nationalization of foreign-owned properties in various lands. In the industrialized capitalist countries, communists have found confirmation of their beliefs in strikes, unemployment, inflation, instances of corruption, the presence of prominent businessmen in high political office, as well as in business failures, corporation mergers, and the alleged growth of monopoly as a result of the elimination of smaller competitors. In each case communists have isolated such events from the total environment and interpreted them in accordance with their own rigid scheme of analysis.

Acceptance of the basic premises of the ideology fulfills the desire for dedication and commitment. Sharing common values, beliefs, enemies, and goals, its adherents see proof enough in the very existence of a mass movement which embraces tens of millions and rules over hundreds of millions. Indeed, if communists do not find the meaning of life in their ideology, it is unlikely that they will obtain it outside of the Party because alternative philosophies of history and politics are excluded. Nor can it be assumed that basic communist beliefs are only propaganda used to deceive the masses and rank-and-file members, but are not believed by the Soviet rulers. These beliefs provide a rationale for the regime's existence and a sense of legitimacy and destiny; anyone having a stake in that political order must accept them.

9. RELEVANCE TO SOVIET POLITICS

Communism has been described by C. E. M. Joad as a "philosophy in action." Its concern with uniting theory and practice was expressed by Marx in the eleventh of his *Theses on Feuerbach:* "Philosophers have only *interpreted* the world in various ways; the point, however, is to *change* it." Thus communist philosophy is reflected in political practice. The refusal to share power and to tolerate other political parties or private economic organizations, the insistence upon forced industrialization, collectivized agriculture, and the propagation of "scientific atheism" in schools and universities—all testify to the influence of ideological requirements. Indeed, the claim to possess "truth" has enabled communists to rationalize their use of repressive measures and their demands for great sacrifices from their subjects in the name of a happy and glorious future.

The dialectic—with its emphasis upon contradictions, abrupt changes, and the transformation of phenomena into their opposites—has influenced Soviet political behavior. It has facilitated sudden shifts in the policies and general line of the Communist Party. Thus, the New Economic Policy, with its concessions to petty capitalism and commerce, could replace War Communism in 1921 and be replaced, in turn, by its antithesis in the First Five Year Plan of 1929. Veteran Party leaders have been praised and decorated only to be denounced and publicly disgraced. The posthumous denigration of Stalin following his adulation during his lifetime provides a graphic example of the transformation of something into its opposite. The dialectic has also enabled Soviet politicians to advocate unabashedly contradictory formulae. Accordingly, Stalin could declare in June, 1930:

> We are for the withering away of the state. And at the same time we stand for the strengthening of the dictatorship of the proletariat, representing the strongest and most powerful authority of all existing state authorities up to the present time. The higher development of state authority for the purpose of preparing the conditions *for* the withering away of state authority—there you have a Marxist formula. Is it "contradictory"? Yes, it is "contradictory." But contradiction is a part of life, and it fully reflects Marxist dialectics.[23]

Men trained in the dialectic with its concern for contradiction and change tend to view the truth as a variable depending upon circumstances. Yet truth must further the cause and must therefore be official and subject to censorship and change. Since in this view the inevitable future is more important than the prosaic present, it is permissible to utter a statement which is false today but is *po-*

[23] I. V. Stalin, *Sochineniia,* XII, pp. 369 ff.

tentially true. Conversely, what is true today may be false tomorrow. In addition, the dialectic with its emphasis upon conflict and struggle promotes a brand of politics preoccupied with enemies and seeing life as characterized by conflict rather than by compromise.

Yet the essentially dogmatic and arrogant character of communist ideology should not blind one to its instrumentalist and manipulative aspects. Lenin modified and developed the teachings of Marx and Engels in applying them to Russia. Stalin modified Lenin's teachings and Khrushchev revised certain of Lenin's and Stalin's doctrines. Yet each Soviet leader claimed that he was remaining faithful to the basic belief. It was possible for Stalin to remove language from the Marxist superstructure; he could also decide to tolerate formal logic and even introduce it as a subject of instruction after it was denounced for years as being contrary to dialectics. In 1955 Einstein's relativity theory was found to be acceptable after having been rejected on the grounds that it was not based on dialectical materialism; its acceptance was made possible by treating energy (into which mass is transformed) as a form of matter in motion. This change was prompted by practical considerations and the need to exploit nuclear energy. A similar change occurred in the case of cybernetics—the science of control and communications in machines and living organisms—which was denounced in 1953 as a "pseudo-science" and later accepted (without its possible ideological or philosophical implications) because of its relevance to computers, automation, and guidance systems.

While it is incorrect therefore to view ideology as static or immutable, its pragmatic aspects should not blind one to such of its axiomatic bases as atheism, historical materialism, historical necessity, the role of the class struggle in history, the supposedly evil nature of private ownership of the means of production, the belief in inevitable progress and in the leading role of the Communist Party as the chosen instrument of the will of history. These tenets have constituted the hard core of doctrine. The practice of combining basic truth with pragmatic truth was well expressed in Engels' assertion that "our doctrine is not a dogma but a guide to action." Thus, all ideological pronouncements are not of equal significance but some are crucial. Khrushchev succinctly summarized the blending of doctrine and policy when he reminded the Twentieth Congress of the Communist Party of the Soviet Union that "Marxism-Leninism teaches that theory divorced from practice is dead, and practice which is not enlightened by revolutionary theory is blind." [24]

Ideology has dictated intervention by the Party in a variety of fields, including literature, the arts, pedagogy, genetics, historiography, architecture, the social sciences, and philosophy. It has required the use of official textbooks in all disciplines and has dictated their revision in more sensitive areas. Power struggles and policy debates have been conducted in doctrinal terms as conflicts between orthodoxy and deviation. Communists, it should be remembered, believe in the importance of ideas and take pains to distinguish between what they regard as "correct" and "incorrect" philosophies. Their beliefs have provided a rationale and justification for the acts of the Soviet government and the Communist Party.

[24] *XX S"ezd Kommunisticheskoi Partii Sovetskogo Soiuza, Stenograficheskii otchet* (Moscow: Gospolitizdat, 1956), I, 112.

CHAPTER 4

THE COMMUNIST PARTY OF THE SOVIET UNION: DEVELOPMENT AND ORGANIZATION

The Communist Party, although mentioned only briefly in the Soviet constitution, has provided the lifeblood of the Soviet regime in the form of the cadres or key personnel which operate the political system. The Party recruits and trains persons, and defines the conditions of advancement for political and administrative positions of responsibility. It determines the regime's basic policies, which are then adopted by the Soviet government. It endeavors to remake its subject populations in its own image. The Party's membership of more than fourteen million is committed to propagating its values and prescriptions for the communist version of the "good life," and is the embodiment of the attitudes and beliefs which are termed "communist ideology." In brief, the party sees itself as exercising a tutelary role in relationship to its subjects, and the Party leaders view their relationship to the rank-and-file membership in a similar fashion.

This remarkable organization began to take shape soon after the turn of the century as a result of the activities of a small number of compulsive and dedicated persons who had embraced Marxism and endeavored to give it substance in the context of the Russian Empire's autocratic political order. To a significant degree the Party was the brainchild of Vladimir Ilyich Lenin (Ulianov), who imposed upon it his organizational blueprint and who abused, chastised, and excommunicated those of its members who would not accept his leadership, ideological formulas, and tactics. The son of a provincial school inspector and by consequence a member of the appointive nobility, Lenin abandoned legal practice and engaged in full-time political agitation in behalf of Marxism.

1. THE EMERGENCE OF LENINIST BOLSHEVISM

The Russian version of a Marxist political party came into being as a reaction against the peasant-oriented Populist movement (*Narodnichestvo*) of the last quarter of the nineteenth century. It was also a response to earlier ineffective efforts to establish such a party. The Marxists of the Russian Empire parted company with other Russian revolutionaries in insisting on the desirability and inevitability of Russia's experiencing capitalism and industrial development with a bourgeoisie and proletariat. They opposed the Populist efforts to socialize Russia on the basis of a rural commune and contended, instead, that Russia's future lay with the urban industrial working class.

The founding in 1883 (the year of Marx's death) of the "Emancipation of Labor" Group in Geneva, Switzerland, by Georgii Plekhanov and other Russian political émigrés was not consequential, although it reflected the break with Populism. Initially, the Russian Marxist movement began in the late 1880's and early 1890's with a few small clandestine study groups confined principally to genuine or would-be intellectuals, as well as a few small workers' circles. In December, 1895, the Union for the Struggle for the Emancipation of the Working Class was formed in St. Petersburg. However, most members of this group of Marxist intellectuals, including Lenin, were soon arrested. Lenin was kept in prison during all of 1896 and spent the three subsequent years in exile in Siberia.[1]

In March, 1898, several unions for emancipation and other Marxist groups held the founding congress of the Russian Social

[1] For the early period of Russian Marxism see Richard Pipes, *Social Democracy and the St. Petersburg Labor Movement, 1885–1897* (Cambridge: Harvard University Press, 1963) and Leopold H. Haimson, *The Russian Marxists and the Origins of Bolshevism* (Cambridge: Harvard University Press, 1955). Also see Donald W. Treadgold, *Lenin and His Rivals: the Struggle for Russia's Future, 1898–1906* (New York: Frederick A. Praeger, 1955).

Democratic Labor Party (RSDLP) in Minsk. This Congress had no practical results, and eight of the nine delegates were arrested soon after it adjourned. Lenin, in exile, determined that the Party would have to be based on particular organizational principles. Upon completing his sentence in 1900, Lenin joined several Russian political émigrés in Western Europe and established *Iskra* (The Spark), a Marxist newspaper which was smuggled into Imperial Russia. Lenin's method was to employ the newspaper to propagate Marxism and also to use its agents and subscribers in Russia as organizers of local groups which would affiliate with the revived Party. The agents would also raise funds and transmit them along with information to the Party center in Western Europe.

Lenin insisted on organizing a new kind of party based upon professionalism and iron discipline and the use of various methods of struggle, including conspiracy. He used the pages of *Iskra* for expressing his views on Party organization and in 1902 published a work, *What Is to Be Done?*, in which he explained his plans in greater detail.[2]

Lenin advocated these views with considerable success at the Party's Second Congress, held in Brussels and London during August, 1903. *Iskra* became the Party's central organ, with Lenin as editor, and a Central Committee was elected. However, the Congress was marked by controversy over the definition of a Party member (Lenin advocated an inelastic definition), over how much autonomy local Party organizations would have (Lenin demanded complete centralism), and on the issues of national self-determination and cultural development of non-Russian nationalities. When seven delegates walked out of the Congress, Lenin and his followers were able to claim a "majority" and as a result of this fateful act, Lenin's faction became known as the *Bolsheviks* (members of the majority). The opponents who remained at the Congress were called *Mensheviks* (members of the minority), and Lenin subsequently was to claim that his Bolsheviks were the majority even when they were in the minority in a badly divided Party.

[2] For a slightly abridged English translation of Lenin's *What Is To Be Done?* see the edition prepared by S. V. Utechin, which also has a lengthy introduction and notes by S. V. and Patricia Utechin (London: Oxford University Press, 1963).

Lenin also sought to reduce the editorial board of *Iskra* from six to three members, with the Mensheviks having but one representative, L. Martov. When Martov refused to serve, the other member (Plekhanov) deserted Lenin and advocated the reinstatement of the ousted Menshevik members of the editorial board. Lenin, outmaneuvered, resigned as editor of *Iskra* and had himself appointed to the Central Committee; he soon began publishing another newspaper, *Vperyod* (Forward), organ of the Bolshevik faction. In April and May of 1905 the Bolsheviks held their own Party Congress in London, which was boycotted by the Mensheviks. Efforts to heal the breach at the Stockholm "Unity" Congress in April-May of 1906 were unsuccessful when the Bolsheviks were outvoted and Lenin was not even elected to the Central Committee. A subsequent Congress (the Fifth by Bolshevik count) was held in London in May, 1907, and was attended by both factions but did not end the schism in the Party.

The division between Bolsheviks and Mensheviks involved differences of degree on many issues which subsequently became differences in kind. Both factions were Marxist and socialist and believed that capitalism, although temporarily beneficial for Russia, would be replaced by the revolutionary order. However, the Mensheviks did not share the impatience of the Bolsheviks to overthrow the regime and were willing to let the bourgeois capitalist epoch run its course and fulfill its purpose in Russia by establishing conditions conducive to the advent of socialism. The Bolsheviks emphasized illicit conspiratorial organization and a tightly organized party of professionals, while many of the Mensheviks favored a mass party of workers, less centralism, and reliance upon legal means. The two factions also disagreed over tactics toward and within the Russian quasi-parliament, the State Duma, and on the issue of electoral alliances with other parties. Another source of controversy was the Bolshevik method of obtaining funds by means of armed raids; on one occasion they also arranged a fictitious marriage in order to gain control of an inheritance. The Mensheviks objected to such methods, as well as to the Bolshevik faction's practice of maintaining its separate treasury, apparatus, and newspaper. Thus the factions in the RSDLP disagreed largely over methods and tactics rather than over ultimate socialist goals.

Lenin had no genuine desire to repair the breach with the Mensheviks. He was able to acquire funds from wealthy donors and from other sources, including foreign governments, in general keeping the various sources of funds secret even from many of his closer followers. The tsarist secret police (*the Okhrana*) succeeded in infiltrating Lenin's Bolshevik movement and was fully aware of his activities in Switzerland, France, and Austria; they even placed a spy in the Central Committee. The police were also interested in promoting the Bolshevik-Menshevik split, with the intention of weakening the social democratic movement. Thus, Lenin did their bidding while promoting the interests of his own faction. In January, 1912, he gathered his followers in Prague for a conference, as a result of which his organization came to be called the Russian Social Democratic Labor Party (of Bolsheviks) and the division of the Russian Marxists into two parties was consummated. In 1912 each group was publishing its own daily newspaper—and that of the Bolsheviks was named *Pravda* (Truth). Subsequent efforts to unite the factions were unsuccessful.

By November, 1917, Lenin was in a position to wrest the reins of power from a weak and indecisive Russian Provisional Government, which did not exercise full powers in its own capital but had to share them with the Petrograd Soviet of Workers and Soldiers Deputies; the latter body gradually came under Bolshevik control. Lenin's success in 1917 was due to several factors. In addition to being ruthless and dedicated, he was preaching a simple doctrine in a time of general confusion and despair.[3]

[3] Lenin had returned to Russia from Switzerland in April, 1917, with the aid of the Imperial German Government, which had clandestinely financed the Russian revolutionary movement (but especially the Bolsheviks) and defeatist elements during World War I in an effort to weaken the Russian political order and compel the tsarist regime to sue for peace. Millions of German marks were invested in this operation, and although Lenin took support from wherever he could find it and crossed Germany by rail on his return to Russia, he was no one's agent but his own and was serving the interests of Bolshevism. See Z. A. B. Zeman, ed., *Germany and the Revolution in Russia, 1915–1918: Documents from the Archives of the German Foreign Ministry* (London and New York: Oxford University Press, 1958) and Stefan T. Possony, *Lenin: The Compulsive Revolutionary* (Chicago: Henry Regnery, 1964). Other studies of Lenin are Louis Fischer, *The Life of Lenin* (New York: Harper and Row, 1964); Robert Payne, *The Life and Death of Lenin* (New York: Simon and Schuster, 1964); and Bertram D. Wolfe, *Three Who Made a Revo-*

The Provisional Government, under the leadership of Alexander Kerensky, was bent upon prosecuting an unpopular war effort, while Lenin advocated immediate peace and promoted disaffection among the troops. Lenin also promised bread to those who were in need and land to the land-hungry peasantry. He had succeeded in creating for the Bolsheviks a private army (the "Red Guard"), and in winning over or demoralizing and neutralizing the troops in the capital, thus depriving the Provisional Government of armed support. Other parties could obtain more votes in Russia's last free election but could not compete with the Bolsheviks' demagogic appeals nor with their organizational talents. Lenin's paramilitary force seized power on the night of November 6–7, 1917 (October 24–25 according to the then-official Julian calendar), by taking the Winter Palace, the seat of the weak Provisional Government, and other key points in the capital.

2. STAGES IN THE PARTY'S DEVELOPMENT

Lenin's Leadership (1917–22). After having spent a decade and a half in Western Europe as an émigré, Lenin was to have but four and a half years to leave his mark upon the Soviet regime, which had now become synonymous with Bolshevism. The Party grew rapidly from approximately 20,000 members in March, 1917, at the time of the monarchy's collapse, to ten times that number by the year's end. It attracted left-wing Mensheviks and renegade Socialist Revolutionaries, and as it grew it acquired an appearance far different from that intended by Lenin when he first expounded the notion of an exclusive, tightly-knit group of dedicated conspirators and agitators.[4]

The Party seized power in a demoralized and war-weary country beset with innumerable problems. The collapse of the army made it impossible to resist the advancing armies of Germany and

---

lution (New York: Dial Press, 1948). Certain aspects of Bolshevik conspiratorial activity are dealt with in Michael Futrell, *Northern Underground* (New York: Frederick A. Praeger, 1963).

[4] For a general treatment of the Party's development, see J. S. Reshetar, Jr., *A Concise History of the Communist Party of the Soviet Union*, rev. ed. (New York: Frederick A. Praeger, 1964).

Austria-Hungary. Thus, it was imperative for Lenin to conclude a peace treaty and dissociate his regime from an unpopular war, in this way improving its chances for survival. With the signing of the Brest-Litovsk Treaty, however, Russia lost certain of her Western non-Russian territories and had to recognize Ukrainian independence. Lenin encountered considerable difficulty in getting the treaty ratified by the Party's Seventh Congress (March, 1918); he had to contend with the opposition of his fellow-Bolsheviks (the "Left-Communists"), who objected to the treaty contending that it was a surrender to imperialism and a denial of revolutionary war. The treaty also caused the fellow-traveling Left Socialist Revolutionaries to resign from Lenin's government.

The peace treaty, which enabled Russia to withdraw from World War I, was but the prelude to a renewed internal armed struggle between Bolshevism and its Russian and non-Russian opponents. The Party, which had adopted the communist label at the Seventh Congress, recruited a new army and imposed a harsh secret police system upon its subjects. It nationalized industry and banking, conscripted labor, imposed rationing, and requisitioned food from the peasants, whom it could not compensate with consumer goods. Yet the policy of War Communism did not prevent Lenin from using tsarist army officers and bourgeois (non-Communist) managers and technical specialists. Such concessions evoked much antagonism among diehard orthodox Bolsheviks, who were not placated by the adoption of a new program at the Eighth Congress in March, 1919. The Congress upheld Lenin's policies and also established a Political Bureau (Politburo)—a body capable of superseding the Central Committee. The Congress also authorized the first full-scale purge (verification and "cleansing") of the membership, which resulted in the ouster of approximately half of the members; however, the admission of new members raised the level to 350,000 by late 1919.

The Soviet regime's ability to retain control of the country's vital core made it possible for Lenin to engage in ineffective efforts to foment world revolution. The Comintern or Communist (Third) International was founded in 1919, just prior to the Party's Eighth Congress, but the failure to establish a communist regime in Poland by military means during the summer of 1920 led to renewed preoccupation with internal problems. The Ninth Congress (March-April, 1920), for instance, witnessed a controversy over the role of trade unions and their relationship to the Party. It was decided that the communist trade union leadership would be subordinate to the Party apparatus and that civilian labor would be mobilized and disciplined. Idealistic communists—members of the Democratic Centralist Opposition—were becoming disillusioned as a result of the growth of a Party bureaucracy, the appointment rather than the election of many Party officials, and the arbitrary transfer of dissident members as a form of administrative "exile." Lenin defeated the Democratic Centralist Opposition, but was soon confronted with strikes and famine as well as an armed rebellion (at the Kronstadt Naval Base), which demanded free elections to the soviets and an end to the Party's monopoly of political power.

The Tenth Congress, in March, 1921, saw the defeat of a new dissident movement—the Workers' Opposition—which was dissatisfied with the influx of nonproletarian elements into the Party. Lenin was incensed by the charge that the Party was losing its character as a workers' organization and denounced his former followers as a "petit-bourgeois anarchist element." He employed several drastic measures: he had the Tenth Congress adopt a resolution forbidding factional and opposition movements; he ordered the suppression of the Kronstadt rebellion; he obtained adoption of the New Economic Policy (NEP). This last measure signaled a relaxation of controls in an effort to restore production; small-scale "capitalism" and private retail trade were to be permitted but the regime retained ownership of heavy industry and large-scale manufacturing, transport, communications, and natural resources; in lieu of the hated agricultural requisitions the peasants were permitted to sell any surplus they had after paying a tax in kind. The NEP was accompanied by a new purge of the Party in 1921, which led to the expulsion of 170,000 members.

At this time Lenin began to show symptoms of the arteriosclerosis which was to cause his death on January 21, 1924. The first of three strokes occurred in May, 1922, and left Lenin an invalid for the remaining twenty months of his life. Unable to exercise leadership, Lenin could only ponder what he had wrought in a lifetime of agitation, polemical activity, and conspiracy combined with utopian visions and a significant appreciation of political realities.

From Collective Leadership to Stalinist Dictatorship (1923–29). During 1922 and 1923, as Lenin lay ill, leadership of the Party was assumed by a triumvirate which consisted of Iosif V. Stalin (Dzhugashvili), Lev B. Kamenev (Rosenfeld), and Grigorii E. Zinoviev (Radomyslskii). Stalin had been elected General Secretary of the Party on April 3, 1922, following the Eleventh Congress (he had become a Marxist in 1898, had been appointed to Lenin's Central Committee in 1912, and had served as a member of the Soviet government since 1917). Kamenev headed the Moscow Soviet while Zinoviev headed the Leningrad Party organization and was the leading figure in the Comintern. All three were Politburo members. Lenin did not designate a successor in his Testament (December 25, 1922) but in a postscript of January 4, 1923, called for Stalin's removal from the General Secretaryship on the grounds that he was too rude and capricious and not sufficiently tolerant, loyal, or polite. However, Stalin's fellow-triumvirs had Lenin's Testament suppressed and saved Stalin's career. (The Testament was not published in the Soviet Union until 1956.)

A fourth leader, Lev Trotsky (Bronstein), figured prominently in the power struggle which occurred after Lenin's death. Trotsky had had disagreements with Lenin since 1903 and did not, in fact, join the Bolsheviks until the summer of 1917. However, he acquired fame as a Politburo member, as the principal organizer of the regime's Red Army, and as its Bolshevik civilian head. Trotsky was Stalin's principal rival, although a bitter personal feud between Trotsky and Zinoviev obscured this conflict—a feud beneficial to Stalin because it assured him of Zinoviev's support during a crucial period. Stalin enjoyed an important advantage as General Secretary because of his control of Party personnel. He also could give the appearance of having had better relations with Lenin—so long as the Testament was suppressed—while the other three leaders had been publicly criticized by Lenin at various times. Indeed, Stalin was able to pose as an advocate and interpreter of

Leninism in his publications and speeches by quoting his teacher and by taking an oath at Lenin's funeral to remain faithful to his teachings. He also had Lenin's body embalmed and placed in a mausoleum in Moscow's Red Square as a "sacred relic" of communism.

It is ironic that in the 1923–25 period it was Trotsky who was thought by many to present a greater danger of aspiring to the role of dictator. Stalin skillfully dissimulated his character and appeared to be a moderate. The exaggerated fear of Trotsky as a Bolshevik Bonaparte held the triumvirate together until the summer of 1925. Kamenev and Zinoviev, in their feud with Trotsky, had acquiesced in the strengthening of the Party's administrative apparatus in Stalin's hands. The Twelfth Congress in April, 1923, and the Thirteenth in May, 1924, resulted in the enlargement of the Central Committee to nearly twice its size (from 27 to 53 members); this gave Stalin an opportunity to reward loyal followers and to use this enlarged (and supposedly more "democratic") body to reduce the influence of his colleagues in the Politburo.

Trotsky challenged the triumvirate only in a spasmodic and ineffective manner. He had failed to oppose Stalin when the dying Lenin had asked him to do so in the winter of 1922–23. Instead, Trotsky criticized the bureaucratic regime in the Party and endeavored to rally the Party youth against Stalin's machine. He also criticized Zinoviev for Comintern failures and was unhappy about the NEP. Finally, in January, 1925, the triumvirate removed Trotsky from his post as Commissar of War. Stalin was now ready to adopt a rightist orientation in agricultural policy by reducing the tax on those peasants who did not hire labor. This course won the support of other Politburo members—the theoretician Nikolai Bukharin, the head of government Alexei Rykov, and the trade union chief Mikhail Tomsky. Stalin was now able to dispense with Kamenev and Zinoviev, who disapproved of these concessions and who had belatedly become aware of the General Secretary's growing power. The triumvirate was replaced by a quadrumvirate, and Stalin's influence was greater in the latter than it had been in the former. Kamenev and Zinoviev, joined by Lenin's widow (Krupskaia), challenged Stalin ineffectively at the Fourteenth Congress in December, 1925, by criticizing the NEP. Stalin defended the NEP as a Leninist policy while Trotsky remained aloof from the spirited debate after having falsely denied the authenticity of Lenin's Testament (which had been published abroad in 1925).

By the spring of 1926 Kamenev, Zinoviev, and Trotsky belatedly joined forces against Stalin—who accused them of being "unprincipled" because they had put aside their earlier disagreements to unite against his rule. However, by now Kamenev had been demoted to the rank of a candidate-member of the Politburo. Zinoviev had been removed from the leadership of the Leningrad Party organization in February and was expelled from the Politburo in July. Although the oppositionists capitulated in the autumn of 1926, they renewed their campaign against Stalin during the summer and autumn of 1927. Demonstrations in the streets of Moscow on November 7, 1927, were broken up by Stalin's supporters; and the oppositionists were expelled from the Party. The Fifteenth Congress in December, 1927, reaffirmed Stalin's victory.

Stalin's triumph over the Trotskyite "Left Deviation" was possible because he had obtained the support of the Right (Bukharin's group), which favored a continuation of the NEP and a slower rate of industrialization based on a prosperous peasantry. The defeated Left had condemned the NEP, the Party bureaucracy, and the *kulaks* ("wealthy" peasants) and had advocated rapid industrialization. While Trotsky had argued the necessity of extending the revolution (communist rule) to other countries, Stalin had responded by insisting that socialism could be built in one country. The disagreement, however, was over tactics and methods and not over goals, for Stalin never rejected world revolution as the ultimate objective, defending "socialism in one country" as the most realistic means of achieving this end.

After Stalin had disposed of the Left in 1927, he was able to dispense with his allies of the Right, who mistakenly thought that he had adopted their policy of less rapid industrialization—paid for by an increased agricultural output made possible by granting concessions (and paying adequate prices) to the middle ranks of the peasantry. Instead, Stalin adopted a policy of forced collectivization of agriculture, under which the peasants would deliver agricultural products to the state at low prices and pay for the program of rapid forced industrialization. By 1929 the NEP was replaced by the First Five Year Plan, Bukharin was expelled from the Politburo, and some of Trotsky's followers had begun to recant and support Stalin now that he had adopted Trotsky's program of industrialization and collectivization. Stalin had changed direction so rapidly that the Right was disarmed and divided before it could coalesce into a well-defined faction. The Secretary General was now in an unassailable position.

Stalinist Socialism and Purges (1930–39). The development of a state-owned heavy industry involved the accumulation of capital on a vast scale by means of expropriation of the peasantry; forced savings in the form of compulsory government loans; inflation; and deprivations in consumption. It also led to an artificial famine in 1932–33, which claimed millions of peasant victims, especially among the Ukrainians, while Stalin exported grain at depressed world prices in order to pay for machinery imports. Increased emphasis was placed upon technical skills, as well as upon acceptance of the Party line as laid down by Stalin's Secretariat and Central Committee. Thus at the Sixteenth Congress in June, 1930, there was no debate, but the delegates heard recantations uttered by the members of the defeated Right Opposition.

At the Seventeenth Party Congress in January, 1934, Stalin warned against "enemies both internal and external" and stressed the selection of personnel and "verification of fulfillment" in organizational work. Within a year he launched the first of a series of blood purges which, ironically, took place under the regime's slogan, "Life has become better, life has become happier." In reality, life had only become cheaper. The mysterious assassination of the Leningrad Party leader, Sergei Kirov, on December 1, 1934, provided the pretext for the first wave of blood purges, many of whose victims did not even know Kirov. Stalin erected monuments to Kirov but may also have played some role in his death.

The blood purges were to last four years and upon attaining their most intensive stage were to be termed the *Yezhovshchina*—in dubious honor of Nikolai Yezhov, the chief of Stalin's secret police from September, 1936, to December, 1938. After he had performed his gruesome task and Stalin no longer required his services, Yezhov also perished. Three "show trials" were staged in Moscow in August, 1936; January, 1937; and March, 1938. The defendants were old Party leaders and oppositionists and included Kamenev, Zinoviev, Bukharin, Alexei Rykov, Christian Rakovsky, Karl Radek, and others—as well as certain obscure persons who were probably provocateurs. The defendants, almost without exception, confessed to having committed treasonable acts and frequently made fantastic and false admissions. The overwhelming majority were sentenced to death and executed. A secret trial of eight leading Soviet generals, including Marshal Tukhachevsky, was held in June, 1937; all of the accused were executed.[5]

The rank-and-file membership also felt the blow of the purges. The membership decreased by more than 1.6 million between 1933 and 1938; but the number purged was greater because new members were admitted after November, 1936 (prior to that—beginning in December, 1932—admission of new members was suspended). Nor were members of the Central Committee immune. It was reported in 1956 that 98 of the 139 Central Committee members and candidate-members elected at the Seventeenth Congress in January, 1934, were executed; ironically, it had been called the "Congress of Victors."[6] Loyal Stalinists perished along with those who had made an unfortunate statement or association in the past. Nor did Trotsky—the star defendant *in absentia* at the Moscow trials—escape Stalin's reign of terror. Exiled from the Soviet Union in 1929, the Red Army's founder took refuge in Turkey, France, Norway, and, finally, in Mexico. There on August 20, 1940, an as-

[5] The Stalinist era is treated extensively in John A. Armstrong, *The Politics of Totalitarianism* (New York: Random House, 1961). On the purges, see F. Beck and W. Godin, *Russian Purge and the Extraction of Confession* (New York: Viking Press, 1951). For the transcript of the March, 1938, show trial see *The Great Purge Trial* edited, and with notes by, Robert C. Tucker and Stephen F. Cohen (New York: Grosset and Dunlap, 1965). For biographies of Stalin, see Isaac Deutscher, *Stalin: A Political Biography* (New York: Oxford University Press, 1949); Boris Souvarine, *Stalin, A Critical Survey of Bolshevism* (New York: Alliance Book Co., 1939); and Leon Trotsky, *Stalin, An Appraisal of the Man and His Influence* (London: Hollis and Carter, 1947).

[6] *Current Soviet Policies II*, ed. Leo Gruliow (New York: Frederick A. Praeger, 1957), p. 176.

sassin drove an ice axe into Trotsky's skull. Stalin had destroyed the last of his old opponents.

War and the "Cult of Personality" (1940–53). The failure of Stalin's efforts to avoid involvement in World War II had a profound impact upon the Party. Its losses were great and new members had to be admitted not only to compensate for the wartime losses, but also to obtain a greater degree of support for the regime—especially in the armed forces. In 1945, Party membership reached a new high of nearly four million members and 1.8 million candidate-members. Much of the new membership consequently had to be screened and part of it expelled during the postwar years. At the same time the educational level rose as the Party acquired intellectuals, technicians, and members of the managerial class.

Beginning in 1946, the Party launched a campaign for ideological purity under the direction of the Leningrad Party leader, Andrei Zhdanov. Philosophers, writers, poets, geneticists, and advocates of "rootless cosmopolitanism" came under attack. Stalin later issued pronouncements on linguistics and economics which at the time were accepted by the professors and ideologists. The General Secretary was now head of the government, generalissimo of the armed forces, credited as author of the official textbook on Party history, and was also dictator of tastes in music and architecture. Celebrated as a "genius," as the "father of peoples," and as the "Lenin of today," Stalin was adulated and became the object of what his successor termed the "cult of personality." In his last years Stalin gave some indication of suffering from some form of dementia. He became increasingly suspicious and allegedly would "look at a comrade with whom he was seated at the same table and say: 'Your eyes are shifty today.' "[7]

Shortly before his death Stalin convoked the Party's Nineteenth Congress—in October, 1952—and eliminated the term "Bolshevik" from the Party's name. The All-Union Communist Party (of Bolsheviks) now became the Communist Party of the Soviet Union (CPSU). The aging dictator installed a large number of new lieu-

[7] *XXII S"ezd Kommunisticheskoi Partii Sovetskogo Soiuza, stenograficheskii otchet* (Moscow: Gospolitizdat, 1962), II, 583.

tenants and made ready to eliminate some of his senior lieutenants who had survived the purges of the thirties and whose careers had benefited from the resultant vacancies.[8]

In January, 1953, the arrest of nine physicians for allegedly having committed medical murder on orders of United States intelligence was announced. Andrei Zhdanov, the Leningrad Party leader who died in 1948, and Alexander Shcherbakov, former political chief of the Soviet Army, were said to have been the victims of this fantastic "doctors' plot." Six of the arrested physicians were Jewish. Fear gripped the entire population and the Party as events pointed to the unleashing of a massive blood purge. Thus, Stalin's death on March 5, 1953, left his subjects both bewildered and relieved. An era of spectacular achievements and of unsurpassed despotism had come to an end.

Collective Leadership Again (1953–57). Before arranging for Stalin's funeral and after removing his hated personal secretary, Alexander V. Poskrebyshev—a powerful and sinister man—Stalin's senior lieutenants divided the heritage of the late dictator. Georgii Malenkov, who had served in the Party Secretariat under Stalin, became head of government, but soon had to relinquish his post as a Party Central Committee Secretary. This left Nikita S. Khrushchev in the most advantageous position within the Secretariat and he soon adopted the title of "First Secretary" of the Party (as distinct from Stalin's title of "General Secretary"). Lavrentii Beria, a deputy premier, was made head of a reunified secret police organization, as interior minister, and also controlled an internal security army. This collective leadership was to lose one member in late June, 1953, when Beria was arrested and subsequently executed. The secret police chief, who had endeavored to gain support by freeing the physicians accused in the "doctors' plot" and by advocating concessions to the non-Russian nationalities and to the collectivized peasantry, had presented a threat to the others.

[8] Khrushchev, in his secret speech at the Twentieth Congress, asserted that Stalin "evidently had plans to finish off the old members of the Political Bureau." He also observed that "had Stalin remained at the helm for another several months, Comrades Molotov and [Anastas] Mikoyan would probably not have delivered any speeches at this Congress." *Current Soviet Policies II*, p. 187.

Beria's place in the collective leadership was taken by Viacheslav M. Molotov, an old Bolshevik and head of government during the 1930's who had succeeded in having himself restored to the post of foreign minister after Stalin's death. The collective leadership lost another member with the removal of Malenkov from the chairmanship of the U.S.S.R. Council of Ministers in February, 1955; he was replaced by Nikolai Bulganin, former defense minister. In September, 1955, Molotov was accused of an "ideological error" and issued a reluctant recantation; in June, 1956, he was compelled to resign from his post as foreign minister. Khrushchev, as Party chief, and Bulganin, as premier, were seemingly inseparable members of a duumvirate in 1955 and 1956.

The membership of the collective leadership had changed as a result of differences over domestic and foreign policy issues and ideological questions (often closely related to policy). Khrushchev and Malenkov disagreed, for instance, over the rate of development for heavy industry versus light industry and the amount of consumer goods that the regime could afford. The extent and nature of the Soviet Union's nuclear deterrent and the consequences of World War III also entered into this debate, which concealed a power struggle.[9] Among the foreign policy issues was the decision to sign the Austrian State Treaty in May, 1955, and to terminate the Soviet military occupation of Eastern Austria. Molotov opposed this decision, as well as the visit of Khrushchev and Bulganin to Belgrade to attempt a reconciliation with Marshal Tito and the excommunicated Yugoslav Communist Party. Domestic policy issues causing disagreement included the decision to denigrate Stalin's memory in the "secret speech" at the Twentieth Congress and in more moderate terms in public addresses at the Congress. Khrushchev's policy of bringing millions of acres of virgin lands under cultivation (in Western Siberia and Kazakhstan) and his scheme to cultivate corn aroused opposition—as did his plan to reorganize economic management in 1957.

The period of collective leadership culminated in an unsuccessful attempt to oust Khrushchev from his post as First Secretary in

[9] For a discussion of these matters, see Herbert S. Dinerstein, *War and the Soviet Union*, rev. ed. (New York: Frederick A. Praeger, 1962).

June, 1957. A majority of seven of the eleven members of the Central Committee's Presidium favored Khrushchev's removal. The wily and ruthless First Secretary, fighting for his political life, contended that he could only be removed by the Central Committee and succeeded in calling a plenary session of that body at which he rallied his supporters and defeated his opponents.[10] Significantly, these opponents had united against Khrushchev despite their disagreements over policies. Malenkov, Molotov, Lazar Kaganovich (an old crony of Stalin's and a deputy premier), and the former foreign minister, Dmitrii T. Shepilov, were then expelled from the Central Committee and denounced as the "anti-Party group." Within eighteen months four other opponents of Khrushchev, including Premier Bulganin and Marshal Kliment Voroshilov, were demoted and publicly denounced. The June, 1957, crisis and Khrushchev's assumption of the premiership on March 27, 1958—while retaining his post as Party First Secretary—marked the end of the period of collective leadership.

The Khrushchev Era (1958–64). Many of the reforms introduced by Khrushchev reflected an effort to revitalize a regime which showed the effects of having been in power for four decades. The First Secretary and Premier adopted a distinctive style of visiting the various union republics and making state visits abroad—in contrast to Stalin's self-imposed isolation in the Kremlin. Khrushchev readily granted impromptu interviews, employed earthy language, gave the impression of being solicitous of his subjects' welfare, and occasionally engaged in studied clowning. His volubility—like Stalin's taciturnity—served to conceal a cunning which had enabled him to plot and fight his way to the top. However, Khrushchev was not able to utilize the secret police as the punitive organ of his personal secretariat in the way in which Stalin had. The demise of Beria and many of his aides (termed collectively the "Beria gang" in official parlance at the time) had enabled the Party as a whole—if not individual members—to acquire a degree of independence from the security police.

During Khrushchev's tenure Party membership (including candi-

[10] On Khrushchev's career, see Lazar Pistrak, *The Grand Tactician: Khrushchev's Rise to Power* (New York: Frederick A. Praeger, 1961) and Myron Rush, *The Rise of Khrushchev* (Washington, D. C.: Public Affairs Press, 1958).

date members) increased from 7.2 million in 1956 to 11.7 million in 1964. An effort was made to recruit more factory workers and peasants as members. Khrushchev departed from the Stalinist pattern of rule by holding regular Party congresses and convening the Central Committee in regular sessions. The Twentieth Congress—in February, 1956—was significant in that it elected a new Central Committee and indicated an effort to dissociate the Party from Stalin's despotism, blaming the regime's failures, cruelties, and shortcomings on the late dictator. The Twenty-first Congress—in January-February, 1959—did little more than approve the Seven Year Plan (1959–65) and denounce the defenseless members of the anti-Party group of Malenkov, Molotov *et al.*, who had attempted to oust Khrushchev in 1957.

The Twenty-second Congress—in October, 1961—adopted a new Party Program and new statutes in an effort to convey the impression of Party "legality" and the "restoration of Leninist norms of Party life." The attacks on the anti-Party group were intensified. The Congress ordered the removal of Stalin's body from the Lenin-Stalin mausoleum in Red Square and its interment in a simple grave near the Kremlin wall—a petty gesture which could hardly eradicate the impact of the quarter-century of Stalin's rule. The Congress was also significant in providing a forum for the excommunication of Albania from the Soviet communist camp. This action, taken by Khrushchev, prompted a public expression of disapproval by the Chinese communist delegation headed by Premier Chou En-lai, who left the Congress prematurely.

The deterioration of the Sino-Soviet relationship became a principal feature of Khrushchev's regime, with the two leading communist powers engaging in undignified mutual recrimination. Khrushchev was denounced as a "revisionist" by the Chinese because of his ideological pronouncements and policies, and the primacy of the CPSU was challenged. The disarray in international communism was paralleled by a host of Soviet domestic problems to which Khrushchev responded with improvised and ineffective solutions. His numerous administrative reorganizations and his vaunted but abortive policies, especially in agriculture, resulted in frustration and confusion.

The abrupt removal of Khrushchev on October 14, 1964, by what was said to have been a plenary session of the Central Committee, coincided with the detonation of Communist China's first nuclear device. Initially it was announced by the Central Committee in *Pravda* of October 16 that it had only complied with Khrushchev's "request" that he be relieved of his duties as First Secretary, Presidium member, and Chairman of the USSR Council of Ministers (Premier) "in view of his advanced age and deteriorating health." Although Khrushchev had turned seventy in April of 1964, the falsity of the "reasons of health" explanation soon became apparent on October 17 when *Pravda* attacked him by innuendo in denouncing "hare-brained schemes, premature conclusions, hasty, unrealistic decisions and actions, boasting and idle talk, a preoccupation with administration, and an unwillingness to consider what has already been proven by science and practical experience. . . ." The Party was said to oppose "subjectivism" and "the ideology and practices of the personality cult," implying, it would appear, that Khrushchev had violated the "collective leadership" principle. At the March, 1965, plenary session of the Central Committee, Khrushchev was criticized implicitly in references to "errors of leadership" in the field of agriculture.

The coup which resulted in Khrushchev's ouster was well planned and had the character of a palace revolution. The First Secretary had been staying at his palatial retreat near the Black Sea resort of Sochi. When he learned what was afoot, his efforts to offer a defense and to prevent his removal were in vain. The coup was organized by Leonid Brezhnev, Khrushchev's successor as First Secretary, and by such other lieutenants as Party Secretaries Mikhail Suslov and Alexander Shelepin. Khrushchev's colorful career of ten eventful years at the very top of the Soviet pyramid ended where it had begun—in the Central Committee.

3. CENTRAL PARTY ORGANIZATION

The central Party bodies and the administrative apparatus stand at the top of a vast hierarchical structure. At the bottom are approximately 350,000 primary Party organizations which do the bidding of the Party apparatus in economic enterprises, institutions, farms, and military units. The primary Party organizations are subordinated to district (*raion*) or city (*gorod*) Party organizations, which are in turn subordinated—except in the case of the largest cities—to province (*oblast'*) or territory (*krai*) Party organizations. The latter organizations number more than a hundred and in the case of the larger non-Russian republics (Ukraine, Belorussia, Kazakhstan, and Uzbekistan) are subordinated to the central committees of the respective republic Party organizations which, in turn, are subordinated to the CPSU Central Committee and its Secretariat in Moscow. The *oblast'* and *krai* Party organizations within the Russian SFSR are subordinated directly to the CPSU Central Committee.

The CPSU Congress. Although the Party statutes define the Congress as the Party's "supreme organ," in practice it is much less than that. The large numbers of delegates and the relative infrequency of Congresses have made this body subsidiary to the Central Committee and the Secretariat. Regular Congresses are convened by the Central Committee "at least once every five years" according to the statutes as amended in 1971. Extraordinary Congresses can be called during the intervening periods—as was the case with the Twenty-first Congress in 1959.

The first six Congresses were held prior to the establishment of the Soviet regime, and only the First in 1898 and the Sixth in 1917 were held on the territory of the Russian Empire. All Congresses since the Eighth have been held in Moscow. From 1917 until 1925 Congresses met annually in accordance with a statutory provision. Stalin initially violated the provision when he convened the Fifteenth Congress in 1927 rather than in 1926. Subsequent violations occurred, and in 1934 the statutes provided for the Congress to meet "at least once every three years." This new provision was first violated in 1937 when Stalin postponed the Eighteenth Congress until 1939. No Congress was held between 1939 and 1952, despite the provision in the 1939 statutes for convening a Congress at least once every three years. The 1952 and 1961 statutes provided for a Congress to be held at least once every four years. Under Khrushchev's leadership a degree of regularity in the convocation of Party Congresses was restored, but his successors failed to convene the

Twenty-third Congress in the autumn of 1965 or the Twenty-fourth Congress in the spring of 1970 as provided for in the statutes. The convocation of the Twenty-fourth Congress in March–April, 1971, was a year overdue.

Spirited debates over leadership, policies, and organizational matters distinguished nearly all Congresses prior to the Fifteenth in 1927. The growth in the size of the Congress and the ability of the Secretariat to control the election of delegates then eliminated the last vestiges of debate and deliberation. After 1925 the Congress became a vast spectacle used to register unanimous support for the General Secretary and his policies, and to proclaim his (and the Party's) wisdom and achievements. Various oppositionists and factionalists were also denounced in accordance with the propaganda requirements of the day.

The Congress, meeting in Moscow's Kremlin, follows a tested format which reflects the circumscribed role defined in the Party's statutes for this "supreme organ." It "hears and approves" the reports of the Central Committee and of the Central Auditing Commission, and also elects these two bodies; it "reviews, amends, and approves" the Party's Program and statutes; it "determines the Party line on questions of domestic and foreign policy and examines and decides on the most important problems in the building of Communism."

The principal document of a Congress is the Report of the Central Committee, which is usually delivered by the leading figure in the Party. Thus, Lenin presented these reports from 1918 to 1922. Zinoviev and Stalin shared the task in 1923, offering separate political and organizational reports. Stalin delivered political reports at the five Congresses between 1925 and 1939. In 1952, at the Nineteenth Congress, Malenkov presented the report under Stalin's watchful eye. Khrushchev, during his tenure as First Secretary, presented the report in 1956, 1959, and 1961; and Brezhnev subsequently performed this task as General Secretary. The Central Committee's Report is really the report of the Secretariat and the Politburo of the Central Committee. It is a lengthy document and provides much information in its three parts, which deal with the general international situation and the Soviet Union's foreign pol-

TABLE 1. PARTY CONGRESSES

	Number of Delegates					*Size of Central Committee*	
Congress	*Voting*	*Non-voting*	*Party Membership*	*Ratio of Delegates to Members*	*Duration (days)*	*Members*	*Candidate Members*
Seventh March 6–8, 1918	46	58	ca. 300,000 (170,000 represented at Congress)	None due to wartime conditions	3	15	8
Eighth March 18–23, 1919	301	102	313,766	1 : 1,000	6	19	8
Ninth March 29–April 5, 1920	554	162	611,978	1 : 1,000	8	19	12
Tenth March 8–16, 1921	694	296	732,521	1 : 1,000	9	25	15
Eleventh March 27–April 2, 1922	522	165	532,000	1 : 1,000	7	27	19
Twelfth April 17–25, 1923	408	417	386,000	1 : 1,000	9	40	17

TABLE 1. (*Continued*)

Congress	*Number of Delegates*		*Party Membership*	*Ratio of Delegates to Members*	*Duration (days)*	*Size of Central Committee*	
	Voting	*Non-voting*				*Members*	*Candidate Members*
Thirteenth May 23–31, 1924	748	416	735,881	1 : 1,000	9	53	34
Fourteenth December 18–31, 1925	665	641	643,000 445,000°	1 : 1,000	14	63	43
Fifteenth December 2–19, 1927	898	771	887,233 348,957°	1 : 1,000	18	71	50
Sixteenth June 26–July 13, 1930	1,268	891	1,260,874 711,609°	1 : 1,000	18	71	67
Seventeenth January 26–February 10, 1934	1,225	736	1,874,488 935,298°	1 : 1,500	16	71	68
Eighteenth March 10–21, 1939	1,569	466	1,588,852 888,814°	1 : 1,000	12	71	68

Nineteenth October 5–14, 1952	1,192	167	6,013,259 868,886°	1 : 5,000	10	125	110
Twentieth February 14–25, 1956	1,349	81	6,795,896 419,609°	1 : 5,000	12	133	122
Twenty-first (Extraordinary) January 27–February 5, 1959	1,269	106	7,622,356 616,775°	1 : 6,000	10	none elected	
Twenty-second October 17–31, 1961	4,394	405	8,872,516 843,489°	1 : 2,000	15	175	155
Twenty-third March 29–April 8, 1966	4,619	323	11,673,676 797,403°	1 : 2,500	11	195	165
Twenty-fourth March 30–April 9, 1971	4,740	223	13,810,089 645,232°	1 : 2,900	11	241	155

° Candidate-members

SOURCES: *KPSS v rezoliutsiiakh i resheniiakh*, 7th ed. (Moscow: Gospolitizdat, 1960); *Politicheskii slovar'*, ed. by B. N. Ponomarev, 2d ed. (Moscow: Gospolitizdat, 1958); and stenographic reports for select Party Congresses.

icy, the domestic situation and problems of Soviet economic development, and ideological questions and the general condition of the Party.

The various Party leaders address the Congress on matters for which they are primarily responsible; secretaries from the non-Russian union republic Party organizations speak on problems within their respective jurisdictions. A carefully planned and controlled agenda also permits a select few of the rank-and-file delegates to deliver brief statements. The Congress also provides a pretext for bringing to Moscow representatives of foreign communist parties, who consume much time speaking of their activities and who usually praise the Soviet leadership and the Soviet Union's way of life.

The delegates are elected on the basis of a norm of representation and in accordance with procedures set by the CPSU Central Committee prior to each Congress; the ratio of delegates to members has varied considerably since 1934 (see Table 1). Voting delegates represent Party members, while nonvoting delegates (possessing the so-called consultative vote) are said to have the right to speak—but not to vote—and represent candidates for Party membership. Delegates are elected at *oblast'* and *krai* Party conferences in the Russian SFSR and at *oblast'* conferences in the larger non-Russian republics such as Ukraine and Belorussia. Delegates from the smaller non-Russian republics are elected at republic Party congresses.[11] Party organizations in military units stationed abroad elect delegates at their own conferences, while those in units on the territory of the U.S.S.R. and in internal security, frontier, and convoy troop units participate in the conference of the local territorial Party organization. Delegates are "elected" by means of a list system, and their nomination is carefully controlled by the Party secretaries responsible for organizing the electing conference or republic congress.

It would appear from the occupational and other data in Table 2

[11] In 1961 the size of the Moscow *city* Party organization (690,000 members) and the Leningrad *oblast'* Party organization required election of delegates at *raion* (district) conferences within these jurisdictions, rather than at a city or *oblast'* Party conference. *XXII S"ezd Kommunisticheskoi Partii Sovetskogo Soiuza, stenograficheskii otchet* (Moscow: Gospolitizdat, 1962), I, 424.

TABLE 2. DATA ON DELEGATES TO PARTY CONGRESSES

	Nineteenth Congress (1952)		*Twentieth Congress (1956)*		*Twenty-first Congress (1959)*		*Twenty-second Congress (1961)*		*Twenty-third Congress (1966)*	
Voting Delegates	1,192		1,355		1,269		4,408		4,619	
Occupational Groups										
Party workers	no		506	37.3%	432	34.0%	1,158	26.3%	1,204	26.0%
Government employees			177	13.1%	147	11.6%	465	10.5%	539	11.6%
Trade Union and Communist Youth officials	data		20	1.5%	19	1.5%	104	2.3%	126	2.7%
industry, transport, and construction			251	18.5%	355	28.0%	1,391	31.5%	1,577	33.0%
agriculture			187	13.8%	175	13.8%	748	16.9%	874	18.9%
military			incomplete data		91	7.2%	305	6.9%	352	7.6%
arts, sciences, and culture			incomplete data		50	3.9%	incomplete data			
Female Delegates	147	12.3%	193	14.2%	222	17.5%	1,073	22.3%	1,154	23.3%
Education										
Completed higher education	709	59.5%	758	55.9%	708	55.8%	2,312	52.5%		55.5%
Incomplete higher education	84	7.1%	116	8.5%	67	5.3%	230	5.2%		} 24.0%
Secondary education	223	18.7%	169	12.4%	155	12.2%	665	15.1%		
Incomplete secondary or elementary	176	14.7%	312	23.2%	339	26.7%	1,201	27.2%		20.5%

TABLE 2. (*Continued*)

	Nineteenth Congress (1952)	*Twentieth Congress (1956)*	*Twenty-first Congress (1959)*	*Twenty-second Congress (1961)*	*Twenty-third Congress (1966)*
Age					
40 or under	23.6%	20.3%	21.1%	38.6%	40.2%
41–50	61.1%	55.7%	47.8%	37.9%	34.3%
over 50	15.3%	24.0%	31.1%	23.5%	25.5%
Year of Admission to Party					
pre-1917	1.2%	1.6%	0.6%	0.9%	0.4%
1917–20	6.2%	4.5%	2.9%	1.3%	4.8%
1921–30	36.4%	24.9%	19.9%	7.7%	
1931–40	36.0%	34.0%	33.8%	22.0%	15.5%
1941–45	16.1%	21.6%	21.7%	26.6%	24.7%
1946–55	4.1%	13.4%	21.1%	23.1%	24.2%
1956				18.4%	30.4%

N.B. Table is based on data in reports of chairmen of Credentials Commissions at Party Congresses.

SOURCES: *Current Soviet Policies I*, ed. Leo Gruliow (New York: Frederick A. Praeger, 1953), pp. 93–95; *XX S"ezd KPSS* (Moscow, 1956), I, 232–239; *Vneocherednoi XXI S"ezd KPSS* (Moscow, 1959), I, 258–262; *XXII S"ezd KPSS* (Moscow, 1962), I, 421–431; *XXIII S"ezd KPSS* (Moscow, 1966), I, 278–285.

that some effort has been made to change the weight of different groups and categories. Thus, there has been a steady effort to increase the number of female delegates. Prior to the Twenty-second Congress, the largest single occupational group among the delegates was that of full-time Party officials. In 1961, however, the industry, transport, construction, and agricultural categories together constituted nearly half of the delegates at the Twenty-second Congress; this resulted in a decline in other categories (including that with higher education). The changes in the body of Congress delegates were also related to an effort to lower the median age of delegates. The Twenty-second Congress, the largest the Party had seen, had 2,045 more voting delegates than the previous Congress of record size. As a result, 32.9 percent of the 4,408 voting delegates were said to be *directly engaged* in agriculture, industry, or construction; this, along with the steady increase in the percentage of delegates having only elementary or incomplete secondary schooling, reflected an effort to give the Party the appearance of a workingmen's organization rather than one of officials, technicians, and managers.

Despite the lack of genuine debate and the hollowness of unanimous voting, the Congress serves a number of functions. In fulfilling the ritual of "electing" a Central Committee, it periodically endows the Party leadership with a degree of apparent legitimacy. It also serves as an important medium for promulgating and approving new policies, programs, and economic plans and launching propaganda appeals. These are then propagated by the delegates when they return to the subordinate Party bodies. The Congress provides delegates with a sense of participation—however passive and modest it may be—and with an opportunity to see and hear (if not question) the Party's leaders.

The Central Committee. The Party has had a Central Committee since its founding Congress in 1898, when three of the nine delegates were elected to serve as its members. Subsequent Central Committees reflected the various divisions within the Party and at times also shared authority with the editorial staff of the Party organ prior to 1917. Under Lenin's leadership, however, the Central Committee developed into the principal instrument for ruling the Party. Stalin enlarged the Committee substantially (see Table 1), rewarding his followers with membership but also demeaning the Central Committee membership by convening joint plenary sessions with the much larger Central Control Commission. In the first years of the Soviet regime Central Committee meetings were to be held twice a month, but the 1922 statutes reduced their frequency to once every two months. By 1934 the statutes provided for meetings once every four months, and in 1952 this was fixed at once every six months. However, the Central Committee fell into a state of desuetude during the latter part of Stalin's rule when plenary sessions were infrequent and brief, occurring at intervals of several years. Following Stalin's death, plenary sessions were convened at least twice a year, although as many as six sessions were held in 1958.

The Central Committee, which is elected by each regular Party Congress, "directs all Party activities and local Party bodies" during the lengthy intervals between Congresses. It also includes representation from various key groups in Soviet society, and its plenary sessions are used to inform and to promote new policies. The Central Committee elects a Politburo and a Secretariat which act in its name. The Secretariat, for its part, selects and assigns Party personnel (leading cadres) and directs the work of governmental and public organizations through the Party groups within them. It controls the Party's press organs and journals, and appoints and removes their editors. It has at its disposal the central Party fund and allocates expenditures.

Plenary sessions held during Khrushchev's tenure usually lasted several days and dealt with a wide range of subjects, including governmental and economic reorganization, economic plans, agricultural policy, the chemical industry, "ideological work," control of the intelligentsia, technical progress, Party organization, internal power struggles, and relations with other communist parties. Some sessions called by Khrushchev were enlarged to include planning officials, local government heads, factory directors, local Party secretaries not included in the Committee's membership, and scientific workers. Such enlarged plenary sessions confirmed the usefulness of the Central Committee as a means of promoting the regime's policies and programs.

"Unanimous" voting has been the rule in the Central Committee as in the Party Congress. However, there have been secret plenary sessions in which heated debates have occurred in the course of a life-and-death political struggle. Such sessions occurred in January, 1955, when it was decided to remove Malenkov from the premiership; in June, 1957, when Khrushchev defeated the members of the anti-Party group; and in October, 1964, when Khrushchev himself was ousted. What were said to be stenographic reports of Central Committee plenary sessions first began to be published following the December, 1958, session (except for the publication of Committee proceedings for a brief period preceding and following the seizure of power in 1917). However, these records reflected the prearranged nature of most Central Committee proceedings, in which speakers vied with each other to do the bidding of those in command of the Party's administrative apparatus. Khrushchev's successors, for all practical purposes, ceased publishing Central Committee stenographic reports.

The Central Committee has become too large and meets too infrequently to be a continuing decision-making body. Yet its importance in the crisis situations of 1955, 1957, and 1964, and the need for the Party's rulers to act in its name at all times, indicate that it is a significant body.

The Central Committee consists of voting members and candidate-members; the latter attend plenary sessions and can speak but do not vote. The Committee's membership, as indicated in Table 3, is derived from several categories of officials. The largest of these is the group of *oblast'* (province) and *krai* (territory) Party committee secretaries, nearly all of whom are first secretaries; the exceptions have been the second secretaries of the Leningrad and Moscow *oblast'* organizations. *Oblasti* consistently represented in the Central Committee—in addition to Moscow and Leningrad—have been Saratov, Gorky, Volgograd (Stalingrad), Tula, Kuibyshev, Ivanovo, Smolensk, Kaliningrad (Koenigsberg), Perm (Molotov), Irkutsk, and Novosibirsk. In 1961 the *oblast'* contingent was increased with the addition of eight Ukrainian *oblast'* secretaries; in 1952, in contrast, only one Ukrainian *oblast'*, Kiev, was represented in the Central Committee. The *krai* (territory) Party secretaries in the Central Committee are usually from the Altai, Stavropol, Krasnoiarsk,

TABLE 3. MAJOR CATEGORIES IN VOTING MEMBERSHIP OF THE CENTRAL COMMITTEE

Year Elected	*1952 (125 members)*		*1956 (133 members)*		*1961 (175 members)*		*1966 (195 members)*	
Oblast' and *krai* Committee Secretaries	39	31.2%	41	30.8%	46	26.2%	45	23.0%
USSR Government Ministers	25	20.0%	31	23.8%	28	16.0%	37	18.9%
Union Republic Central Committee Secretaries	16	12.8%	16	12.0%	19	10.9%	19	9.8%
CPSU Central Committee Secretaries and Department Heads	16	12.8%	11	8.0%	15	8.6%	13	6.6%
Union Republic Premiers	5	4.0%	5	3.8%	8*	4.6%	9**	4.6%
Military	5	4.0%	6	4.5%	14	8.0%	15	7.8%
Female Members	2	1.6%	4	3.0%	6	3.4%	5	2.5%

* includes two Ukrainian vice premiers

** includes three R.S.F.S.R. vice premiers and one Ukrainian vice premier

SOURCES: *Current Soviet Policies I*, ed. Leo Gruliow (New York: Frederick A. Praeger, 1953), pp. 237–240; *Bulletin, Institute for the Study of the USSR*, Supplements for May, 1956; November, 1961; and September, 1966.

Maritime, and Krasnodar territories. The first secretaries of the central committees of the Party organizations in the non-Russian union republics are *de facto ex officio* members of the CPSU Central Committee.

Among the most influential members of the Central Committee are its own secretaries and certain of the Secretariat's department heads. The membership also includes the Soviet Union's premier, its chief of state, and the premiers of the leading non-Russian republics. A few workers and a collective farm chairman are included for the sake of appearance. The Central Committee has also never included many females among its membership (see Table 3).

There has always been a turnover in Central Committee membership, although the rate has varied. The Central Committee elected in 1934 had a survival rate of only 22.5 percent when its successor body was elected in 1939; only 16 of the 71 voting members elected in 1934 were reelected in 1939. The Committee elected in 1939 had a survival rate of 47 percent, with 33 of its members reelected to the enlarged Central Committee of 125 members in 1952. Sixty-four percent of the 1952 Central Committee was reelected in 1956, but only 49.6 percent of the 1956 Central Committee was reelected in 1961. The rate of turnover, as reflected in the percentage of *newly elected* members, is indicated in Table 4.

The 1961 Party statutes provided for the "systematic renewal" of the membership of Party bodies. In the case of the Central Committee and its Politburo, "at least one-fourth" of the membership was to be replaced at each regular Party Congress and a limit of three consecutive terms was adopted. However, an exception was provided for "Party workers [who] by virtue of their recognized

TABLE 4. NEW MEMBERS IN CENTRAL COMMITTEE

Year Committee Elected	*Number of Newly-elected Members*	*Percentage of Total Membership*
1918	2	13.3
1919	7	36.8
1920	6	31.6
1921	10	40.0
1922	7	25.9
1923	16	40.0
1924	16	30.2
1925	14	22.2
1927	19	26.8
1930	14	19.7
1934	15	21.1
1939	55	77.5
1952	92	73.6
1956	53	39.8
1961	109	62.3
1966	48	24.6

SOURCE: Adapted, with modifications, from Zbigniew Brzezinski and Samuel P. Huntington, *Political Power: USA/USSR* (New York: Viking Press, 1964), Table 10, p. 179.

authority, high political, organizational or other qualities" could be elected for more than three terms if they received three-quarters of the votes cast in the election of the Central Committee at the Congress. In practice the Central Committee was renewed at a rate in excess of 25 percent. In 1966 the statutes were amended to eliminate the fixed rate of turnover in membership while affirming the "principle of systematic renewal . . . and continuity of leadership" for all Party bodies from the bottom to the Central Committee.

The Central Committee's size and composition are not defined in the Party statutes; and the degree to which various geographic areas, institutions, and interests will be represented in it is a political issue of great importance in the Soviet Union and one that is resolved behind the scenes. Committee meetings are not scheduled at any fixed time on the Soviet calendar, as the convoking of a plenary session depends upon when the leadership summons the members to Moscow. The Committee's proceedings can be secret or published in part, or in what is purported to be their entirety—all at the discretion of the leadership. The statutes' vague and laconic provisions regarding the Central Committee reflect its unstructured nature, as well as its instrumental role in behalf of whoever controls the Committee's apparatus.

The Politburo of the Central Committee. This body—called the Presidium from October, 1952, until April, 1966—is elected by the Central Committee "to direct the . . . [latter's] work" during the lengthy intervals between Committee plenary sessions. Such a body first came into being in 1917 on the eve of the seizure of power. It was made permanent in March, 1919, by the Eighth Congress; and its size gradually increased to 10 full members and 5 candidate-members in 1934. As in other Party bodies, candidate-members do not vote. The Politburo's size has remained relatively constant at 11 or 12 full members and 6 to 9 candidate members—with the exception of the five-month period between the Nineteenth Congress and Stalin's death, when there were 25 full members and 11 candidate-members. A slight increase occurred again after the June, 1957, crisis—when there were as many as 15 full members and 10 candidate-members—and again in 1971.

Apparently experience has confirmed the desirability of having ten to twelve members as an optimum number for deliberation. Under Stalin the Politburo-Presidium atrophied; it rarely met in the last years of his life. During World War II it was superseded by the State Committee for Defense (GKO). Stalin divided the Politburo membership into small specialized committees and in this way retained the ability to act as arbiter and adopt decisions independently. After Stalin's death the Presidium was reconstituted with ten members and four candidate-members. It became the setting for a fierce inner-Party struggle for power, but it also began to meet regularly (often at weekly intervals) and to adopt policy decisions by majority vote while seeking unanimity.

The Politburo membership includes the General Secretary of the Party, the head of government (premier or chairman of the U.S.S.R. Council of Ministers), and the chief of state (chairman of the Presidium of the U.S.S.R. Supreme Soviet). It usually includes several Central Committee secretaries (under Khrushchev the number varied from two to nine) and two or more first deputy premiers. The First Secretary of the Ukrainian Communist Party is usually a member. The chairman of the Party Control Committee has held Politburo membership.

Although the Politburo is, in practice, the highest Soviet policy-making body, relatively little is known about it apart from its membership and the fact of specific decisions of great import which obviously originated within it. It meets secretly and its minutes are not published. Some of its members—and especially candidate members—are not always in Moscow, since they hold positions in the union republics; in all probability some Politburo meetings are held in their absence. Prominent members have been demoted abruptly and consigned to oblivion.

Central Committee resolutions usually reflect Politburo decisions, and the Politburo also issues directives to various government ministries and agencies. It takes up urgent problems brought before it by the departments of the Party Secretariat, by a ministry, or by the Council of Ministers. Individual Politburo members often have a field of specialization for which they are responsible, deciding matters of lesser import independently and referring difficult cases to the entire Politburo. On occasion the Politburo has discussed matters that would appear to be trivial in other regimes. When the Politburo has not been able to resolve internal conflicts involving a struggle for power, those conflicts have been taken to the Central Committee. The presence of a dominant personality such as Lenin or Stalin (or even Khrushchev at certain times during the height of his career) has determined the way in which the Politburo would function and has restricted its freedom of action. In the absence of such a dictator, arbiter, or strong personality, decisions have been arrived at "collectively" with more deliberation and less dispatch.

The Secretariat. The Party's administrative apparatus, with approximately 200,000 or more full-time officials and employees, is directed by the Central Committee's Secretariat, which is headed by the General Secretary (between 1953 and 1966, by the First Secretary). Party administration is in the hands of the Secretariat and it is second only to the Party's Politburo in importance. The Party statutes say almost nothing about this body and did not even mention the powerful post of General Secretary prior to 1966. The Secretariat is elected by the Central Committee and is authorized "to direct current work, chiefly the selection of cadres and the verification of the fulfillment of Party decisions." In practice, this means that the Secretariat serves as the Party's executive arm and controls the activities and key personnel of all union republic, province, city, and district Party organizations. It issues directives to them and receives their reports.

Lenin never held the position of Party secretary. As principal founder of the Party, his position was that of leading member of the Central Committee and Politburo. The first person to serve as Party secretary during 1918 was Iakov Sverdlov, who was also chairman of the Soviet legislature (the Central Executive Committee of the Congress of Soviets). Sverdlov relied more on the well-financed governmental machinery than on the small central Party staff. His death in March, 1919, resulted in the appointment of Nikolai Krestinsky, who was succeeded by Molotov in 1921. Their inability to organize the Secretariat effectively led to the election of Stalin as General Secretary in April, 1922. Originally the Secretariat was to have been a service organization and a records department subordinate to the Organizational Bureau (Orgburo), established in March, 1919, along with the Politburo. While the Politburo was to decide policy, the Orgburo was to decide organizational questions and allocate the Party's forces. The appointment of two additional Secretaries in March, 1920, made the Secretariat a potential rival of the Orgburo.

Stalin's appointment as General Secretary made him a member of all four leading Party bodies: the Central Committee, the Politburo, the Orgburo, and the Secretariat. Under his command the Secretariat became a power unto itself and overshadowed the other bodies. The abolition of the Orgburo in October, 1952, gave belated recognition to its having been superseded by the Secretariat. For most of Soviet history, especially under Stalin and Khrushchev, the Secretariat has provided the principal vehicle for the establishment of a personal dictatorship or the advancement of one's career as a political lieutenant.

The Secretariat has varied in size from three to as many as fourteen members. At times—especially in the winter of 1952–53 and from July, 1957, to 1959—all or most of the Secretariat members have been members or candidate-members of the Party Presidium-Politburo. Usually the Secretaries have been in a minority in the Politburo, however, although the General Secretary and certain subordinate Secretaries (whose positions are not rank-ordered) exercise substantial influence in that body.

The Secretariat is organized into a number of departments (*otdely*), each of which is headed by one of the Secretaries or by a department head. The division of responsibilities between Secretaries is usually not revealed, but is often evident from their activities and pronouncements. Usually the designation of a department head is made public in an indirect manner and after the fact rather than by formal announcement. The number of departments has varied but has always included a group devoted to various sectors of industry and to agriculture, construction, transport, and communications. The Party-Organizational Work Department (formerly known as the "Party Organs" Department) is responsible for supervising the subordinate Party organizations, the Komsomol (Communist Youth), and trade unions; it is also charged with staffing these and governmental organizations; and it keeps dossiers on all of the regime's leading officials. The Administrative Organs Department exercises guidance and control over the courts, prosecuting agencies, and certain nonindustrial government agencies. The Department of Propaganda and Agitation (*Agitprop*) is responsible for the communications media and ideological training. A separate department is in charge of science and education, and there is also a department for culture. Relations with ruling communist parties in other countries and with foreign parties not in power are the responsibility of separate departments. In all likelihood, a Foreign Affairs Department deals with foreign policy questions. The Main Political Administration of the Armed Forces, although formally in the Defense Ministry, is really a branch of the Secretariat. An Administrative (Affairs) Department functions as a general services and housekeeping organization.

There is hardly any sector of Soviet life for which some branch of the Secretariat cannot claim responsibility. The secretariat prepares reports for the Politburo, as well as background papers on current problems, policy proposals, and recommendations. It oversees the entire Party machine and is responsible for the execution of Party policy decisions. It allocates the Party's manpower and controls its resources. It mobilizes the rank-and-file membership and enables the Party to act with a high degree of unity.

Control Bodies. The Central Committee also elects a Party Control Committee. The precursor of this latter committee was the Central Control Commission, which came into being in 1921 along with local and regional control commissions established in the autumn of 1920. These bodies were responsible for the enforcement of Party discipline and were to be independent of the Party committees which functioned at their level. In practice they became adjuncts of the Party bureaucracy. The Central Control Commission began to meet with the Central Committee in joint plenary session in October, 1923, and was used by Stalin to combat critics and oppositionists. The Commission's membership was increased to 50 in 1923 and to 151 in the following year; by 1925 it had 163 members. In 1934 it was renamed the Party Control Commission, and after 1939 it was elected by the Central Committee rather than by the

Congress. In 1952 it became the Party Control Committee. The function of the Committee is to verify and enforce Party discipline, and to hear appeals regarding penalties or regarding the expulsion of members by union republic and province Party organizations.

The Central Auditing Commission. This committee of inspection is elected by the Congress and is charged under the Party statutes with verifying "the speed and correctness of the conduct of affairs in the central bodies of the Party and the treasury and institutions of the CPSU Central Committee." The Commission's chairman reports to each regular Congress on the conduct of the Party's business in a speech which is not particularly informative. Since the Party is very secretive about its finances and expenditures (as has been the case since Lenin's time), the Auditing Commission's report is correspondingly vague and incomplete. Although most unsatisfactory as a financial statement, the report does include references to the Party's publishing enterprises, the payment of dues (which item constituted 85 percent of the Party's income in 1952, 73 percent in 1955, and 65 percent in 1966), and repeated warnings regarding the failure of local secretaries to deposit funds promptly. Income from Party publications has gradually risen and is the second source of funds after membership dues. The Auditing Commission has usually criticized local Party officials for delays in dealing with letters of complaint and proposals, while giving the Central Committee apparatus a clean bill of health in such matters.

4. SUBORDINATE BODIES

The Primary Party Organizations. These bodies, called "cells" prior to 1939, are the foundation stones on which the Party structure stands. They number approximately 350,000 and are to be found in every Soviet enterprise and institution—including government ministries, factories, schools and universities, institutes, farms, military units, and Soviet embassies. Wherever three Party members are similarly employed, a primary party organization (p.p.o.) is formed. However, territorial p.p.o.'s are to be found in some villages and in cities; the latter are in housing developments and consist of party members who are housing officials, pensioners, or housewives.[12] The *functionally* organized p.p.o. contrasts with the higher Party bodies, which are organized exclusively on a *territorial* basis. Thus, the authority of the p.p.o. is limited to the particular functional enterprise, while the jurisdiction of a local Party committee extends over a given territory and embraces a number of primary party organizations.

Every Party member must belong to a p.p.o. Those having at least fifteen members elect a "bureau" or committee for one year to conduct the Party business in the particular enterprise; the bureau meets two or three times each month. Those having fewer than fifteen members elect only a secretary and a deputy. If the p.p.o. has more than 150 members, one or more secretaries are relieved of all regular duties within the enterprise to concentrate on Party work as full-time employees who work for the Party but are kept on the enterprise's payroll. The members of smaller p.p.o.'s hold a closed Party meeting once a month, but in larger organizations meetings of the entire membership are called less frequently.

The p.p.o. serves as the eyes and ears of the Party in every enterprise, institution, or public organization. In organizations "directly connected with production [they] have the right of control over the activities of administrations" (article 59 of the 1961 Statutes). In governmental bodies and in organs of economic administration, the p.p.o. "must actively influence the perfecting of the work of the apparatus" and must inform the "corresponding Party organs" of any "shortcomings" rather than intervene directly. Thus, each p.p.o. intervenes actively in the operations of the particular enterprise and must be reckoned with. The p.p.o. enlists new members and is responsible for their training in Marxism-Leninism. It can also expel members by a two-thirds vote of those present at a duly constituted general meeting of the p.p.o.; before coming into force, expulsions must be approved by the territorial Party Committee to which the p.p.o. is subordinate. Lesser penalties, such as a reprimand with or without a recorded entry in the member's file, can be imposed by the p.p.o. without the approval of the appropriate district or city Party committee. The p.p.o. can investigate the personal life of a Party member and can expose and censure his

[12] *Organizatsionno-ustavnye voprosy KPSS* (Moscow: Politizdat, 1968), p. 10.

conduct. The p.p.o. must engage in mass agitation and propaganda in support of Party decisions and public appeals; it must mobilize the masses to fulfill economic plans, combat waste and laxity, and strengthen both labor and state discipline.

The *Raikom* and *Gorkom*. At the district (*raion*) level, which is comparable to a small rural county or an urban ward or borough, the Party is organized on the territorial principle. All p.p.o.'s in the *raion* are subordinated to the Party's *raion* committee (*raikom* is the Russian acronym for this body), which places an "instructor" in charge of each group of p.p.o.'s. Larger cities are divided into *raiony*, each of which also has a Party *raikom*. At the municipal (*gorod*) level there is a Party committee which is called a *gorkom*. The *raion* (district) and *gorod* (city) Party committees are elected at biennial conferences to which the p.p.o.'s send representatives. The *raikom* and *gorkom* are elected at the district or city conference for a two-year term and meet in plenary session at least once every three months. The daily work of the Party is conducted by a bureau or smaller committee, which at the local level corresponds to the Central Committee Politburo in Moscow in the same way that the conference and *raikom-gorkom* plenary session correspond to the Party Congress and Central Committee plenary session, respectively.

The *Obkom* and *Kraikom*. At the provincial level (including the autonomous soviet republics) there are more than one hundred *oblast'* Party committees and several *krai* (territory) Party committees. The *oblast'* or province is a basic administrative-territorial unit which varies in area and population. Approximately half of the *oblasti* are in the Russian S.F.S.R. and another twenty-five are in the Ukrainian S.S.R. The *krai* is generally larger than the *oblast'*, though often more sparsely populated, is more remote from the center of Soviet power; and is generally located in the Russian S.F.S.R. The *oblast'* committee (*obkom*) and the *krai* committee (*kraikom*) of the Party are elected at biennial conferences to which the *raion* Party organizations elect delegates. The *obkom* and *kraikom* meet at least once every four months; the daily business of the Party is conducted by the bureau. The Party apparatus at this level mirrors much of the Central Committee Secretariat apparatus in Moscow with its various departments, and the first secretary of the *obkom* or *kraikom* is usually the most influential person in the province.

The Union Republic Central Committee. Each non-Russian union republic Communist Party has a Central Committee which is elected by the republic Party congress. However, in the smaller union republics, which are not divided into *oblasti*, the Central Committee is treated by Moscow as the equivalent of an *obkom*. The non-Russian union republic Party congresses are held every five years. The Russian Republic does not have a separate Central Committee nor does it hold its own Party congress. The dominance of the CPSU Central Committee and Congress by the Russian *oblast'* Party organizations makes a Russian Republic Party organization with its own congress and central committee unnecessary.

The organizational scheme described above has served the Party well and has enabled it to impose its will upon millions of subjects. It has kept the Party leadership sufficiently informed of conditions throughout the land to permit it to cope with dissident elements, to satisfy or suppress enough of the demands emanating from the population, and to control its own officials. When the Party's leadership has erred—as it has egregiously on occasion—it has been able to retain power largely because of its ability to command the numerous forces available to the Party apparatus. The ability to deploy Party cadres and to obtain the support of the rank-and-file membership has been due in large measure to the organizational machine.

CHAPTER 5

THE COMMUNIST PARTY AND THE STRUCTURE OF POWER

The quasi-monopoly of power enjoyed by the Soviet Communist Party has been jealously guarded. In the 1936 Constitution the Party defined itself as the "leading core of all organizations of the working people, both public and state" (article 126). It is not bound by any constitutional requirements; for it can change the constitution of the Soviet polity at will, reorganizing the government, replacing or abolishing existing agencies or practices, or even writing a new constitution. The Party retains control of the government and gives direction to its administrative machinery, determining which Party leaders will hold particular governmental positions. It recruits, trains, and advances (or demotes) members of the Soviet political class. The Party develops public policies and defines goals; Party decisions have the force of law. It resolves the conflicting interests of various subordinate organizations and segments of Soviet society, often counterposing and weakening them to its own advantage.

1. GENERAL CHARACTERISTICS

Centralism and Antifederalism. Under Lenin's leadership the Bolsheviks in 1903 adopted a position opposed to federalism based on ethnic distinctions. The walkout of the Jewish Social Democrats (the Bundists) from the Second Congress had been precipitated by Lenin's and Plekhanov's rejection of the proposal that the Marxist movement in the Russian Empire be based on coequal organizations representing the various nationalities. Lenin's professed "proletarian internationalism" provided the theoretical basis for what was to become, in practice, a Russian-dominated central Party apparatus. Bolshevism's founder was acutely aware of the centrifugal forces inherent in an ethnic conglomerate such as the Russian Empire and hoped to prevent their operating within the Party. A federal type of organization would, in Lenin's view, concede too much to non-Russian national interests and would be a denial of what he chose to call the international solidarity of the working class. If, subsequent to the seizure of power, separate Communist Party organizations were established for the various non-Russian nationalities, they were nevertheless strictly subordinated to the Party's center in Moscow.

The principle of "democratic centralism" which reflects this subordination was first defined in the Party statutes in 1919, although the term was first introduced but not explained in the 1906 statutes. The centralist side of the coin is evident in the provision for "periodic accountability of party organs to their Party organizations and [to] higher organs" and in the stipulation that "the decisions of the higher organs are absolutely binding on lower organs" (article 19 of 1961 Statutes). The Party statutes (article 2) obligate members to combat "localism" (*mestnichestvo*)—that is, the tendency to place local or regional interests ahead of those of the center or other areas. Local Party organizations "are autonomous in deciding local matters provided they are not contrary to Party policy" (article 21)—a very broad qualification.

Antifactionalism. From its beginnings Bolshevism was plagued with opposition, from within the ranks, of Russian Marxists who adopted different views regarding tactics and priorities. In the late 1890's Lenin did battle with the "Economists," who advocated economic reforms by means of trade unionism, strikes, and boycotts for the purpose of improving the workers' lot. Lenin insisted upon the primacy of the political struggle over economic demands, fearing that the latter would become an end in itself rather than a means of promoting political conflict. The Mensheviks—whom Lenin called "Liquidators" because of their desire to abandon illicit conspiratorial activity and dissolve the underground apparatus—were another factional group which was regarded as harmful.

However, factionalism broke out among the Bolsheviks themselves after the 1905 revolution. When Lenin decided in June, 1906, to end his boycott of the tsarist quasi-parliament, the Duma, and to sponsor Bolshevik candidates for legislative seats, he was confronted with a movement among those of his followers who opposed such "bourgeois" methods. These Recallists (*Otzovisty* in Russian) and Ultimatists were more "Bolshevik" than Bolshevism's founder in their desire to pursue a purely leftist policy of boycotting the Duma. Lenin, on the other hand, wished to employ the bourgeois parliament as a tribune for revolutionary agitation, using legal means along with conspiratorial methods. Disagreements over philosophical questions—especially regarding the nature of cognition and perception—in 1908 and 1909 prompted Lenin to denounce some of his followers as Machists (followers of Ernst Mach's Empiriocritical philosophy) and as philosophical "idealists" and betrayers of dialectical materialism. An effort to deify human potential in the form of a humanistic quasi-religion resulted in the "God-building" movement led by the Bolshevik A. Lunacharsky; this, too, aroused Lenin's ire. When several of these factionalists organized a Party school on the island of Capri with the help of the writer Maxim Gorky, Lenin denounced the effort and succeeded in disrupting the school's work.

The pattern of factionalism persisted after the Bolsheviks came to power. "Left-Communists," led by the theoretician Nikolai Bukharin, opposed Lenin's decision to sign a peace treaty with the Central Powers in March, 1918. In 1919 a Military Opposition expressed dissatisfaction with Lenin's policy of organizing a standing army and hiring tsarist officers rather than relying on an armed popular militia. In 1920 the Democratic Centralist Opposition unsuccessfully took issue with the growing centralism and authoritarian practices of the Party apparatus. The Workers' Opposition of 1920–21 objected to the limited role of industrial workers in the Party, to its increased bureaucratization, and to the policy of hiring bourgeois technicians and specialists. These opposition movements prompted Lenin to adopt harsh measures at the Tenth Congress in March, 1921, including a resolution which outlawed all factions and provided for the expulsion of offenders from the Party. Although factionalism was outlawed it could not be prevented;

there subsequently emerged such factions as the Left Opposition (Trotsky, Kamenev, and Zinoviev), the Right Opposition (of Bukharin, Rykov, and Tomsky) and the so-called anti-Party group of 1957.

The 1961 Party statutes, like earlier such documents, declared that "any manifestation of factionalism and group activity is incompatible with Marxist-Leninist party principles and party membership." The preamble refers to "the ideological and organizational unity and monolithic cohesion" of the Party's ranks as an "immutable law of the [Party's] life." Thus, dissent is forbidden once a policy has been adopted and the current line laid down. Although the "free and businesslike discussion of the questions of Party policy" (article 27) is said to be the "inalienable right" of each Party member, it would be unwise for the rank-and-file member to question the wisdom of the current leadership. If the statutes grant to members the supposed right "to criticize at Party meetings, conferences, congresses, and committee meetings any Communist, irrespective of the post he occupies" (article 3), it is difficult to reconcile this provision with the outright condemnation of factionalism. In practice the Party line is laid down by those in control of the central apparatus, who are able to equate differences of opinion and judgment with factionalism.

Obligations of Membership. The statutory definition of the Party as "the militant, tried, and tested vanguard of the Soviet people" implies a highly selective approach to the recruitment of members. Although the Party inevitably attracts many careerists, it also imposes obligations upon its members. Applicants undergo a one-year period of candidacy during which they familiarize themselves with the Party's program and statutes and with the current official version of its history. Each candidate must obtain recommendations from three members of at least five years' standing who have been acquainted with him professionally and socially for at least one year.

Members' duties include the following: "to struggle to create the material-technical base of Communism," increase labor productivity and master technology, and "safeguard and augment public socialist property"; to "carry out Party decisions firmly and undeviatingly" and strengthen ties between the Party and the people; to participate actively in "political life" and in "economic and cultural construction," setting an example in the fulfillment of public duty; "to master Marxist-Leninist theory, raise the ideological level [and] . . . combat resolutely any manifestations of bourgeois ideology, vestiges of a private-property psychology"; to promote "socialist internationalism and Soviet patriotism, combat the survivals of nationalism and chauvinism"; to protect the Party's "ideological and organizational unity," to guard against the penetration of the Party by those "unworthy of the high title of Communist," and to "display vigilance and keep Party and state secrets."

Members are required to "develop criticism and self-criticism" (limited in practice to means rather than to policies) and to combat "ostentation, conceit, complacency and localism . . . [and] oppose any activities prejudicial to the Party and state and report them to the Party bodies up to and including the CPSU Central Committee." Other obligations include the observance of "the Party line in the selection of cadres [key personnel] on the basis of their political and professional work (*delovye*) qualifications," the observance of "Party and state discipline," and the strengthening of the "defensive might" of the U.S.S.R. Members and candidate-members are also required to pay monthly dues ranging from 0.5 percent to 3.0 percent of their income.

The Party is a harsh taskmaster, viewing itself—in Lenin's definition of September, 1917—as "the intelligence, honor, and conscience of our epoch." [1] It is a jealous ruler, brooking no rivals and exacting many demands, as well as offering the possibility of real rewards along with the prospect of some hazards and risks. Members are not only required to propagate convincingly the rationale for current Party policies, but are expected to carry out decisions irrespective of whether or not they may approve of them. This is the price of discipline. Members of a "minority"—by definition those who may be in disagreement with the Party's administrative apparatus—have no recourse but to accept the current line and remain silent, or risk expulsion for continuing their activities. Party discipline may even require that a member condemn himself, as

[1] V. I. Lenin, *Sochineniia* (Moscow: Gospolitizdat, 1949), 4th ed., XXV, 239.

the victims of the Moscow purge trials did in the 1930's. The members of the anti-Party group in 1957 voted *for* the resolution of censure and *for* their expulsion from the Central Committee—with the exception of Molotov, who abstained but would not cast a solitary vote in his own defense. Khrushchev, upon being summarily ousted in October, 1964, could offer no public defense of his policies and conduct, but had to retire in humiliating silence. The strange spell cast by one's affiliation with the Party has frequently paralyzed the will to resist those who act in its name.

2. "KREMLINOLOGY"

The study of the current alignment of forces within the Soviet ruling circle and the significance of the promotion or demotion of individual leaders and aides has sometimes been referred to as "Kremlinology." However, the struggle for power and influence, and the elimination of actual and potential rivals, occurs irrespective of what it may be called. Although frequently only the surface manifestations of this struggle are evident, its consequences (in the form of ousters, personnel transfers, and shifts in policy) ultimately provide confirmation of its having occurred. Thus, the student of "Kremlinology" is compelled to rely on fragmentary data and clues which he must interpret cautiously, with a full awareness of the many pitfalls to be encountered.

Various criteria and clues reflecting prestige and protocol have proved useful in determining the relative positions of individual Soviet politicians. In addition to the order in which leaders are listed (alphabetical versus nonalphabetical) in public pronouncements, their status is sometimes revealed by their absence or presence at official functions and by their positions in photographs which appear in the Soviet press. The Party Congress has provided one means of distinguishing between leaders, in terms of the adjectives used to describe the amount and quality of applause given to individuals as recorded in the official stenographic report.[2] The

[2] Thus at the Twentieth Congress in 1956 there were the following gradations: "applause"; "continued applause"; "stormy applause"; "stormy, continued applause" (Molotov, Malenkov, Voroshilov, Suslov); "stormy, prolonged applause" (Mikoyan); "continued, lasting applause. All rise." (Premier Bulganin);

length of a leader's speech at the Congress and its subject matter also serve as a status index. Appointment to certain positions—such as first secretary of an important *oblast'* Party organization or of a large union republic central committee—is usually a sign of advancement in the Party hierarchy.

Leaders who are advancing often promote subordinates with whom they were associated in the past. The careers of these men become dependent upon that of their sponsor, at least for a time. The number of lieutenants and aides who obtain higher positions as a result of their sponsor's support is an index of his influence. However, it is also possible for lieutenants to shift allegiance if their mentor's star is declining and that of his rival is ascending. Although the charting of personal relationships between Soviet leaders in terms of past associations is subject to many provisos, it can serve as one indicator of the shifting currents of Kremlin politics.

Another index of status is the number of honorary nominations received by leading Soviet politicians at the time of elections to the U.S.S.R. Supreme Soviet. In the end each leader declines all nominations but one, although the ritual has been indicative of the relative standing of the various leaders. Thus in the 1954 election Premier Malenkov received 50 nominations, as compared with 43 for Khrushchev; in 1958 Khrushchev received 84 nominations, while Marshal Voroshilov was second with 31; in 1962 Khrushchev was nominated in 136 constituencies and Leonid Brezhnev was second with 39 nominations. In 1966 Brezhnev led the field with 170 nominations, followed by Kosygin with 94 and Podgorny with 52; Suslov had 41, Voronov 34, Kirilenko 31, and Shelepin 29. Still another criterion for determining status is the treatment accorded to prominent Party leaders in successive editions of the frequently revised official Party history.

Critics of "Kremlinology" have disparaged the study of power relationships within the Soviet inner elite as being overly deterministic, to the exclusion of chance and contingency. The critics

---

"Stormy, prolonged applause transforming itself into an ovation. All rise." (Khrushchev). Following Khrushchev's ouster, the gradations became less pronounced at the Twenty-third Congress in 1966.

contend that "Kremlinologists" read far too much significance into minor events. Yet one such event—the transfer of Khrushchev from Kiev to Moscow in December, 1949—was to have far-reaching consequences which were not perceived at the time. It is difficult to determine which events, at the time of their occurrence, are of minor or major significance, but the Kremlinologist is acutely aware of the possibility that an obscure and seemingly unimportant piece of information may be of great potential significance. He proceeds on the basis of theoretical constructs and hypotheses, fully aware of the possibility that the regime may falsify some data as well as suppress information.[3]

Another criticism of "Kremlinology" is based on the contention that Soviet politics are determined, not by personalities, but by sweeping socio-economic forces. These are identified as industrialism, urbanization, a state-operated economy, the existence of a technical intelligentsia and a managerial class, the possession of nuclear weapons, and a capability in rocketry and space flight. Thus, in this view, policies and problems which result from such forces are far more important than the personalities dealing with them. Yet if one concedes both the importance of socio-economic forces and the technical apparatus which accompanies those forces, it does not follow from this that personalities can be ignored. Indeed, the proponents of the socio-economic forces thesis may be said to ignore the role of individual leaders in a quasi-Marxist manner. They neglect the possibility that the winner in the Soviet power struggle may have a very different political style, method, and program from those of the loser. It is quite likely that the Soviet Union would have developed along different lines had Bukharin rather than Stalin emerged as the victor, or had Molotov or Malenkov defeated Khrushchev. The study of the careers and power-relationships of the Soviet leadership, if it is pursued to the exclusion of other factors, can obscure the purposes for which power is sought. However, to ignore the means by which individual Soviet leaders place themselves in a position to determine ends and adopt policies, is to neglect the essence of Soviet politics.

[3] See the excellent study by Robert Conquest, *Power and Policy in the U.S.S.R.; The Study of Soviet Dynastics* (New York: St. Martin's Press, 1961).

3. THE SOVIET GAME OF POLITICS

That Soviet politics involve anomalies, surprises, and irony is seen in the fact that two men—Stalin and Khrushchev—who together ruled the Soviet Union for more than forty years, subsequently fell into disgrace. Only Lenin, who ruled less than five years, remained as an uncorrupted figure worthy of praise on the basis of his role as the regime's founder. In this context it would appear that the process for recruiting the top Soviet leadership and the general political environment leave something to be desired. Indeed, leading Soviet politicians do not often retire voluntarily. If charged with failures and errors, they have no opportunity to call a press conference and explain their actions, or to publish memoirs in their own defense.

The Soviet game of politics is played for high stakes and is essentially what theorists have termed a zero-sum game—one in which the winner takes all and the loser receives nothing. It involves a fierce struggle in which no holds are barred; and it assures the rise of vigorous and resourceful men, although many of them may later be demoted or disgraced. Those who are removed make way for ambitious men seeking to rise in the hierarchy.

Various weapons are employed in the game at the highest level. One of these has been ideology and the charge of ideological deviation used to compromise one's opponents. Power struggle cannot be depicted officially as a clash of personalities but only as a conflict between orthodoxy and deviation, between the "correct" Party line and the proponents of "factionalism" or "distortion" of "Leninist norms of Party life." Soviet politicians who emerge triumphant can claim that they are pursuing ideologically "correct" policies, although such "correct" policies cannot be adopted without first obtaining office. Thus Malenkov was accused by Khrushchev of advocating a "Rightist" line in 1954–55 and was removed from the premiership. The "anti-Party group" of 1957 was said to have opposed the Twentieth Party Congress and the campaign against the "cult of personality." Khrushchev could claim that his policies were "correct" after he was able to oust his opponents.

At various times in the past—especially during Stalin's regime—opponents have been executed, although political blackmail can also serve as an effective method of silencing one's opponents. It is probable that the large volume of information gathered by the Soviet secret police and by Party officials has provided much material which those with access to the files have been able to use effectively at times. Thus Khrushchev could implicate Malenkov, Molotov, and Kaganovich in Stalin's crimes while giving himself a not entirely deserved clean bill of health. The opportunities for intrigue and blackmail have not usually been missed in Soviet politics.

The practice of "criticism and self-criticism," in addition to giving support to the pretence of intraparty democracy, permits officials to be singled out for allegedly ineffective performance of their duties. Central Committee members who are associated with a losing individual or group in the Politburo may therefore find themselves subjected to criticism on performance grounds and may subsequently be removed. The ability of the Secretariat to shift personnel and effect periodic shake-ups and reorganizations gives it a powerful weapon in dealing with opponents. The system of *nomenklatura* gives the Secretariat—and at lower levels the corresponding Party officials—the right to control the appointment of all persons to a stipulated series of positions. In addition, the practice of systematic transfers serves as a convenient cover for removals and appointments, which can affect the distribution of forces within the Central Committee. The tenure of an *obkom* first secretary's appointment varies considerably, and what may appear to be routine transfers may in fact have political consequences at Party headquarters in Moscow. The economic reorganization of 1957 was used by Khrushchev to remove many of the supporters of the anti-Party group from Moscow. Involuntary exile abroad by appointment to Soviet ambassadorships has at times also been a means of removing prominent politicians from the Moscow scene. Stalin employed this device in the 1920's, and Khrushchev also used it.[4]

[4] Thus Molotov was sent to the Mongolian People's Republic and to the International Atomic Energy Agency in Vienna. Pervukhin, also a member of the anti-Party group, was named ambassador to East Germany. P. K. Ponomar-

Transfers and removals of personnel are prompted not only by personal associations but by disagreements within the Soviet leadership on policy issues. In Stalin's time such issues were usually debated in a rather cryptic manner, although in the 1920's they were discussed quite openly (the future of the NEP). After World War II differences existed among Stalin's lieutenants regarding the appropriate labor unit in agriculture—the smaller "link" (*zveno*) or the larger "brigade"—and over whether or not collective farmers should be permitted to manufacture their own construction materials. A somewhat abstract discussion in the Soviet leadership in 1948–49 on the "law of value" under socialism reflected very real disagreement over the degree of rigidity in economic planning and the role of profit in determining what should be produced.

Disagreements in Khrushchev's time dealt with the anti-Stalin campaign, the virgin lands program, the economic reorganization of 1957, the Party reorganization of 1962, the sale of state-owned agricultural machinery to the collective farms, the level of steel production, and investment allocations for the various sectors of the economy (agriculture, heavy industry, and consumer goods production).[5] Foreign policy issues such as nuclear deterrence, arms reduction, the nuclear test ban, the Austrian State Treaty of 1955, and the problem of Germany have also provoked differing viewpoints within the leadership.

Oligarchical decision-making is not likely to produce unanimity, although oligarchies have been necessary whenever one man or several have had to rule by means of a coalition—in the absence of a strong dictator. Yet an oligarchy or "collective leadership"

enko, one of Malenkov's supporters and a former Central Committee Secretary, was sent successively to Poland, India, and the Netherlands as Soviet ambassador.

[5] For a series of case studies see *Soviet Policy-Making*, ed. Peter H. Juviler and Henry W. Morton (New York: Frederick A. Praeger, 1967). Also see Sidney I. Ploss, *Conflict and Decision-Making in Soviet Russia: A Case Study of Agricultural Policy* (Princeton, N.J.: Princeton University Press, 1965). Disagreement among Soviet leaders is often revealed—or poorly concealed—by criticism of anonymous persons ("certain comrades," "certain theoreticians," "some people") or by the fact that a member of the leadership deliberately remains silent on a particular issue. Differences in emphasis or in the choice of an adverb or adjective may appear to be slight, but may also reflect disagreement. Thus, the careful study of verbal formulae is an important concern of those who seek clues indicating disagreements within the Soviet leadership.

usually requires a spokesman and arbiter in the person of its leading member, and the composition of its coalitions is subject to change. The more weakly structured the oligarchy, the more likely it is to result in disequilibrium as coalitions shift from one issue to another. The addition or removal of a member can change the relationships among the oligarchs. Alliances within the oligarchy have not usually been stable. This is testified to by the changing coalitions of the 1920's and of the 1950's and 1960's in the Soviet Politburo.

Apparently one cannot be sure of one's allies and lieutenants, especially in the absence of the sanction of terror as wielded by a dictator with a personal secretariat of the kind Stalin had. Thus Beria aroused the suspicions of his fellow oligarchs in 1953. Molotov and Kaganovich supported Khrushchev in the ouster of Malenkov from the premiership, but were later to break with Khrushchev and join forces with Malenkov. Premier Bulganin deserted Khrushchev in 1957 and joined the "anti-Party group." Dmitrii Shepilov, one of Khrushchev's most trusted aides, also turned against his mentor in 1957; originally in the Malenkov camp, he then joined Khrushchev, and finally rejoined Malenkov. In the end Khrushchev placed too much trust in his subordinates, who ousted him in October, 1964, and demonstrated the ephemeral nature of personal loyalty among Soviet politicians. The First Secretary had spent too much time away from Moscow, and by not employing terror within the Party he was to seal his political fate by being unable to prevent the coalescence of the conspiracy which removed him from office.

The tactic of playing off lieutenants and associates against each other, developed most fully by Stalin, has been an important feature of Soviet politics. Stalin, for example, encouraged a rivalry between the Leningrad Party leader Andrei Zhdanov and Malenkov in 1946–48. Following Zhdanov's death, Stalin brought Khrushchev to Moscow from Ukraine in 1949, presumably to check the ambitions of Malenkov.[6] Khrushchev attempted to employ the same tactic in 1963, when he brought the Ukrainian Party secretary N. V.

[6] See Myron Rush, *Political Succession in the U.S.S.R.* (New York: Columbia University Press, 1965), p. 137.

Podgorny to Moscow, in an apparent effort to counterbalance the growing influence of Party Secretary Leonid Brezhnev. The rivalry of lieutenants, if cultivated and utilized successfully, can enhance the position of the Party's leading figure; but it can also result in instability since no lieutenant can be entirely sure of his position.

4. TYPES OF CAREER PATTERNS

A political career in the Soviet Union depends upon the fulfillment of certain prerequisites. Although membership in the Party is a *sine qua non,* it is in itself inadequate to assure success. At least initially, one who aspires to high political office must be associated with a person who is rising in the hierarchy. In contrast with many other political systems, lawyers are not only few in number, but their chances of having a political career are limited. Although Lenin was a lawyer by training and Stalin made use of Andrei Vyshinsky in the purge trials and as foreign minister, the Soviet legal profession is a source of technicians rather than of politicians and policy-makers. In addition, the chances of a woman's pursuing a political career are severely limited, despite the claim that the Soviet regime promotes women's rights. Only Madame Furtseva succeeded in attaining full membership in the Politburo in 1957, for example, and served there only four years although continuing as U.S.S.R. Minister of Culture.

Once a leading Soviet politician has been downgraded, it is unlikely that he will be able to stage a comeback. The exceptions to this rule are mostly officials of middle rank who have managed to survive a setback and then found a new sponsor among the top leadership. The need to have an elder or two in the leadership as a sign of legitimacy and as a tie with the Party's past, brought to or kept in the Politburo such figures as Otto Kuusinen (who entered it in 1957 at the age of 76), Anastas Mikoyan, Nikolai Shvernik, Kliment Voroshilov, and Arvid Pel'she. However, since Stalin's time there has been an increased emphasis upon demonstrating technical competence at least at some stage in one's political career. Leonid Brezhnev, for instance, was a metallurgical engineer before becoming a Party official; Madame Furtseva began her career as a chemical engineer; Party Secretary Andrei Kirilenko was originally trained as an aviation engineer; and N. V. Podgorny graduated from the Kiev Institute of Food Industry Technology and served as engineer in Ukrainian sugar refineries. In addition to attaining a measure of success in one's nonpolitical field of specialization, a career in Soviet politics requires appropriate openings, a mentor-sponsor, and good fortune; it is usually disadvantageous to be a non-Russian. Designation as a representative for an important region or city may also improve one's career opportunities. For those who aspire to the highest ranks it is essential to have a personal following, consisting of former associates who can be brought into the Central Committee and placed in key posts. Thus it is advantageous to have Party field experience.

There are four broad types of career patterns, although there are also subgroups within these patterns. One type is that of the central Party apparatus official, whose rise is attributable to his obtaining a responsible position in the Central Committee's administration and then becoming a member of the Secretariat. The case of Malenkov provides a classic example; although he studied in a higher technical school, he joined the Central Committee apparatus immediately upon graduating in 1925. Beginning in 1934 Malenkov headed the important Department of Leading Party Organs, and in 1939 he became a member of the Secretariat; by 1941 he was a candidate-member of the Politburo, becoming a full member in 1946 and remaining such until his ouster in 1957. The career of Alexander N. Shelepin is another example of one based on the Moscow apparatus. After graduating from the Moscow Institute of History, Philosophy and Literature in 1935, Shelepin began work as an official of the Communist youth (Komsomol) organization in the capital. In 1943 he became a Komsomol secretary; from 1952 to 1958 he was Komsomol First Secretary, which position qualified him for membership in the CPSU Central Committee. After serving nearly three years as chief of the Soviet secret police, Shelepin became a Party Secretary in October, 1961, and a full member of the Politburo in November, 1964, following the removal of Khrushchev.

The "ideocrat" represents a second type of career pattern. His career is made primarily in Moscow—although it might commence in the provinces—and it is distinguished primarily by the fact that in his training and experience he is primarily an ideologist-theoretician-propagandist. The career of Mikhail A. Suslov offers an example of this species of Soviet politician. Suslov obtained secondary and higher education as a result of joining the Party, and after a brief experience as a university lecturer was appointed in 1931 as a Party and government official in charge of various purging operations. From 1937 to 1944 he served in *oblast'* Party organizations as secretary and later as first secretary. During World War II he was given special assignments in the North Caucasus and in Lithuania. In 1944 he became a Central Committee apparatus official, and in 1947 he was appointed Party Secretary—probably with the help of Zhdanov. Although he was elected to full Politburo-Presidium membership in 1952, he was dropped along with others after Stalin's death; in July, 1955, however, he was restored to full membership. His responsibilities have included supervision of propaganda campaigns, enforcement of ideological purity, control of Soviet journalism and culture, and relations with foreign communist parties (including the Chinese).[7]

A third type of career pattern is that of the specialist or highly placed technician who does not serve in the Secretariat or in the Central Committee apparatus, but whose value to the Party as-

[7] Another example of the ideocratic career was that of Peter N. Pospelov, who joined the Party in 1916, despite a middle-class background. He attended the highest Party schools and served in the Agitprop Department. From 1940 to 1949 he was editor of *Pravda* and then became head of the Marx-Engels-Lenin Institute. He served as a Central Committee Secretary from 1953 to 1960, but never became more than a candidate-member of the Politburo. Pospelov's career illustrates the limits of the ideocrat's role and the relative safety with which the truly cautious member of this species can pursue his lifework.

The career of Leonid F. Ilyichev, on the other hand, illustrates the fate of the intrepid and miscalculating ideocrat. Ilyichev joined the Party in 1923 and attended the Institute of the Red Professorate. He became a candidate-member of the Central Committee in 1952 after serving as chief editor of *Izvestiia* (1944–48) and of *Pravda* (1950–52). Following service as press chief in the Foreign Ministry (1953–58), he became head of the Agitprop Department, after winning Khrushchev's backing. Khrushchev brought Ilyichev into the Secretariat in 1961 and employed him as a counter to Suslov. Apparently antagonizing Suslov, Ilyichev tipped his hand too early in emerging as Suslov's rival. Following the ouster of Khrushchev, Suslov therefore had Ilyichev removed from the Secretariat and demoted to the Foreign Ministry.

sures him membership in the Central Committee or even in the Politburo. Probably the most outstanding example of such a career was that of Anastas Mikoyan, an Armenian who graduated from a theological seminary and joined the Party in 1915. Following a career as a revolutionary in the Caucasus, during which he narrowly escaped death in 1918, he held various regional Party posts. Between 1926 and 1930 he headed the U.S.S.R. Commissariat of Foreign and Internal Trade. He subsequently was responsible for food supply, food industry, and foreign trade; in 1937 he became a deputy premier. He became a Central Committee candidate member in 1922 and a full member in 1923. Stalin brought him into the Politburo in 1926 as a candidate-member; he achieved full membership in 1935, survived purges and power struggles, and retired with distinction in April, 1966. Had Mikoyan been in the Secretariat or less adept as a communist businessman, his career in the leadership would probably have been of shorter duration.

Another example of the specialist's career is that of Premier Alexei Kosygin, who joined the Party in 1927 after working in the cooperative movement. In 1935 he graduated from the Leningrad Textile Institute, and by 1937 he was director of a textile factory. In 1938, as a result of the purges, he moved into Leningrad Party and government work and served as mayor of that city (Chairman of the Executive Committee of the Leningrad City Soviet). In 1939 he assumed the first of a number of positions in the U.S.S.R. government: these included the post of Minister of the Textile Industry, deputy premier, Minister of Finance, Minister of Consumer Goods Industry, and head of the State Planning Commission (*Gosplan*). This administrative experience in government enabled him to become premier in 1964. Kosygin was first elected to the Central Committee in 1939. He was a candidate-member of the Politburo from 1946 to 1948, a full member from 1948 to 1952, and a candidate-member again from 1957 to May, 1960, when he regained full membership.

Another Soviet premier, Nikolai Bulganin, headed the government from 1955 to 1958 and prior to that served in a variety of non-Party positions. After serving in the secret police from 1918 to 1922, Bulganin shifted to economic activity and in 1927 became director of a Moscow electrical plant. From 1931 to 1937 he served as mayor of Moscow, and from 1938 to 1941 he headed the U.S.S.R. State Bank and was a deputy premier. The Party put him in uniform in 1941 as a political general; he was Minister of Defense from 1947 to 1949. Bulganin never served in the Party Secretariat; he was elected to the Central Committee in 1934, along with Khrushchev, and survived the purging of that body. He was a Politburo member from February, 1948, until his ouster in 1958. The protection which the role of "specialist" gave Bulganin ceased when he became involved in the attempt to unseat Khrushchev in June, 1957. Thus, this type of Soviet politician can have a relatively "safe" career so long as he does not choose the losing side in a crucial division within the Politburo.

A fourth type of career is that of the Party official who attains a responsible position in the Secretariat and/or Politburo following field experience in *oblast'* and/or union republic Party and governmental organizations. The careers of both Khrushchev and Brezhnev are representative of this type of politician. Khrushchev gained invaluable field experience as head of the Ukrainian Communist Party and also had the advantage of heading the Moscow *oblast'* and city Party organizations.

Leonid Brezhnev joined the Party in 1931, the same year in which he entered the metallurgical institute in his Ukrainian home city of Dnieprodzerzhinsk. Following employment as an engineer from 1935 to 1937, he became deputy mayor of Dnieprodzerzhinsk. In May, 1938, he left local government for a Party post as department head in the Dniepropetrovsk *obkom,* and as a result of the purges he became a secretary of that *obkom* in 1939. During World War II he served as a political officer and attained the rank of major general. In 1946 he became first secretary of the Zaporozhe *obkom* and in 1947 he headed the Dniepropetrovsk *obkom* under Khrushchev's tutelage. He followed Khrushchev to Moscow in 1950 and served in the Central Committee apparatus, but from July of that year to October, 1952, he was first secretary of the Moldavian Communist Party. He attained Central Committee membership in October, 1952, at the age of 45; he also became a candidate-member of the Politburo-Presidium and a Central Committee Secretary but lost both positions four months later following Stalin's death. Brezhnev spent most of 1953 as deputy chief of the Main Political Administration of the Armed Forces. In February, 1954, Khrushchev appointed Brezhnev second secretary of the Kazakhstan Communist Party, and in August Brezhnev became First Secretary with responsibility for the republic's virgin lands program. In February, 1956, he regained the positions he had lost in March, 1953—candidate-member of the Politburo and Central Committee Secretary. He became a full member of the Politburo in June, 1957, following the expulsion of the anti-Party group. Although he was out of the Secretariat from May, 1960, until June, 1963 (he served as chief of state from November, 1960, until July, 1964), he returned to that body and within sixteen months engineered the ouster of Khrushchev. (Brezhnev's reappointment to the Secretariat was made possible by the illness of Frol Kozlov.) The varied nature of Brezhnev's career experiences in the field and in Moscow, in Party and in government, provided him with skills and associations which he put to effective use.

A related type of career is represented by Party officials and secretaries who, after lengthy experience in the Party apparatus, are given highly responsible government positions. Two examples are provided by the careers of Dmitrii S. Poliansky and Kirill T. Mazurov. Both became first deputy chairmen of the U.S.S.R. Council of Ministers in 1965 after holding important regional Party secretaryships. Poliansky, a graduate of the Kharkov Agricultural Institute and of the Moscow Higher Party School, served in the Central Committee apparatus and in several *obkom* secretaryships. He became a U.S.S.R. deputy premier in 1962 after serving four years as head of government of the Russian SFSR. Mazurov, a graduate of a road-building technical school and of the Moscow Higher Party School, acquired experience as a Komsomol leader and guerrilla organizer in Belorussia during World War II. He subsequently rose in the leadership of the Belorussian Communist Party to be first secretary in 1956 after serving three years as head of government of the Belorussian S.S.R. After nine years as first secretary of the Belorussian Party organization, he was transferred to Moscow to serve with Poliansky as chief deputy to Premier Kosygin.

These two careers illustrate the interchangeability of Party and government key personnel, and the Party's efforts to keep a close watch on governmental specialists.

5. THE SYSTEM OF PARTY SCHOOLS

Millions of Soviet citizens, including non-Party members, are exposed to political instruction as a result of the regime's need for trained agitators. An extensive network of "universities of Marxism-Leninism" provides a two-year program of evening courses in which dialectical and historical materialism and the Party's history and program are studied. Party functionaries require more thorough and advanced training, which is provided by a system of inter-*oblast'* and union republic Party schools. At the apex of the system is the Higher Party School attached to the Central Committee in Moscow; it offers a two-year course of study and its students must have completed higher education, must not be more than forty years of age, and must have been in the Party at least five years. Applicants for admission are carefully screened and must have the approval of their *obkom, kraikom,* or union republic Party organization. The Party therefore provides a variety of specialized quasi-academic training for its own officials, as well as for government employees and journalists.[8]

The Party also maintains an Academy of Social Sciences attached to the Central Committee. Its students must not be more than thirty-five years of age, must have higher education, and must have been in the Party at least three years; approval by the applicant's Party organization is also required. The Academy is for Party officials concerned with propaganda and for journalists whose interests are said to lie in a quasi-scholarly career. The three-year course of study includes Party history; economics; Marxist-Leninist philosophy and a critique of bourgeois philosophy; the bases of scientific communism; the history of Soviet society; the history of the international communist, workers', and national liber-

[8] The entire system of Party-sponsored schools is described in Ellen Propper Mickiewicz, *Soviet Political Schools, The Communist Party Adult Instruction System* (New Haven: Yale University Press, 1967).

ation movements; journalism; and literature. The Academy also has an Institute of Scientific Atheism.

6. PARTY MEMBERSHIP: SOCIAL AND ETHNIC VARIATIONS

The CPSU membership can be divided into four main groups. The top and middle-rank leadership consists of Central Committee members, responsible Central Committee apparatus officials, influential members of union republic central committees and of *oblast'* Party committees; this leadership numbers several thousand. A second group, which is both dependent upon and indispensable to the first group, consists of the Party apparatus itself and includes Party officials at the *raion* and city levels. Estimates of its size have varied from 100,000 to 250,000. A third group consists of the well-rewarded members of the "new class" who are not Party officials but who are active in the professions, in economic management, in the military, and in governmental ministries. Millions of rank-and-file members constitute a fourth group; many members are not privileged and often have a living standard below that of those members of the "new class" who are not Party members.

The Party recognizes three social categories of members: workers, peasants, and employees (salaried persons). The size and relative weight of these three groups have varied. Following the establishment of the regime, the Party in January, 1918, claimed the following social *origin* for its membership: worker, 56.9 percent; peasant, 14.5 percent; employees, 28.6 percent. During the 1920's, the employee category declined to a low of 16.8 percent, while the membership of worker *origin* rose to a high of 61.4 percent. The peasant category ranged from 19 to 28.8 percent during the first decade of Soviet rule. However, the percentage of Party members actually *employed* as workers engaged in production at the bench never exceeded 48.8 percent (in 1930).[9] The 1930's witnessed a decline in the worker component because the Party membership card

[9] Merle Fainsod, *How Russia Is Ruled*, rev. ed. (Cambridge: Harvard University Press, 1963), pp. 250–252.

has served as a ticket to social advancement. As the demands of economic growth required more technicians and managers, the employee (salaried) group grew steadily at the expense of the worker and peasant categories. The social composition of the Party has varied as follows:

	January, 1956	*July, 1961*	*January, 1966*	*January, 1969*
Workers	32.0%	34.5%	37.8%	39.3%
Collective Farmers	17.1	17.5	16.2	15.6
Employees and Others	50.9	48.0	46.0	45.1

SOURCES: Merle Fainsod, *How Russia Is Ruled,* rev. ed. (Cambridge: Harvard University Press, 1963), p. 276; *XXIII S"ezd KPSS, stenograficheskii otchet* (Moscow: Gospolitizdat, 1966), I, 86; and *Yezhegodnik Bol'shoi Sovetskoi Entsiklopedii, 1969* (Moscow, 1969), p. 23.

Women have always been a minority within the Party membership. They constituted 8.2 percent of the membership by 1924; 15.9 percent in 1932; 14.9 percent in January, 1941; 17 percent in January, 1945; 20.7 percent in July, 1950; and 20.9 percent in 1967.

The ethnic composition of the CPSU membership has not accurately reflected the ethnic composition of the Soviet Union (see Table 5). Russians have constituted more than 60 percent of the Party membership, although their percentage of the population of the U.S.S.R. is less. Russians constituted 72 percent of the membership in 1922 and 65 percent in 1927. Armenians and Georgians have also been overrepresented in the Party membership. Uzbeks, Ukrainians, Lithuanians, Moldavians, Latvians, Estonians, Belorussians, Tadjiks, Kirghiz, Turkmens, Azerbaidjanians, and Kazakhs are all underrepresented in varying degrees as compared with their weight in the total population.

The largest city and provincial Party organizations in the Russian Republic are those of the city of Moscow; the *oblasti* of Leningrad, Moscow, Rostov, Gorky, and Sverdlovsk; and that of the Krasnodar *krai.* The largest non-Russian union republic Party organizations are, in order of size, those of Ukraine, Kazakhstan, Belorussia, Uzbekistan, Georgia, and Azerbaidzhan.

TABLE 5. ETHNIC COMPOSITION OF PARTY MEMBERSHIP (January 1, 1967)

		Percentage of Party Membership	*Percentage of Population (1959 Census)*	*Percentage of Population (1970 Census)*
Russians	7,846,292	61.86	54.5	53.3
Ukrainians	1,983,090	15.64	18.0	16.8
Belorussians	424,360	3.34	3.8	3.7
Uzbeks	219,381	1.73	2.9	3.8
Georgians	209,196	1.65	1.3	1.3
Armenians	200,605	1.60	1.4	1.5
Kazakhs	199,196	1.57	1.7	2.2
Azerbaidjanians	162,181	1.28	1.4	1.8
Lithuanians	71,316	.56	1.1	1.1
Latvians	49,559	.39	.7	.6
Tadjiks	46,593	.36	.7	.9
Moldavians	46,562	.36	1.1	1.1
Kirghiz	39,053	.31	.5	.6
Estonians	37,705	.28	.5	.4
Turkmens	35,781	.28	.5	.6
Others	1,113,263	8.79	9.9	10.3
Total	12,684,133 Members and Candidate-Members			

SOURCE: Based on "KPSS v tsifrakh," *Kommunist* No. 15 (October, 1967), p. 97.

7. THE MASS AUXILIARY ORGANIZATIONS

The CPSU relies on a series of auxiliary mass organizations which are designed to serve as transmission belts to win popular support for the Party's policies, although each of these organizations also performs functions peculiar to it. These organizations enable the regime to mobilize millions of its subjects who are beyond the sanctions and inducements of Party membership. Although they are said to be non-Party organizations—and are such in the strict sense of the term—their leadership consists of Party members whose task it is to make certain that the auxiliary bodies remain in a subordinate role and perform their assigned functions.

The Soviet trade union movement embraces nearly all workers

and salaried employees in the U.S.S.R. and is based on the production principle. A countrywide congress elects the All-Union Central Council of Trade Unions (VTsSPS),[10] which serves as a counterpart of the Party's Central Committee; the Council elects a Presidium and Secretariat. The trade unions promote Soviet patriotism as well as fulfillment of the economic plan by sponsoring "socialist emulation" among workers (the word "competition" has invidious connotations in the Soviet lexicon and when used is associated with "capitalism"). The trade unions administer part of the state's social insurance program and sponsor a variety of facilities and activities, including athletic and sports contests, "palaces of culture," libraries, clubhouses, resorts and camps, cinemas, excursions, and lectures on atheism and other subjects. The Council publishes the newspaper *Trud* (Labor) and also operates its own publishing house, *Profizdat.* Decisions of the CPSU Central Committee are approved at Council plenary sessions, and the entire trade union movement provides an effective means of mobilizing mass support.

The *Komsomol* (VLKSM or All-Union Leninist Communist League of Youth) brings more than 24 million of "progressive Soviet youth" under Communist influence.[11] It was founded in October, 1918, and by the 1930's became a mass organization useful to the regime in the collectivization of agriculture and in the anti-*kulak* campaign (directed against more prosperous peasants who opposed collectivization), as well as in World War II. Its membership embraces youth from 14 through 28 years of age, although the Komsomol leadership is often beyond the maximum age. The Komsomol is not confined to student membership but includes employed youths as well. Despite official assertions that the Komsomol is non-Party, its organizational structure parallels that of the CPSU from primary party organization to central committee. The First Secretary of the Komsomol is a member of the CPSU Central

[10] *Vsesoiuznyi Tsentral'nyi Sovet Professional'nykh Soiuzov.* For a somewhat uncritical but useful study, see Emily Clark Brown, *Soviet Trade Unions and Labor Relations* (Cambridge: Harvard University Press, 1966).

[11] *Politicheskii slovar'*, 2nd ed. (Moscow: Gospolitizdat, 1958), p. 97.

Committee. The Party closely supervises the youth organization and recruits most of its own members from the Komsomol.[12] The Komsomol official organ is *Komsomolskaia pravda,* which is published daily on weekdays.

The Komsomol is used to control the social and political behavior of youth and to guide its energies into channels useful to the regime. It promotes labor productivity among its members in factories and on farms, combats antisocial attitudes and conduct, and aids in the dissemination of propaganda. Study of the works of Marx and Lenin is encouraged in terms of their relationship to the current Party line. The Komsomol mobilizes "volunteer" labor for special projects, as in bringing the virgin and fallow lands under cultivation in the late 1950's and aiding collective and state farms during harvesting seasons or in special construction projects. The Komsomol is closely related to secondary and especially to higher education; it is nearly impossible to obtain admission to a university unless one is a member. Social control is high on its list of objectives and it has sought to impose orthodox tastes not only in political attitudes but in dress, the arts, dancing, and in personal conduct.

The Pioneers, also officially named in honor of Lenin, is the mass communist organization of children of the Soviet Union.[13] Its ranks consist of more than 20 million Soviet schoolchildren from the ages of 9 through 14, and it serves as a training and recruiting ground for the Komsomol. It was founded in 1922 as a result of the Party's concern over child-rearing practices and its desire to limit familial influence in the interests of indoctrination. In the Pioneer organization the child is conditioned to subordinate himself to the group pressures of the "collective" and to accept public shaming and civic rituals at an early age.

Pioneers wear special uniforms and an emblem with a hammer

[12] For the history of the Party-Komsomol relationship, see Ralph T. Fisher, Jr., *Pattern for Soviet Youth; A Study of the Congresses of the Komsomol, 1918–1954* (New York: Columbia University Press, 1959). A general treatment of the Party's youth organizations is provided in Allen Kassof, *The Soviet Youth Program, Regimentation and Rebellion* (Cambridge: Harvard University Press, 1965).

[13] *Politicheskii slovar', op. cit.* (above, n. 11), 2d ed., p. 429; also see *Pionerskaia organizatsiia imeni V. I. Lenina* (Moscow: Uchpedgiz, 1950), p. 5.

and sickle emblazoned upon a star and inscribed with the organization's slogan, *Vsegda gotov!* ("Always ready"). They take a ceremonial pledge upon being initiated. The children are organized into brigades (*druzhiny*) by schools; each grade in a school is organized into a detachment (*otriad*); and at the classroom level there is the "link" (*zveno*), which is the basic unit of the Pioneers and consists of from 5 to 12 children. Older Komsomol members are assigned to work with Pioneer detachments and brigades, and the teachers and school director also supervise their activities.

The Pioneers serve as the Soviet Union's answer to the scouting movement, which is regarded as bourgeois and counter-revolutionary—although Pioneers and scouts share certain common characteristics. Pioneers are not concerned primarily with recreational activities, although the organization does operate camps with the financial support of the trade unions and has "Pioneer palaces" used for handicrafts, study courses, and work in the various arts. More important are the organization's efforts to inculcate discipline, seriousness, punctuality, and respect for work. Socially useful labor is performed as, for example, tree planting and the collecting of scrap metal when required. Excursions are organized and, in accordance with the slogan "the Pioneer is an example for all children," children are urged to excel in school work. Each Pioneer detachment has a banner, and drum and bugle are used in marching exercises; commands are conveyed by means of the bugle.

The work of the Pioneers organization embraces one of the vital periods in the process of political socialization experienced by Soviet youth. No opportunity is lost to introduce children to a favorable view of Soviet history, the life of Lenin, and to group observance of political holidays. Pioneers are told that they live in the best of all possible societies and that bourgeois society is evil and corrupt.[14] Nature studies are conducted in a manner designed to

[14] Pioneers have for years been told of the "heroism" of Pavlik Morozov, a boy who betrayed family loyalties during the collectivization campaign when he informed on his father; the father was shot and villagers then killed the son in vengeance in September, 1932. On the Morozov case, see *Pionerskaia organizatsiia imeni V. I. Lenina, ibid.*, pp. 25–27 and Kassof, *op. cit.* (above, n. 12), pp. 37ff.

propagate the materialist world outlook and atheistic belief. Children are prepared for membership by spending three years in the Little Octobrists (*Oktiabriata*), which embraces the 7 to 9 age group. A semiweekly newspaper, *Pionerskaia pravda,* is published by the organization. The relationship to the Party is evident in the practice of having a delegation of Pioneers appear at each Party Congress, marching into the auditorium and filling the aisles and stage before the dais, the children greeting the delegates and leadership and extolling the Party by reciting especially composed verses.

The mass civil defense organization, DOSAAF (Voluntary Society for Assistance to the Army, Air Force, and Navy),[15] is said to have more than 30 million members. Its organization closely parallels that of the Party but is subordinate to the Ministry of Defense. It publishes a newspaper, *The Soviet Patriot,* as well as several journals and maintains close ties with the Komsomol. DOSAAF is a paramilitary organization that trains its members in physical culture, marksmanship and weapons, skiing, parachuting, gliding, diving, and in military history, as well as in the operation of aircraft, motorcycles, trucks, and radio and electronic equipment. It also promotes interest in the breeding of dogs for military use. However, it is concerned primarily with manning evacuation and shelter facilities, with anti-air defense, and with fire-fighting and decontamination. Members receive training and, in turn, train nonmembers in the population. DOSAAF's activities indicate the seriousness with which Soviet leaders regard civil defense; they also provide a means of promoting patriotism and disseminating a variety of skills.

8. THE SECURITY POLICE

From its inception the Soviet regime has employed a special political police force to suppress its internal enemies and to frighten

[15] *Dobrovol'noe obshchestvo sodeistviia armii, aviatsii i flotu*—formed in 1951 as the result of a merger of the civil defense organizations of the three services, which existed separately after 1948. The predecessor organization was *Osoaviakhim* (*Obshchestvo sodeistviia oborone i aviatsionno-khimicheskomu stroitel'stvu SSSR*), the Society for Assistance in the Defense and Aviation-Chemical Construction of the U.S.S.R., founded in 1927. Activities of DOSAAF are discussed in Leon Gouré, *Civil Defense in the Soviet Union* (Berkeley and Los Angeles: University of California Press, 1962).

potential opponents into compliance. This organization—known since March, 1954, as the Committee of State Security or KGB (*Komitet Gosudarstvennoi Bezopasnosti*)—had its origins in the *Cheka*, which was established on December 20, 1917. The name *Cheka* was derived from the Russian term *Chrezvychainaia Komissiia;* its full title was the Extraordinary Commission for the Struggle against Counter-Revolution, Sabotage, and Breach of Duty by Officials. In February, 1922, it was renamed the GPU (*Gosudarstvennoe Politicheskoe Upravlenie*) or State Political Administration, although members of the secret police continued to be called "Chekists." With the establishment of the Soviet Union at the end of 1922 the GPU formally became the OGPU—the additional initial standing for the word "Unified" (*Ob"edinennoe*). In July, 1934, it was renamed the NKVD (People's Commissariat for Internal Affairs) and became a ministry (NMVD) when the new designation was adopted in March, 1946.

However, a separate Commissariat of State Security (NKGB) was established in April, 1943, probably because of the special security police responsibilities resulting from Soviet reoccupation of territories held by the Nazis during the war. The NKGB had the task of uncovering wartime collaborators, as well as agents left behind by the Nazi forces; it was also necessary to establish a new and larger network of Soviet secret police informers (*seksoty*), who were often recruited by blackmail to spy upon the population. The ordinary police functions were performed by the NKVD's militia, which combated crime and maintained public order, regulated traffic, and administered the internal passport system (introduced in late 1932). The NKVD also had within its jurisdiction the fire departments, automobile and driver licensing, the state archives, and the registry of vital statistics (conducted by civil registry offices known as ZAGS—*Zapis' aktov grazhdanskogo sostoianiia*).[16]

The division of functions between NMGB and NMVD was terminated in March, 1953—following Stalin's death—when a unified Interior Ministry (MVD) was created under Lavrentii Beria. It was

[16] The history of the Soviet secret police is described in Simon Wolin and Robert M. Slusser, eds., *The Soviet Secret Police* (New York: Frederick A. Praeger, 1957). Also see Robert Conquest, *The Great Terror; Stalin's Purges of the Thirties* (New York: Macmillan, 1968).

subsequently redivided on March 13, 1954, with the establishment of the KGB.

The Soviet regime has, in general, preferred to rely upon constraint and terror only as means of last resort; to obtain compliance it has also utilized indoctrination and psychological conditioning, social inducements, and material incentives. However, it has not hesitated to employ repressive measures and under Stalin at times the organs of terror were permitted to run rampant. The reliance upon secret police methods had its origins in the Bolshevik experience with the *Okhrana* (the tsarist secret police) and in the fear of factionalism and penetration which Lenin bequeathed the Party. Revolution was to breed various forms of counterrevolution and to justify their elimination by whatever means regarded as necessary. The Party leadership long viewed itself as commanding a fortress under siege and repeatedly issued calls for "vigilance."[17] The fear of being contaminated by the non-Soviet world and the need for the Party to protect its claim to a monopoly of power have served to rationalize the perpetuation of the regime's political police apparatus. The police have also had a certain utility in keeping officials alert and in facilitating circulation among the elite.

Under Stalin the NKVD became the country's largest "employer," using millions of persons in forced labor camps for lumbering, gold and coal mining, and construction projects (including canals, roads, and railways). Nor did the Party itself escape the toils of the secret police. Although originally the Cheka and OGPU were directed against the former ruling class and the old intelligentsia, oppositionists within the Party felt its oppressive hand in the late 1920's and many of them perished in its execution chambers during the 1930's. The secret police also played the leading

[17] The 1961 CPSU Program included the following provision regarding the use of repressive measures: "The general trend of class struggle within the Socialist [i.e., Communist-ruled] countries in conditions of successful Socialist construction leads to consolidation of the position of the Socialist forces and weakens the resistance of the remnants of the hostile classes. But this development does not follow a straight line. Changes in the domestic or external situation may cause the class struggle to intensify in specific periods. This calls for constant vigilance in order to frustrate in good time the designs of hostile forces within and without."

role in uncovering so-called wrecking (sabotage) activities allegedly engaged in by Soviet engineers in behalf of foreign powers. The political police spearheaded the collectivization of agriculture, arresting and deporting millions of recalcitrant peasants who were arbitrarily classified as *kulaks* (wealthy peasants). The NKVD also prepared the defendants for Stalin's three show trials of Old Bolsheviks held between August, 1936, and March, 1938.[18]

The NKVD developed a variety of techniques for breaking men, including the writing of autobiographies, the practice of holding prisoners incommunicado for lengthy periods, and the alternating of threats with blandishments during protracted interrogations often held at night.[19] Its methods have included the "conveyer method" of interrogation, by which a succession of interrogators would confront the isolated and fatigued prisoner who has been systematically deprived of sleep. The practice of having prison cells constantly illuminated and of having guards maintain frequent surveillance of prisoners through cell doors—at least in Moscow's infamous Lubianka Prison—is indicative of the kind of regime maintained in prisons of the secret police. Nor have the police hesitated to employ outright fabrications and provocateurs and to prompt prisoners to compromise each other.

There are also two known instances of mass murder perpetrated by the NKVD—the massacre of more than 10,000 Ukrainians in 1937–38 in the city of Vynnytsia and the mass execution of 4,000 Polish army officers in the Katyn Forest west of Smolensk in 1940.[20] The number of other such mass atrocities perpetrated by the Stalinist regime remains buried with the victims.

[18] For the incomplete stenographic record of the March, 1938, trial of Bukharin, Rakovsky, Grin'ko, and others, see *The Great Purge Trial,* ed. Robert C. Tucker and Stephen F. Cohen (New York: Grosset and Dunlap, 1965).

[19] There is a very substantial literature dealing with the practices of the Soviet security police. Among the knowledgeable authors are F. Beck and W. Godin, Margarete Buber, Rev. Walter J. Ciszek, David J. Dallin, Peter Deriabin, Rev. Gerhard Fittkau, Evgeniia S. Ginzburg, Jerzy Gliksman, Albert Konrad Herling, Valentin Gonzalez ("El Campesino"), N. N. Krasnov, Jr., Elinor Lipper, Anatoly Marchenko, Allan Monkhouse, John Noble, Unto Parvilahti, A. Pidhainy, Nicholas Prychodko, David Rousset, Joseph Scholmer, Zbigniew Stypulkowski, and Alexander Weissberg.

[20] The Vynnytsia massacres have been accorded little attention as compared with Katyn. See *The Crime of Moscow in Vynnytsia* (Edinburgh: Scottish

The subordination of the secret police to Stalin (and to his personal secretariat) was one of the most important elements in his dictatorship. Yet the men who have headed the security police have generally not held very high positions within the Party leadership. The *Cheka*'s founder, Felix E. Dzerzhinsky, was a Central Committee member from 1917 to his death in July, 1926; he attained Politburo candidate-membership only in 1924. His successor and deputy, Viacheslav R. Menzhinsky, headed the OGPU from 1926 until his death in 1934 and became a full member of the Central Committee in December, 1927. Menzhinsky was succeeded as NKVD chief by Genrikh G. Yagoda, a bookkeeper who had joined the *Cheka* in 1920 and became deputy chief in 1924. Yagoda was removed in September, 1936, and stood trial in March, 1938, on fantastic charges of having killed Menzhinsky, the writer Maxim Gorky, and Valerian Kuibyshev; he was condemned to death. Yagoda's successor was Nikolai Yezhov, a Central Committee secretary who had headed the Cadres Department. Yezhov attained Politburo candidate-membership in October, 1937, and had the dubious distinction of having the most sanguinary Soviet purge, the *Yezhovshchina,* named for him in the popular lexicon. After serving his purpose Yezhov was removed in December, 1938, and perished.

Yezhov's successor was Lavrentii Beria, who served in the secret police during the 1920's and headed the Party apparatus in Transcaucasia in the 1930's. Beria headed the NKVD until 1945 and in that year also attained full membership in the Politburo. He was also a deputy premier and continued to supervise police activities. Thus Beria rose higher in the Party leadership than any previous Soviet secret police chief. Although he was nearly purged in the last period of Stalin's reign, he succeeded in retaining control of

---

League for European Freedom, 1952), as well as testimony heard by the Committee on Un-American Activities of the United States House of Representatives, 86th Congress, First Session, on September 9, 1959, *The Crimes of Khrushchev* (Washington, D.C.: Printing Office, 1959), pp. 17–37. Also see Zbigniew K. Brzezinski, *The Permanent Purge* (Cambridge: Harvard University Press, 1956), pp. 109 and 228. On Katyn, see J. K. Zawodny, *Death in the Forest* (Notre Dame, Ind.: University of Notre Dame Press, 1962) and the volumes of testimony and documentation amassed by the Select Committee of the U. S. House of Representatives, 82nd Congress, Second Session (1952).

the secret police following Stalin's death. Beria as Minister of Internal Affairs was a threat to Stalin's other heirs, and he was executed in 1953 even though previously he had been decorated with the Order of Lenin on five occasions. The unified MVD was headed by General Sergei N. Kruglov following Beria's demise until the KGB was established.

The KGB was headed by General Ivan Serov from its inception in March, 1954, until December, 1958. Serov began his career in the military but became a professional police officer in the 1930's; although a Russian, he headed the Ukrainian NKVD in 1940–41 when he developed an association with Khrushchev which proved to be advantageous. In 1952 he attained Central Committee candidate-membership; as KGB chief he became a full member in 1956.[21] When Serov was appointed chief of the Military Intelligence Directorate (GRU), he was succeeded in the KGB by a Party apparatus official, Alexander Shelepin, who had served as First Secretary of the Komsomol from 1952 to 1958. Shelepin's successor as Komsomol First Secretary, Vladimir Semichastny, also succeeded him as KGB head in November, 1961. Semichastny was removed in May, 1967, and was succeeded by Yuri Andropov, a Secretariat member who became a Politburo candidate-member in June, 1967.

The decision to place the secret police under the direction of professional Party officials was undoubtedly related to the shake-up which the police organs had experienced following the execution of Beria and his aides. Yet the police have not been able to play an independent role in Soviet politics. The military has served as a counterforce and check on the police, and the Party has never hesitated to deal harshly with its police chiefs. Only Beria, while head of the police, enjoyed full Politburo membership, while Shelepin obtained a post in the Secretariat and later in the Politburo only after leaving the KGB chairmanship.

Although the head of the police is usually at least a full member

[21] Serov was subsequently compromised as a result of his associations with Colonel Oleg Penkovskiy, Soviet military intelligence General Staff officer who served Anglo-American intelligence organizations in 1961 and 1962. Serov was expelled from the Party in 1965. See *The Penkovskiy Papers* (Garden City, N.Y.: Doubleday, 1965), pp. 70, 90–91, 188–191, 210–211, 239, 279, 282.

of the Central Committee, his position is not in itself likely to serve as a vehicle for advancement. Indeed, the incumbents have been among the more expendable Soviet politicians. The position entails great responsibility, and tends to elicit fear and distrust within the leadership because of the opportunities it provides for collecting information of a compromising nature that can be used against opponents. The police representation in the Central Committee is limited and could be important only if it were to act as a bloc and if it should hold the balance during an internal crisis. If the role of the police is circumscribed within the leadership, it nevertheless remains an indispensable component of the Soviet system.

The soviet secret police organization exercises vast powers and has at its disposal personnel numbering in the hundreds of thousands. The KGB includes foreign intelligence and counterintelligence, and the political police who deal with offenses against the state, censor the mails, and guard the Soviet leadership. The border guards control the world's longest frontier, preventing persons from entering the country illegally and Soviet citizens from leaving it without permission. Special frontier zones two kilometers in width have been maintained to control the movement of all persons.[22] The police also control the Army of Internal Security, a special force used to maintain order in the event that the militia cannot do so; it also serves as a counterforce to the regular army and as a means of suppressing internal revolt. The KGB maintains its own communications facilities and operational air force. It has even been known to reach out into foreign lands in order to dispose of persons regarded an enemies of the Soviet regime.[23] An organization of this type also of necessity conducts many operations that remain unknown to the general public.

[22] *Sbornik zakonov SSSR, 1938–1961* (Moscow: "Izvestiia Sovetov Deputatov Trudiashchikhsia SSSR," 1961), pp. 371–372.

[23] Illustrations are provided by the kidnapping of the Russian émigré General Paul Kutepov off a Paris street by Soviet police agents on January 26, 1930 (see the admission by Colonel-General N. Shimanov in *Krasnaia zvezda*, September 22, 1965, p. 3) and by the assassinations in Munich of the Ukrainian émigrés Lev Rebet and Stepan Bandera (in October, 1957, and October, 1959, respectively) by the Soviet agent Bogdan Stashinsky. The confessed assassin was tried in the Supreme Court of the Federal Republic of Germany in Karlsruhe. The German Foreign Ministry protested to the USSR on April 23, 1963; see the *Bulletin des Presse und Informationsamtes der Bundesregierung* of April 25, 1963, No. 73.

9. THE MILITARY

Most polities—with the possible exception of long-established constitutional systems—are confronted with the problem of preventing the military from challenging civilian control. In numerous Afro-Asian and Latin American countries, civilian politicians have been ousted and replaced by juntas or by a single dominant military figure. The role of the armed forces vis-à-vis the Party has troubled the Soviet leadership since Lenin's time. The problem has been one of utilizing the military with its indispensable professional knowledge and its weaponry, and stimultaneously preventing it from challenging the Party.

Initially, Lenin favored establishment of a nonprofessional people's army and the abolition of standing armies. The Soviet regime had owed its establishment to the demoralization of the old army and the organization of the Party's own paramilitary force, the Red Guard. However, the need to employ substantial military force to preserve the regime and extend its domain necessitated the establishment of the Red Army, based on conscription, and the hiring of approximately 50,000 commissioned officers and more than 200,000 noncommissioned officers of the tsarist army. This fact, together with the Party's fear that it might lose control of its new military forces, led to the establishment of the system of political commissars. These officials were instructed to prevent the defection of army officers, to sign orders and reports along with the commander, and to conduct propaganda among the troops.

The system led to friction, but it enabled the regime to defeat its domestic enemies by 1921. Subsequently, professional army officers who joined the Party and gained its confidence were given independent authority to make military decisions ("single command" or *edinonachalie*), while non-Party members were checked by the commissars. These gains made by the professional military were quickly eroded with the establishment of Stalin's dictatorship, although the armed forces were increased in size and given larger appropriations. The purges of the 1930's resulted in the ouster or elimination of fully half of the officer corps; eight of the leading officers, including Marshal Tukhachevsky, were executed in June,

1937.[24] Stalin also enhanced the role of the political commissars, making them coequal with commanding officers in August, 1937. The system of dual command did not function well during the Soviet-Finnish war of 1939–40; it was modified in August, 1940, when the office of commissar was replaced with that of the deputy commander for political affairs (*zampolit*), who dealt with propaganda and morale while the commander was responsible for military decisions. Stalin's lack of confidence in the military was testified to in July, 1941, following the Nazi invasion of the Soviet Union, when the commissar system was reintroduced. However, the *zampolit* system was restored in October, 1942. Although the Soviet Army was given much latitude during World War II, stringent controls were reimposed in 1945.

Party-military relations have followed an uneven course which has depended upon the degree to which the Party has had to rely on military support.[25] In order to maintain its traditional dominance over the military, the Party developed a variety of controls and techniques. Foremost among these has been the effort to recruit nearly all officers as Communist Party members and bring them within the ambit of party discipline through the primary Party organizations in military units. A classic example of the kind of control the Party exercises was provided in the case of M. V. Frunze, who in 1925, as Commissar of the armed forces, was ordered by the Politburo to undergo surgery—from which he never recovered. A second method is that of political indoctrination, which is part of professional military training and is conducted under the supervision of the Main Political Administration (MPA) or *Glavnoe Politicheskoe Upravlenie* of the Soviet armed forces. The MPA, although housed in the Ministry of Defense, is in fact a

[24] For a personal account of a Soviet officer who was arrested and released only during World War II when trained commanders were in great demand, see the memoirs of General A. V. Gorbatov, which appeared in an abridged English translation, *Years off My Life* (New York: W. W. Norton, 1965).

[25] For a thorough historical treatment of the Soviet military, see John Erickson, *The Soviet High Command: A Military-Political History, 1918–1942* (New York: St. Martin's Press, 1962). The system of political control and the party-military relationship are treated in Roman Kolkowicz, *The Soviet Military and the Communist Party* (Princeton, N.J.: Princeton University Press, 1967).

department of the Central Committee apparatus. It is charged with evaluating the political reliability of responsible military personnel. It directs the work of the deputy commanders for political affairs (*zampolity*), who function at the divisional, brigade, regimental, and battalion levels. Through them it controls the primary Party organizations and the Komsomol units in the armed services. A third method used at various times is to have the territorial Party organizations check on the military units within their jurisdiction. Related to this type of control is the institution of the military council—established by Stalin in May, 1937—which functions at the regional level. This body includes the regional commander and his chief of staff, representatives from the local (*oblast'* or *krai*) party organizations, and usually a member from the security police. The commander's decisions must have the Council's approval.

Other techniques of control include the practice of promoting those officers who are "politically reliable," the implicit threat of transfer to the reserves with loss of privileges, as well as the use of personal rivalries between leading military figures (as between Marshals Zhukov and Konev). The regime has also employed political marshals among the professional military. It has introduced secret police informers into the armed services in order to promote conformity and uncover the disaffected. The Soviet practice of "criticism and self criticism" (*kritika-samokritika*) at Party meetings, in which one can criticize others but must also admit one's own errors, is used to put one military rank against another; in this way a state of tension is institutionalized, and Party meetings are used to mix ranks and to cut senior officers "down to size." The regular army is also held in check by the separate army of the interior. However, direct and indirect controls and indoctrination are accompanied by inducements and rewards. The officer corps of the Soviet armed services constitutes a privileged class valued by the regime. At the same time measures must be exercised to prevent the military from becoming a caste which could dictate policy to the Party leadership.

The degree of latitude permitted the military within the system of controls and the degree of influence on policy exercised by the leading generals depend upon the state of the Party leadership and the extent to which the regime is *immediately* dependent upon military support. If the Party oligarchy is divided and one or another faction seeks the backing of the armed forces leadership, the military is in a position to exact concessions. The varying degree to which controls have been applied in relationship to the domestic political situation is reflected in the direction of the MPA. Its heads have been "political generals" during periods of intensified control, and the post has been sensitive to changes in Party leadership.[26] The head of the MPA is usually a Central Committee member.

Marshal Georgii K. Zhukov was the sole professional army officer to attain full membership in the Politburo-Presidium, and that

[26] As early as 1924 Stalin removed Antonov-Ovseenko, a Trotskyite, as head of PUR (*Politicheskoe Upravlenie Raboche-Krestianskoi Krasnoi Armii*), the precursor of MPA, thus indicating the importance of the post in the developing power struggle with Trotsky and in the system generally. A. S. Bubnov, a Stalinist and nonmilitary figure, held it until 1929. Bubnov's successor was Jan B. Gamarnik, a Party official and army commissar, who held the post until 1937, when he committed suicide at the time of the execution of eight of the Soviet Union's leading generals. From 1937 to 1940 the MPA was headed by Lev Z. Mekhlis, a former Party official and member of the editorial board of *Pravda,* who presided over the purging of the officer corps. From 1942 to 1945 the MPA was headed by Alexander S. Shcherbakov, a member of the Party Secretariat and a veteran official of its apparatus. Shcherbakov, unlike his predecessor, remained a Central Committee Secretary while heading MPA, in addition to serving as Moscow city and *obkom* secretary; he also attained candidate membership in the Politburo.

Controls were tightened in the postwar period, when Iosif V. Shikin headed MPA from 1946 to 1949, and leading military figures were given obscure posts. Shikin, a protégé of Andrei Zhdanov, was removed in 1949, along with other of Zhdanov's followers; but he made a comeback after Stalin's death and served as ambassador to Albania in 1960. The MPA was subsequently headed by a military man, Colonel General F. F. Kuznetsov, and in the same year Marshal Vasilevsky replaced the political Marshal Bulganin as Defense Minister. Following Stalin's death the MPA was headed by Colonel General Zheltov, who remained at the post until January, 1958, when he was succeeded by General (later Marshal) F. I. Golikov. Both of these chiefs presided over a weaker MPA; but in May, 1962, Golikov, a professional army officer, was succeeded by Alexei A. Yepishev, a political general who tightened controls. Yepishev had served with Khrushchev in the Ukrainian Party apparatus after World War II and was brought to Moscow in 1951, apparently by Khrushchev, to be Deputy Minister of State Security (MGB). He left that post in 1953 and became first secretary of the Odessa *obkom* in Ukraine; in 1955 he was appointed ambassador to Rumania and in 1961 ambassador to Yugoslavia. Yepishev's career illustrates the kinds of political qualifications and experience which the Party requires of the MPA chief when it has wished to reimpose more rigid controls over the military.

briefly, from July to October 1957; he was soon regarded as a threat to the Party and to Khrushchev's rule.[27] His summary removal from the post of Minister of Defense and from the Central Committee was accomplished in October, 1957, when he was sent to Yugoslavia and Albania on an official mission. Zhukov was later accused of pursuing a "Bonapartist policy." His rapid advance had been due to the fact that the Party needed the support of the army against Beria. Khrushchev also required it in his struggle for power with Malenkov, which led to the latter's removal from the premiership. The military did not approve of Malenkov's budget cuts or his views in 1954, which regarded Soviet nuclear deterrence as adequate to deal with any external threat and advocated the diversion of resources from heavy industry to the production of consumer goods. The military also favored the rewriting of Soviet history in 1956–57 to take into account its role, in contrast to that of Stalin, in achieving victory in World War II. Zhukov insisted, moreover, that the Party posthumously rehabilitate the generals executed in 1937. While the military had supported Khrushchev against the "anti-Party group" in 1957, Khrushchev's victory made it possible for the Party to reassert its control over the armed forces. The improved conditions and the emancipation from indoctrination obtained for the military by Zhukov were thus shortlived.

The military's sense of professionalism and exclusiveness and its awareness of how important a role it might play still lead to disagreements with the Party leadership. The military often dislike political controls and ideological indoctrination, which consume much time and detract from professional activities and interests. The military may sometimes represent views which conflict with those of Party leaders regarding military policy, questions of strategy, and estimates of risk and capabilities. Both Party and military leaders have views regarding the country's defense needs, what the

[27] Although Marshal K. Voroshilov was in the Politburo from 1926 to 1960, he was less a representative of professional military interests and more of a crony of Stalin's. His military experience was limited and his advancement was due more to his revolutionary past than to military expertise. Voroshilov's appointment as Soviet chief of state, following Stalin's death, was probably designed to accord greater recognition to the military.

size and nature of the defense establishment should be, how resources and investments should be allocated, and what the level of defense expenditures should be. There are opportunities, in other words, to differ over the extent to which international tension can be reduced, and over what the conditions of deterrence and détente might be. The military does not always trust the judgment of Party leaders in military matters; it wishes to apply its professional expertise and has a natural distrust of the amateur.

Although there are disagreements *within* the military, which the Party can often manipulate to its own advantage, the Party must constantly act to preserve its monopoly of authority and its system of controls. By means of a skillful granting and retraction of concessions, as well as by encouraging personal rivalries, the Party has been able to maintain its dominant position. The military and the secret police are among the more influential interest groups in Soviet politics, but they are also indispensable attributes and instruments of Party rule.

CHAPTER 6

THE CENTRAL GOVERNMENT

Knowledge of the Communist Party's leadership and organization, while indispensable for a thorough understanding of Soviet political structures, is not in itself adequate for that understanding. For, while it is commonplace to assert that the Soviet regime and its Communist Party are synonymous, in practice, the Party and government are distinct organizational entities. Within the government there are bodies that fulfill many functions not performed by the Party organization. And while the Party apparatus exercises vast power and ultimate decision-making ability, it lacks juristic authority; this requisite of its rule it obtains only by dominating the vast governmental structure that it originally created.

1. THE SOVIETS: ORIGIN AND MEANING

It is indicative of the nature of language and of the mutable nature of semantics that the ordinary and politically neutral Russian word *soviet,* denoting "council," should have acquired a highly specific political meaning. For the term has come to be synonymous with communist dictatorship and is at times even used interchangeably with the adjective "Russian."

The term *soviet* was used by the Imperial Regime in naming the State Council (*Gosudarstvennyi Sovet*), a purely advisory body established by Alexander I in 1810. With the proclamation of the Duma in 1906, the State Council became the upper house of the Imperial legislature. The tsarist regime also had a Council (soviet) of Ministers. However, the term began to acquire a politically tendentious meaning originally as a result of the 1905 Revolution. In October of that year, there emerged in St. Petersburg a Soviet of

Workers' Deputies, which assumed leadership of the general strike that prompted concessions from Nicholas II. The most important of these were the establishment of the Duma and the recognition of circumscribed freedom of expression. The 1905 Soviet vainly proclaimed the eight-hour workday and advocated a constituent assembly and a republic. When its chairman, a lawyer, was arrested, the Menshevik Trotsky became its spokesman. The tsarist government arrested the entire Executive Committee of the Soviet when it issued a financial manifesto calling upon the public not to pay taxes.

The institution of the soviet made its appearance again in the Russian capital in 1917, with the establishment of the Petrograd Soviet of Workers' and Soldiers' Deputies. This was a spontaneous body whose members were not elected in accordance with any established procedures. In the period following the tsar's abdication, the Petrograd Soviet and the Provisional Government, which had emerged from the Duma, constituted a dyarchy. The Soviet, initially consisting largely of Socialist Revolutionaries and Mensheviks, had vague objectives, such as defending the revolution, but would not enter the Provisional Government. While refusing to accept the responsibility of governing, the Soviet succeeded in paralyzing the Provisional Government and in bringing about the collapse of authority in the Russian capital. The assumption was that authority would be assumed by the All-Russian Constituent Assembly, but the Provisional Government was dilatory in organizing the popular election of that body. Soviets were organized in other cities and in peasant communities; factory committees and soldiers' committees added to the general confusion.

The return of Lenin to Russia in April, 1917, prompted the Bolsheviks to utilize the Petrograd and other soviets. Lenin declared war on the Provisional Government and advocated the slogan of "All Power to the Soviets." Although the Bolsheviks were a small minority in the principal soviets, Lenin gradually built up a following in factory committees and in the Petrograd garrison. By using street mobs Lenin succeeded in pressuring both the Provisional Government and the Petrograd Soviet. As the Provisional Government, headed by Alexander Kerensky, lost strength and prestige in the early autumn of 1917, both the Bolsheviks and the Soviets (which included many non-Bolsheviks) gained ground. In September, Trotsky, who had now joined the Bolsheviks, succeeded in becoming chairman of the Petrograd Soviet after the Menshevik Chkheidze resigned ill-advisedly and helped preempt the situation.

The Bolshevik seizure of power occurred as the Second All-Russian Congress of Soviets of Workers' and Soldiers' Deputies was being convened. The Bolsheviks did not have a clear majority in the Congress, but Lenin seized power in the name of the soviets rather than relying upon the Congress to determine Russia's future. Lenin succeeded in gaining control of the Congress when most of the Mensheviks, the Socialist Revolutionaries, and the Jewish Bundists walked out—again preempting the situation rather than resisting the Bolsheviks. While claiming to have seized power in behalf of the Congress of Soviets, the Bolsheviks had it acclaim their new, supposedly provisional, government—a soviet of people's commissars (*sovnarkom*). The rump Congress also approved a Bolshevik-dominated Central Executive Committee, which was to serve as an interim legislative body.

Thus began the long association of the Russian Communist Party (of Bolsheviks) and the institution of soviets, which has enabled the ruling party to claim that it is not actually the government of the U.S.S.R., and that, rather, its regime is "soviet power." Indeed, when Lenin dispersed at bayonet point the popularly elected All-Russian Constituent Assembly on January 19, 1918, he justified his action as a defense of "soviet power." His regime would submit its policies for approval only to Congresses of Soviets, whose membership it would control. Thus, at the Third Congress of Soviets, which met in late January, 1918, Lenin's Bolsheviks had 61 percent of the seats. In subsequent convocations of Soviets at all levels of government, the Bolsheviks were to fashion ready instruments to transform their Party decisions into law.

In Lenin's theory the system of soviets was to serve as communism's answer to "bourgeois parliamentarism" and was to provide the organs of "proletarian power." Although soviets are nothing more than elected councils, it was claimed that they provided a "state of a new and higher type" which would lead to socialism. Soviets did, in fact, give to the communist regime a mass participation basis, while not permitting the masses any choice in the matter of Communist Party rule. Yet it is claimed that "state authority" resides in the "soviets of toilers' deputies" (*sovety deputatov trudiashchikhsia*)—although they do not participate directly in the decision-making process of the CPSU.

2. THE FUSION OF POWERS

The system of soviets extends from the U.S.S.R. Supreme Soviet (the country's bicameral legislative body) to the unicameral supreme soviets of the union republics and of the autonomous republics, down through the province and city soviets to the rural and urban district level, and to the smallest village and hamlet. At each level, from the highest to the very lowest, there is an elected soviet that serves to legitimize governmental authority. Yet all of the soviets, irrespective of their territorial jurisdiction, are said to constitute a single unified system that supposedly gives substance to the claim regarding the unity of the Soviet state and people. The centralism that characterizes Communist Party organization has thus been extended to the government, and the lower soviets are "strictly subordinate" to the higher soviets. At the same time, all soviets, including the U.S.S.R. Supreme Soviet, are in fact subordinate to the Communist Party organization at each jurisdictional level.

The soviets embody the principle of the fusion of legislative and executive power that is a basic characteristic of the Soviet regime. Thus, Lenin is quoted approvingly as having asserted in 1917 that "there *cannot be* two powers (*vlastei*) in a state." [1] While a differentiation of functions and competence is recognized as existing between legislative, administrative, and judicial bodies, it is still claimed that state authority is unified. The soviets are said to "control" the executive because the executive bodies (the councils of

[1] V. I. Lenin, *Polnoe Sobranie Sochinenii,* 5th ed. (Moscow, 1961), XXXI, 155; italics in original. See Ia. N. Umanskii, *Sovetskoe gosudarstvennoe pravo* (Moscow; Gosiurizdat, 1959), p. 235.

ministers of the U.S.S.R. and of the various republics, and the executive committees of the soviets below the republic level) are elected by them and consist of persons from their membership. However, legislative initiative rests with the executive and, ultimately, with the Party organization, which is the embodiment of the fusion of powers.

3. SOVIET CONSTITUTIONS

The first Soviet constitution was adopted in July, 1918—for the Russian Socialist Federated Soviet Republic—and, by Lenin's admission, was not drafted by jurists or based on any other constitution. Instead, it was said to be based on the experience of revolutionary struggle and did, in fact, give evidence of having been drafted hastily. It proclaimed the "dictatorship of the proletariat" and claimed to have replaced "bourgeois democracy" with "proletarian democracy." The land, resources, and banking system were nationalized, and the factories, mines, railways and other means of production and transport were placed under "workers' control" and under the Supreme Soviet of the Public Economy (VSNKh) as the first step toward complete state ownership. The 1918 Constitution provided for "universal labor service" as a means of "destroying the parasitic strata of society." It also endeavored to have international appeal by vowing to "deliver humanity from the claws of finance capital and imperialism" and by "insisting upon a complete break with the barbaric policies of bourgeois civilization which have built the prosperity of the exploiters in a few privileged nations on the enslavement of hundreds of millions of the toiling population of Asia, in the colonies in general and in small countries." [2]

The soviets were proclaimed to be truly popular organs of government, and the norms of representation established in 1918 were to persist until 1936. Thus, the "bourgeoisie" and "exploiters" (including persons hiring labor for profit or living on unearned income, tradesmen, clergymen, tsarist police officers, and employers) were denied the right to participate in such direct elections as

[2] *Sovetskie konstitutsii, spravochnik* (Moscow: Gospolitizdat, 1963), pp. 130–131.

were held. Lenin justified this prohibition as providing "proof" that the soviets were "not organs of petit bourgeois compromise with the capitalists and [were] not organs of parliamentary chatter." [3] Why such discriminatory denial of suffrage should have been necessary when the bourgeoisie was but a small minority in Russia was not explained.

A second Soviet constitution was adopted in January, 1924, as a result of the formation of the Union of Soviet Socialist Republics and the need to restructure the political order in accordance with the Union's multinational nature. The Ukrainian and Belorussian communist regimes, whose nominal independence had been recognized by Moscow, adopted their own constitutions in 1919; that of Azerbaidjan did so in 1921; and those of Armenia and Georgia followed suit in 1922. Although the non-Russian communists expressed preference for a confederation in 1923 during the drafting of the constitution, Moscow succeeded in imposing a federal order characterized by a high degree of centralism.

The 1924 Constitution consisted of two principal parts: a declaration of an ideological nature that reflected the "two camps" doctrine ("capitalism" and "socialism," with the latter purporting to represent "mutual confidence and peace, national freedom and equality, peaceful coexistence and the fraternal collaboration of peoples") [4] and a treaty between the Russian S.F.S.R. and the Ukrainian S.S.R., the Belorussian S.S.R. and the Transcaucasian S.F.S.R. (Azerbaidjan, Georgia, and Armenia). The treaty contained the actual U.S.S.R. constitution, which was modeled on the 1918 R.S.F.S.R. constitution.

The 1924 Constitution established an All-Union Congress of Soviets (as the previous All-Russian Congress had functioned only on the territory of the R.S.F.S.R.), but the norms of representation were fixed to the advantage of the urban population. Delegates to the All-Union Congress of Soviets were elected indirectly (by provincial and republic congresses of soviets) on the basis of one delegate per 25,000 *voters* in the cities, while for the rural areas there was one delegate per 125,000 *inhabitants.* Official commentators

[3] Lenin, *Polnoe Sobranie Sochinenii, op. cit.* (above, n. 1), XXXVII, 290.
[4] *Sovetskie konstitutsii, spravochnik* (above, n. 2), p. 183.

have endeavored to justify these ratios of representation on the grounds that they were adopted in 1917 for the elections to Congresses of Soviets prior to the establishment of Lenin's regime. However, the Bolsheviks were not bound to retain such discriminatory norms of representation except for the fact that they were advantageous for a regime that distrusted the peasantry.

The All-Union Congress of Soviets, which functioned until 1936, was to meet annually until 1927 and, subsequently, biennially. Its voting membership ranged from 1,540 to more than 2,000 and was elected for each specific congress. The All-Union Congress was said to be the "supreme organ of authority," but during the lengthy intervals when it was not in session its authority was exercised by the All-Union Central Executive Committee (CEC). The CEC was bicameral; the Council of the Union was elected by the Congress itself on the basis of the population of each republic; the Council of Nationalities was elected by the congresses of soviets of the union republics and of the autonomous republics and by the congresses of the autonomous *oblasti* on the basis of fixed representation.

The CEC was to hold at least three sessions during each of its convocations between the All-Union Congresses of Soviets. During the lengthy intervals between CEC sessions, "supreme legislative, executive and administrative" authority was vested in the Presidium of the CEC, which issued decrees. The Presidium's membership varied from 21 to 27. The CEC elected both its Presidium and the Council of People's Commissars at a joint session of the Council of the Union and the Council of Nationalities, with both chambers voting separately. Under the 1924 Constitution, the Council of People's Commissars was responsible to the Presidium of the CEC and to the CEC when that body was in session. The Presidium, although a continuously functioning body, was said to be responsible to the CEC and the latter, in theory at least, was responsible to the All-Union Congress of Soviets. This elaborate pyramid of indirectly elected bodies was retained by Stalin until 1936, when the All-Union Congress of Soviets was abolished and the CEC was replaced by the U.S.S.R. Supreme Soviet.

The Stalin Constitution was adopted by the Extraordinary Eighth

Congress of Soviets on December 5, 1936, but only after the Central Committee of the CPSU had initiated the proposal at its February, 1935, plenary session. Although Stalin presided over the constitutional commission, Nikolai Bukharin and Karl Radek contributed much to its drafting. The new document was supposedly the "constitution of victorious socialism" and reflected the profound changes that had occurred in the country's class structure and economy—with the supposed liquidation of "exploiting classes," the development of technology and heavy industry, and the collectivization of agriculture. The draft constitution was approved by the Party's Central Committee and by the Presidium of the CEC of the Congress of Soviets in June, 1936. There followed five months of controlled public discussion in which more than 50 million persons were said to have "participated."

The 1924 Constitution was declared to have been a document for the transitional period from capitalism to socialism. With the proclaimed achievement of socialism it was expedient, therefore, under the 1936 Constitution to provide for general, equal, and direct suffrage in the election of all soviets, from the village to the U.S.S.R. Supreme Soviet. Secret suffrage was introduced in lieu of the open voting used previously, although the absence of a choice between candidates hardly required secrecy at the polls. The previously disfranchised classes (clergy, entrepreneurs, and persons who were allegedly privileged under the tsarist regime) were henceforth permitted to participate in elections.

Although all Soviet constitutions have probably concealed more than they have revealed regarding the true nature of the Soviet polity, this does not mean that they can be ignored. The nature of the Soviet constitutions reflects certain of the regime's characteristics. All of the constitutions have been permeated with Marxist-Leninist ideology. The 1936 Constitution proclaimed work to be a duty and declared that "He who does not work neither shall he eat" (article 12)—but without attributing the quotation to Holy Writ (II Thessalonians 3:10). Soviet spokesmen have repeatedly claimed that their constitution has "enormous international significance," supposedly offering the world an ideal and providing an inspiration to all "progressive humanity."

The instrumental nature of the Soviet constitution is seen in the assertion that "new constitutions are adopted when substantial changes occur in the relationship of class forces in the country." [5] Thus, a constitution is not regarded as a repository of certain sacrosanct political norms and principles but simply as a device designed to fulfill the alleged needs of a particular stage of historical development. The Soviet constitution has been able to be amended with great ease (the 1936 Constitution provided for amendment by a two-thirds majority of both chambers of the Supreme Soviet); amendment has been frequent and at times has even been initiated by executive decree. Soviet constitutions have little relationship to constitutionalism, for they have not effectively restrained the country's rulers.

Frequently, the 1936 Constitution has been honored more in the breach than in the observance, and some of its provisions have a decidedly hollow ring. Not the least of these is the assertion (article 3) that "All power in the U.S.S.R. belongs to the working people of town and country. . . ." Other passages of low credibility in the 1936 Constitution include article 15, which refers to the "sovereignty" of the union republics although article 14 stipulates 24 areas in which they are decidedly not sovereign. The right of the union republics to secede from the Soviet Union was incorporated into both the 1924 Constitution (article 4) and the 1936 Constitution (article 17), but an attempt to exercise the "right" would be treated as treason. The union republics have been empowered to enter into diplomatic relations with foreign states and to have their own military formations (articles 18-A and 18-B), but none has been permitted to exercise these constitutional "rights." The rights supposedly "guaranteed by law" in article 125 of the 1936 Constitution—including freedom of speech, press, assembly, and street processions and demonstrations—were rigorously limited by the provision that they be exercised "in conformity with the interests of the working people" and "to strengthen the socialist system." Most important, the 1936 Constitution says nothing meaningful about the vital role of the Communist Party in Soviet politics.

Although the above examples might prompt one to conclude that

[5] *Ibid.*, p. 216.

the 1936 Soviet Constitution is little more than a sham and a fraud, it can nevertheless be said to fulfill certain functions. Any constitution—even one that is violated—can serve as a useful device in giving a regime the appearance of a conventional political order and in prescribing certain formalities. A constitution is also a mark of respectability, serving as a symbol of "moral and political unity" and as a source of legitimation, even if only in a contrived manner. In the case of the 1936 Constitution, its adoption was also designed to impress gullible foreigners, who mistook constitutional provisions for Soviet political reality. It was also issued at a time when Moscow was seeking allies among the Western democracies. Stalin and his successors unabashedly proclaimed their constitution to be the "world's most democratic."

Yet this immodest claim did not prevent Khrushchev from asserting that the 1936 Constitution was "obsolete" and did not reflect the numerous changes that had occurred in the country. Accordingly, the Supreme Soviet established a constitutional commission in April, 1962, to draft a new document. Following the ouster of Khrushchev in October, 1964, the commission chairmanship was assumed by Leonid Brezhnev. However, the observance of the Soviet regime's fiftieth anniversary in 1967 did not include the promulgation of a new constitution. The failure to issue a new document probably reflected an inability to agree on its provisions—especially as they concerned the division of powers between Moscow and the union republics. Nor is it an easy task to prepare a constitution that is to prescribe the political order for a society supposedly on the threshold of "communism."

4. THE U.S.S.R. SUPREME SOVIET

Although the Supreme Soviet is referred to in the 1936 Constitution as the "highest organ of state power in the U.S.S.R." (article 30), this can be said to be true only in a highly formal and legalistic sense. It is a meaningful statement only insofar as all acts of the Soviet government are done in the name of the Supreme Soviet and are ultimately given blanket approval by that body. The largely honorific role of the Supreme Soviet in Russian political practice is seen in the fact that it meets for but a few days each year—usually eight or ten days at the most. Indeed, probably the most significant fact regarding the Supreme Soviet is that it consists of part-time legislators. Soviet spokesmen endeavor to justify this unusual, but highly revealing, fact by claiming it to be a virtue. By not being professional legislators, Supreme Soviet deputies are said to be closer to their constituents; and it is seriously argued that as amateur legislators, they can retain their jobs in the regular economy, can observe the laws in action, and remain closer to the electorate. "Bourgeois parliamentarians" are said to form a "caste of officials divorced from the people."[6] Why the CPSU should have a professional officialdom when professional full-time lawmaking by a legislative assembly is frowned upon has never been satisfactorily explained by Soviet spokesmen.[7]

The anomalous nature of the Supreme Soviet and its modest role should not prompt its being dismissed as irrelevant or as redundant. Potentially it could serve as a conventional parliament under the relevant provisions of the 1936 Constitution—if the duration of its meetings were lengthened and made more frequent and if freedom of debate and of legislative initiative were permitted. The Supreme Soviet is probably the most representative body in the Soviet political system and is certainly far more representative than the Party's Central Committee because of its large size, the broader nature of its membership, and its closer relationship to the constituencies.

Organization and Procedure. The U.S.S.R. Supreme Soviet consists of two chambers, the Soviet of the Union and the Soviet of

[6] V. Kotok, *The Soviet Representative System* (Moscow, n.d.), pp. 34 and 36. P. S. Romashkin, ed., *Fundamentals of Soviet Law* (Moscow, n.d.), p. 70. A. I. Lepeshkin, A. I. Kim, N. G. Mishin, and P. I. Romanov, *Kurs sovetskogo gosudarstvennogo prava* (Moscow, 1962), II, 395.

[7] Stalin asserted in an "election speech" following the adoption of the 1936 Constitution (on December 11, 1937) that "bourgeois deputies" (legislators) are "independent" of the voters once they are elected (after allegedly "fawning before them [the voters], swearing loyalty to them, and making a heap of promises"). By contrast, the Soviet deputy would have no such "independence." Although Stalin misunderstood—or chose to misunderstand—the relationship of the legislator and constituency in a democracy, he established a precedent regarding the deputy's dependence that was to survive his rule. I. V. Stalin, *Sochineniia* (Stanford, Calif.: The Hoover Institution, 1967), I [XIV], 261.

Nationalities, that have equal powers under the 1936 Constitution. The deputies of both chambers are elected at the same time for four-year terms. The newly elected Supreme Soviets are numbered consecutively, and each such convocation (*sozyv*) of four years' duration is divided into sessions, the numbering of which begins anew with each new convocation. The duration of each session has varied from a day or two to approximately one week. Ordinarily the Supreme Soviet meets twice a year, but prior to 1953, it was meeting hardly more frequently than once a year (five sessions in the course of four years). Both chambers commence their sessions and adjourn simultaneously.

The Soviet of the Union was originally elected on the basis of population, in accordance with a constitutional provision that set a ratio of "one deputy for every 300,000 of the population" (article 34). Consequently, the Soviet of the Union increased in size every four years, reflecting increased population. This occurred in all elections between 1937 and 1962, when the Soviet of the Union's membership rose from 569 to 791. The process was then reversed and the constitutional provision abandoned in the election of the Seventh Convocation in 1966, when the size of the Soviet of the Union was reduced to 767 deputies. The membership of the Soviet of Nationalities, on the other hand, is based on fixed representation for the various national territorial units. Each of the fifteen union republics has had 32 deputies since 1966 (25 prior to that); each autonomous republic has 11 deputies, each autonomous *oblast'* has 5, while each national area (*okrug*) has 1. The Soviet of Nationalities increased in size from 574 deputies in 1937 to 750 in 1966 as a result of the establishment of new union republics and the increase in the number of union republic deputies in 1966. It appears that the regime prefers that both chambers be of approximately equal numerical size. Thus the number of deputies in the Eighth Convocation, elected in 1970, remained at 767 in the Soviet of the Union and 750 in the Soviet of Nationalities.

The two chambers have equal, if limited, rights and neither exercises any special prerogatives. Both chambers employ the same procedures and organization and sit jointly as well as separately. Joint sessions are held to elect the Presidium of the Supreme Soviet and the U.S.S.R. Supreme Court and to appoint the U.S.S.R. Council of Ministers. The two chambers also meet jointly to hear reports on the economic plan, on the state budget, and on "important socio-cultural questions," as well as the report of the U.S.S.R. foreign minister. The Chairman of the Council of Ministers addresses joint sessions. These reports are discussed by the chambers meeting separately; if a law is adopted at a joint session, the chambers vote separately. Joint sessions are held in the large conference hall of the Great Kremlin Palace.

However, voting in the U.S.S.R. Supreme Soviet is, significantly, by show of hands only. Every vote in the Supreme Soviet has been said to be unanimous, and it is seriously—if not very convincingly—claimed that this practice is indicative of the country's "moral-political unity."[8] Actually it demonstrates the readily admitted fact that the Supreme Soviet conducts its business under the close direction of the Central Committee of the CPSU.[9] The Central Committee frequently meets prior to a session of the Supreme Soviet. Approximately three-quarters of the deputies are Party members, and this proportion has persisted in each of the quadrennial elections. Thus, the Party effectively dominates the so-called electoral bloc of communists and non-Party people. The unanimity in open voting renders irrelevant the provision in the 1936 Constitution (article 47) which calls for the use of a conciliation commission in the event of disagreement between the two chambers and for dissolution of the Supreme Soviet and the ordering of new elections by the Presidium of the Supreme Soviet if the commission should fail.

Disagreements do not arise in the plenary sessions of the chambers because of the Party's use of the Council of Elders and the committee system. A Council of Elders (*Sovet Stareishin*) is formed in each chamber in accordance with custom and not on the basis of any constitutional provision. It has approximately 150 members and consists of leaders of groups of deputies from the various republics, territories (*kraia*), and provinces (*oblasti*). This body rec-

[8] Lepeshkin et al., *op. cit.* (above, n. 6), II, 414.

[9] *Ibid.*, II, 399–400, 412. Also see D. A. Gaidukov et al., *Vysshie predstavitel'nye organy vlasti v SSSR* (Moscow: izd-vo "Nauka," 1969), p. 53.

ommends to its chamber the candidates who are elected as chairman and as vice chairmen (four) and the candidates who are elected to membership in the various standing committees. It also determines the agenda and approves the candidates of the various bodies and officials elected by the Supreme Soviet.

The committees—termed "commissions"—are identical in both chambers, although from 1957 to 1966 the Soviet of Nationalities alone had an Economic Commission, designed to take into account the particular needs of the republics in economic planning. The number of commissions was substantially increased in 1966 and made more specialized. Prior to 1966, both chambers had commissions on credentials, legislative proposals, the budget, and foreign affairs. The post-1970 roster of standing commissions is indicated in the diagram on p. 203. Most of the commissions deal with economic matters, although the Legislative Proposals Commission deals with all matters that do not come within the jurisdiction of other commissions. The commissions, which because of their large size also rely on subcommissions, are used to review bills that usually originate elsewhere. It is at the commission stage that amendments to a bill are more likely to be made and that additional relevant information is assembled and specialists are consulted. A unique feature of the Soviet commission system is the practice of referring a bill to more than one commission of the same chamber.[10] Commissions often meet prior to sessions of the Supreme Soviet.

The work of the commissions is coordinated by the Supreme Soviet's Presidium. Deputies do not initiate legislation as individuals. The vast majority of bills adopted by the Supreme Soviet are initiated by its Presidium or by the Council of Ministers (at times formally in conjunction with the Party's Central Committee) and by the Council of Elders. Very few bills have been initiated either by the commissions or by the union republics.[11] Informally, it is the Communist Party that determines whether any of these is to initiate a particular bill.

[10] *The Soviet Parliament, A Reference Book* (Moscow: Progress Publishers, 1967), pp. 55, 64.

[11] Lepeshkin et al., *op. cit.* (above, n. 6), II, 411.

SUPREME SOVIET OF THE U.S.S.R. AND THE BODIES IT ELECTS, FORMS, OR APPOINTS
(EIGHTH CONVOCATION, 1970-74)

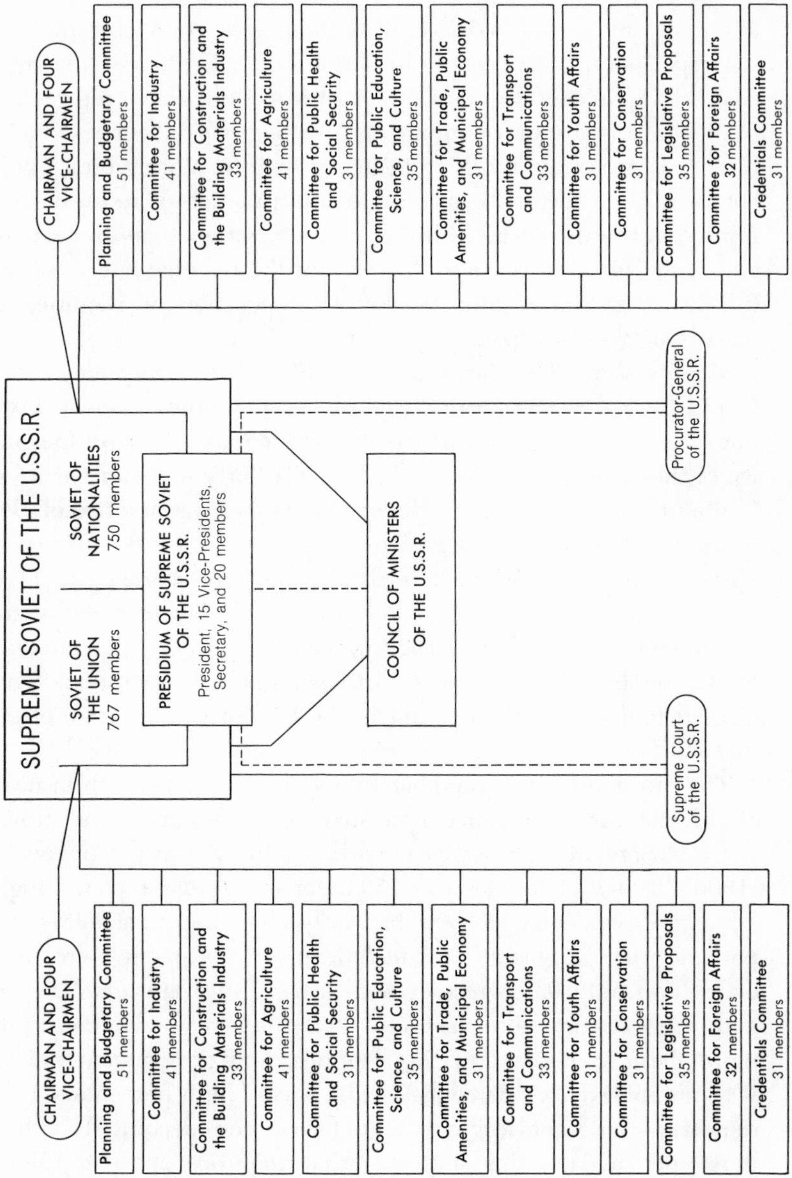

SOURCE: Adapted from *The Soviet Parliament* (Moscow: Progress Publishers, 1967), facing pp. 68–69; and *Izvestiia*, July 15, 1970.

The process of enactment involves the presentation of the bill by a rapporteur (*dokladchik*), and at times also by a co-rapporteur, who speaks on behalf of the initiating body. In the case of important bills sponsored by the Council of Ministers, they are presented by its Chairman or by ministers. All legislation concerning the budget is presented by the minister of finance. Voting on a bill becomes a mere formality in view of the practice of requiring unanimity; voting is on the bill in its entirety rather than on each article. The discussions on bills can hardly be characterized as a full-dress legislative debate, for the speeches of deputies are usually of a stereotyped nature.

Membership. The large membership of the Supreme Soviet would in itself severely limit the role of the deputy even if it were not circumscribed by the rigors of Party controls and by the brevity of the sessions. A person who is not a Party member has a very limited chance to become a deputy in view of the practice of electing three-quarters or more of the deputies from the ranks of the CPSU leadership and membership. Soviet spokesmen can claim, however, that no "bourgeois" legislative body has so many women in its membership as does the Supreme Soviet. The percentage of female deputies has risen from 16.3 percent in the Supreme Soviet elected in 1937 to 30.5 percent in the Eighth Convocation elected in 1970.

The Supreme Soviet membership consists of persons from nearly all of the Soviet Union's non-Russian nationalities and from a great variety of occupational fields. In the Seventh Convocation (1966–70) half of the deputies (50.2 percent) had completed higher education, while 5.9 percent had only elementary schooling; 20.5 percent were engineers and technicians; 2.2 percent were physicians; and only 0.9 percent (14 deputies) were lawyers. The Seventh Convocation also included Party officials, who constituted more than 18 percent of the deputies, and government officials, who numbered 15.1 percent. Usually a very high percentage of the deputies—three-quarters or more—have been decorated with orders and medals; this indicates that deputies are carefully recruited in the nominating process and that an effort is made to select persons of some distinction, including milkmaids and factory workers.

Yet, the tenure of the average deputy is not at all secure. Only the Communist Party leaders, high government officials, or nonpolitical eminent persons are likely to be reelected to the succeeding convocation of the Supreme Soviet. If the Soviet Union's rulers have quotas for the election of various groups of deputies, they have also established a high rate of turnover, eliminating approximately two-thirds of the deputies at each election by denying them nomination. Thus, in 1958, 62.3 percent of the Supreme Soviet deputies were newly elected; in 1962, the deputies who had not been previously elected numbered 70 percent; and in 1966, the newly elected deputies constituted 65.4 percent of the membership.[12] It is evident that the position of deputy is viewed as an award that should be rotated in the case of rank-and-file deputies and conferred repeatedly only in the case of the regime's luminaries.

The honorific nature of the deputy's position is also confirmed by the modest emolument that he receives. Deputies are paid 100 rubles per month but also continue to receive their salaries at their place of employment while attending Supreme Soviet sessions. They also receive a per diem of 15 rubles while attending sessions. In addition, deputies are given free rail, water, and air transportation. However, they are subject to recall by a majority of the electorate in their constituency. Thus, if a deputy should conduct himself improperly or in some way lose the confidence of the Communist Party leaders who arranged his nomination, his removal from office can be effected without difficulty.

Functions of the U.S.S.R. Supreme Soviet. Although Supreme Soviet deputies are hardly the "masters of the country" that the regime's pronouncements claim them to be, the Supreme Soviet performs certain important functions. Like the constitution, it serves as a source of legitimation by giving its approval to the acts and policies of the Soviet government. The Supreme Soviet enacts laws including constitutional amendments, organic laws that define the structure and jurisdiction of state organs, and a variety of ordinary laws. In addition, it enacts economic planning and budgetary laws, including tax measures. The Soviet government's fiscal year coincides with the calendar year; the state budget is usually

[12] V. Kotok, *op. cit.* (above, n. 6), p. 35 and *The Soviet Parliament* (above, n. 10), p. 42.

adopted in December, although in Stalin's time it was adopted as late as the summer, when more than half of the fiscal year had expired. The annual and long-range economic plans have the force of law, even though the goals are not always fulfilled.

The Supreme Soviet also has the task of approving, but not discussing, the numerous decrees (*ukazy*) issued by or in the name of its Presidium during the lengthy periods when the "Soviet parliament" is not in session. The decrees are issued and signed by the Chairman and Secretary of the Presidium, are published within seven days, and have the force of law. The Supreme Soviet is thus presented with a series of *faits accomplis;* its approval of the decrees, while apparently necessary, can hardly be said to add appreciably to their legal force. Yet such formalities can be important, and the Supreme Soviet gives its approval with the usual unanimous vote. Often as many as half or more of the laws enacted by the Supreme Soviet are Presidium decrees that it summarily approves.[13]

The Supreme Soviet must give its approval to the appointment of the Council of Ministers (ratifying the entire slate of ministers at once) and to the establishment of new ministries and government agencies, and the definition of their competence and jurisdiction. It approves the appointment of the Procurator-General of the U.S.S.R., the country's leading legal official, for a seven-year term; it also elects the U.S.S.R. Supreme Court every five years. The Presidium of the Supreme Soviet must also be elected every four years so that the parent body's "supreme authority" can be readily exercised on a permanent proxy basis.

The infrequent sessions of the Supreme Soviet provide an opportunity for the public criticism of individual ministers and ministries whom the Party leadership has singled out for embarrassment. While this practice hardly demonstrates that the Supreme Soviet exercises initiative in performing a "control" function, it provides a useful means of occasionally calling an administrator to account. Although relatively few deputies are able to obtain recognition to address the Supreme Soviet, those who do so can use the opportunity to place in the stenographic record specific requests emanat-

[13] Lepeshkin et. al., *op. cit.* (above, n. 6), II, p. 418.

ing from their constituencies. Such requests frequently deal with budgetary items, and they provide a means of bringing to the attention of particular ministries the needs and complaints of a republic, *oblast'*, or city. The greater participation of deputies in the work of the standing commissions since 1966 has also provided opportunities for making officials in the Moscow ministries more aware of the concerns of the deputies' constituencies.

The Supreme Soviet provides a medium through which the regime can issue foreign policy pronouncements, as well as serving as a sounding board for its foreign minister. Joint sessions of the Supreme Soviet have approved declarations, appeals, statements, and messages dealing with particular problems and issues; expressing support for the regime's foreign policy; and denouncing the alleged "aggressive actions of international reaction." The usefulness of the Supreme Soviet in this respect has been especially evident since June, 1955, with its participation in the Inter-Parliamentary Union. Soviet membership in that international body has given the regime greater respectability at home and abroad and has led also to the establishment of the Parliamentary Group of the U.S.S.R. Thus, although this organization of deputies mainly attempts to promote the Soviet regime's foreign policy objectives in the annual conferences of the Inter-Parliamentary Union, it also provides a means of promoting among its members greater awareness of their role as deputies.

The modest enhancement of the Supreme Soviet's role that has occurred in the post-Stalin period has not enabled it to compete effectively with the Communist Party apparatus as an initiator of legislation or as a source of authority to whom the highest office holders are directly responsible. The head of government is not required to answer random questions put to him by individual deputies, although the practice of having him deliver a report to the Supreme Soviet does offer a quasi-precedent for having him defend his statements. However, the Party leadership, especially insofar as it does not hold high governmental positions, is not accountable to the Supreme Soviet in any way. The Party apparatus continues to fill self-appointed roles and operates beyond the purview of the regime's truncated legislature. Despite this, the Supreme Soviet does provide a medium for the muted articulation of regional and group interests.

5. THE PRESIDIUM OF THE SUPREME SOVIET

The Soviet regime is somewhat unique in possessing a collegial chief of state or titular executive in the form of the U.S.S.R. Supreme Soviet's Presidium. This body—elected from its membership by the Supreme Soviet at a joint session, for the duration of the convocation—consists of a chairman, 15 vice chairmen, a secretary, and 20 members (16 prior to 1966). It performs many different functions and illustrates well the fusion of legislative, executive, and even quasi-judicial powers in a single body.

The Presidium's role as a legislative body is exercised on the basis of powers delegated to it by the Supreme Soviet, although the 1936 Constitution solemnly proclaimed that "the legislative power of the U.S.S.R. is exercised exclusively by the Supreme Soviet" (article 32). The delegation of legislative authority is necessitated by the fact that the Supreme Soviet is only rarely in session. During the lengthy intervals between sessions the Presidium can issue decrees (*ukazy*) and even amend the Constitution—as it did on October 10, 1945, when it raised the age requirement for deputies from 18 to 23 years or whenever it hastily creates a new ministry or executive agency. It can issue decrees on any matter, including taxation, economic policy, organization of industry, agriculture and transportation, and law enforcement. The Chairman and Secretary sign all decrees. The Presidium also issues ordinances (*postanovleniia*), which are designed to reinforce its actions in organizational and administrative questions. At times important decisions are adopted and enacted jointly by the Presidium and the U.S.S.R. Council of Ministers and the Central Committee of the CPSU. Although in theory the Presidium is accountable to the Supreme Soviet, in practice it exercises independent powers much of the time.

In addition to acting as an interim legislative body, the Presidium performs such functions as convoking regular and extraordinary sessions of the Supreme Soviet and in general supervising the work of the parent body and its commissions. It calls for new elections upon expiration of the deputies' four-year terms; it determines the constituencies for both chambers and approves the composition of the Central Election Commission. It appoints and dismisses ministers at the suggestion of the Chairman of the Council of Ministers, while the Supreme Soviet is not in session. The Presidium also appoints and recalls ambassadors, and receives foreign envoys accredited to the Soviet Union; it ratifies and denounces treaties, although this is a formality. The Presidium grants Soviet citizenship and can deprive persons of it or permit its renunciation. It also establishes and grants awards, decorations, and titles of honor.

The executive function of supervising the military is conducted by the Presidium. It appoints and removes the high command of the armed services, although the relevant decisions are initiated in the Party apparatus dealing with personnel. The Presidium fixes the order of service ranks and confers the rank of Marshal of the Soviet Union. It is empowered to order general or partial mobilization and can proclaim a state of war or martial law in all or part of the country in the interests of defense, public order, or state security.

The Presidium receives petitions for justice, exercises the right of pardon, and can issue partial or full amnesties. It performs an important function in receiving letters, appeals, complaints, and requests from ordinary citizens. Many of these communications are simply transmitted to the administrative agency concerned. The Presidium is in a position to collect a variety of information and proposals useful to the leadership of Party and government. It also serves as a means by which the ordinary citizen might obtain redress of a grievance.

Although the Presidium is primarily a legislative and executive body, it also performs quasi-judicial functions. The 1936 Constitution states that the Presidium "gives interpretations of the laws of the U.S.S.R. in operation" (article 49). In practice it is simpler for the Presidium to interpret laws by issuing new laws by decree. The Supreme Court of the U.S.S.R. is, according to the Judiciary Law of February 12, 1957, responsible to the Supreme Soviet and (in practice) to its Presidium. The Court is also obligated to refer to the Presidium suggestions on matters that should be determined by legislative procedure and suggestions on questions of the interpretation of the laws.[14] The Presidium is empowered to annul acts of the U.S.S.R. and union republic councils of ministers, as well as orders and instructions of the U.S.S.R. Procurator-General that it finds contrary to law.

The Presidium publishes all of its own decrees and the laws adopted by the Supreme Soviet. These are to be found in the *Gazette of the Supreme Soviet of the USSR* (*Vedomosti Verkhovnogo Soveta SSSR*); the Presidium also publishes the newspaper *Izvestiia,* official organ of the Soviet government. The Presidium's staff records all changes in the laws, including those decrees and laws that have been rescinded or superseded.

In practice the Presidium is supposed to meet at least once in two months, although it is said to be a "continuously acting" body. Its meetings are not public and little is known about them. On occasion it has functioned through committees. It is very likely that when decrees have had to be issued without delay they have simply been signed by the Presidium's Chairman and Secretary, and have subsequently been approved by the entire body as a formality. It is evident that the Presidium's staff and its various departments function on a permanent basis.

The Presidium's membership is rather diverse and is intended to reflect that of the parent body. It usually includes several women, as well as members from ordinary walks of life (as, for example, a weaver, tractor driver, collective farm chairman), in addition to a military figure and an academic person. The Presidium also includes a substantial number of non-Russian members.

The leading Party Secretary (General Secretary of the CPSU prior to 1953 and since 1966) is a member of the Presidium, if he is not also head of government as Chairman of the U.S.S.R. Council of Ministers. Thus, Khrushchev was a Presidium member until he became head of government in 1958, and Brezhnev remained a Presidium member after becoming First Secretary of the CPSU in 1964. This practice is designed to provide the Party chief with a nominal but quasi-prestigious position in the government so that

[14] *Sbornik zakonov SSSR i Ukazov Prezidiuma Verkhovnogo Soveta SSSR, 1938 g.–1961 g.* (Moscow, 1961), pp. 789–790.

he can participate in purely state and diplomatic functions as the occasion may warrant. A substantial majority of the Presidium's members are members or candidate members of the CPSU Central Committee.

The Chairman of the Presidium performs many of the ceremonial functions of a President, including, more recently, state visits to foreign countries. However, the use of a collegial body to fulfill the functions of chief of state places certain limitations on the Chairman's role. The Presidium is collegial because of the Soviet rationalization that collegiality is the equivalent of "democracy"—a position that conveniently ignores the crucial criterion of the accountability of a popularly elected president.[15] The multinational nature of the Soviet Union, however, provides a more practical reason for a collegial executive. The fifteen vice chairmen of the Presidium represent the union republics; by custom they are the chairmen of the presidiums of the republic supreme soviets.

The Chairman of the Presidium, although a member of the Party's Politburo on what might be termed in practice an *ex officio* basis, has not always exercised the same power and influence. Such chairmen as Mikhail I. Kalinin (1938–46), Nikolai M. Shvernik (1946–53), and Kliment Voroshilov (1953–60) were not members of the inner ruling circle, despite being Politburo members and chiefs of state. More recent Presidium chairmen such as Leonid I. Brezhnev (1960–64), Anastas I. Mikoyan (1964–65), and Nikolai V. Podgorny (who succeeded Mikoyan) have played important roles in policy-making. Although the chairmanship has served both as a sinecure and as a figurehead post for a somewhat benign Party leader useful to the regime as a front, its real and potential significance should not be ignored. In a highly formalized regime any chief of state is in a position to exercise some degree of influence, and if the role of the Supreme Soviet should be enhanced, it is

[15] During the discussion preceding the adoption of the 1936 Constitution, Stalin displayed a certain sense of humor when he expressed opposition to the popular election of the Presidium's Chairman on the grounds that such a president might counterpose himself to the supposedly omnipotent Supreme Soviet. Stalin reasoned that a collegial executive would be "most democratic" and subordinate to the Supreme Soviet. I. Stalin, *Voprosy Leninizma,* 11th ed. (Moscow: Gospolitizdat, 1952), p. 569.

likely that the Chairman of the Presidium would gain as a result. However, enhancement of the authority of a governmental body would be at the expense of the Party apparatus; and the Soviet chief of state would, moreover, have a rival beneficiary within the central government in the person of its head, the Chairman of the Council of Ministers.

6. THE U.S.S.R. COUNCIL OF MINISTERS

The government of the Soviet Union is usually equated with the Council of Ministers, which, according to the 1936 Constitution, is said to be the "highest executive and administrative organ of state authority." It is appointed by the Supreme Soviet at a joint session at the beginning of the first session of each new convocation, although ministers are obviously initially selected by the Party leadership and apparatus officials responsible for personnel. The practice of having the Council of Ministers go through the motions of resigning and of being formally reappointed is designed to provide an innocuous means of demonstrating its "responsibility" to the U.S.S.R. Supreme Soviet. Stalin, during the most frightening years of his brutal dictatorship, would perform this ritual of "resigning" as head of government as if to mock his subjects and "their" deputies who had no choice but to sanction his reappointment.

While in terms of constitutional theory, the Council of Ministers appears to function like a cabinet under the parliamentary system, in reality it has little to do with the "Soviet parliament." It oversees the functioning of a vast state bureaucracy and carries out the Party's policies at the administrative level. It resolves legal problems in cooperation with the Presidium of the Supreme Soviet, and it initiates much legislation, although undoubtedly this is usually done at the Party's behest. The Council of Ministers supervises the economy by determining human and material resources allocation, investment, and prices. It is responsible for carrying out the Party's policies in cultural and in military matters as well as in relations with foreign states. It also supervises a substantial part of the activities of the councils of ministers of the union republics and can annul those of their acts that it can claim fall within its own competence.

The Council of Ministers is empowered to issue ordinances (*postanovleniia*) and regulations (*rasporiazheniia*) based on its decisions in the areas within its competence. Ordinances are generally normative acts and are said to be collegial; while regulations usually are nonnormative, have a more specific and concrete application, and are simply signed by the chairman or his deputy. Both kinds of acts are supposedly based on law, have the same juridical standing, are enforceable over the entire territory of the Soviet Union, and provide one of the bases for enactments of the governments of the union republics. Highly important matters are dealt with by joint ordinances adopted by the Central Committee of the CPSU and by the U.S.S.R. Council of Ministers.

The Council of Ministers is a large and unwieldy body headed by a Chairman and consisting of several First Deputy Chairmen and of as many as eight or nine Deputy Chairmen and numerous ministries, state committees, and other administrative agencies. The total membership has reached more than ninety. It includes as *ex officio* members the chairmen of the councils of ministers of the fifteen union republics; this unusual practice is based on a constitutional amendment of May 10, 1957.

The size of the Council of Ministers has made necessary the establishment of an "inner cabinet"—the Presidium of the Council of Ministers—which consists of the Chairman, First Deputy Chairmen, and Deputy Chairmen. Although such a body and its Bureau apparently existed in Stalin's time after 1946, the present Presidium was established in March, 1953. Its exact relationship to the Council of Ministers is not known, but it appears to direct the Council's work and determine its organization and composition. It also operates through committees that consult with particular ministries before recommending the issuance of regulations by the Presidium. It is likely that the Presidium functions with considerable flexibility and that it frequently acts in the name of the entire Council of Ministers.

The Chairman of the Council of Ministers is in a sense the "premier" or "prime minister" of the Soviet Union. However, the one-party system and the fact that the incumbent Chairman need not be the leading figure in the CPSU render the use of the term misleading. The Chairmanship has been held by Lenin, Stalin, and

Khrushchev, as well as by secondary leaders. As the first Chairman of the Council of People's Commissars (renamed Council of Ministers in March, 1946) Lenin exercised great influence because of his generally undisputed role in the Party Politburo. His successor as head of government was Alexei Rykov, who held the post from 1924 to 1929, when he was ousted from the Party for having participated in the "Right Opposition." Rykov was succeeded by Viacheslav Molotov, who served as Chairman from 1930 to 1941, and as foreign minister from 1939. (It suited Stalin's purposes to have the Soviet government headed by a colleague during the 1920's and 1930's while he established and consolidated his personal dictatorship as the Party's General Secretary.) Stalin retained the highest Party post and also headed the government from 1941 to his death in 1953. Georgii Malenkov held the Chairmanship from March, 1953, to February, 1955, when he was succeeded by Nikolai Bulganin, who served until March, 1958. Nikita Khrushchev was Chairman and also CPSU First Secretary from 1958 to October, 1964, when he was succeeded as head of government by Alexei Kosygin.

The Chairman is a member of the Politburo. Although he nominally heads the government apparatus, his position is not necessarily secure because of that fact. His influence in the Politburo may be limited and his position may become untenable should he align himself with an unsuccessful opposition group within the leadership—as happened to Rykov and Bulganin. Most Chairmen have been summarily removed or demoted, as they do not have fixed terms of office. A Party chief who simultaneously heads the government undoubtedly has enhanced powers as well as greater prestige than one who does not head the government. The head of government who has not made his career in the Party apparatus (Rykov, Molotov, Bulganin, Kosygin) is especially vulnerable. The Chairman risks the possibility of being accused of opposing the government to the Party, of advocating or pursuing policies that are inimical to the Party, or of having perpetrated administrative failures.

The Chairmanship is potentially a powerful position if the incumbent should succeed in mobilizing the interests of the administrators and economic managers. It is also a position that could possibly retain its viability and prestige in the event that the party leadership were to experience a degree of fragmentation that would prove fatal. The Party apparatus seeks to prevent any independent development of the government by providing for an interlocking arrangement under which most members of the Council of Ministers are also members or candidate members of the Central Committee. While this practice does not in itself guarantee an identity of interests between Party and government apparatus, it does appear to be an effort to apply Lenin's advice to the Party's Tenth Congress to foster a "fusion" of the Party and soviet "summits." [16]

7. MINISTRIES AND RELATED AGENCIES

State ownership of the economy in the Soviet Union has made necessary the establishment of a great variety of ministries and other governmental agencies. Their number and the names of many of them have been subject to fairly frequent change despite the fact that this is done by constitutional amendment. Originally these bodies were called commissariats, at Trotsky's suggestion, in order to emphasize the regime's uniqueness and revolutionary nature. However, Stalin decided to adopt the "bourgeois" term "minister," and this was done on March 15, 1946. The move was rationalized on the grounds that various local bodies were also termed commissariats and that it was advisable to use the conventional term "ministry" to clarify the status and competence of the union and republic agencies of government.

There are three types of ministries in the Soviet Union: the All-Union, Union-Republican, and Republic ministries. The All-Union ministries are to be found only in Moscow and are exclusively in the jurisdiction of the U.S.S.R.; they function directly over the entire territory of the Soviet Union and do not operate through republic ministries of the same name. Examples of All-Union ministries are foreign trade, merchant marine, railroads, and a variety of industrial ministries—including aviation industry, chemicals,

[16] V. I. Lenin, *Polnoe Sobranie Sochinenii, op. cit.* (above, n. 1), XLIII, 15.

electronics, shipbuilding, machine-building, and electrical engineering. The second type of ministry, the Union-Republican, is a joint type found both in the U.S.S.R. Council of Ministers and in the union republic councils of ministers. Each such ministry in Moscow functions in the field through the union republic ministries of the same name. The Union-Republican category includes such ministries as foreign affairs, culture, finance, public health, higher and specialized secondary education, and a variety of economic ministries. The third type of ministry is found exclusively at the republic level and includes social insurance, communal (municipal) economy, and vehicular transportation and highways.

The U.S.S.R. Council of Ministers consists of ministries of the first and second categories, while the union republic councils of ministers consist of ministries of the second and third type. Ministries have been transferred abruptly from one category to another. Foreign Affairs was in the first category until 1944, when it was placed in the second group. The Ministry of Justice was shifted from the second to the third category in 1956 and was abolished by 1963; however, it was reestablished as a ministry of the second type in September, 1970, as part of an anticrime campaign. The Ministry of Internal Affairs (MVD) was transferred from the second to the third category in 1960 and was subsequently renamed Ministry for the Protection of Public Order (MOOP). However, in July, 1966, MOOP was restored to the second category and became a joint Union-Republican ministry; and in 1968 it was again renamed the MVD. The practice of changing the status of ministries reflects the apparent need to enhance control by Moscow or to encourage local initiative in an attempt to find more effective solutions to problems.

Some ministries of the first and second type have been consolidated or divided at times. The regime has also employed a variety of "state committees." Those committees that are "of the Council of Ministers" have the status of ministries, while others have had subordinate status, indicating that they are "attached to the Council of Ministers." The Committee of State Security provides an example of a "committee" that is actually a powerful ministry of the second (Union-Republican) type and that has subordinated to it "committees" of the same name in the republic councils of ministers. Cinematography, for instance, is a Soviet Governmental endeavor that has been at various times a separate ministry, a unit in the Ministry of Culture, and a state committee. The civil air fleet (*Aeroflot*—the government-owned Soviet commercial air line) was organized as a Main Administration (*glavnoe upravlenie*) attached to the Council of Ministers until 1964, when it was given the status of an All-Union Ministry of Civil Aviation. These examples illustrate the variety of organizational forms available to the governmental leadership and the flexibility with which they are sometimes employed.

The importance of individual ministers varies with the ministries headed by them. Certain ministers have enjoyed rather long tenure and have a degree of technical expertise, while others have held ministerial posts on a "probationary" status. In general, a career in the governmental apparatus is not compatible with one in the Party apparatus, and it is relatively rare to find a Party secretary or Central Committee department head appointed to a ministership. Women have rarely served as ministers, although in the post-Stalin period they have headed the ministries of health and culture. Ministers are generally members of the Central Committee of the Party and are usually deputies to the U.S.S.R. Supreme Soviet.

The minister bears sole responsibility for the conduct of the ministry's work before the Council of Ministers and is indirectly responsible to the Supreme Soviet. This is in accordance with the principle of "unitary headship" (*edinonachalie*) advocated by Lenin in order to assure effective and rapid action and the fixing of responsibility. The principle of collegiality is also recognized and finds application in the institution of the collegium (*kollegiia*), which is found in each ministry. The collegium has from nine to eleven members and consists of the minister (who presides over its meetings), several of the deputy ministers (usually numbering from two to five), and the heads of important departments. It is expected to discuss important questions affecting the ministry's work, but it is not to involve itself in operational matters. Collegium decisions can be carried out only by an order (*prikaz*) issued by the minister because the collegium as such has no authority. In the event of disagreement, the minister is authorized to carry out his own decision but is required to inform the Council of Ministers of this. Members of the collegium can appeal the matter to the Council of Ministers, although the likelihood of this occurring is not great.[17]

8. SOVIET ELECTIONS: THEIR CONDUCT AND MEANING

Although the results of Soviet elections are already known prior to election day, the regime has nevertheless developed what is probably the most elaborate electoral system known to any one-party system. That this is not entirely a matter of sham and political ritual can be seen from the rationale for Soviet elections offered at the conclusion of this section. Soviet spokesmen and political writers frequently attack the electoral systems of Western European countries and the United States, presumably on the assumption that such attacks will somehow make the obvious fundamental defects in the Soviet system of elections less evident or more acceptable. They cite the phenomenally high percentage of voter participation in Soviet elections (uniformly no less than 99 percent) as contrasted with other countries and contend that bourgeois elections are often determined by pluralities rather than by absolute majorities, and that the suffrage is limited by residence and other requirements, as well as by gerrymandering. The Soviet argument ignores the fact that Russian elections provide no incentive to gerrymander constituencies because the outcome is determined in advance through the nomination of but one candidate. Advocates of the Soviet system, in effect, assert that a "genuinely democratic" electoral system is one that, like theirs, permits no choice between political parties or even between two candidates from the single ruling party.

Despite the lack of any electoral contest, the Soviet rulers have made suffrage general, equal, direct, and secret since 1937. Prior to the adoption of the 1936 Constitution, the suffrage was unequal (at the expense of the rural population), a small percentage of the

[17] I. N. Ananov, *Ministerstva v SSSR* (Moscow, 1960), p. 160.

population was disfranchised, only the lowest soviets were elected directly while the higher soviets were elected indirectly, and voting was open and by lists and not by secret ballot for individual candidacies; voting prior to 1937 was in electoral assemblies often convened in production enterprises. The right of suffrage now applies to all persons who are 18 years of age. The sole restriction in law is that mentally ill persons are denied the right to vote on the basis of legal certification of such a condition. There is no literacy test, although the Soviet Union is a country having a high rate of literacy. Persons under court sentence for crimes are not disfranchised, although they were denied the right to vote prior to a constitutional amendment adopted on December 25, 1958. Thus, persons serving sentences in Soviet forced labor camps and prisons for political and criminal offenses apparently have the right to vote for the regime that has incarcerated them.

The nearly all-inclusive electorate votes for deputies to the various local soviets and to the republic and U.S.S.R. supreme soviets; it also votes for the judges of the courts of first instance, the People's Court. All other officials are appointed or elected by the various soviets. Deputies to the U.S.S.R. Supreme Soviet must be at least 23 years of age, while for those elected to the union republic and autonomous republic supreme soviets the age requirement is 21 and members of local soviets must be at least 18 years of age.

The election of deputies to the various soviets is based on the single-member district, with one deputy from each constituency or election district (*izbiratel'nyi okrug*). In view of the fact that more than two million deputies are elected to the entire range of soviets from villages to the U.S.S.R. Supreme Soviet, the number of overlapping constituencies is very great.[18] A voter must vote for one deputy to each of the two chambers of the U.S.S.R. Supreme Soviet and for one deputy to the unicameral supreme soviet of the union

[18] The origins of the Soviet system of elections are discussed in George B. Carson, Jr., *Electoral Practices in the USSR* (New York: Frederick A. Praeger, 1955). For the results of a field study of Soviet elections, see Max E. Mote, *Soviet Local and Republic Elections* (Stanford, Calif., 1965). Also see Jerome M. Gilison, "Soviet Elections as a Measure of Dissent: The Missing One Percent," *American Political Science Review*, LXII, No. 3 (September, 1968), 814–826.

republic in which he lives. If he lives in an autonomous republic he must vote for a deputy to its supreme soviet. He will also vote for a deputy to his *oblast'* or *krai* soviet and if he lives in a city he will vote for a deputy to the city soviet; if the city is large enough to be divided into boroughs (*raiony*), he must also vote for a deputy to the *raion* soviet. If he lives in a rural area he will vote for the deputy to the *oblast'* or *krai* soviet, but will also vote for a deputy to the rural *raion* (district) soviet and for one to his village soviet.

Nomination is tantamount to being elected and is accomplished not through primary elections but by means of a unique process. An individual cannot simply file for a deputy's seat and present the voters with his candidacy. Only "public organizations" such as the Communist Party's local organizations, trade unions, cooperatives, the Komsomol (Communist youth organization), and "cultural societies" down to the *raion* level propose candidates for nomination, although in the less populous constituencies the individual's role may be somewhat less circumscribed by the nominating process. The qualifications of potential candidates are discussed in factory and other nominating meetings. The process, always conducted under the watchful eyes and pervasive tutelage of the responsible Communist Party officials, leads to an official public nominating meeting. This is a very formal public meeting in the large constituencies, complete with ceremony and entertainment. The candidate who has the Party organization's approval is nominated by acclamation, the matter having been decided in advance.

The nomination is then presented to the election commission for the particular constituency. The officials of the nominating meeting certify that it was conducted in accordance with the election statute, and the nominee agrees in writing to accept the candidacy. In practice there is but one candidate for each position. The sole exception is the practice of also nominating prominent members of the Party leadership as supreme soviet deputies in certain constituencies. The number of such honorary nominations that a particular leader receives is significant, but all such nominations are declined, except for the one in the constituency which the leader will represent. Soviet election laws do not exclude the possibility of electoral contests within a single electoral district, but political practice has served to prevent the registration of more than one candidate for each position.

Registration of candidates is one of the functions of the election commission that is found in every constituency. Election commissions are also established in every precinct and are charged with the actual conduct of the particular election; their membership is unpaid and thus elections cost the Soviet regime very little. The commissions are appointed by the executive body of the soviet that is being elected; their volunteer membership comes from the same public organizations that participate in the nominating process and numbers more than eight million persons for the entire country. Their administration of the electoral machinery is supervised by the All-Union Central Election Commission for elections to the U.S.S.R. Supreme Soviet and by republic central election commissions for the elections to republic supreme soviets and to local soviets.

The size of constituencies varies. The largest are for the election of deputies to the two chambers of the U.S.S.R. Supreme Soviet. The smallest may have but one hundred voters in the case of a remote village soviet. The size of the constituencies for the Council of Nationalities varies with each republic, as does the size of the constituencies for the republic supreme soviets. The boundaries of the constituencies for each soviet are determined prior to each election by the executive body of the soviet that is being elected.

The lack of electoral contests does not preclude election campaigning. The network of agitators is fully activated during the ten days preceding the election. Agitators must visit each voter in the precinct explaining the virtues and qualifications of the sole candidate. The mass media publicize the biography of each candidate to the larger soviets and urge a resounding vote of confidence for the regime. The candidate spends no money campaigning but holds meetings with voters; in the smaller constituencies the voters are able to apprise the candidate of their needs and expectations, although he cannot usually offer them very effective assurances that their wishes will be heeded during his term of office. While such meetings do provide one means of determining the grievances of a particular constituency, they are also used to explain and justify the regime's policies.

The voting is administered by the electoral commission of several members that functions in each precinct (*uchastok*). Lists of voters prepared by the commission on the basis of local records are posted in public prior to the election and are subject to correction. Elections, which are held on Sunday, have a festive quality. The voter usually identifies himself by showing his domestic passport, the possession of which is required by law, and he is given as many ballots as there are candidates (and positions to be filled). The printed form of the ballot provides space for more than one candidate and the voter is instructed to cross out all names except that of the candidate for whom he is voting, but in practice each ballot contains only one name. Thus, the voter has no need to go into a booth unless he possibly wishes to cross out the name of the sole candidate as an act of protest—and this can attract unfavorable attention. Indeed, the ballot need not be marked but can simply be deposited in the ballot box. A write-in candidacy as an alternative to the Communist Party's candidate would be futile and is not recognized by law because only organizations can nominate candidates and each nomination must be registered by the appropriate election commission. Crossing out the name of the candidate and writing in the name of another is regarded as invalidating the ballot.

The high percentage of voter participation in Soviet elections is due to the practice of checking off the names of those on the list of voters who have voted (thus the authorities know who has not voted). Usually most persons vote by mid-afternoon; but if it is evident that the voting is slow, agitators and "activists" are dispatched to call on those who have not yet voted and remind them of their civic obligation. Refusal to vote is regarded as an unpatriotic act. Even the sick are expected to vote and ballot boxes are brought to the bedside of hospital patients. Voting occurs on ships that are at sea on election day if there are at least twenty-five voters aboard; the votes are added to those cast in the ship's home port. Passengers on long-distance trains vote in special precincts while in transit.

A unique feature of Soviet elections is the provision for absentee voters who before embarking on their journey apply for a certificate which they present at the polls wherever they may be on election day. Thus, the absentee voter votes not for the candidates in the several constituencies in which he actually resides, but for the candidates on the ballot in the precinct in which he happens to present himself. Election commissions in resort areas have had to print additional ballots in order to accommodate the influx of voting tourists. Under such a system it is possible for the candidate to obtain more than 100 percent of the (registered) vote in his constituency. The practice of being able to vote in a constituency in which you do not reside obviously demeans the concept of a mandate conferred on a deputy by his constituents. In the view of the Soviet rulers, whom one votes for is not important; what is important is that a person votes somewhere to register his support of the regime.

Despite the fact that all candidates are unopposed and are favored by 99 percent of the voters (assuming that there is no falsification of returns), a minute fraction of the candidates fails to obtain a majority of the votes cast. This can occur only in small constituencies where the candidate is well known to the electorate and does not enjoy its confidence despite the endorsement given him by local CPSU officials. In such cases—and there have been more than two hundred in certain elections to local soviets—a second election must be held in those constituencies after a new candidate has been nominated. However, it is virtually impossible for a candidate to be rejected in the average-sized constituency. Indeed, his chances of winning are usually better than 9,999 in 10,000. The regime's principal leaders fare even better, for they are assured election not only to the U.S.S.R. Supreme Soviet but to republic and local soviets as well.

Recall of deputies is provided for both by the 1936 Constitution and by a law of October 30, 1959. Recall can be initiated by any of the public organizations that nominate deputies or by "assemblies of toilers." Deputies can be recalled for having engaged in conduct unworthy of their position or for having lost the confidence of constituents (in practice, the confidence of the ruling hierarchy in the case of larger constituencies). Meetings of voters are convened by organizations and the recall proposal is voted on by a show of hands; a special election commission determines whether or not a majority of the voters in the constituency favor the recall. The practice of recall is another means of disciplining the deputy and keeping him dependent.

Soviet elections do serve certain functions despite their general failure to give the voter a choice between candidates, political parties, and alternative policies. The ritual of voting is maintained because the regime must hold elections of some kind in order to give itself the appearance of being democratic. Although the outcome of Soviet elections is never in doubt, the elected representatives who sit in the numerous soviets can claim to enjoy popular support, as demonstrated in their victory at the polls. The election campaign permits the regime to explain its policies and to justify the correctness of its actions. The holding of such plebiscitary elections serves to enable the regime to claim that its policies have earned the overwhelming—and for their purposes unanimous—support of its subjects. By regularly holding such rituals of acclamation the regime can assert that its mandate to rule has been renewed. Elections are also used as a means of supposedly demonstrating the "unparalleled moral-political unity" of Soviet society. It is probably for this reason that electoral contests, even between communist candidates, have not occurred; they would nullify this mass exercise in contrived unity and also terminate the so-called bloc of communists and non-Party people. The elections also have a psychological significance because the voter is not permitted to boycott the balloting ritual but must participate and make a commitment to the regime. Thus, the voter is periodically reminded that there is no alternative to the Communist party and its regime, and that dissent is not permitted.

If Soviet elections require no manipulation, apart from assuring the nearly total turnout, the same cannot be said of the nominating process, where a behind-the-scenes choice is actually made. At that stage an effort is made to select a candidate who will inspire public confidence and who has achieved recognition in his or her profession or vocation. The purpose is to select as deputies people who will generate support for the regime's policies and contribute to their implementation. Deputies to the various soviets are not genuine legislators insofar as they do not initiate bills and are not policy-makers. However, the regime endeavors to nominate and elect to the soviets the "best people," who will then endorse the government at each level and approve its conduct. Nomination and election as a deputy is both a reward and a duty, but it does not confer power. Those deputies who hold administrative posts in the government and in the CPSU apparatus do wield power, but not by virtue of their elective positions as deputies. It is in the Party and government bureaucracies that decisions are made, and it is the elected soviets that are responsible for their fulfillment.

CHAPTER 7

ADMINISTRATION: CENTRAL AND LOCAL

The Soviet regime operates one of the world's largest and most complex bureaucratic structures. It functions by means of ministries and related agencies, as well as government corporations and state-owned economic enterprises. Each soviet at every level has an executive committee (*ispolkom*) that, in theory, supervises the administrative departments required by its particular jurisdiction and economy. In practice these departments are also subordinate to the corresponding body at the next higher level and indirectly are subordinate to the appropriate ministry or agency of union republic or All-Union jurisdiction. The size and scope of the Soviet administrative apparatus and its many distinctive features set it apart from the more conventional administrative structures found in constitutional systems.

1. THE RUSSIAN ADMINISTRATIVE TRADITION

Historically, Russian public officials served an imperial political order at the discretion of the ruling autocrat or of persons capable of influencing him or acting in his name. Officials were not responsible to the public but to a regime upon which they were utterly dependent—but one which also gave them considerable authority in dealing with its subjects. Although their authority could be withdrawn abruptly should they be discredited, the powers exercised by local officials were sufficient to promote arrogance, arbitrariness, inefficiency, and corruption. The condition of the Russian bureaucracy was reflected in Russia's defeat in the Crimean War and in the Russo-Japanese War and in the events antecedent to the 1905 Revolution. The lack of an effective administrative apparatus resulted, furthermore, in the shortages of food and munitions that played such an important role in bringing about the Russian collapse in 1917.

Russians and the non-Russian subject peoples have traditionally been at the mercy of an officialdom against the excesses of which they have had little redress. The autocrat, whose good intentions they were willing to assume, was unapproachable in his distant capital but presumably would remove overbearing and corrupt officials were he aware of their conduct. The centralism of the autocratic order and the nature of its officialdom deprived its subjects of any opportunity to identify effectively with the political order. Thus there developed an attitude—often still evident in the Soviet Union—of viewing the regime, the administrative apparatus, the system of controls, and the rulers as "they." This term has been used to refer to the entire communist establishment and its all-pervasive bureaucracy that constantly pries and interferes and makes unreasonable demands.

The distrust of bureaucracy and the "we"–"they" dichotomy have found expression both in classical Russian and in Soviet literature. The satirization of Russian provincial officialdom achieved prominence in Gogol's comedy, *The Inspector-General,* and the tradition was continued by Saltykov-Shchedrin, who was himself an official and therefore had to employ "Aesopean" language in his satires. The stories of Nikolai Leskov, who was also in the civil service, contain unflattering portraits of officials. The tradition of ridiculing the bureaucrat has been perpetuated under the Soviet regime by such writers as the humorist Mikhail Zoshchenko and the novelist Vladimir Dudintsev.

The Soviet regime has followed certain of the administrative patterns established by the imperial regime. The collegial form of ministry was introduced by Peter I and was used until the reign of Alexander I, when in 1802 the collegium was initially reduced to subordinate status, and in 1811 abolished under the influence of Speransky. Significantly, Lenin restored the collegial principle in a form comparable to that existing between 1802 and 1811 with the college subordinate to the minister. Both the tsarist and soviet regimes followed the principle of recognizing a division of functions but not a separation of powers. In local government both regimes have exercised wide powers. The tsar appointed provincial governors who enjoyed considerable autonomy although they could be arbitrarily dismissed. The Soviet counterpart of the provincial governor is the first secretary of the *oblast'* committee of the CPSU. Thus, the local administration has represented the central government more often than it has served as an agent of local assemblies.

2. THE SOVIET BUREAUCRACY

Although the Soviet regime abounds with Communist Party, government and economic officials and managers, it finds the term "bureaucracy" distasteful because it stubbornly refuses to admit the obvious: that it actually is a form of "government by officials." Instead, the term *apparat* is used to refer to administrative structures and officialdom and is generally synonymous with Western usage of the term "bureaucracy" in a dispassionate and technical sense. In order to identify the unfavorable traits of officialdom, the Soviet regime has introduced the term *bureaucratism,* which is synonymous with the use of "bureaucracy" as an epithet.

The phenomenon of *bureaucratism* has been under attack since Lenin's time. It includes red tape, delay, inefficiency, preoccupation with formalities and routine, apathy, "loss of contact with the masses," and neglect of the people's needs.[1] The Soviet press abounds with criticism of *bureaucratism* and such related practices as evasion of responsibility and falsification of reports. Bribery and reliance on "family-type relationships" (*semeistvennost'*) that involve mutual accommodations at the regime's expense have been frequently condemned; "localism" (*mestnichestvo*), the promotion of local interests at the expense of the center, has also been a problem for the Soviet rulers. The Russian term *ochkovteratel'stvo* is used extensively in the Soviet Union and means "throwing dust in someone's eyes"; its literal definition is "to smear someone's eyeglasses so as to obscure his vision," and is used to refer to efforts to

[1] *Politicheskii slovar',* 2nd ed. (Moscow, 1958), pp. 63–64.

hoodwink one's superiors and the regime. Other abuses include nepotism, cronyism, pilfering, embezzlement, and bribery.

The need to combat such dysfunctional practices requires that the regime closely control personnel and be able to transfer it at will. This is done by means of the Party's ability to deploy administrative cadres through use of the *nomenklatura* system, under which there are lists of specific positions to be filled at the various administrative levels only with the approval of the corresponding Party body. The Ministry of Finance has a Central Administration of the Civil List (*Tsentral'noe shtatnoe upravlenie*) that determines personnel classification and fixes the number of employees and the size of the wage and salary fund. The Administration does not recruit personnel, as this is done by the agencies themselves, but it does set standards. The Finance Ministry also seeks to eliminate superfluous positions and administrative units both in the government and in the economy.[2] Soviet civil servants are subject to many restrictions. Superiors are responsible for the level of achievement of their subordinates, and both are responsible for not carrying out orders and regulations that are contrary to the law.[3]

Although the regime confers various awards and honors on state employees, it also insists that they bear full "administrative, disciplinary, criminal, and material responsibility" for those of their acts that are said to be illegal. State employees can be required to compensate with up to three months' salary for damage or loss inflicted on the state; this amount is fixed either by an administrative act or through a judicial determination. If a state employee inflicts loss or damage upon a citizen or public organization, he is liable only if his act involves "abuse of authority" (*zloupotreblenie vlasti*), nonfeasance, or neglect; however, this must be determined by a court. Officials are not liable if they can claim that they erred while acting in good faith, although they may still be subject to disciplinary action of some kind. In general, it is difficult for a Soviet citizen to obtain redress against the administrative acts of officials.

[2] V. A. Vlasov and S. S. Studenikin, *Sovetskoe administrativnoe pravo* (Moscow: Gosiurizat, 1959), pp. 103–104.

[3] *Ibid.*, p. 112.

Soviet administration is unique not only because of its size but because it does not distinguish between public and private administration; consequently it is public administration *par excellence.* It is also distinctive because the Soviet administrator operates under a system of multiple controls of a magnitude and variety not encountered in more conventional polities. The rulers distrust the regime's administrators and managers and have found it advisable to place them under near-constant surveillance.[4]

3. TYPES OF CONTROLS

The surveillance of Soviet officialdom is conducted at all levels, both by Party and governmental bodies. While each of these inspection agencies is not operating in the same administrative unit simultaneously, it is reasonable to assume that the Soviet administrator cannot be certain when he might be called to account and what the consequences might be. However, the size and complexity of the Soviet bureaucracy often work to the advantage of the administrator and to the disadvantage of the "control" bodies. It is not always possible for the latter to uncover the often subtle and concealed forms of evasion and corruption employed by administrators. While much remains undetected, when the errant administrator is found out he is dealt with summarily.

Party Controls. Party loyalty has always been an important criterion in Soviet personnel assignments, although technical and professional qualifications have been given increased importance with the development of the economy. The notion of the politically neutral civil servant has been alien to Soviet public administration. However, the Party does not rest with the appointment of its members to all positions of trust and responsibility in the governmental and economic apparatus. They are subject to the surveillance of the primary party organizations whose role and functions were discussed in Chapter 4; for among those functions is the task of checking on the fulfillment of Party decisions. In production and commercial enterprises the primary party organization is required to advise the management on the means best suited to fulfill the con-

[4] For further discussion of the Soviet bureaucracy see the section on the bureaucratic model on pp. 345–348.

cern's objectives; it is also required to inform the Party *raikom* or *gorkom* of conditions in the enterprise that require attention. In the state apparatus the primary Party organizations are expected to alert the superior Party body, so that it can deal with the problem through the appropriate governmental administrative channels. However, there is no assurance that a primary party organization will function effectively or that it will not engage in collusion either with plant management or with government officials.

Governmental Control Bodies. In the Soviet lexicon the term "control" is employed to mean verification in the nature of an audit or a check on performance and the fulfillment of decisions. It does not imply the ability of the "control" body to direct or restrain the administrative or production organization that is under its surveillance. Various bodies have exercised this function on behalf of the U.S.S.R. government since the early years of the Soviet regime. The Commissariat of Workers' and Peasants' Inspection (*Rabkrin*), headed by Stalin from 1919 to 1922, was the first such formal body. On Lenin's advice, it was subsequently merged with the Party's Central Control Commission, but both bodies later functioned separately; *Rabkrin* exercised financial "control" from 1926 to 1933, when this function was restored to the Commissariat of Finance. *Rabkrin* was abolished in 1934 by a decision of the Seventeenth Party Congress. As the economy developed, *Rabkrin's* efforts to intervene in all sectors proved ineffective.

The reduced functions of *Rabkrin* were performed by a Commission of Soviet Control, attached to the U.S.S.R. Council of People's Commissars, which had its plenipotentiary representatives in the locales; these officials were not responsible to the union republic governments, as there was no comparable body within that jurisdiction. The All-Union Commission of Soviet Control was charged with overseeing the fulfillment of governmental decisions and functioned largely through the ministries. The Commission was itself renamed the Ministry of State Control and was later headed by the secret police official V. N. Merkulov (a lieutenant of Lavrentii Beria) in 1950–53 and by V. M. Molotov in 1956–57.

In August, 1957, the Ministry was renamed Commission of Soviet Control, and similar bodies were established in the union republic councils of ministers. These agencies sought to find unused or hoarded reserves and to promote economies, eliminate shortcomings, and defend state interests. They could issue instructions to the organizations and enterprises subject to their inspection, directing that they cease the violations and rectify the shortcomings uncovered. The commissions were also to inform the appropriate ministry and could impose financial penalties on persons responsible for losses suffered by an organization.

In November, 1962, the Commission of Soviet Control was replaced by a Party-State Control Committee, which functioned until December, 1965, and was headed by Alexander Shelepin, a CPSU Secretary and Politburo member. Despite its title, this body confined itself to the inspection of state agencies and did not inspect the Communist Party apparatus or replace the Party Control Committee. However, it did possess broad powers and could fine, demote, and remove officials.[5] It endeavored to develop "control from below" with mass participation by part-time volunteers numbering five million. This "control" arrangement was the offspring of Khrushchev's economic and Party reorganization of 1962 and could not long survive his ouster in 1964.

The fact that the Party-State Control Committee was headed by a prominent CPSU official like Shelepin raised the possibility that he could develop a personal power base in this mass organization possessing broad and discretionary inspection authority. During 1965, it became necessary to resolve the question of whether or not this central governmental inspection body would operate independently of the CPSU organization or whether local Party officials would truly control the local "control committees." Party Secretary Brezhnev won the conflict over control of appointments and made certain that the "control committees" would direct their efforts under the guidance of the Party.[6] Shelepin was eased into the

[5] See Howard Swearer, "Who Controls Whom?" *Problems of Communism*, XII, No. 4 (July–August, 1963), 46–50; and Jan S. Adams, "'People's Control' in the Soviet Union," *Western Political Quarterly*, XX, No. 4 (December, 1967), 919–929.

[6] The nature and form taken by this conflict is documented in Christian Duevel, "The Dismantling of Party and State Control as an Independent Pillar of Soviet Power," *Bulletin, Institute for the Study of the USSR* (Munich), XIII, No. 3 (March, 1966), 3–18.

lesser position of chairman of the All-Union Council of Trade Unions. In December, 1965, the Party-State Control Committee was replaced by a "Committee of People's Control" headed by a Central Committee member. Brezhnev asserted that this body would not inspect the work of Party organs.

The "control" function seeks to promote efficiency, reduce costs, increase labor productivity, improve quality, and increase output. Yet it can be asked whether these objectives can be accomplished more readily by delegating sufficient powers to management or by promoting the activities of a mass of "controllers" who often duplicate existing inspection and auditing arrangements. "People's control" has been known to disrupt operations; it can be questioned whether such large numbers of controllers possess the knowledge and experience needed to audit complex operations and to introduce more efficient methods.

A number of other governmental agencies also perform specialized inspection functions. The U.S.S.R. State Committee for Labor and Wages can send inspectors to plants and enterprises as well as ministries to determine whether work forces are being utilized efficiently and labor norms are fixed at appropriate levels. It can also inquire into training programs for the preparation of qualified personnel. The State Planning Committee (*Gosplan*), found in the U.S.S.R. Council of Ministers and in those of the union republics, exercises broad inspection powers in determining fulfillment of the economic plan. It is also charged with enforcement of "state discipline" in production matters. *Gosplan* has the aid of the Central Statistical Administration, an agency of ministerial rank in the U.S.S.R. Council of Ministers, which collects statistical performance data and sets standards for evaluating accounting records.

Financial Controls. The promotion of economies is the responsibility of the U.S.S.R. Ministry of Finance and its counterparts in the union republic councils of ministers; the U.S.S.R. State Bank also exercises financial controls and promotes "financial discipline." The Control and Auditing Department within the Ministry of Finance plays a key role in checking on the observance of the U.S.S.R. state budget. It also oversees the work of the state insurance system, the savings banks, and banks of long-term deposits.

The accounts of all ministries and other agencies and organizations are subject to audit. The union republic Finance Ministries also have Control and Auditing Departments, which inspect the accounts of the republic ministries and their subordinate organizations and enterprises.

The U.S.S.R. State Bank is responsible for overseeing the use of financial credits and the rate of accumulation of capital. In enterprises that are experiencing excessive losses, it can impose a special accounting regime for credits and disbursements and can insist that the agency responsible for the enterprise guarantee the loan. In the absence of such a guarantee the State Bank refuses to grant new credits and seeks recovery of funds already lent. It can declare such an enterprise to be insolvent if the special financial regime fails to restore solvency, and it can then use the enterprise's receipts to satisfy creditors.

Legal Controls. The principal role in the application of legal controls is played by the Procuracy. This is the centralized and unified system of state's attorneys that is headed by the Procurator-General of the U.S.S.R. He is the government's chief legal officer and is elected for a seven-year term by the U.S.S.R. Supreme Soviet; he is responsible to the Supreme Soviet or its Presidium and is, in theory at least, not a part of the executive. He appoints the procurators of the union republics, autonomous republics, provinces, and territories for five-year terms and confirms the appointment of area (*okrug*), district, and city procurators (who are appointed by the procurators of the union republics).

The Procuracy is authorized to exercise surveillance or "supervision" (*nadzor*) over all activities of ministries and their agencies to determine whether their acts are in accordance with Soviet law. This power extends to the operations of economic enterprises and to the organs of local government. The Procuracy can demand that any administrative agency submit to it any order, instruction, decision, regulation, ordinance, or other act to determine its legality. Such acts can be protested by the Procuracy and the protest must be considered by the responsible ministry, agency, or superior body within ten days. However, the Procuracy is not empowered to annul orders and decisions of administrative bodies; in the event, though, that there is a violation of the criminal code, prosecution of officials can be instituted. It can also recommend that disciplinary measures be employed. The Procuracy is aided by the silent surveillance exercised by the Soviet security police. The Procuracy can submit representations to a ministry or to the Council of Ministers regarding the circumstances and conditions that lead to illegal acts, and that body is required to take action on the causes within one month.

The vagueness of the Procuracy's powers in dealing with administrative decisions that are based on a liberal interpretation of the law and its inability to discipline errant administrators directly limit its role as a guardian of "legality." However, its ability to influence the Soviet courts does give it an effective sanction whenever there is the possibility that a basis for criminal prosecution exists in a case. Since the Procuracy functions under the direction of the Communist Party's Administrative Organs Department and is also an agency of the Supreme Soviet and its Presidium, it can be expected to serve both Party and state interests. There is no system of administrative courts in which the aggrieved Soviet citizen can sue officials or obtain redress for alleged wrongs done him and damage suffered as a result of arbitrary acts. He can protest to the official himself and to the Procuracy, but the latter can only present the matter to the Council of Ministers, which has the last word. Officials can be sued in the courts only for a limited group of acts, such as illegal dismissal of an employee, eviction from a dwelling, illegal imposition of disciplinary penalties, and inaccuracies in public records.[7]

A form of legal control is also provided by the system of state arbitration (*Gosarbitrazh*) established by Stalin in 1931 and which is not part of the regular judicial system. It provides a special type of administrative court which adjudicates disputes between economic enterprises concerning deliveries, accounts, the quality of goods, and the interpretation and fulfillment of contracts. Arbitration bodies are attached to each executive organ, from the U.S.S.R. and republic councils of ministers to the executive committees of regional and city soviets. Arbitral panels are appointed by the executive;

[7] V. A. Vlasov and S. S. Studenikin, *op. cit.* (above, n. 2), p. 193.

when a dispute arises, each litigant designates a representative, and an arbiter is also named. Decisions of such panels are final, except that the chief arbiter in each jurisdiction can suspend a decision within one month acting either on his own initiative or on a petition for review; review of an arbitral decision can also be undertaken by the executive agency to which the arbitration organ is attached. The costs of arbitration are borne by the litigants and determined by the arbitral body.

While legal principles are supposed to govern Soviet arbitration, it has in practice been influenced by criteria of economic policy and plan fulfillment. When evidence of serious violations of law is uncovered, the arbitration bodies refer the matter to the Procuracy. The arbitration body of the U.S.S.R. Council of Ministers takes only the most important cases involving institutions or organizations of different union republics or of All-Union subordination or those cases brought at the request of union republic councils of ministers; it also generalizes arbitration experience for the benefit of the lower arbitral bodies.

There is also a system of intraagency arbitration (*vedomstvennyi arbitrazh*), under which disputes arising between enterprises and organizations of a particular ministry or agency are resolved by its own arbitral body; as in state arbitration, discussed above, the chief arbiter designates one arbiter and each party to the dispute appoints a representative and together they arbitrate the dispute. The two types of arbitration keep property disputes between enterprises and state organizations out of the regular courts and also provide a fairly rapid means of administrative adjudication which functions under executive control. Arbitration also serves to uncover various administrative shortcomings.

The Soviets. In theory the standing commissions of the various elected soviets are regarded as able to exercise a form of control. They are specialized bodies whose number and membership vary with the size of the soviet; a village soviet will have several commissions, a *raion* or city soviet will have approximately ten, and an *oblast'* or *krai* soviet can have as many as fifteen. Commissions deal with such matters as local industry, budget and finance, education, cultural affairs, health, communal economy and welfare, and commerce. Although commissions as such have no special powers and are merely organs of the parent soviet, they can investigate any matter that comes within the competence of the soviet and verify the work of the institutions and enterprises responsible to the executive body of the particular soviet.

In practice, the role of the soviets as watchdogs over administrative agencies is severely circumscribed. There are several reasons for this. As part-time legislators, the deputies are not likely to acquire the kind of expertise needed to understand and scrutinize the ways of administrators. The budgetary powers of the lower soviets are limited and their taxing powers nonexistent; thus, the deputies cannot exercise the power of the purse that is normally used by a legislative appropriations committee over administrators.

The soviets are also limited by the nature of their system, which strictly subordinates lower soviets to higher soviets—and in practice subordinates them to the executive committee of the higher soviet. Since the executive and administrative organizations of each lower soviet are also subordinate to those of higher soviets, each administrative department of a soviet's executive committee can thus claim a certain degree of independence from its own soviet on the grounds that it is responsible to the department of the same name attached to a higher soviet and, ultimately, to a union-republican or All-Union ministry.[8] The principle of "dual subordination" —subordination to the soviet of an administrative unit's own jurisdiction and to a higher administrative body—severely limits the soviet's role as a controlling organ.

4. THE ADMINISTRATION OF JUSTICE

If the inclusion of the Soviet legal and judicial system in a chapter dealing with administration might at first appear to be unusual, there are nonetheless some persuasive reasons for doing so. For, in the highest degree, the Soviet system of justice is administered. The courts, law schools, judges, procuracy, and legal profession all function as parts of an integrated system that is administered

[8] Ia. N. Umanskii, *Sovetskoe gosudarstvennoe pravo* (Moscow: Gosiurizdat, 1959), p. 336.

under the close guidance of the ruling Communist Party. Because of its limited tenure and its being subject to recall during its five-year term of office, the judiciary has little independence. If judges can readily be removed because of their "errors," they are hardly independent. Indeed, Soviet judges are little more than civil servants. The fact that the U.S.S.R. Procurator-General has a seven-year term of office while judges of the U.S.S.R. Supreme Court are elected for only five years is indicative of the status of the Soviet judiciary. The Soviet legal and judicial system can be regarded as administered because the judiciary is closely supervised; the higher courts and Communist Party directives provide the lower courts with instructions regarding judicial policy (leniency or harshness in sentencing) in certain types of cases. The Ministry of Justice also keeps the judiciary under surveillance. The contents of the legal codes of the union republics also reflect the centralism of a highly administered system, for they must conform to general principles laid down in Moscow and adopted by the U.S.S.R. Supreme Soviet.

The Russian Legal Tradition and the Marxist View of Law. Russian legal and judicial institutions developed in the shadow of autocracy. Although Imperial Russia had a ponderous collection of detailed laws (the *Svod Zakonov Rossiiskoi Imperii*), this fact did not make it less of an autocracy. Thus, Russia did not cultivate the ideal of the *Rechtsstaat,* in which the government itself must be subordinate to a fundamental law. Instead, there developed an instrumental view of law which reproached the West for being preoccupied with "legalisms" rather than pursuing "truth" and "justice." The implication of this point of view is that a regime that claimed to represent "truth" and "justice" could ignore legal niceties and procedural safeguards, and could justify its every action by the allegedly virtuous nature of its motives. This has led to a situation in which the Soviet rulers have made themselves the sole judges of the legality of their conduct—except when they have quarreled among themselves. It has given continuing meaning to the old Russian proverb: "Law is like a wagon tongue, it goes wherever you turn it." It is this quality that may have prompted one Soviet commentator to observe approvingly that Soviet laws are "not a collection of congealed norms, but are characterized by pliability." [9]

Russian legal practice has meant ignoring laws at times. Thus, popular election of judges of the People's Courts was provided for in the 1936 Constitution but went unheeded for more than a decade. Although Soviet citizens are supposedly guaranteed a public trial, there have been instances of closed trials and in certain cases the prosecution and the security police have been known to pack the courtroom with spectators hostile to the defense.[10] At times in the law there has been neglect, as when the antiquated legal codes of the 1920's were not replaced with revised codes until the early 1960's. All decisions of the U.S.S.R. Supreme Court have not been published, and there have been times when Soviet judges have not been certain how particular types of cases should be decided.

Russian law developed in the European continental tradition—but with certain distinctive features—under the influence of Roman law. The Soviet rulers initially attempted to apply the tenets of Marxism-Leninism to what was supposed to be a legal system of a new type. In the Marxist view, law is little more than a phase of politics and is a tool designed to promote the interests of a particular ruling class rather than to achieve justice. It was naively assumed that with the advent of Communist Party rule (in the name of the "proletarian masses") the need for law would decline, as "exploitation" and class conflict were supposedly eliminated and state functions would be assumed by "society." The notion of the "withering away" of the state also contributed to the belief that law and courts would disappear along with standing armies, money, bureaucracy, and crime.

Lenin's regime dissolved the courts, dismissed government attorneys, and disbanded the organized bar. A rough brand of justice was meted out by local popularly elected courts in ordinary cases and by revolutionary tribunals designed to combat counterrevolution. It soon became evident, however, that a system of regular

[9] A. I. Lepeshkin, A. I. Kim, N. G. Mishin, and P. I. Romanov, *Kurs sovetskogo gosudarstvennogo prava* (Moscow, 1962), II, 409.

[10] For examples, see Viacheslav Chornovil, *The Chornovil Papers* (New York: McGraw-Hill, 1968).

courts was necessary along with legal counsel and codes. As a result, the judicial and legal institutions that had been discarded so hastily had to be reestablished, albeit in a form designed to promote the interests of the Soviet state. However, the tendency to view law and courts as temporary, if necessary, nuisances persisted —as did the notion of the gradual withering away of the state.

The principal spokesman for this latter viewpoint and the leading Soviet jurist in the 1920's and early 1930's was Eugene B. Pashukanis. His advocacy of the withering away of the Soviet state even led him to predict that 1937 would be a turning point in this process because all economic classes would supposedly disappear by then. However, it was in that year that Pashukanis was denounced for his errors in the important field of legal theory. One of these errors was his statement that the Soviet state had commenced to wither away from the first moment of its existence. Contending that law had resulted from exchange in the free marketplace and had reached its most developed form under the bourgeoisie, he suggested that it could be expected to disappear with the last remnants of the bourgeoisie. Pashukanis' heresy was his unwillingness to regard the state as the source of law; and when he finally did so, he still regarded Soviet law as bourgeois in form though socialist in content. For this he was accused of the philosophical error of separating form from substance and of confusing the similarity in terminology between bourgeois and Soviet legal codes with similarity in form. His heresy was his failure to regard Soviet law as socialist in both form *and* substance. He had also ignored the "capitalist encirclement" of the U.S.S.R.—which played a prominent role in Stalin's thought—and its logical consequence in the form of a (Soviet) state of unprecedented strength.

Stalin's insistence that the Soviet state would not wither away in the condition of "capitalist encirclement" but would make laws, required that Pashukanis be replaced by a new legal theorist. This role was bestowed upon Andrei Vyshinsky, a Menshevik who converted to Bolshevism and who became the high priest of Soviet jurisprudence after a career as a law professor and as chief prosecutor in Stalin's purge trials. Vyshinsky had the task of eliminating Pashukanis' influence from the law schools and from legal publications. Soviet socialist law was declared to be socialist in both form and substance and to express the will of the entire people. The role of law and the state was to be enhanced and not diminished, and legal norms would protect socialist property and assure its defense against foreign and domestic enemies. Law was to serve as a weapon in the "struggle against the remnants of capitalism" in life and in the minds of men, and as a means of educating the masses in "socialist discipline."

The Soviet Legal System. One of the basic characteristics of the Soviet view of law is to regard it as an instrument of the state and as an executor of state policies. The term *zakonnost'*, which is usually translated as "legality," implies an ordering and strengthening of the state rather than the notion of law as the means of circumscribing the role of the state and protecting the individual. Law is to further state interests, and the courts and the Procuracy are regarded as the instruments through which this is accomplished. The Soviet Union's legal system is therefore based on a variety of legal codes that are adopted through legislation, but that are also supplemented and amended by means of decrees and orders of a normative nature.[11] Thus, while the codes possess a certain conciseness, clarity, and simplicity, they must also be viewed as incomplete repositories of the law that can be substantially modified and even negated by new enactments and by judicial practice.

The Soviet regime's policy regarding capital punishment illustrates well the fluid quality of Soviet law. The death penalty, while initially abolished for a brief period, was originally applied only to crimes against the state; but by 1932, it was extended to the theft of state and collective farm property in the absence of mitigating circumstances. On May 26, 1947, a decree of the Presidium of the U.S.S.R. Supreme Soviet abolished the death penalty, supposedly because of the "exceptional devotion" of the population toward the Soviet regime. However, the death penalty was restored on January 12, 1950, for treason, espionage, and sabotage; in 1954, it was

[11] For general treatments of the Soviet legal system, see Harold J. Berman, *Justice in the USSR*, rev. ed. (New York: Vintage Books, 1963) and Wayne R. La Fave, ed., *Law in the Soviet Society* (Urbana: University of Illinois Press, 1965).

extended to persons committing murder under aggravating circumstances. In a series of subsequent enactments capital punishment was extended to a number of other crimes, including so-called economic crimes (counterfeiting, embezzlement, bribery, black market activities, currency speculation) committed under aggravating circumstances. The criminal codes of 1960 retained application of the death penalty in a variety of crimes ranging from espionage and terrorist acts to rape, bribery, and attempting to take the life of a policeman.[12] The severity of the punishment and the types of crimes to which it has been applied have varied, but cannot be said to have been generally and progressively lightened under the Soviet regime.

Soviet law as code law has required the preparation of numerous codes and manuals dealing with criminal law, criminal procedure, civil law, civil procedure, family law, agrarian law, labor law, housing law, and administrative law. The revision of the codes in the early 1960's reflected a tendency to strengthen and regularize legal procedures evident since the abolition of the special three-man administrative tribunals of the secret police in September, 1953. Thus, confession alone was no longer regarded as an adequate proof of guilt as it had been under Stalin and Vyshinsky. The principle of analogy was abandoned; under this principle it was possible for judge and prosecutor to find a person guilty of a "crime" not specifically mentioned in the criminal code but analogous to specific criminal acts. However, the Soviet codes, despite their detail, contain certain vague provisions, such as those regarding "crimes against the state," "subverting or weakening the Soviet authority," "participation in an anti-Soviet organization," and circulating "slanderous fabrications which defame the Soviet state and social system." [13]

The Soviet Courts. The Soviet judicial system has a fairly simple structure because there is a single integrated system rather than parallel hierarchies of All-Union ("federal") and republic courts. The U.S.S.R. Supreme Court is the sole regular court of nonre-

[12] See Harold J. Berman, *Soviet Criminal Law and Procedures; The RSFSR Codes* (Cambridge: Harvard University Press, 1966), pp. 61–62.
[13] *Ibid.*, pp. 178–181.

public jurisdiction. All other (lower) courts function within particular territorial jurisdictions in the union republics. Soviet courts are collegial. The court of first instance in most civil and ordinary criminal cases (in approximately 90 percent) is the People's Court, the judges of which are the only jurists popularly elected in the Soviet Union. Judges in all higher Soviet courts are elected by the corresponding soviet; thus, the judges of an *oblast'* court are elected by the *oblast'* soviet, while the members of the supreme court of a union republic are elected by the republic's supreme soviet.

The People's Court functions at the district (*raion*) or municipal level, and the number of judges attached to it is determined by the volume of cases heard; if a *raion* has more than one judge, each is elected from a separate constituency. More than a half million judges staff the People's Courts. Judges must be at least twenty-five years old, and the overwhelming majority (95 percent of those elected in 1965) are members or candidate-members of the CPSU. Many judges of the People's Court are women (31 percent of those elected in 1965).[14] Soviet judges do not wear robes, and there is a degree of informality in the courtroom that is sometimes obtained at the expense of judicial dignity. It is not uncommon to have a graduate fresh out of law school sent to a remote area to be "elected" as a judge. Soviet judges do not create law but only apply existing statutory law to specific cases. Judicial precedent is not recognized because it would make the judiciary a less flexible instrument and hinder changes in governmental policy as applied in the courts.[15]

[14] V. A. Boldyrev, *Sovetskii sud* (Moscow: izd. "Iuridicheskiia literatura," 1966), pp. 37–38.

[15] A quasi-judicial institution, outside of the formal structure of the Soviet judiciary, is the so-called Comradely Court, which is not bound by legal codes or procedural requirements. It deals with antisocial acts and attitudes but not with any truly criminal offenses, and also takes up minor quarrels between citizens. It can levy small fines and determine minor claims for damages but often simply issues reprimands and attempts to conciliate petty disputes. The Comradely Courts are held in housing developments, on collective and state farms, and in factories; the "judges" are elected at public meetings in each locale or institution. They follow a highly informal procedure, with the audience actually participating, are designed to promote "communist morality," and supposedly provide a model for the Soviet court of the future. Comradely Courts were first established by Lenin but fell into disuse under Stalin; they

A distinctive feature of Soviet courts is the institution of the assessor (*zasedatel'*), designed to introduce an element of popular participation in the judicial process through judgment by one's "peers." Each case—whether criminal or civil, other than the hearing of appeals—is heard by a judge and two assessors; the latter are lay persons without legal training. Assessors are, in theory, the judge's equals and have a vote which enables them to outvote the judge in deciding a case. They enjoy all the rights of a judge while serving and can interrogate witnesses and litigants. Assessors determine questions of law and of fact, and differ from a jury, which would determine only questions of fact; there are no juries in Soviet courts. Panels of assessors for the People's Courts are elected at public assemblies by open voting for two-year terms; assessors hear cases for but two weeks out of the year and do not receive a special salary for their services. They are to be found not only in the People's Courts but in all higher courts, including the U.S.S.R. Supreme Court, and participate whenever the higher courts serve as courts of first instance but not when appeals are being heard. Assessors for the higher courts are elected by the corresponding soviet.

Soviet judicial procedure is generally flexible and is in keeping with the unprepossessing and at times drab physical attributes of the average Soviet courtroom. Cases are usually handled with dispatch and at times even with haste because in criminal cases the court is presented with a lengthy case record and the testimony of witnesses compiled by the pre-trial investigator (*sledovatel'*). The court's task is to determine the validity of the investigator's findings, thus in a sense the actual trial is little more than an appeal from a *de facto* "conviction" rendered by the prosecution. Yet it is the court's responsibility to determine guilt or innocence and to render, at least in theory, a judgment not unduly influenced by the prosecution.

Soviet courts employ the inquisitorial procedure common to the

---

were revived in 1959 by Khrushchev. For a graphic and detailed firsthand account of the Comradely Courts' activities and of the workings of the People's Courts, see George Feifer, *Justice in Moscow* (New York: Simon and Schuster, 1964).

Western European continental civil law systems; it is designed to establish the facts of the case with a minimum of procedural delay —although this is not always in the defendant's interests. The Soviet judge plays an active role in the proceedings—unlike the relatively passive role of the judge in the British and American courts. He or she questions witnesses, civil plaintiffs, and the accused, and at times may give the appearance of a prosecutor rather than a judge. The court can summon witnesses and elicit expert testimony on its own initiative—apart from testimony provided by the prosecution and the defense. The rules governing evidence admissible in Soviet courts are very broad and flexible, and judges are empowered to determine freely what evidence is admissible and relevant; there are no formal rules regarding exclusion of evidence or providing for evaluation of specific kinds of evidence. Indeed, Soviet courts seek to obtain all kinds of biographical data regarding the defendant that would be treated as inadmissible in a British or American court.

Soviet courts permit a form of popular participation in trials in addition to that provided by the two lay assessors who sit with the judge. Since 1958, Soviet judicial practice has provided for community accusers and community defenders, who participate along with the defense counsel and prosecution when admitted to the trial by the court. Such accusers and defenders represent "public" or "social" (voluntary) organizations, as distinct from governmental bodies; they speak in the name of the "collective" which they represent and can urge either clemency, leniency, or severe punishment. If the "collective" can testify to the defendant's good character and record, this can be to his advantage. Other aspects of Soviet judicial procedure are not always to the defendant's advantage. Thus, while the 1960 R.S.F.S.R. Code of Criminal Procedure gives the accused the "right to give testimony," it does not explicitly grant him the right to remain silent on the grounds of possible self-incrimination. Indeed, the Soviet court can compel relatives (including spouses) to testify against the accused; it does not recognize professional confidence (of a physician or clergyman) as grounds for refusing to testify. Only defense counsel or a physically or mentally incapable person may not be interrogated as witnesses.

Litigant's right of appeal is limited in the Soviet Union; he is permitted only one appeal—to the court of next instance. Thus a case originating in the People's Court can be appealed to the *oblast'* or other regional court (at the *krai*, autonomous republic, autonomous *oblast'*, or national area level). However, in union republics that are not divided into *oblasti*, cases are appealed directly from the People's Court to the Union Republic Supreme Court. Few cases go beyond the Union Republic Supreme Court. The U.S.S.R. Supreme Court is primarily an appellate court, but it hears cases on appeal only if they are taken to it by the Procuracy (under its right to "protest" decisions) or if the President of the Court decides to exercise its broad powers of supervision (*nadzor*) over all lower courts. Appeal in its Soviet version can actually be to the defendant's disadvantage because the appellate court can remand the case for retrial, and the court of first instance can impose a heavier sentence or retry the defendant for a graver offense. Appeals are generally handled with dispatch.

The U.S.S.R. Supreme Court is a large body and includes the presidents of the supreme courts of the fifteen union republics. It is divided into civil, criminal, and military divisions, and acts as a court of first instance only in the most important cases. Espionage cases of importance are tried before the Military Division of the U.S.S.R. Supreme Court, which also supervises a separate system of military tribunals for service-connected offenses. The Supreme Court sits in plenary session to supervise its divisions and to pass final judgment on their rulings. Plenary sessions are also convened for the purpose of issuing general legal interpretations that are binding upon all lower courts.

The Procuracy. The Soviet legal system is unique in its institution of the Procuracy, which performs a variety of functions. It is difficult to find in other legal systems a single institution that merges so many diverse functions. The Procuracy is specifically charged with guarding "socialist legality" and with making certain that public officials observe the law and fulfill the government's directives. This aspect of the Procuracy was discussed earlier in this chapter in the section dealing with legal controls over administration. The Procuracy is centralized, and local procurators are supposedly made independent of the local soviets and of their officials; this is said to assure strict observance of the law. However, this arrangement is more effective as a rationale for centralism than as a means of creating a responsible officialdom.

The Procuracy is best understood in terms of its being a pre-Soviet institution established by Peter I in 1722, abolished by Lenin in 1918, and restored in 1922. Indeed, the Soviet Procuracy has much in common with the tsarist Procuracy of the eighteenth century. Peter I was interested in promoting autocratic centralism and in combating those who resisted his administrative reforms; he viewed his General Procurator "as Our eye, and lawyer in matters of state." Thus, the Soviet practice of having the Procuracy exercise supervision over administrative acts and serve as an organ of control had its origins in Peter's imperial brand of tsarism.

The other functions of the Soviet Procuracy include serving as legal counsel to the executive bodies of the various soviets and prosecuting persons who are alleged to have violated the law. The Procuracy approves the arrest of persons by the ordinary and security police forces; the Soviet substitute for a bench warrant, the Procuracy's approval is not issued by a court and can be given after the fact of arrest. Prosecution for criminal offenses is the responsibility of the Procuracy, and it also supervises the pre-trial investigation of persons charged with such offenses. Yet it is known that the Procuracy in Stalin's time failed to control the security police, and the question of the degree to which the Procuracy imposes legal norms and due process upon the KGB is not readily answered. Indeed, collusion between the Procuracy and the secret police is very possible.

The relationship of the Procuracy to the Soviet courts is an unusual one, and in many ways the Procuracy is more important than the judiciary. The Procuracy is actually a large, centralized judicial bureaucracy that exercises considerable supervision over the courts. It is responsible for the legality and validity of all court judgments, decisions, rulings, and decrees. The Procuracy is constantly scrutinizing judicial acts to determine whether or not they are "legal" and meet with its approval. Procurators can enter civil suits at any time to urge the court to adopt a particular decision on the grounds that it is in the interests of the state or security, although this practice is a common feature of code law systems.

The Procuracy's influence over judicial practice is especially evident in its role in appealing court decisions. If the Procuracy is not satisfied with a decision in a civil or criminal case, it can protest it to a higher court and continue protesting under its powers of supervision. However, presidents of supreme courts can also initiate reviews of cases. Even an acquittal can be protested and the higher court can vacate the judgment. Supreme courts of union republics and of the U.S.S.R. cannot meet in plenary session in the absence of the republic procurator or the U.S.S.R. Procurator General. If the U.S.S.R. Procurator General is of the opinion that a decree of the U.S.S.R. Supreme Court is not in accordance with the law, he is obliged to take the matter to the Presidium of the U.S.S.R. Supreme Soviet. He can also propose to the Supreme Court that it issue new instructions regarding judicial practice.

Among the Procuracy's other functions is the supervision of the execution of all criminal sentences and the supervision of detention facilities, prisons, and prison colonies. It also publishes a journal, *Socialist Legality*, which is indicative of its role as a fountainhead of judicial doctrine. The Procuracy receives complaints from citizens and has been likened to the *ombudsman* in other systems, but the analogy is not very apt because the *ombudsman's* role is not performed well by state's attorneys. Indeed, one can ask whether the procurator, as the government's legal counsel and prosecutor, can really fulfill the role of "guardian of legality." In many ways a truly independent judiciary is in a better position to perform this vital function if legality must be protected not only against encroachments by individuals but by government as well.

The Legal Profession. Although Lenin distrusted lawyers despite the fact that he himself was trained in the law, the Soviet regime has not been able to dispense with their services. The Soviet legal profession includes judges and procurators, as well as those engaged directly in legal practice. Practicing lawyers are of two types: the *advokat*, who is a trial lawyer, and the *iuriskonsul't*, who is the Soviet version of a corporation counsel and is employed by government agencies and economic enterprises. The *iuriskonsul't* confines himself largely to administrative law and labor law but does enter the courtroom when enterprises are involved in litigation. The *advokat* serves as defense counsel in criminal cases and as counsel for plaintiff or defendant in civil suits, and also prepares documents and gives legal advice to clients. The Soviet courts hear civil suits dealing with evictions, inheritance claims, payment of alimony, libel, reinstatement in place of employment, and almost every other conceivable matter; thus, under these circumstances, lawyers have much to do.[16]

The practice of law is conducted through legal consultation offices that function under the jurisdiction of collegiums of advocates organized on a territorial basis. The collegiums are supposedly "voluntary" organizations, by which is meant that they are not agencies of the state, although they are under the supervision of the courts, union republic councils of ministers, and regional and local executive bodies. The Soviet *advokat* cannot practice privately but must be a member of a legal "collective" or consultation office; he must also be a member of the local (city or regional) collegium. Disbarment is by administrative action and the courts do not participate directly in the procedure as they do in the United States.

Soviet lawyers, although they include men of wit, intellectual subtlety, and rhetorical talent, do not enjoy the high fees received by many American attorneys and trial lawyers specializing in criminal law and in personal liability suits involving generous awards and commissions. The Soviet legal profession is closely regulated by the state and the fees for various types of legal service are fixed by law. The fees are paid to the legal consultation office and not directly to the *advokat;* they are then apportioned among the law-

[16] The Soviet Union also has a system of *state notaries* for the purpose of preparing and certifying documents (including sales and other agreements and wills), taking depositions, and attesting to matters of fact and record. Notaries are under the jurisdiction of the *oblast'* and *krai* courts (including appointment and removal) and notarial offices are state organs. Notaries also accept documents for safekeeping and hold sums of money and valuable papers in trust for transfer. Fees, fixed by law, are charged for nearly all notarial services, and a register is kept of all notarial acts. Notaries must have a certain minimum of legal training and experience because they are required to determine the legality of all transactions and agreements notarized.

yers. A limited number of routine legal services must be performed gratis for certain specified categories of clients. Nevertheless, the Soviet *advokat* earns at least as much or more than the highly skilled Soviet worker; he may even obtain a generous gratuity from an especially appreciative client, although this practice can have unpleasant consequences and lead to disbarment.

The *advokat,* furthermore, often enjoys a far better income than does the Soviet judge or ordinary procurator, neither of whom is well paid. Indeed, the judge of the People's Court often aspires to enter legal practice as an *advokat* or *iuriskonsul't.* A barrier separates the *advokat* from the procurator and judge because the latter are more often than not serving the Soviet state and its policies, while the *advokat* is endeavoring to protect the rights and interests of his client and is doing this for remuneration. So long as civil litigation and criminal prosecution persist in the Soviet Union and the defendant is said to have certain rights, the *advokat* therefore plays an indispensable role in the administration of justice.

In addition to the matter of remuneration, the regime has circumscribed the role of the legal profession in a variety of other ways. As befits a planned and state-owned economy, it controls the size of the enrollments in law schools and limits the number of persons permitted to practice law. The regime also prescribes the curricula of law schools and endeavors to influence the character and ethos of the legal profession. Lawyers, the Procuracy, and the courts are periodically mobilized to combat those practices and forms of conduct that the Communist Party leadership regards as especially undesirable or as a threat to the regime's stability.

Yet the *advokat* inevitably finds himself in conflict with the regime and with its officials, including the Procuracy and the security police, when endeavoring to protect his client and when the client's interests and those of the Soviet state are at variance. The state claims that the Procuracy must prosecute the guilty but must also protect every last innocent person suspected of having broken the law. Since it is unlikely that even a dictatorial regime seeks to punish innocent persons for ordinary crimes, it then becomes a question of whether or not there are adequate procedural safeguards to protect the accused from the chronic suspiciousness and desire to convict that often characterize the agencies of detection and prosecution. In theory the investigator is supposed to conduct an "impartial" examination of the case and is to serve as the suspect's "defense counsel" while simultaneously determining whether there are sufficient grounds to convict. If the procurator is convinced that such grounds exist and that the suspect is guilty, the latter is placed on trial.

The Soviet lawyer's role as defense counsel in criminal cases is circumscribed, and it is hampered by his inability to help his client at an early stage in the proceedings. In Soviet procedure the suspect is denied access to legal counsel during the initial inquiry and pre-trial investigation. It is only after the investigation of the case has been completed and the procurator has confirmed the indictment that defense counsel can enter the case. Only if the accused is a minor or under a physical or psychiatric handicap can he or she have access to legal counsel during the investigation. Thus, by the time the investigation is completed and the case against the accused is developed, both defense counsel and defendant are at a disadvantage.

Although Soviet judicial procedure contains many aspects of a fair trial and appears to permit the defendant his "day in court," the right to legal counsel is not absolute. This is especially true in political trials and in cases involving interests of state. In ordinary cases, defense counsel may present a spirited defense; but when the Procuracy, a dependent judge, and the Communist Party regime make it patently clear that a defendant must be convicted for reasons of state, defense counsel is likely to offer a halfhearted defense and to confine himself to pleading for leniency on the grounds of mitigating circumstances. The situation is made even more disadvantageous, especially for the political defendant, by the absence of a free press that would report on the arbitrary activities of procurators, judges, and assessors.

The Soviet lawyer practices law before courts that seek to shame the defendant and that employ procedures designed to render the accused contrite. Soviet law has therefore been termed "parental law" by Professor Harold J. Berman. Soviet judges often employ a didactic approach, with the courts expected to help make the "new

Soviet man" who will presumably be worthy of communism. Thus, the Soviet lawyer is caught in conflicting roles; he is an aid to a court that seeks to reeducate while punishing and he is also expected to serve his client as an advocate. In certain circumstances also, the confidential nature of the lawyer-client relationship involves ambiguities and can therefore be violated; an individual is not free to select counsel of his own choice, for instance, and a lawyer doesn't have the choice of cases that he will accept. Soviet lawyers are not members of a free profession as ordinarily understood, and they do not possess the equivalent of a countrywide bar association. Yet many of their number continue an old tradition of civic courage and seek to defend the individual against the state and against miscarriages of justice perpetrated by the courts.

5. THE QUESTION OF SOVIET "FEDERALISM"

The question of whether the Soviet Union can be regarded as a federal system is one of considerable importance for an understanding of the nature of the Soviet regime. If something resembling a federal polity was adopted by Lenin and Stalin, it was in reluctant recognition of the linguistic and cultural diversity of the population and the vast size of the country over which they ruled. The Soviet Union is at least a quasi-federal system insofar as it consists of constitutionally recognized territorial units (the union republics) that exercise certain functions, with the distribution of powers between the republics and the central government defined in the constitution.

However, there are many features of the Soviet system that in practice qualify or even nullify its federal character. It can be asked whether federalism, a political order that emerged in democratic systems, is possible under a system of party dictatorship that frequently denies political rights to those who openly question its policies. The application of the adjective "federal" to the Soviet Union is of limited validity if only because the meaning of the Russian term *soiuz* (sometimes translated as "federal") is vague and can be used to refer to a loose alliance of sovereign states or to a very close union; the choice of this ill-defined term with reference to the union republics contributes to the lack of a precise definition of the powers of those republics.

In practice, Moscow has encroached upon the union republics in a variety of ways. The republics have no independent taxing power, although their ministries of finance are used to collect revenues for the taxation monopoly enjoyed by the Union. The budgets of the republics are subordinate parts of the unified All-Union budget that reflects the countrywide economic plan. The centralism that characterizes the Soviet taxation, planning, banking, and budgetary systems is also evident in the Communist Party organization, which expressly rejects federalism. The non-Russian union republic Party organizations enjoy no more real powers than do *oblast'* Party organizations within the Russian Republic. The non-Russian republic Party organizations are expected to carry out the will of the center even when this conflicts with the interests of their republic.

Soviet "federalism" is also characterized by a division of powers that leaves few matters exclusively within the jurisdiction of the republics; it is a division that can be shifted to the center's advantage with ease. The numerous powers that are directly exercised by Moscow through the All-Union ministries and indirectly through the joint Union-Republican ministries make it possible for the center to intervene in nearly all of the activities of the republics.[17] The republics are not even permitted to appoint their principal legal officers, the procurators, who are instead appointed by the U.S.S.R. Procurator-General; as a result Soviet centralism in the legal field is unparalleled.

An important characteristic of genuine federalism is the right of the states or provinces to participate in the process of formal constitutional amendment in a role apart from their membership in the federal legislature. If a federal legislature alone has the right to amend the constitution, this can be detrimental to the component parts of the federation and can endanger their existence.[18] In the

[17] I. N. Ananov, *Ministerstva v SSSR* (Moscow, 1960), p. 92, note, and p. 171, states that the U.S.S.R. Union-Republican ministries have at times brusquely interfered in the republic ministries of the same name, even to transferring personnel.

[18] See William S. Livingston, *Federalism and Constitutional Change* (London: Oxford University Press, 1956), pp. 13–14, 298–302.

Soviet Union the Supreme Soviet or its Presidium amends the constitution and has done so on innumerable occasions. Although the republics are accorded separate representation in the Soviet of Nationalities, the republic governments and legislatures play no role in the amendment of the U.S.S.R. Constitution. Thus, there is no Soviet counterpart to the provision in the American amending process that requires three-quarters of the states to ratify amendments through their legislatures or by special conventions. By denying the governments or populations of the union republics a special and direct role in the amending process, the Soviet constitution fails to protect the republics' rights and maintain a fixed division of powers.

The "federalism" of the Soviet Union has been further attenuated by the fact that Moscow is the Union's capital. Instead of establishing a new capital on relatively neutral territory, Lenin selected the traditional seat of Russian despotism and absolutism as the seat of his regime. It is revealing that the Supreme Soviet of the Russian S.F.S.R. meets in the same chamber in the Kremlin in which the U.S.S.R. Supreme Soviet holds its joint sessions. While this fact may reflect the all too frequent Russian attitude expressed in the idiomatic phrase *vse ravno* ("it's all the same"), it also reveals a lack of appreciation of constitutional distinctions. Indeed, the presence of a dominant member in the federation, like the Russian Republic, creates the condition for the subversion of the federal principle.

There is no right of judicial review that can be invoked by the union republics in defense of their powers against encroachments by the central government. The U.S.S.R. Supreme Court does not hear constitutional cases. The Presidium of the U.S.S.R. Supreme Soviet can annul decisions of the councils of ministers of the union republics "if they do not conform to law." Thus the republics have no recourse when their interpretation of their constitutional powers might conflict with that of the central government. Nor are there any provisions governing the nature of the federal system that are specifically exempted from amendment.

Although federal systems are not identical, they do share certain common characteristics. It is evident therefore that the Soviet

Union possesses many features of a unitary system and falls short of qualifying as a genuine federal system. Yet even a quasi-federal system such as the Soviet Union is comparable to authentic federalism in being a compromise between homogeneity and diversity, centralism and secession, integration and the preservation of identity. Such compromises are neither easily maintained nor necessarily stable and are reflected in changing institutional structures.

6. REPUBLIC AND LOCAL ADMINISTRATION

Although the union republics are said to be "independent" and "sovereign"—apart from the vast enumerated powers held by the central government and the strictures imposed upon the republics by the U.S.S.R. Constitution—they constitute an integral part of the countrywide administrative system. The vast majority of ministries are either joint (Union-Republican) or republic bodies; consequently most of the business of Soviet government is conducted through ministries that are to be found in the republic councils of ministers. However, the Union-Republican joint ministries function in conformity with directives issued by the U.S.S.R. ministry of the same name in Moscow and hence their administrative competence is subject to limitations and change because of their status of "dual subordination" to the republic and to the Union.

The government and administration at the union republic level manifest many of the features that characterize the central government. The unicameral republic supreme soviets function in a manner similar to that of the U.S.S.R. Supreme Soviet, meeting but twice a year in regular sessions; their presidiums, while varying in size, investigate questions and complaints referred to them by deputies regarding the activities of ministries and government agencies. The presidiums issue decrees, interpret the laws of the union republics, and can rescind ordinances and regulations issued by the republic councils of ministers as well as the decision of lower soviets. Councils of ministers of union republics can rescind decisions and regulations of the executive committees of *oblast'* (and *krai*) soviets, as well as the orders and instructions of its own ministries.

The union republics are said to be "sovereign" and "independent," when in fact they enjoy little more than autonomy. The autonomous soviet socialist republics are said to possess "state-political autonomy" and to enjoy "self-government in internal affairs." Lesser autonomous units—such as the autonomous *oblast'* and the national area (*okrug*)—are said to enjoy "administrative-political autonomy," though lacking the status and trappings of statehood conferred on soviet republics.

The autonomous soviet socialist republics have their own constitutions (that must be approved by the supreme soviet of the union republic in which they are located), supreme soviets, presidiums, supreme courts, and councils of ministers. To these attributes of "nonsovereign statehood" can be added separate representation in the U.S.S.R. Supreme Soviet's Soviet of Nationalities. However, autonomous republics do not have the state seal and flag that union republics are permitted to have. Unlike the union republics, the autonomous republics do not possess the "right" to secede from the Soviet Union. Their councils of ministers include a number of the ministries to be found in the union republics, such as health, culture, education, social security, finance, the KGB, and others.

Most of the autonomous republics are in the Russian S.F.S.R. and vary greatly in size of territory and population. Among the more populous autonomous republics are the Tatar, Bashkir, Daghestan, Chuvash, Komi, Mordvinian, Chechen-Ingush, and Karelian republics. Although six of the union republics were once autonomous republics or part of such republics, it is unlikely that others will be given such status. The presence of autonomous republics within the Russian S.F.S.R. does not make it a federation—despite the use (or semantic abuse) of the adjective "federated" in its name.[19] The claim that the Russian Republic is a federation is negated by the fact that it does not consist of coequal autonomous re-

[19] The adjective was initially introduced by Lenin in 1918 to provide a means of reintegrating seceded non-Russian territories, while paying lip service to national self-determination. The formation of the U.S.S.R. in 1922 rendered the federal form of the Russian Republic largely redundant, reducing it to a type of semantic abuse. See Walter R. Batsell, *Soviet Rule in Russia* (New York: Macmillan, 1929), pp. 61 and 81 and Chap. III.

publics; the autonomous republics comprise but part of the R.S.F.S.R. and are not accorded separate and equal representation in its supreme soviet (representation is based exclusively on population).

The "autonomous *oblast'*" is not to be confused with the ordinary *oblast'*. It represents a form of administrative autonomy based on the recognition of numerically small nationalities that occupy fairly large regions. It is subordinate to the government of a territory (*krai*) or directly to a union republic. The autonomous *oblast'* has a statute (*polozhenie*) that distinguishes it from the ordinary *oblast'* and provides for recognition of its nationality. Unlike the ordinary *oblast'*, it has separate representation in the U.S.S.R. Soviet of Nationalities and can delimit its districts (*raiony*). Most autonomous oblasts are in the R.S.F.S.R. and are included in territories (*kraia*). Thus the Jewish Autonomous *Oblast'*, which has attracted very few Jews, is located in the Khabarovsk *krai* on the Sino-Soviet frontier. Tuva, located on the frontier of the Mongolian People's Republic—and itself a "people's republic" prior to October, 1944—became an autonomous *oblast'* when it joined the Russian Republic during World War II; in October, 1961, it became the Tuvinian Autonomous Soviet Socialist Republic—one of several such Turkic republics.

The least of the ethnic autonomous administrative units is the "national area" (*okrug*). They have been established for the numerically small peoples of the Soviet Far North and Far East who inhabit large and sparsely populated areas. They are actually multinational units and are included within regular *oblasti* and *kraia*. Each such area has one deputy in the U.S.S.R. Soviet of Nationalities. It differs from the autonomous *oblast'* in not having a separate statute for its legal basis (instead, a single law pertains to all national areas). The administration of the *krai* or regular *oblast'* in which the national area is located exercises greater powers over it than are exercised by the *krai* over the autonomous *oblast'*.

The ordinary *oblast'* is the most numerous of the important units of Soviet administration, both in Party and governmental organization. The more than one hundred *oblasti* and the far less numerous *kraia* (territories) occupy a crucial place in the hierarchy of Soviet administrative jurisdictions. They are subordinate to the union republic governments (in the R.S.F.S.R. and the other union republics that are divided into *oblasti*); but they, in turn, are superordinate in relationship to the *raiony* (districts) and to the cities of *oblast'* subordination. The smaller union republics—like Estonia, Latvia, Lithuania, Moldavia, and Armenia—do not have *oblasti* but are divided into *raiony*. The administration at the *raion* level has within its jurisdiction small towns, the *poselok* (settlement), and rural villages. The workers' *poselok* is a populated area usually near a factory, mine, electric station, or railroad center.

Local administration functions in the name of the soviet or council that is popularly elected within each jurisdiction in the administrative hierarchy. Formally known as the "soviets of toilers' deputies," these bodies vary in size and in the frequency of their meetings. *Oblast'* and *krai* soviets have 100–300 deputies and meet at least once every three months. *Raion* (rural) soviets have 40–80 deputies, while *poselok* and village soviets are usually half that size; both hold bimonthly meetings. City soviets have from 50 to several hundred deputies; and if the city is large enough to have boroughs (*raiony*), they also have soviets. The norms of representation for local soviets are set by the presidium of the supreme soviet of each union republic and are subject to change from one election to another.

The local soviets must approve their annual budgets and the economic plan for their jurisdiction. They also determine the use to which land (all of which is state-owned) shall be put. The soviets directly administer many important economic enterprises and provide a variety of public services. Each soviet elects an executive committee (*ispolkom*) that varies in size with the importance of the local soviet. The executive committee is a body of "dual subordination" being responsible both to its own soviet and—more significantly—to the executive committee of the next superior soviet, which can annul its decisions. The entire structure of soviets is rigidly hierarchical and is based on the subordination of one soviet to another.

The executive committee serves as the interim decision-making body when its soviet is not in session—which is most of the time.

It administers the local budget and is responsible for the fulfillment of the economic plan and for law enforcement. It directs the subordinate administrative agencies—the departments (*otdely*) and administrations (*upravleniia*) that are found in all soviets above the *poselok* and village level. Although their number and nature vary, the departments and administrations at the *oblast'* level usually include the following: health, social security, education, finance, communal economy, culture, road construction, agriculture, local industry, fuel industry, and construction materials industry. *Oblast'* and *krai* departments and administrations are subordinate not only to their executive committee but to the appropriate union republic ministry. Departments of *raion* soviets are subordinate to the *oblast'* departments of the same name.

Oblast' and *krai* executive committees have organizational-instructional departments that inspect and oversee the work of subordinate soviets. "Instructors" are sent to the local soviets to organize elections and meetings of deputies with constituents and to train newly elected deputies—of whom there are many. These instructors conduct preparations for the infrequent sessions of the soviets and aid in the organization and work of the standing commissions. Deputies in the soviets are expected to explain the regime's policies to their constituents and to win their support; instructors check on the effectiveness with which deputies fulfill this task. Instructors also work with the staffs of subordinate soviets, conveying to them relevant decisions of the *oblast'* soviet executive committee and supervising their handling of complaints and requests received from citizens. They aid in the organization of the agendas of the executive committees. Seminars are organized for the chairmen, vice chairmen, secretaries, and staffs of lower soviets in an effort to improve their qualifications.

City soviets and their executive committees are subordinate to *raiony, kraia, oblasti,* or republics—depending upon their size and significance. Municipal soviets in the larger cities are responsible for a wide range of activities and have administrations or departments for housing, housing renovation, capital construction, retail trade, various sectors of industry, bakery goods production, water and sewage systems, gas, heat and electric power, streets and bridges, public transportation, parks, education, and social security. Municipal administration includes "culture"—the functioning of reading rooms, mass libraries and museums, the organization of literary evenings, publishing, and the cinema, and the preservation of historical and artistic monuments. The soviets of cities provide such services as bath houses, laundries and dry-cleaning shops, funeral services and operation of cemeteries, repair shops for personal items (watches, shoes, radios), photo shops, pawnshops, and barber shops. Soviets also maintain records of vital statistics and direct the local law enforcement organization.

The administration or department of a local or city soviet is responsible both to its own executive committee and to the *oblast'* or union republic administrative unit that deals with the same subject matter. Dependence of local governmental bodies is especially evident in taxation and finance. Although the finance departments of local soviets collect all taxes, revenue policy is highly centralized because only the central government is empowered to levy taxes; local soviets enjoy no independent taxing power. The budget of each local soviet is merely a minute component of the total U.S.S.R. state budget administered under the U.S.S.R. and union republic ministries of finance. Local soviets are permitted by the central government to retain a stipulated portion of the taxes collected within their jurisdiction but are limited in what they can spend. Although each local soviet adopts a separate budget ordinance, decisions on expenditures are preempted as a result of their having been predetermined by higher echelons of government.

The Soviet administrative system is generally characterized by excessive centralization. The autonomy granted to local soviets, especially in fiscal matters, is tentative in addition to being circumscribed. The acts of soviets and of their administrative bodies and departments can readily be annulled by superior bodies such as higher soviets and their executive committees, and republic councils of ministers and ministries. Each superior soviet acquires a large administrative apparatus because in addition to conducting its own business it must concern itself with the work of all subordinate soviets. Such autonomy as is required by administrative necessity can readily be vitiated by the intervention of local Party officials who also hold key positions in the local soviets. Indeed, the local soviets are essential instruments for the fulfillment of Party decisions.

CHAPTER 8

THE SOVIET POLITY: FUNCTIONS AND POLICIES

The wide scope of the many and diverse activities engaged in by the Soviet government gives to the polity a character very different from that of other industrial mass societies. The Soviet government forbids individuals or groups from owning the means of production or from engaging independently in entrepreneurial activities. The few exceptions are the collective farms, which are in theory agricultural cooperatives, and certain consumer and handicraft cooperatives. State ownership of the means of production and of all natural resources has resulted in an economy that is a virtual state monopoly. The denial of freedom of economic enterprise has made nearly all citizens the equivalent of government employees, and very few are permitted to be self-employed.

The Soviet government is, indeed, a gigantic economic "conglomerate" or corporate "trust" that defies imagination. Its largest single source of revenue is the profits from economic enterprises. It is landlord to most of the country, having entered the housing business on a vast scale especially in the cities. It owns the entire banking system, operates all savings banks, and sells various kinds of insurance. It is a carrier having a monopoly on all forms of transportation and has a single state-owned airline for the entire country as well as for foreign routes. The Soviet regime owns the various communications media, including newspapers, magazines, and radio and television stations; if organizations subsidiary to the Communist Party have their own publications, they do not challenge the Party's monopoly position in the media.

Yet the functions of Soviet government are not confined to state-ownership of the economy and to profit-making. State-ownership is viewed as a means of achieving certain social ends and of effecting a transformation in human nature. The abolition of the stock market by the Soviet regime and the impossibility of private ownership of common stocks and of the means of production are viewed, for instance, as contributing to these ends. Centralized planning of a nationalized economy is but one of the means employed to promote the regime's objectives. There is much inculcation designed to persuade workers that their interests are for all practical purposes identical with those of the management of the state-owned enterprises; strikes are not an activity of the Party-controlled trade unions and there is no recognized right to strike.

The Soviet government's policies also extend far beyond the economic sphere and embrace the broad area of political socialization. By making (nearly) all education public and secular and by frequently giving it a political and ideological content, the regime seeks to reinforce the activities of its communist youth organizations (discussed in Chapter 5). Indeed, political socialization begins with the preschool nurseries at which many employed mothers must leave their children. The propagation of so-called scientific atheism, and the inculcation of a sense of civic obligation and loyalty to the regime are primary functions of Soviet schools. Moreover, by endeavoring to control the content of belles lettres and the arts, the Party leadership involves itself in many activities that would not be the concern of democratic politicians. It is the regime's involvement with so many different areas of human conduct, and its constant meddling and insistence upon the politicization of activities that might better remain nonpolitical, that distinguish the Soviet polity.

1. ECONOMIC DECISION-MAKING AND CONTROLS

The Soviet economy is sometimes described as a "command economy," by which is meant that all important decisions affecting the economy are determined by administrative directives issued by public officials rather than by the actions of consumers and of countless private individuals and corporations acting through the mechanism of the market. Centralized planning by the governmental bureaucracy made it possible to develop heavy industry at rapid tempos, at the expense of light industry and consumer goods production, however. Like the so-called capitalist countries, the Soviet Union accumulates and invests capital for economic return and development, but its capital is state-owned and is allocated among the various sectors of the economy on the basis of investment decisions made by planning officials. There is no market for capital in the Soviet Union, and capital is not raised through the sale of stocks and debt instruments as it is in other countries. High rates of capital formation and investment have been possible as a result of forced "savings" and deprivations imposed upon the population by the government's planners. Since capital in the Soviet Union is state-owned and is allocated by government officials, the system might be described as "state capitalism."

Economic planning per se is not unique to the Soviet Union. American and European corporations engage in planning in deciding when and where to build a new factory or in adopting long-range production schedules. Governmental budgets in democratic countries are based on planning in that they often reflect deliberate choices affecting research and development, or the granting of subsidies to a particular sector of the economy (e.g., the merchant marine or aircraft industry). However, the Soviet brand of planning is distinguished by its extensiveness and centralized nature, by the myriad of economic decisions made by the planners, and by the array of controls and devices available to them.[1]

Soviet planners have their decisions embodied in the central government's annual budget and in the subordinate budgets of the union republics. Unlike some "bourgeois" governments, the Soviet government operates with a balanced budget or has a surplus at the end of the fiscal year. The budget provides the guidelines for

[1] On the nature and problems of Soviet economic planning, see Abram Bergson, *The Economics of Soviet Planning* (New Haven: Yale University Press, 1964) and Gregory Grossman, ed., *Money and Plan: Financial Aspects of East European Economic Reforms* (Berkeley and Los Angeles: University of California Press, 1968). Also see Nicholas Spulber, *The Soviet Economy: Structure, Principles, Problems,* rev. ed. (New York: W. W. Norton, 1969), and Alfred Oxenfeldt and Vsevolod Holubnychy, *Economic Systems in Action,* 3rd ed. (New York: Holt, Rinehart & Winston, 1965), pp. 74–166.

the annual economic plan or, more correctly, series of plans, for there are financial, labor, output and consumption plans, as well as plans for separate regions. Planning is facilitated by a state monopoly of foreign trade that makes possible strict controls over imports and exports. Thus, Soviet foreign exchange holdings are expended upon those imports that are essential to the fulfillment of the regime's economic objectives.

Soviet planners have at their disposal a wide variety of economic tools enabling them to exact sacrifices, stimulate economic growth rates, and to determine what shall and shall not be produced by the state-owned factories. Prices and wages are controlled; but while inflation is suppressed, many of the conditions that promote it tend to persist. Arbitrarily fixed prices serve to encourage or discourage consumption of particular commodities and also serve as a form of indirect rationing. Arbitrarily fixed foreign exchange rates, as well as the Soviet price system, have been used to promote or discourage certain imports from and exports to particular countries.

The Soviet government has employed drastic currency reforms and has revalued the ruble in order to reduce or wipe out accumulated savings. Thus in December, 1947, and in January, 1961, a new ruble was introduced; in both reforms the new ruble was issued at the rate of 1:10 in relationship to the old ruble. In 1947 larger sums could be exchanged for the new ruble on the basis of reduced rates designed to eliminate large holdings of rubles, especially those accumulated as a result of the condition of the wartime and postwar economies. The 1961 currency reform was based on a fixed ratio of 1:10 and not on a scale of varying ratios, but persons with large ruble holdings were usually reluctant to exchange them so as not to arouse the interest of the security police in how such sums might have been acquired. Such drastic currency reforms also disposed of foreign ruble holdings and gave the ruble the appearance of a more substantial currency with a higher value in relationship to other currencies.

The state banking monopoly provides an important means of effecting a variety of monetary controls. The State Bank of the U.S.S.R. (*Gosbank*) serves as the sole bank of emission issuing coin and paper currency; it provides a means of combating inflation by controlling the money supply (and the issuance of money is a vital factor in the economic plan). The State Bank also handles all foreign exchange transactions and deals in gold and other precious metals; the Bank of Foreign Trade is its subsidiary. The State Bank and its more than 6,000 branches service the accounts of enterprises and enforce the economic plan; directors of enterprises must expend accounts as earmarked, and the Bank provides a means of ascertaining fulfillment of the *financial* plan in exercising "control by the ruble." It also provides short-term (one-year) credits to enterprises, but the State Bank official has little discretion in making loans because they must be for purposes provided in the plan. Long-term credits for capital investment are extended by the Investment Bank (*Stroibank*), which transfers such funds from the state budget and also serves as a control agency.

The need to raise large sums of capital and to control consumption has dictated the Soviet regime's taxation policies. The principal tax in the Soviet Union is the turnover tax (*nalog s oborota*), which is in fact a sales tax levied on a massive scale. It is an important source of the government's revenue and provides large quantities of needed capital. Prior to 1967 the turnover tax was the largest single source of revenue, but in that year it was exceeded by the government's share of the income from the profits of economic enterprises. The income tax has provided a modest share of less than 10 percent of the government's revenue. A variety of direct taxes and miscellaneous sources of revenue such as profits from the sale of insurance by the government, social insurance revenues paid by enterprises, customs duties, automobile registration fees, and the like provide additional funds.

The turnover tax is a largely hidden indirect tax that is included in the sales price of commodities and manufactured articles. It was introduced by Stalin in 1931 and has survived. Rates are not generally publicized but they are usually high, and the tax often constitutes half or much more than half of the total sales price. Such a tax absorbs much of the excess money that is more abundant than the supply of available goods. Thus the turnover tax is a substitute for rationing. From the point of view of the regime the turnover tax is preferable to the income tax because it is concealed, presumably less painful, and is easily administered. It enables the regime to influence consumer preferences and consumption patterns and to limit demand by bringing it into balance with the available supply of consumer goods. Thanks to the turnover tax and to planners' decisions, the Soviet Union tends to remain a seller's market.

Soviet finance is, by definition, public finance, and the revenues generated and the expenditures made reflect the government's current economic plan. While the central planning authorities in Moscow have the responsibility for setting longer-term economic goals, many decisions must be delegated to republic planning officials and to industrial managers. Thus managers must determine the product mix and the specific quantities to be produced in particular colors, sizes, and styles. In practice, only the short-term operational plans (up to one year) can be detailed. Long-range planning can only set approximate production targets. For the most part the Soviet regime has relied on five-year plans, the first of which was introduced by Stalin in 1928. A seven-year plan was adopted in 1959, but was abandoned early in 1963 when it was decided to revert to the five-year plan system.

The attempt to plan the manufacture of hundreds of thousands of items—indeed, millions of items if one includes all components and parts—is a formidable undertaking to which task Soviet planners have not always been equal. The need to mobilize and allocate resources and to maintain a near-perfect balance between the various factors of production (capital, labor, transportation) requires that planning be based on accurate data and valid assumptions. In practice many imbalances have resulted and Soviet planners and managers have not always been able to innovate and introduce new techniques. The high degree of centralization in Soviet planning has often resulted in inflexibility, in excessive preoccupation with one or another sector of the economy, and in high costs.

A case in point is provided by Soviet agriculture. In the name of socialist planning a collectivization campaign was undertaken in the early 1930's that, according to Stalin, may have taken as many as 10,000,000 lives.[2] For years Soviet planners neglected to invest adequate funds in agriculture; it was only in the 1960's that substantial increases were made in agricultural investments. Chemical fertilizers were neglected and collective farmers were underpaid and deprived of any incentive to produce. Expensive and hastily conceived crash programs—such as Khrushchev's campaign to bring virgin lands under cultivation or the futile attempt to grow corn in northern latitudes—have misdirected resources and mobilized effort in ways hardly conducive to economic problem-solving.

In industry excessive preoccupation with increasing steel production led to a neglect of plastics and nonferrous metallurgy. A preference for huge plants (gigantomania) led to a failure to develop smaller enterprises that could provide the economy with greater flexibility. The fetish of economic self-sufficiency (autarky) resulted in the Soviet Union's exporting raw materials and surplus commodities rather than finished goods—despite the fact that the country is the world's second industrial power. Such exports have prevented the Soviet Union from developing stable export industries that would provide adequate and regular means of earning foreign exchange.

By stimulating exports the Soviet economy would of course be competing with foreign producers; innovation would moreover be promoted in ways not required by a domestic "captive" market. Insofar as the Soviet Union has retained a "closed economy," then, its domestic prices have borne little relationship to those of other countries and have not been permitted to determine decisions regarding what should be exported or imported. The lack of realistic and flexible prices has meant that the price structure reflects the preferences and decisions of economic planners and not market conditions. Administered prices can serve as regulators, but if they are deliberately set too low they lead to shortages and queues, or can involve subsidization of an item that remains in limited supply. Soviet prices have not adequately identified scarcities in the

[2] Stalin in a moment of frankness informed Churchill of this horrendous statistic in August, 1942. See Winston S. Churchill, *The Hinge of Fate* (Boston: Houghton Mifflin, 1950), p. 498.

economy and have not served so effectively as regulators as they would if they were to reflect consumer demand and market conditions.

With certain exceptions, the tendency has been to sacrifice economic flexibility and even the promise of increased productivity and greater profitability in order to maintain centralized control. The controls have, in turn, led to the development of evasive and protective tactics by managers. Accounts have frequently been padded in order to improve performance records. Managers have been known to underestimate their plant's productive capacity in order to prevent the fixing of a higher production quota. A lower quota is easier to fulfill, assures attainment of the production bonus, and makes next year's quota more readily attainable as it is based on a percentage increase of that of the previous year. Hoarding of inventories of parts and supplies has been widespread because managers have not wished to be dependent on suppliers and have wanted to be in a position to fulfill their production quota. Such hoarding enhances the manager's bargaining position in dealing with other enterprises. Thus plan fulfillment is made possible by evading the plan. Technology and innovation have often lagged because managers have feared that production would decline (though only temporarily) and the economic plan be disrupted. The tendency of both planners and managers too often has been to continue to produce what has been manufactured in the past but at a higher rate of output. The development of new and improved products has suffered as a result.

The Soviet economy has been characterized by disproportionate growth, overinvestment in certain sectors and underinvestment in others, growing demand as the population's purchasing power increases, and the manufacture of producer goods having low profitability and the neglect of consumer goods having high profitability. The state has tended to subsidize too many inefficient producers, and the returns on invested capital (often in the form of outright government grants rather than interest-bearing loans) have often been low. Capital, which Marx held not to be a source of value, has been known to lie idle rather than being put to work with dispatch. Capital has been wasted as in the construction of huge dams and hydroelectric facilities that have proved to be more expensive than thermal generating plants.

In the last analysis Soviet economic planning must be judged by its ability or failure to provide the population with a great variety of products and services. The persistence of various forms of speculation and black market activity and the regime's need to rely on the peasant collective-farm free market (which charges higher prices than the state-owned food stores and sells fresher produce) in order to feed the urban population testify to serious shortcomings in the planning process. If Soviet savings bank deposits have increased, it indicates that consumers have postponed purchases and are dissatisfied with the supply, range of choice, and prices of goods available.

Too often Soviet planners have been guided by quantitative indices in measuring production and have ignored quality control and consumers' tastes. Large inventories of shoddy goods have accumulated. The inadequacy of the Soviet television set's longevity and warranty provisions became proverbial. The failure to manufacture automobile spare parts in sufficient quantities or to produce prescription lenses in adequate numbers reflects an indifference to the plight of the consumer. As if to add insult to injury, Soviet citizens have too often had to tolerate rude and surly sales personnel who care little whether the individual customer is satisfied. The ability to pay has not assured one's ability to buy, and it has often been useful to have friends in retail outlets.

Despite such shortcomings, Soviet planners have demonstrated the ability to concentrate resources on certain priority projects. Among these are the ability to engage in space exploration; to develop supersonic aircraft and nuclear energy facilities; to produce machine tools and some export items of adequate quality; to organize a modern merchant marine, an impressive horological industry, and fleets of hydrofoil rivercraft. However, as the Soviet economy seeks to develop greater diversifications of output and to satisfy consumer demands, it will require more sophisticated and accurate planning methods. To some degree the use of the most modern data-processing methods and the application of cybernetics can be expected to contribute to improved planning. The growing complexity of the task is reflected in the need to combat reduced growth rates, and to make greater outlays for research and development and for automation.

Increasingly, planning requires an ability to revise priorities, rectify imbalances, and meet more diverse needs. It is one thing to maintain high growth rates and to keep increasing the production of electric power, steel, coal and cement annually; but it is a very different task to retail large quantities of unpopular consumer goods or to produce the variety and quality of goods desired by consumers. The shortcomings of using quantitative fulfillment of the economic plan (in terms of gross output) as the index for measuring performance became increasingly evident during the 1960's. Yet to rely on profits and costs as providing a more effective index would mean permitting prices to reflect scarcities and relying upon market conditions.

The crucial questions in Soviet economic decision-making remain. Who will allocate raw materials? Will central planners do so by directive or will enterprises bid for raw materials in seeking to conclude supplier contracts? How will prices be fixed? Will plant managers be able to fix wages or will the central authorities do so? Can plan and market be reconciled? Despite much discussion by Soviet economists of alternative and improved methods of operating enterprises, the concept of centralized planning remains a sacred cow that cannot be directly challenged. Yet even if a novel species of "market socialism" should ultimately emerge in the Soviet Union, certain questions will still remain. For example, will employees in the state-owned enterprises identify with the management? Will these enterprises be responsive to human costs (in contrast to financial costs) and be guided by the public interest (as against that of the enterprise) in such matters as air and water pollution and the interests and safety of the products' users? It is in terms of the answers to questions such as these that the utility of Soviet economic decision-making must ultimately be judged.

2. THE SOCIAL SERVICES OF DICTATORSHIP

The Soviet regime in its post-Stalin variant could not base itself exclusively on the security police and other organs of repression and on propaganda. It has endeavored to raise real income and improve living standards and has rashly promised Soviet citizens that ultimately their material level of living will be the world's highest. Although Soviet living standards have been low when compared with those of many industrial countries (in terms of housing, diet, clothing, and automobile and appliance ownership, and various amenities), there is no reason to believe that the Soviet leadership is committed to the perpetuation of relative poverty. The Soviet regime has endeavored to provide its subjects with a variety of social services and benefits that are subsidized by the government and are paid for indirectly by the beneficiaries or by other citizens. Although social service outlays have been rising steadily in the Soviet Union, they have done so within *balanced* government budgets. But if capital equipment accumulation and the production of producers' goods have been at the expense of the consumer and if living standards have suffered in the "guns versus butter" dilemma, the regime has nevertheless been committed to "abundance" and to improving social services.[3]

Housing. Housing must be regarded as a social service because of the large amount of publicly-owned and municipally-administered apartment buildings. Since rents are usually unrealistically low and cannot even finance the maintenance of housing structures, construction and repairs are subsidized by the government. It is little wonder, then, that Soviet housing—especially in the large cities—has been inadequate both in terms of the amount of per capita living space and in the quality and variety of construction. If Soviet citizens often pay only nominal rents, their housing is frequently of a commensurate nature and their choice of a dwelling is limited. Some citizens are able to obtain better housing from their place of employment, and those who have the financial means can join housing cooperatives that erect apartment buildings for their members.

Government-operated housing provides a means of claiming that Soviet workers have a real income that is greater than their money income because much of the housing cost (above the nominal rents

[3] On Soviet living standards, see Janet G. Chapman, *Real Wages in Soviet Russia since 1928* (Cambridge: Harvard University Press, 1963), and Arvid Brodersen, *The Soviet Worker* (New York: Random House, 1966).

paid by tenants) is really a form of social benefit. Of course, if Soviet workers were paid higher money wages and less housing were government-owned, there would probably be greater choice between various kinds of housing and more money would be invested in the housing industry. However, the Soviet housing system has the possible added advantage, from the regime's point of view, of enabling officials to know who resides where, as this current information is kept by the local housing offices.

Medical Care. The health of a country's population is a vital resource because it affects economic productivity and is an important factor in military capability. The Soviet government operates a centralized health service that functions through the ministries of health of the U.S.S.R. and of the union republics. Medical care is provided for in each successive economic plan and in the annual governmental budgets. The system of medical care is financed from government revenues and taxation. Although the physician's services and hospital care are generally free to the patient, all Soviet taxpayers pay indirectly for medical care. Drugs for out-patient use and eyeglasses are paid for directly by the patient. All hospitals and clinics are state-owned or are operated by state-owned enterprises. The state trains all physicians, who then become salaried state employees.

The Soviet Union's system of medical care is impressive in a number of ways. The country has more than 20 percent of the world's physicians, and the ratio of physicians to population is among the very highest in the world. Per capita expenditures for medical treatment have constantly risen. Life expectancy has increased markedly and infant mortality has declined. Epidemic and endemic diseases have been eliminated in a country in which malaria, cholera, and typhus were a serious problem in the past. The number of hospital beds in relation to population has increased. Medical practice is conducted through district polyclinics that serve as out-patient facilities for several thousand persons and operate in two shifts in urban areas.

Despite many positive features, the Soviet system of public medical care has certain shortcomings. Thus the patient cannot usually select his physician because they are simply assigned to each other; this tends at times to give the doctor-patient relationship an impersonal quality. Physicians of each specialty are expected to adhere to norms regarding the average number of patients they are to treat in an hour. The physician is placed in the position of having to certify medical excuses for employees and to determine who is malingering. Medical personnel and not the system of medical practice are blamed for shortcomings. The system is highly bureaucratized and many physicians serve as administrators. While standardization has certain advantages, it can also stifle innovation and medical research.[4]

The effectiveness of the public health system is weakened as a result of various conditions of Soviet life. Among these is the general diet, which is high in carbohydrates and fats and low in protein; nor do crowded housing conditions promote health. Admission to a hospital is not always an easy matter. A patient who is seriously ill and requires the services of a highly skilled specialist might find it preferable to pay for such medical care rather than rely on the government-operated system. By contrast, members of the Soviet elite are assured the best available medical care through a network of special facilities.[5] Although the medical profession is generally responsible for improving sanitary conditions and maintaining health standards, factory managers and economic planners often ignore medical recommendations regarding working and health conditions because of cost considerations. Soviet physicians are not paid very well, although they do not work the long hours that physicians in private practice in Western countries do. The system is staffed largely by female physicians, most of whom must also rear families and cannot devote much time to professional activities outside of office hours. Some Soviet physicians, especially highly skilled specialists, are able to conduct a limited private practice in their spare time; but the income from it is heavily taxed and such practice is only tolerated. The Soviet medical profession is not permitted to organize an association capable of defending its professional interests.

[4] See Mark G. Field, *Soviet Socialized Medicine, An Introduction* (New York: Free Press, 1967).

[5] *Ibid.*, pp. 94–96.

Social Welfare. Work is an obligation of the individual that is enshrined in the Soviet constitution; consequently there is no unemployment compensation despite the fact that jobs may be scarce in areas in which economic development has been retarded as a result of decisions of planning bodies. While "full employment" is a goal of the regime and labor shortages do exist in certain areas, in those areas that are plagued by a shortage of jobs, individuals who cannot find employment of the type sought have the choice of settling for a less desirable job or moving to an area in which jobs are in supply. It is assumed that unemployment compensation might discourage persons from working.

Various types of social benefits are provided through the union republic ministries of social welfare.[6] These include pensions for retired persons and for invalids and the permanently disabled, allowances to unmarried mothers for their children, providing institutional care for retarded and severely handicapped children, and manufacturing various prosthetic devices for welfare recipients. Institutional care is also provided for the aged and disabled. The republic ministries of social welfare offer vocational rehabilitation to persons who are injured but can still be employed; placement facilities are also available for invalids, although in the Soviet Union, as in other countries, some reluctance is encountered in hiring the handicapped. The blind and deaf have separate membership organizations, the All-Union Society for the Blind (VOS) and the All-Union Society for the Deaf (VOG), which operate training and workshop facilities. Although these organizations function under the supervision of the republic ministries of social welfare, they come closest in the Soviet Union to being interest group organizations that seek to protect the well-being of their members.

Pensions and other forms of social insurance are financed by the Soviet employing enterprises and institutions as a percentage of the total payroll. However, there are minimum periods of employment, as well as different age requirements for men and women and for various industries, that must be met in order to qualify for

[6] For a general survey and evaluation of Soviet welfare programs and policies based on a field study, see Bernice Q. Madison, *Social Welfare in the Soviet Union* (Stanford: Stanford University Press, 1968).

a pension. Pension payments are part of the economic plan and deficits are financed from the regular state budget. A worker who is ill or injured is paid a sickness benefit, the amount of which is determined on the basis of length of employment and the level of one's earnings, and on whether or not one is a trade union member. If one is injured in connection with one's work, full earnings are paid and trade union membership is not required. The principle of liability awards to compensate for harm and pain is not recognized; only the loss of wages is regarded as a basis for compensation.

Soviet trade unions perform various functions that prompt their inclusion with bodies responsible for welfare programs. The unions administer benefits paid to workers who are temporarily ill or disabled. In addition they operate numerous resort facilities, sanatoria, and rest homes for convalescent care; it is the trade union organization that determines which workers are entitled to use such facilities. Although the unions do not engage in collective bargaining for wage contracts, they do bargain with management over fringe benefits, factory-sponsored housing, bonuses, working conditions, and club and cafeteria facilities. Workers cannot be discharged by management without the union's approval, and unions, in general, seek to make the lot of workers more tolerable.

Despite state-sponsored social welfare programs, many social ills persist in the Soviet Union, and welfare programs are needed in spite of the claims made for communism as a universal remedy. Poverty has not been abolished, although some of its most unfortunate consequences have been mitigated. Welfare services in rural areas are far below the level of those available in cities. Soviet pensions and benefits for the elderly are inadequate and are generally well below the minimum wage—and this in a country in which food costs are the largest single item in the average family's budget, at times constituting nearly half of its expenditures. Collective farmers were excluded from the state pension system prior to 1965. While the Soviet Union may not be alone in neglecting retired persons, it is nevertheless evident that the Soviet regime is not devoting adequate resources to pension systems and welfare programs. Institutional facilities are often crowded and do not meet high construction standards. Yet the regime is committed to providing a wide variety of social benefits, and if resources permit, it is likely that levels will be raised.

Family Policy. Initially, the Soviet regime adopted a hostile attitude toward the family as the principal instrument of socialization. It apparently took seriously Marx's and Engels' prediction that the family was essentially a "bourgeois" phenomenon and was therefore obsolete; socialization would be accomplished more readily and more effectively in state institutions for the rearing of children. Lenin's government reduced marriage to a simple act of registration and made divorce easily accomplished by a simple declaration by one of the spouses made at the civil registry office. Abortion was fully legalized, and the distinction between legitimate and illegitimate children was eliminated. The Soviet regime made an effort to undermine the conventional urban family, fearing that it could be used to develop antiregime attitudes. The presence of several millions of homeless children in the postrevolutionary period gave the state an opportunity to experiment in institutional child-rearing. The undertaking proved to be costly, however, and the results far from satisfactory.

As the country concentrated on rapid industrialization, it was decided to strengthen parental authority and to stress the family's responsibilities as an agent of socialization. Juvenile delinquency and low moral standards contributed to the change in policy. Beginning in 1935 parents were held responsible for the acts of their children, and abortion was forbidden in 1936 except for narrowly-defined medical reasons. In 1944 divorce was made difficult and costly and could be obtained only in the courts and not, as previously, in registry offices. Abortion was legalized again in 1955 for nonmedical reasons; divorce was simplified somewhat in 1965 so that the court of first instance, the People's Court, could grant divorces and determine questions of custody, alimony, and property settlement, and the cost was also reduced.

Although allowances are paid by the state to families having more than three children up to the age of five, most mothers find it necessary to work because prices and wages in the Soviet Union are such as to compel a family to have two sources of income.

Pregnant women are given maternity leave for 112 days under the social insurance system.[7] Preschool nurseries are numerous, and since 1960 extended-day schools have been developed to keep children occupied after classes until parents can take them home in the late afternoon or evening. Thus children are exposed from an early age to nonfamilial rearing and are influenced by the collective. This is in accordance with the Soviet practice of stressing the rights of society and of restraining the individual's interests, desires, and feelings—subordinating them to what are said to be social ends.

That the regime continued to be dissatisfied with the family as the agent of socialization was evident in the establishment of boarding schools (*internaty*) by Khrushchev. However, these schools tended to attract "problem children" and were quite costly to operate.[8] Thus the upbringing of children in an institutional environment has not been the panacea that Engels thought it would be in proposing that society care for children. The less costly extended day school does not eliminate the family's role, but like the boarding school it reflects the regime's unwillingness to rely exclusively upon the family in the crucial area of socialization.[9]

The Soviet family suffers from many ills, especially in the urban milieu. The shortage of adequate housing has often created or contributed to family crises. The fact that many mothers work and must also perform household chores means that children are frequently deprived of the warm maternal nurturing that is so important in the development of a child's personality and attitudes. Although the regime does not publish statistics on the problem, juvenile delinquency occurs with sufficient frequency—and among those who are not deprived in a material sense—to indicate that the family is subject to great pressures and strains. Divorce, illegitimacy, sexual promiscuity, conjugal infidelity, and suicide occur often enough to testify to the weaknesses and failings of the "new

[7] Paid leave for maternity was reduced from 112 days to 70 days in 1938 and the more liberal benefit was not restored until 1956.

[8] Madison, *op. cit.* (above, n. 6), pp. 73–75.

[9] See H. Kent Geiger, *The Family in Soviet Russia* (Cambridge: Harvard University Press, 1968), and Donald R. Brown, ed., *Women in the Soviet Union* (New York: Teachers College Press, Columbia University, 1968).

Soviet man." The family has felt the scourge of alcoholism adopted as a "solution" to problems. While the regime condemns alcoholism, it also operates a highly profitable state liquor monopoly and maintains sobering-up facilities (*vytrezviteli*) as if to demonstrate the dilemmas of social policy.

Education. In the Soviet Union the distinction is made between upbringing or rearing (*vospitanie*) and education (*obrazovanie*). While both family and school are expected to contribute to upbringing, formal education is exclusively the province of the state-operated school system. Private education—with the exception of a few theological seminaries—is not permitted. The state assumes total responsibility for education because trained manpower is an important asset, and the schools can contribute significantly to the regime's success and perpetuation. Apart from providing the personnel needed for the country's economy, the educational system endeavors to provide a communist upbringing, and the inculcation of communist values and Soviet patriotism. The history of the CPSU and Marxist-Leninist philosophy are required subjects.

Education is a social benefit to those who are enabled to study in that it is free, although Stalin did impose tuition for secondary and higher education in 1940 and it was not abolished until 1956. Living expenses of students are frequently provided for by state scholarships, and as a result the authorities have a means of controlling student conduct and of promoting conformity. Although most Soviet citizens have completed only seven or eight years of schooling, the complete secondary education has become more commonplace. Secondary schools teach difficult subjects, and there are some urban schools in which nearly all instruction is given in a foreign language. Soviet education is highly centralized, although it is administered through the union republic governments. Curricula are standardized and textbooks are prescribed by administrators.

Soviet higher education is not entirely accessible and, as it is specialized, does not offer a liberal arts education. Most Soviet institutions of higher education are polytechnical or specialized institutes, including those for medicine, teacher-training, engineering, law, agronomy, construction, foreign languages, economics (including business administration), and conservatories of music. Institutes specialize in applied sciences and the training of practitioners. The less numerous universities offer training in the pure and theoretical sciences and in the humanities. Many Soviet students in higher education are enrolled in part-time correspondence courses in special tuition-free correspondence course institutes.

The enrollments in higher and specialized education are based on the manpower needs of the economic plan. While education is free and in theory accessible to all, in practice admission is limited to those who can compete effectively or whose families have influence and means. Despite centralization and the regime's assumption of responsibility for education, there are disparities in the system, especially between rural and urban schools. Secondary schooling in rural areas is often inadequate. The general emphasis on scientific and technical training in Soviet education means that certain subjects in the humanities and social sciences are neglected or are taught in a biased manner.

3. SOVIET NATIONALITY POLICY: THEORY AND PRACTICE

The interaction of communism and nationalism has been one of the salient features of the twentieth century and has profoundly influenced developments both within the international communist movement and in the CPSU. The problem of resolving national differences in a manner that would serve the interests of the communist cause was of concern to Lenin and Stalin and has required the attention of their successors. The Soviet rulers have had to govern a multinational state and lead an ethnically mixed Communist Party. Since the communist world expanded in the aftermath of World War II, the Soviet Union has had to deal with other ruling communist parties and cope with the disruptive effects of various forms of national communism.

Nationalism and Communist Theory. The founders of Marxism, Marx and Engels, assumed that the interests of the international proletarian class struggle would make nation-states and nationalism obsolete. In the *Communist Manifesto* they asserted that "the workingmen have no country" and contended that "national differences and antagonisms between peoples are daily more and more vanishing, owing to the development of the bourgeoisie, to freedom of commerce, to the world market, to uniformity in the mode of production and in the conditions of life corresponding thereto." [10] Thus Marx and Engels approved of some national movements and disapproved of others. The German and Italian national movements were regarded as "progressive" because they led to the integration of small principalities into larger economic units. The Polish and Hungarian national movements were viewed favorably because they were aimed at Russian autocracy and at the rule of the Hapsburgs; Irish nationalism was regarded as beneficial because it was directed against the British Empire and the center of capitalism. However, Marx and Engels did not approve of Czech or South Slavic nationalisms because of their failure to support the revolutions of 1848; and the founders of Marxism, furthermore, supported the Ottoman Empire as a bulwark against Imperial Russia. Thus, Marxism provided its Russian followers with a purely instrumental and opportunistic approach to national claims, recognizing only those national movements that might further the cause of the revolution.

Lenin and his Bolsheviks had to face the fact that the Russians were in a minority in their own empire and recognize that the grievances of the non-Russian subject nationalities could be utilized in the struggle against the tsarist autocracy. While Lenin would not recognize the principle of nationality in his Bolshevik Party organization, he did recognize the right of national self-determination for such non-Russian peoples as the Poles, Finns, Ukrainians, and others, including freedom of secession from the Russian Empire. Lenin branded Russia a "prison-house of nations" and he quoted Marx and Engels approvingly that "a people who oppresses other peoples cannot itself be free." [11] He held that Russians had to cease oppressing other nationalities and permit the

[10] Emile Burns, ed., *A Handbook of Marxism* (New York: International Publishers, 1935), p. 43.

[11] V. I. Lenin, *Polnoe Sobranie Sochinenii*, 5th ed. (Moscow, 1961), XXVI, 108.

free cultural development of the non-Russian peoples, abandoning the policies of russification and economic exploitation. While recognizing that Russia was a colonial power, Lenin nevertheless cherished the illusion that there could be an "international culture" of the world's toiling masses that would be reflected in the "unity and fusion of the workers of all nations." [12] "National culture" was regarded as a weapon of the bourgeoisie designed to weaken the class struggle.

Lenin apparently believed that the struggle against capitalism would in itself lead to an automatic "solution" of the problem of national oppression. He naively thought that after the overthrow of the old order Russian workers and peasants would somehow, as if by means of a miraculous transformation, acquire an immunity against the Russian great-power chauvinism that was supposedly the monopoly of Russian "capitalists, landowners and exploiters." True to his centralist convictions, Lenin advocated only the right of secession of the non-Russian nationalities but not its practice. He assumed that the right of self-determination would not be exercised and that, instead, there would occur a merger of nationalities into a large centralized state under the leadership of the messianic Russian proletariat.

Stalin in his theoretical writing on the nationality problem in 1913 generally followed Lenin's line and wrote under the latter's tutelage. Stalin defined the nation as an aspect of "the epoch of rising capitalism" and contended that the doom of capitalism would sound the death knell of the nation. While recognizing in the short run the right of nations to autonomy, federalism, or even to secession, Stalin contended that the solution in each case had to be consistent with "the concrete historical conditions in which a given nation finds itself" and suggested that such conditions were subject to change.[13] Thus the Party was to reserve the right to determine when and where application of the "right" of national self-determination was expedient or inexpedient. Stalin noted: "If the dialectical approach to a question is necessary anywhere it is required

[12] *Ibid.*, XXIV, 10.

[13] I. V. Stalin, *Sochineniia* (Moscow, 1946), II, 313.

here in the nationality question."[14] Ultimately Lenin and Stalin were to hold that self-determination could be decided only by the "proletariat" or "toiling population" of a nation—obviously on the advice of the Communist Party—in terms of whether exercise of the right was "revolutionary" or "counterrevolutionary."

The Development of Soviet Nationality Policy. The establishment of the Soviet regime by the Bolshevik Party prompted most of the non-Russian nationalities to secede and establish independent states in 1917–18. They took seriously the Bolshevik claim to respect the right of national self-determination but were soon confronted with the opposition of the Russian minority in the non-Russian areas and with the intervention of such armed forces as Lenin's government could muster. The Bolsheviks, furthermore, had an abundance of agitators who preached the class struggle and who endeavored to equate each non-Russian national movement with the non-Russian and Russian "national bourgeoisie," claiming that all must be subordinate to the "revolutionary centers" of Petrograd and Moscow.

Thus, what was said to be a civil war, and the national conflicts between Russians and the non-Russian subject peoples, became intertwined. However, it was Russian military forces that by 1920–21 imposed Soviet rule upon the non-Russian peoples. Lenin and Stalin had both expressed opposition to a federal system, but the realities of the relations between the nationalities and the intense resistance offered to Soviet rule led them to modify their position. By December, 1919, it became evident to Lenin that an effort had to be made to enable the Soviet regime to become "indigenous" in each non-Russian republic. The policy of "indigenization" (*korenizatsiia*) was designed to build popular support for the regime by promoting use of the non-Russian languages and personnel in public administration and by furthering non-Russian cultural development.

However, this policy met with resistance from the more doctrinaire Bolsheviks and from Russians who had conveniently attached themselves to the new regime. As a result, Lenin at the end of 1922

[14] *Ibid.*, p. 314.

had grave misgivings regarding the practices that had developed in the regime's nationality policy. On December 30–31, 1922, Lenin dictated notes in which he stated frankly that Russian chauvinism had reared its head and that Soviet bureaucrats were behaving like scoundrels and bullies and committing "acts of violence and insults" at the expense of non-Russians.[15] The poor state of Lenin's health did not permit him to attempt to reorient Soviet policy, however. Although nationality conflicts persisted even within the CPSU, the non-Russian nations did make certain gains during the 1920's in terms of education; official use of their languages; and an enhanced, if still very modest, role in the Party.

As Stalin's control of the Party took hold, there began a gradual but relentless shift in Soviet nationality policy. Thus as early as April, 1926, Stalin warned that in view of the "weakness of the basic Communist cadres in Ukraine" the movement for the development of Ukrainian national culture was often led by noncommunist intellectuals and would alienate Ukrainian culture from "general Soviet culture and social life."[16] At that time Stalin was already defending the right of Russian minorities in the non-Russian republics to oppose and actually hinder the process of indigenization and to claim special privileges for themselves. Yet throughout the 1920's and at the Sixteenth CPSU Congress in June, 1930, Stalin continued to insist that in the area of nationality policy Russian chauvinism was a more dangerous deviation than local (non-Russian) nationalism. This formulation was in accordance with Lenin's dictum on the need to distinguish between the nationalism of the oppressing nation and the nationalism of the oppressed nation, between the large nation and the small nation.[17]

By the time of the Seventeenth CPSU Congress—in January, 1934—Stalin in effect reversed the Leninist line by asserting that the question of which nationalism was the greater danger was "a formal and therefore an empty controversy" and that "the major

[15] For the text of Lenin's notes, first published in the Soviet Union in 1956, see Robert Conquest, ed., *Soviet Nationalities Policy in Practice* (New York: Frederick A. Praeger, 1967), pp. 144–147. Also see Richard Pipes, *The Formation of the Soviet Union*, rev. ed. (New York: Atheneum, 1968), Chap. 6 and especially pp. 263–293.

[16] I. V. Stalin, *Sochineniia* (Moscow, 1948), VIII, 149–154.

[17] Conquest, *op. cit.* (above, n. 15), p. 146.

danger is the deviation against which one has ceased to fight."[18] Thus, the advantage was to be given to the large nation; and Stalin undertook a revival of purely Russian national heroes, including St. Alexander Nevsky, Ivan IV (the Terrible), and Peter I (the Great). The Marxist school of Russian historiography (headed by Mikhail Pokrovskii) was condemned for having denigrated Russian national heroes and for depicting Russian expansionism and colonialism not as "progressive" phenomena but as the predatory exploits of the Russian land-owning and commercial ruling class. Stalin sponsored an official Soviet Russian nationalism that depicted his regime as the embodiment of Russian national interests while it continued to lay claim to the loyalties of those who might be inspired by the slogans of "revolutionary internationalism."

To this end Stalin had developed in the late 1920's the formula that defined the cultures of the various peoples of the Soviet Union as "national in form and socialist in content." By 1930 this formula gained acceptance at the Sixteenth CPSU Congress and it provided a convenient means of condemning as "bourgeois nationalism" those aspects of a particular "national form" of which the regime disapproved. While claiming to support the "flourishing" of national cultures, Stalin also asserted that the Soviet regime favored their fusion into a single culture with a single common language. Although the development of such fusion was a long-range goal, it was hardly a consolation to those among the non-Russian peoples who wished to preserve their national identity.

Soviet nationality policy as explicated by Stalin's successors has been similar to Stalin's policy regarding socialist content and national form. The 1961 CPSU Program asserted that "the Party neither ignores nor exaggerates national characteristics," but also advocated the "closer drawing together" of all Soviet nationalities "until complete unity is achieved" with common (communist) cultural traits. The (national) boundaries of the union republics—which often correspond to ethnic frontiers—are said to be "increasingly losing their former significance," but it is conceded that the "obliteration of national distinctions, and especially of language distinctions" will require more time than the obliteration of

[18] I. V. Stalin, *Sochineniia* (Moscow, 1951), XIII, 362.

class distinctions. It is claimed that an "international culture common to all the Soviet nations is developing" and that ultimately there will be a fusion of nations. While the Soviet regime professes to reject "all privileges, restrictions, or compulsions in the use of this or that language," in practice it has promoted the use of Russian as a *lingua franca* and as the principal means of effecting the "fusion" of nations that it advocates.

Nationality Policy in Practice. It is the avowed purpose of the Soviet regime to endeavor to control the content of the non-Russian national cultures—and that of the Russians as well—while attempting to promote greater cultural homogenization by employing assimilatory practices. Various manifestations of non-Russian nationalism are condemned as "bourgeois"—despite the supposed absence of a bourgeoisie in the Soviet Union—while the "single family" of nations that is said to be the "Soviet people" in practice assumes a Russian rather than an "international" form. However, the relations between nationalities in the Soviet Union are far too complex to be characterized by a simple formula, and the elimination of everyone's national identity—except that of the Russians—is not a readily realizable goal.[19]

Soviet nationality policy has varied markedly. It has included the development of alphabets for isolated and numerically small Northern peoples, the establishment of extensive systems of primary and secondary schools using non-Russian languages as the media of instruction, and the organization of national theaters, choirs, ballet companies, dancing troupes, and instrumental groups. The Soviet regime has given non-Russians access to higher education. Soviet policy has also included mass deportations, the arrests of large numbers of non-Russian intellectuals, and the use of cruel and unconscionable measures against less numerous peoples, such as the Crimean Tatars, Chechens, Kalmyks, and others—measures that border on genocide.[20]

[19] For a treatment of Soviet nationality policy see Erich Goldhagen, ed., *Ethnic Minorities in the Soviet Union* (New York: Frederick A. Praeger, 1968), as well as the special issue of *Problems of Communism*, XVI, No. 5 (September–October, 1967).

[20] For example, see Robert Conquest, *The Soviet Deportation of Nationalities* (London: Macmillan; and New York: St. Martin's Press, 1960). During World War II seven nationalities were deported *en masse* from their territo-

Language, education, the arts, and culture are interrelated areas in which nationality policy can be evaluated most readily. A people's language is one of its priceless treasures, and whenever the use and development of the native language is restricted there is a corresponding impoverishment in the diversity and richness of human experience. A non-Russian Soviet citizen has the choice, language-wise, of using and defending his native tongue, and refusing to use Russian; *or* becoming bilingual by acquiring fluency in Russian in addition to his native language; *or* opting for identification with the dominant Russian ethnic group and sending his children to Russian schools. While the use of one's native language is supposedly a constitutional right in the Soviet Union, the non-Russian who insists upon this right is likely at the very best to arouse suspicion or to be accused of "bourgeois nationalism" and encounter discriminatory treatment or worse. Although instruction in the non-Russian languages is available in primary and secondary schools, it is markedly less available in higher education.[21] In the

ries and had their republics dissolved: the Chechens, Ingushi, Crimean Tatars, Kalmyks, Balkars, Karachai, and Volga Germans. Khrushchev criticized most of these deportations in his 1956 "secret speech," and the republics were restored except those of the Crimean Tatars and Volga Germans. The Volga Germans were "rehabilitated" and absolved of guilt by decree on August 29, 1964, and Stalin was blamed for their deportation; but they were not permitted to return from Central Asia and Siberia to the land that they had inhabited since the eighteenth century. The Crimean Tatars were absolved by a decree of September 5, 1967, but were forbidden to return to the Crimea. Khrushchev offered a most revealing observation regarding the failure of Soviet nationality policy in discussing the deportations. He noted: "the Ukrainians avoided meeting this fate only because there were too many of them and there was no place to which to deport them. Otherwise he [Stalin] would have deported them also." Stalin's dislike of the Ukrainians was prompted by widespread opposition among them which for several years during and after World War II took the form of guerrilla warfare conducted in Western Ukraine by the UPA (Ukrainian Insurgent Army). See John A. Armstrong, *Ukrainian Nationalism,* 2nd ed. (New York: Columbia University Press, 1963), Chaps. 6 and 13; also see Yaroslav Bilinsky, *The Second Soviet Republic: The Ukraine after World War II* (New Brunswick, N.J.: Rutgers University Press, 1964), Chap. 4.

[21] It is evident that fluency in Russian improves an individual's life chances, educational and career opportunities. Khrushchev developed the formula of Russian as "the second native language" for non-Russians, although this has prompted the question of why Russians should also not be required to have a second native language. See Yaroslav Bilinsky, "Education of the Non-Russian Peoples in the USSR, 1917–1967: An Essay," *Slavic Review,* XXVII, no. 3 (September, 1968), 411–437.

case of Yiddish and Hebrew no instruction is available. Most important, if Russian is the language of instruction in much of higher education, the graduates of non-Russian secondary schools are placed at a disadvantage in admissions examinations; discrimination is evident both in language use and in the ethnic composition of student bodies in higher education.

Cultural development is circumscribed in various ways, not all of which are subtle.[22] Russian loan-words—especially in technological and socio-political fields—are imposed upon the non-Russian languages, for in the Soviet Union linguistics is not far removed from politics. The Slavic Cyrillic alphabet has been imposed upon the Turkic and other non-Slavic peoples. The repertoires of non-Russian artistic companies are controlled and are required to include Russian offerings. Important historical and architectural monuments have been destroyed or permitted to fall into disrepair; archives have been destroyed. Non-Russian Soviet historians cannot treat the history of their own peoples objectively if doing so directly challenges the biased tenets of Russian national historiography as propounded by the Soviet regime. The numbers of copies of published non-Russian literary and historical works and textbooks have been deliberately limited; the circulation of certain magazines and journals has been impeded and their sale on newsstands limited while Russian publications are generally available in unrestricted quantities. Once non-Russians leave their own republic they are often subjected to greater cultural deprivation even if they reside in compact groups. Thus, Ukrainians who reside in the Russian S.F.S.R. are not permitted to have their own schools or publish their own newspapers.

Although most of the nationalities have their own republics, they are not assured control over their economic development or republic governments, for political rights are as circumscribed as cultural rights. While it is true that industry has been introduced into non-Russian areas that were economically underdeveloped, the di-

[22] The entire range of discriminatory policies and practices is discussed in detail with ample documentation by the Soviet Ukrainian literary critic Ivan Dzyuba in his work *Internationalism or Russification?* (London: Weidenfeld and Nicolson, 1968).

vision of labor is often to Moscow's advantage and has often resulted in highly skewed development. Prominent posts in the Party and governmental organizations of the non-Russian republics are held by Russians, who usually serve Moscow's interests. The Russian leadership of the CPSU has deliberately promoted the mingling of peoples by largely involuntary population transfers, by not maintaining adequate employment opportunities in all parts of the non-Russian republics, and by sending Russians and Ukrainians to settle in the various non-Slavic republics.

The regime's nationality policy has yet to run its full course, and it has generated reactions that have on occasion prompted modifications and some concessions. Parents, teachers, linguists, and non-Russian intellectuals as well as some CPSU officials have resisted the regime's language policy, for instance. Encyclopedias and new journals have appeared in the non-Russian languages, and the non-Russian component in the CPSU membership has increased. The Soviet regime has had to republish the literary classics of the non-Russians and permit them a contemporary literature. If the regime has been able to promote bilingualism among many non-Russians, this cannot be equated with their becoming Russian. Indeed, the presence in the various republics of Russians, who often show little respect for the indigenous population's history, language, and culture (and who do not always conceal their arrogance) breeds resentment—as does the invidious official formula that depicts the Russians as the "elder brother" to the non-Russian nationalities. The latter are frequently—and annoyingly —reminded of their alleged cultural "debt" to the Russians. In many ways the deplorable condition described by the great Ukrainian poet Taras Shevchenko in his poem "The Caucasus" (1845) still prevails:

> We teem with prisons and with peoples beyond all counting!
> From Moldavian to Finn
> In all languages each keeps his silence . . .

It is impossible to determine to what extent the Soviet regime's efforts to denationalize and russify non-Russians will succeed. Those peoples who are sufficiently numerous and who retain an awareness of their past that includes periods of national independence, cultural renaissance, and armed resistance to Russian rule cannot be entirely subdued by efforts to stunt their cultural development. They cannot but ask why nationalism should be regarded by Soviet leaders as "progressive" in Asia, Africa, and Latin America, but condemned as "bourgeois" among non-Russians in the Soviet Union. It is natural for non-Russian Communist Party cadres to desire greater authority in their own republics at Moscow's expense. There is considerable evidence indicating that national antagonisms and frustrations persist within the Soviet Union and that the regime has not "solved" its nationality problem despite the claims regarding the "friendship of peoples."

4. COMMUNISM AND CONSCIENCE

Freedom in matters of conscience implies the right of individuals to determine for themselves or within groups their attitudes and personal beliefs regarding right and wrong, fairness and justice, and what constitutes moral goodness. It also implies the existence of a pluralistic society in which diverse beliefs are tolerated by mutual understanding within the framework of generally accepted rules of conduct.

In contrast, communist doctrine dictates that beliefs regarding such matters must be determined for society by the Communist Party which, according to Lenin's dictum, is "the intelligence, honor and conscience of our epoch." [23] The notion of a morality transcending social classes is specifically rejected. Morality is viewed as a class phenomenon based upon property interests, with the ruling class imposing moral principles designed to serve its interests. An allegedly exploiting class seeks to impose its own moral code designed to promote, disguise, and rationalize its particular interests and dupe the exploited class. Thus what is "moral" is that which advances the interests of the ruling class of the future, which has "history" on its side. For communists—who see themselves as a new ruling class whose avowed purpose is the unity of humanity

[23] V. I. Lenin, *Polnoe Sobranie Sochinenii,* 5th ed. (Moscow, 1962), XXXIV, 93.

and the abolition of all ruling classes—doctrines of morality are not to hinder the pursuit of their objectives and the defeat of their enemies.

The communist attitude toward religious belief is related to that taken toward the class enemy. Religious faith is viewed crudely as nothing more than a rationalization of the interests of the old ruling classes designed to make the exploited forget who is exploiting them. Thus religion is regarded by communists as an "opiate" used to make the exploited submissive and satisfied with their lot. Belief in God and membership in the Communist Party are incompatible. It is assumed by communists that religious belief is a "remnant of capitalism" which should disappear once changes in the economic base and in the mode of production have made its presence unnecessary in the Marxist superstructure.

Apart from the question of the validity of atheism, communism fails to explain certain facts of religious history which do not accord with its scheme of historic development. Religion has transcended historical epochs in spite of its allegedly being part of a changing superstructure dependent upon the mode of production; thus Christianity has persisted from the slaveholding epoch through feudalism and capitalism and possibly into communism. If religion is supposedly an instrument of the ruling class, why did Christianity begin not with the rulers but with the poor and enslaved? Similarly, many religious leaders have not identified themselves and their churches with the ruling class or with a particular economic order, but have opposed them or have been indifferent to such purely secular matters.

Yet atheism is an essential component of communist belief and is derived from its philosophical materialism. For communist doctrine only the material world exists and man is viewed as nothing more than an earthly, physical being who is part of the matter of which the universe consists. In denying what cannot be perceived by the physical senses, communism confines itself to the human flesh, to the satisfaction of physical appetites. In its obsession with man, society, and economic development, it rejects the possibility of divine creation or intercession.

Dialectical materialism holds that only matter itself is eternal and infinite, having neither a beginning nor an end, and that the source of its movement is internal and spontaneous (auto-dynamism). Indeed, its insistence upon self-movement is derived from its denial of all that is divinely ordained and its refusal to recognize God. It ignores the question of how the material world came into being, and how it could exist and be ordered without a prime mover and a first cause. Instead, science is substituted for religious belief and is held by communists to be incompatible with belief in God. Science is seen as holding the key to a complete understanding of the material universe of which man is regarded as a part. Religion is equated with superstition. Thus, Soviet "scientific atheism" claims to be creating a paradise on earth in contrast to Christ's injunction: "My Kingdom is not of this world."

In politicizing matters of conscience Soviet communism has demonstrated that it is itself a creed claiming to be a complete system of thought. Its atheism is actually a pseudo-religious phenomenon in that it requires a fervently held belief that God does not exist. Communism rejects the Christian injunction to render unto Caesar what is Caesar's and unto God what is God's, and, instead, makes an unlimited claim on man which justifies its being termed a totalitarian system. In claiming to give meaning to life and to explain all social phenomena, communism can hardly tolerate competing creeds or systems of thought, whether these be Christianity, Buddhism, Islam, or Judaism.

One of the early acts of Lenin's regime was to separate church and state in February, 1918, by disestablishing the Russian Orthodox Church and secularizing education. A variety of tactics have been employed against the Church, including acts of sacrilege and the physical destruction of church buildings or their conversion into clubs, theaters, or warehouses; lectures and propaganda designed to promote atheism; and divisive measures in supporting reformist and sectarian movements and "progressive" clergy against the traditional Church. The decree of disestablishment also nationalized all Church property and made religious bodies entirely dependent upon the government in obtaining use of church buildings. Many clergymen experienced deprivations and oppression and many were executed. At times the crudest kinds of blasphemous propaganda have been employed in an effort to discredit religious belief.

World War II saw the Soviet regime hard pressed for support, and in September, 1943, Stalin arrived at a *modus vivendi* of sorts with the Russian Orthodox Church, permitting it to reestablish a central organization and to elect a Patriarch—which office had been vacant for two decades. This concession was related to the upsurge of Russian nationalism during the war and to the fact that the Russian Church had demonstrated its loyalty to Stalin's regime; it was also prompted by the spontaneous religious revival that had occurred in the large area under German military occupation. The dictator was also interested in demonstrating to Westerners that "freedom of religion" existed in the Soviet Union, and he undoubtedly recognized that the Moscow Patriarchate could serve as a useful instrument in foreign policy. Two councils were established under the U.S.S.R. Council of Ministers—one for Russian Orthodox Church affairs and the other for the "affairs of religious cults." In 1966 they were merged into a single Council for Religious Affairs headed, ironically, by a Party member who must be an atheist.[24]

The Soviet authorities have employed a variety of techniques in combating religious belief. Church buildings have been converted into museums of atheism; and most churches, synagogues, mosques, monasteries, and seminaries have been closed. Religious instruction of children is forbidden and Soviet schools teach "scientific atheism." The Soviet constitution provides for "freedom of religious worship and freedom of antireligious propaganda" (article 124) and, in effect, implicitly forbids the active propagation of religion. Religious literature cannot be published and sold freely. All congregations must be registered and are kept under close surveillance. They can be accused of "disturbing public order" and can be subjected to administrative restrictions and pressures designed to bring about their closing. Periodic efforts are made to discredit

[24] The most thorough study of Soviet policy toward religious bodies is Walter Kolarz, *Religion in the Soviet Union* (New York: St. Martin's Press, 1962). For a brief treatment see Bohdan R. Bociurkiw, "Church-State Relations in the USSR," *Survey*, No. 66 (January, 1968), 4–32.

clergymen; police agents have been known to enter the clergy and subsequently commit apostasy. In the case of the Russian Orthodox Church the regime is in a position to control episcopal appointments, interfere in its internal administration, and censor its publications that are printed on the government's presses.

Although the Russian Orthodox Church experienced renewed repression in the 1960's, it continued to be useful to the regime in communist-inspired international "peace" movements and in the World Council of Churches and elsewhere, where it has endeavored to further the interests of Moscow's foreign policy. If the Russian Orthodox Church is treated with less intolerance, the same cannot be said of other denominations. The Ukrainian Autocephalous Orthodox Church has been suppressed and its hierarchy liquidated. The Ukrainian Catholic Church was compelled to go underground in 1946 and its hierarchy was arrested; its primate, Joseph Cardinal Slipyj, was held in prison camps until released in 1963, following eighteen years of imprisonment, when he was permitted to reside abroad. The Islamic, Judaic, and Buddhist faiths have also experienced severe restrictions. Yet despite repressions and decades of antireligious indoctrination, tens of millions of Soviet citizens remain religious believers.

5. THE POLITICS OF CULTURE

The Soviet regime seeks to control the content of literature in accordance with the doctrine of "socialist realism" that became official policy in 1934. "Socialist realism" resulted from the attempt to apply to the arts Lenin's concept of *partiinost'* (party-mindedness). According to this doctrine, the writer and artist are expected to depict "reality" in such a way as to promote the communist cause. Often the result is insipid and synthetic literature with a "positive hero" and a happy ending extolling the "builders of communism." Literature and the arts are viewed not only as activity comparable to economic production—as, for example, the manufacturing of tractors or washing machines—but as potentially harmful and requiring constant supervision. The writer cannot be himself and has difficulty portraying life as it is with its occasions of senselessness, misery, pain, personal tragedy, cruelties, unfaithfulness, and coarseness in human conduct. The writer who seeks to depict life honestly runs the risk of being accused of permitting himself to be used by enemy propaganda. If he endeavors to be truly creative, he can be accused of ideological errors and of seeking to subvert the Soviet system. The satirist can find it dangerous if he should direct his satire against certain subjects or practices.

The techniques employed to control writers have varied greatly and have included prosecution and confinement to prison camps, as in the case of Andrei Siniavsky and Iulii Daniel' in 1966, as well as confinement to mental hospitals. Intimidation and vilification have been employed against Anna Akhmatova, Mikhail Zoshchenko, Boris Pasternak, and many others; official criticism has been levelled against individual writers. By owning all publishing houses the regime can refuse to publish certain works, as for example, the novels of Alexander Solzhenitsyn, who spent a decade in Stalin's concentration camps and in exile. While his *One Day in the Life of Ivan Denisovich* was published in 1962 because it was useful to Khrushchev, his novels *The Cancer Ward* and *The First Circle* could only be published abroad, although they have circulated among Soviet officials in a limited edition apparently published by the security police. Pasternak's novel *Doctor Zhivago* and Evgeniia Ginsburg's memoirs of prison camp experiences were published abroad but not in the Soviet Union.

When authors are published the authorities are not above bowdlerizing the texts of their manuscripts and removing entire passages that they deem to be politically inexpedient or ideologically harmful, and even rewriting and adding entire passages.[25] However, the regime prefers to have authors engage in self-censorship. This is accomplished through the U.S.S.R. Union of Writers and its affiliates in the union republics, established by Stalin in 1932 as part of the effort to regiment the arts. In order to receive recognition and enjoy the status of an author or literary critic, each writer

[25] The Soviet writer Anatolii Kuznetsov, who defected in Great Britain in 1969, provided graphic proof of this practice when he brought with him on film the ***unexpurgated*** texts of his works published in the Soviet Union in expurgated form. See his personal account in the *New York Times,* August 7, 1969, pp. 1 and 14.

must be a member of the Union. It reprimands errant writers, distributes awards and perquisites including vacations and travel abroad, and supposedly defends authors' rights. However, the Union has failed to defend the creative rights and professional interests of Soviet writers against the demands of the Communist Party.[26] The poet Evgenii Evtushenko expressed the plight of the Soviet writer in his poem "Winter Station" (1956) when he observed: "And what is a writer now? Not master, but a keeper of thought."

If self-censorship proves to be ineffective, the regime can generally rely on the politically responsible editors of journals, newspapers, and publishing house directors to publish only what serves the Party's interests. Nearly every Soviet publication bears a code number referring to the individual censor who represents the organization still known as *Glavlit* (the Chief Administration of Literary and Publishing Affairs). This organization, officially renamed the Chief Administration for the Protection of State Secrets, is responsible for determining that an approved publication does not contain any classified material. Decisions on the publication of controversial writings are taken only at the highest Party organizational levels.[27] As a result publication of individual issues of journals has been delayed while the decision was pending. The journalism profession serves as a watchdog through the Union of Soviet journalists established in 1959.

In the arts the Union of Soviet Composers includes both composers and musicologists, and determines which persons and what kinds of music shall be accorded professional recognition. The Union decides what will be published and performed. The CPSU condemns "formalism" and modernism in music, and endeavors to have composers incorporate political themes into their music and combat "alien ideology." It keeps a close watch on the Union and

[26] The Union's inability to defend writers and the nature of Soviet literary censorship are discussed in Alexander Solzhenitsyn's letter of May 16, 1967, addressed to the Fourth All-Union Congress of Soviet Writers. For the full text see *Bulletin of the Institute for the Study of the USSR* (Munich), XV, No. 8 (August, 1968), 39–43.

[27] For a survey of Soviet ideological and thought control methods, see Robert Conquest, ed., *The Politics of Ideas in the USSR* (New York: Frederick A. Praeger, 1967).

its leadership. In painting and sculpture the controls are exercised through the Union of Soviet Artists, which enforces official aesthetic standards and rewards conformity. Loss of membership in the Union means loss of an assured income, a studio, commissions for new works, and the right to exhibit in museums and exhibitions. In general, it is "art for the people," art that can be understood by the masses, is "realistic," and conveys a political message that is sanctioned. Nonrepresentational and abstract art can exist only in a semiunderground.

In literature and the arts, as in other areas, official policies encounter resistance. Prominent writers have remained silent, refusing to write, or do translations. Manuscripts that the censors will not approve for publication circulate, often surreptitiously, in limited, usually typewritten, editions. Although Alexander Solzhenitsyn could be expelled by the Writers' Union in November, 1969, his literary stature and his talents could hardly be diminished by such an arbitrary act—as testified to by his being awarded the 1970 Nobel Prize for Literature. Works of art in unorthodox styles are sold by artists to private collectors who are members of the Soviet cultural and scientific elite. Although the inducements to conformity and the various other methods of control are much in evidence, they have neither stifled artistic creativity entirely, nor produced the kinds of art and literature that fully meet the Party's expectations.

CHAPTER 9

SOVIET FOREIGN POLICY

The emergence of the Soviet Union as one of the great powers can be viewed against the record of the Russian Empire of the tsars. The acquisition by the tsars of the world's largest territorial mass under a single sovereignty was an essential antecedent to the Soviet regime's foreign policies. Although Imperial Russia suffered humiliating defeat in the Russo-Japanese War of 1904–05 and had advocated international "disarmament" as early as 1899 at the Hague Conference due to its own weakness, it nonetheless succeeded in retaining its vast holdings until the advent of the 1917 Revolution brought the Empire to an end. Once the Soviet regime established itself in the ethnically Russian territories, it succeeded in time in reacquiring all of its lost territories except Poland, Finland, Kars, and Ardahan (the latter came under Russian rule in 1878 but were regained by Turkey in 1918).

The Soviet Union's great-power status cannot be explained simply in terms of its various territorial acquisitions, for its influence has extended well beyond the Soviet frontiers. Initially Moscow had the advantage of the fact that the Western Powers, although disapproving of Lenin's regime, were too exhausted following World War I to undertake an effective military effort to eliminate Soviet rule. Another advantage enjoyed by the Bolsheviks lay in the disunity from which the various anticommunist forces suffered, while Lenin and Stalin were able to identify with Russian national interests. The ability to utilize foreign communist parties in obtaining support for Soviet foreign policy undertakings (by means of strikes, demonstrations, and propaganda) provided an advantage that was of particular value when the Soviet Union was weak.

World War II provided the Soviet leadership with its most significant opportunity. Although Moscow was sought after as an ally by the French and Czechs in 1934 and by the British in 1939, it signed a nonaggression pact with Nazi Germany on August 23, 1939; this enabled the Soviet regime to annex lands with a non-Russian population of more than 22 million. Not only were Estonia, Latvia, and Lithuania regained—along with Bessarabia and Western Belorussia—but the Soviet Union also acquired the Western Ukrainian lands (Eastern Galicia, Northern Bukovina, and Carpatho-Ukraine—the latter in 1945) that had not been part of the Russian Empire. Thus the Pact not only postponed for twenty-two months Soviet entry into World War II, but it offered territorial gains that were to survive both the Pact and the war.

After the Soviet Union became involved in the war as a result of the Nazi invasion of June 22, 1941, it had the advantage—despite a year and a half of retreats—of having the Germans pursue brutal occupation policies that offered no real alternative to Soviet rule. American Lend-Lease aid, valued at nearly $12 billion and offered unconditionally, also contributed significantly to Soviet victory, although the Soviet sacrifice of approximately 24 million lives and much physical destruction meant that great-power status was prepaid. The total defeat of Germany and Japan, and the weakened condition of France and Italy following the war, resulted in a United States-Soviet bipolarity in place of the multipolar international system of the prewar period and redounded to Moscow's advantage. The inability of the Western Powers to prevent the establishment of communist regimes in eight East European countries and in North Korea led to the emergence of a Soviet bloc under Moscow's leadership. Growing Soviet industrial might and scientific and technological achievements were testified to by the detonation of a Soviet atomic bomb in 1949. This was followed by Soviet development of a hydrogen bomb in 1953 and the acquisition of ballistic missile and space-flight capabilities. As a great power the Soviet Union in the mid-1950's also became a money lender and an exporter of conventional weapons.[1]

[1] General works on Soviet foreign policy include the unique work by Louis Fischer, *The Soviets in World Affairs* (reprinting; Princeton, N.J.: Princeton University Press, 1951); Max Beloff, *The Foreign Policy of Soviet Russia* (Lon-

The Soviet Union's admission to great-power status has been the result of the regime's policies in that human and material resources were mobilized and military capabilities enhanced in support of this objective. However, it was also made possible by the policies (and errors) of others from which the Soviet Union has profited. Thus, the failure of the Western Powers and of Nazi Germany to pursue limited objectives in World War II and the American demand that Germany surrender unconditionally were advantageous to Moscow and resulted in a Soviet military presence in Central Europe. Military strategy employed during the war also contributed to Soviet gains—as did concessions made to Stalin (mostly at China's expense) at the Yalta Conference on the basis of faulty estimates of the Japanese ability to prolong the war.

1. OBJECTIVES OF SOVIET FOREIGN POLICY

Like any great power, the Soviet Union seeks to preserve and, if possible, enhance its security and the area under its influence and prosper. At the very least, it wishes to retain its domains and to persuade the Western Powers (especially the United States, Great Britain, and the Federal Republic of Germany) as well as Japan—and possibly Communist China—to recognize its various acquisitions and accept its current frontiers. It would also like to see communist regimes granted general *de jure* diplomatic recognition. In addition to this minimal objective Moscow seeks to extend its influence wherever possible, even if at times this is accomplished at the expense of the local communist party. However, it has generally not been willing to do this at the risk of precipitating a nuclear showdown with the United States. The goal of increased influence has often been referred to as "world communism" (the establishment of new communist regimes), although since 1955 Moscow has been more interested in influencing the foreign policies

don: Oxford University Press, 1947 and 1949); Jan Librach, *The Rise of the Soviet Empire*, rev. ed. (New York: Frederick A. Praeger, 1965); Alvin Z. Rubinstein, ed., *The Foreign Policy of the Soviet Union*, 2d ed. (New York: Random House, 1966); Jan F. Triska and David D. Finley, *Soviet Foreign Policy* (New York: Macmillan, 1968); Adam B. Ulam, *Expansion and Coexistence, The History of Soviet Foreign Policy, 1917–1967* (New York: Frederick A. Praeger, 1968); and the various writings of George F. Kennan.

of capitalist states and of "bourgeois national anticolonialist" regimes in Africa and Asia than in establishing a host of new communist governments.

A third Soviet objective is to divide its capitalist opponents by driving wedges between them and by disrupting alliance systems established to deter the possible threat of communist blackmail or outright aggression. Moscow has always sought to isolate the state that it regards as its principal enemy. Great Britain was cast in this role in the 1920's, Nazi Germany in the 1930's, and the United States after World War II. Related to this goal is the continuing Soviet effort to prevent the Federal Republic of Germany from effecting a complete military recovery by obtaining a nuclear arsenal. By keeping noncommunist regimes weak and divided, Soviet power is enhanced. By encouraging neutralism in Africa, Asia, and Latin America, Moscow seeks to isolate the United States and to deprive anticommunist defensive alliances of additional support.

A fourth objective of the Soviet Union is to retain its primacy in the communist world, especially among the East European states and over as many nonruling communist parties as possible. For example, Hungary was not permitted to leave the Warsaw Pact and adopt neutral status under the U.N. in November, 1956. Moscow also seeks to defeat or reduce the Chinese challenge to its leadership of the international communist movement and to render ineffective the Yugoslav attitude that encourages polycentrism (the existence of several communist centers). A fifth Soviet objective has been to minimize risks and generally to avoid serious involvement on more than one of its several fronts at any given time. Thus in April, 1941, it sought a neutrality pact with Japan as the danger of involvement in the European war increased. Moscow has pursued a policy of expansionism by military means, as in 1939–45, only when it has involved little risk and been directed against weak victims.

2. MOTIVE FACTORS AND TACTICS

Soviet foreign policy may be said to have several motive factors, although it is unwise to isolate any of these determinants; it is, instead, preferable to view them as an amalgam of interests, drives, and responses. One determinant is identified as the "national interest" syndrome, although it is somewhat inaccurate to refer to the national interests of a multinational state like the U.S.S.R. However, what is usually meant is that the national interests of the Russians, as those of the dominant ethnic group within the U.S.S.R., have often been furthered by the Soviet regime. This explanation of Soviet conduct in international relations assumes that communist doctrinal writings do not determine Soviet policy in all its aspects and that in certain respects the Soviet Union employs conventional diplomacy. Moscow is said, in this view, to base its policies more on what is feasible and practicable and only secondarily on what might be ideologically desirable.[2]

Geopolitical and strategic factors might be said to explain certain parallels between tsarist Russian and Soviet policies, and the fact that Russia was a problem for its neighbors long before the Soviet regime appeared on the scene. Thus, the tsarist regime acquired a sphere of influence in Northern Iran in 1907 and the Soviet regime sought such a sphere in 1945–46. The tsars and Catherine II were obsessed with obtaining the Turkish Straits, and

[2] The issue of "national interest" versus doctrinal considerations is discussed by R. N. Carew Hunt, Samuel L. Sharp, and Richard Lowenthal in *Problems of Communism*, VII, No. 2 (March–April, 1958), 10–30. The discussion is reprinted in DeVere E. Pentony, ed., *Soviet Behavior in World Affairs* (San Francisco: Chandler Publishing Co., 1962), and in Alexander Dallin, ed., *Soviet Conduct in World Affairs* (New York: Columbia University Press, 1960). Of course, the simple assertion that a country's foreign policy has but one purpose, namely to promote the "national interest," raises the question of whether this criterion can be used to justify the violation of treaty obligations and whether or not decisions do in fact serve that interest. Thus, was it really in the "national interest" of the U.S.S.R. to wage war against Finland in 1939–40 in violation of treaty obligations? Was it in Moscow's interest to sever relations with Communist Yugoslavia in 1948 or to promote the dispute with Peking? A related question may be raised regarding the extent to which the Nazi regime in Germany promoted German national interests. Thus, it would be necessary to distinguish between those of Hitler's actions and policies that might be said to have furthered German interests and those that had a clearly detrimental effect; the problem for the student of *Realpolitik* would be to determine the year in which Hitler "went wrong" and committed gross errors (rather than mere blunders) that proved to be irreparable. In other words, how many errors of judgment or breaches of faith can be perpetrated in the name of the national interest without bringing about a debacle or near-debacle?

the Soviet regime also sought military bases in the Dardanelles between 1945 and 1953. Both regimes annexed Estonia, Latvia, Lithuania, and Bessarabia; Alexander II attempted to establish Bulgaria as a Russian satellite in 1877 and the Soviets succeeded in doing so after World War II. Tsarist interests in Korea, Manchuria, Sakhalin, and the Kurile Islands preceded Soviet demands involving those areas.[3]

A second determinant, or series of determinants, is derived from the Soviet view of international politics, which is based largely on ideological tenets. In general, this view, insofar as it is expressed in terms of Marxism-Leninism, assumes a significant level of tension and conflict as a "normal" condition in the relations between states. This is a logical corollary of the view that class conflict is the prime mover of history and that the class struggle should be extended into the realm of interstate relations. However, tension should be kept within limits and not be permitted to involve Soviet foreign policy in unplanned or high-risk military conflicts or in "adventurist" undertakings or confrontations; it should also lead to deterrence of military actions on the part of capitalist countries, especially the United States. The tense and hostile condition of international relations can be viewed in Moscow as a natural consequence of the dialectical materialist outlook; the conflict between countries governed by capitalist and socialist ruling classes is seen as an unfolding of the dialectic and as the hallmark of "progress" and of historical development.

The Soviet leaders perceive themselves as exponents and executors of a "peace-loving foreign policy," even though they generally view international politics as a species of warfare conducted by other than purely military means. To the extent that they are guided by ideological considerations, they view their foreign policies as based on the "science" of Marxism-Leninism and as taking into account the "laws of social development." The Soviet leadership views the international situation as developing in terms of his-

[3] On tsarist foreign policy, see Barbara Jelavich, *A Century of Russian Foreign Policy, 1814–1914* (Philadelphia: J. B. Lippincott, 1964). For a comparison of various aspects of tsarist and Soviet foreign policy, see Ivo J. Lederer, ed., *Russian Foreign Policy, Essays in Historical Perspective* (New Haven: Yale University Press, 1962).

torical forces interpreted by them as operating in their favor in the long run, despite certain setbacks, necessary retreats, and postponements.

The noncommunist world is said to be suffering from the malaise discussed by Lenin in his *Imperialism, the Highest Stage of Capitalism.* Capitalism is said to be in its "ripest" and last stage when it is allegedly driven to obtain colonies.[4] This "need" to exploit dependent peoples that lack investment capital and weapons supposedly leads to "inevitable" conflict between capitalist states. Communist states are by their own self-serving definition not imperialistic or given to promoting conflict, because of their claim to have abolished capitalism.[5] Wars and militarism are said to be bred by capitalism, and the danger of war is said to exist so long as capitalism is not removed from the face of the earth. At the

[4] As a result of the growth of monopoly finance capitalism. See p. 94 *supra.*

[5] This self-deluding viewpoint (which is also used to mislead others) ignores the residual imperialism that has characterized both the Soviet and Chinese Communist regimes as legatees of the Russian and Han empires. It also fails to explain the disagreements and overt conflicts that have developed between communist regimes as, for example, between China and the Soviet Union, the Soviet Union and Albania, the Soviet Union and Yugoslavia, the Soviet Union and Rumania (over Bessarabia and Rumania's desire to industrialize fully), the Soviet Union and Czechoslovakia, and between Albania and Yugoslavia. Lenin's definition of imperialism as a characteristic of capitalism failed to explain the many forms of imperialism that preceded capitalism (those of the Assyrians, Greeks, Romans, Spain, Portugal, and Sweden). With respect to the weaknesses in this definition, it is important to note that Lenin published *Imperialism, The Highest Stage of Capitalism* in Switzerland in 1916 and based it largely on data from the last quarter of the nineteenth and the first decade of the twentieth centuries. He relied heavily on data from Germany, where banking and industry had coalesced to an exceptional degree. For discussions of various theories of imperialism, see Archibald P. Thornton, *Doctrines of Imperialism* (New York: John Wiley, 1965), and E. M. Winslow, *The Pattern of Imperialism* (New York: Columbia University Press, 1948).

In defining imperialism in terms of the need to export capital, Lenin ignored the fact that Russia acquired a vast empire over a period of four centuries and did not export capital in the process; indeed, while the Empire was being completed, the Russians were importing capital from France, Belgium, and Great Britain. The Leninist theory of imperialism also fails to take into account the fact that in the 1930's such countries as Japan and Italy undertook to establish empires despite the fact that they were poor in capital and had no need to export it. It ignores the fact that colonies have usually been economic liabilities and have attracted fewer investments than have noncolonies. In reducing imperialism to a single cause, Lenin failed to comprehend a complex phenomenon that has spanned many centuries.

same time capitalism and its species of imperialism are said to be in decline due to continuing crises. Two world wars, said to have resulted from two general crises of world capitalism, have led to the establishment of communist regimes ruling at least one-third of the human race and constituting a "whole system of socialist states."

The increased strength of communist states is said to deter capitalist states from precipitating World War III. Indeed, a general nuclear war has been declared not to be inevitable by Soviet spokesmen—at least since 1956—although wars of liberation are viewed as both desirable and inevitable.[6] Thus, the wars in Korea, Vietnam, and Algeria; the advent of the Castro regime in Cuba; and guerrilla operations in various countries have enjoyed Soviet support. They are seen as a vital counter in the changing balance of international forces that is said to be occurring to the Soviet Union's advantage.

However, the Soviet views on the demise of capitalism and on the allegedly salutary nature of "wars of liberation" have not

[6] Khrushchev explicated this viewpoint in an official address delivered on January 6, 1961 (see Pentony, *op. cit.* [above, n. 2], pp. 242–248): "There will be wars of liberation as long as imperialism exists, as long as colonialism exists. These are revolutionary wars. Such wars are not only possible but inevitable . . ." (p. 245). The 1961 CPSU Program states: "The CPSU and the Soviet people as a whole will continue to oppose all wars of conquest, including wars between capitalist countries, and local wars aimed at strangling people's emancipation movements, and consider it their duty to support the sacred struggle of the oppressed peoples and their just anti-imperialist wars of liberation." *Programme of the Communist Party of the Soviet Union* (Moscow: Foreign Languages Publishing House, 1961), p. 58.

These statements were, in effect, reiterations of a position expressed by Stalin three decades earlier in a letter (dated January 17, 1930) which the dictator sent to the writer Maxim Gorky. Stalin offered the following literary criticism and political advice: "As to war stories, they will have to be published with great discrimination. The book market contains a mass of literary stories describing the 'horrors' of war and inculcating a revulsion against *all* war (not only *imperialist*, but *every other kind* of war). These are bourgeois-pacifist stories that are not of much value. We need stories which will lead readers from the horrors of *imperialist* war to the necessity of overcoming the *imperialist* governments which organize such wars. Besides, we are not against *all* wars. We are *against* imperialist war as being counterrevolutionary war. But we are *for* a liberating, anti-imperialist, revolutionary war, despite the fact that such war, as we know, is not only not exempt from the 'horrors of bloodshed' but even abounds in them." I. V. Stalin, *Sochineniia* (Moscow, 1949), XII, 176 (italics in original).

prompted the leadership to adopt a rigid timetable for foreign policy operations and revolutionary strategy. Indeed, Soviet tactics have varied markedly, and dual policies have frequently been pursued as if to exemplify the dialectic in action. Thus, Moscow could negotiate simultaneously with Nazi Germany and with Great Britain during 1939 in the period preceding the Nazi-Soviet Pact. Similarly, Stalin endeavored to negotiate with the Germans in 1943 in an apparent attempt to withdraw from the war and only went to Teheran to confer with Churchill and Roosevelt after these efforts failed to produce the appropriate response from Hitler. While supposedly developing common postwar policies for Germany with the United States and Britain in 1943–44, the Soviet Union organized and utilized a Free Germany National Committee, part of which served as the nucleus for the Communist East German regime established subsequently by Soviet occupation authorities. The Kremlin has simultaneously wooed Wall Street and American businessmen with promises of trade, while denouncing the policies of an American government that is said to be the "instrument" of Wall Street.

Other examples of Soviet tactical flexibility can be cited. Moscow has developed cordial relations with neutralist countries that have suppressed local communist parties (as in Egypt, Iraq, and Indonesia); it has sought closer relations with monarchies, such as Afghanistan and Ethiopia, in which communist parties have not been active. While supporting the regime in Iraq which followed the overthrow of the monarchy in 1958, the Soviet Union also sought to utilize the Kurdish national movement against the Baghdad government. The classic example of dual policy was that of the 1920's when the Kremlin established diplomatic relations with various countries while working for the overthrow of their governments (as in Germany and Estonia) and playing host to the Communist International.[7]

[7] Lenin provided relevant advice on tactical measures and splitting efforts in his "*Left Wing" Communism, An Infantile Disorder* (1920): "A more powerful enemy can be conquered only by exerting the utmost effort and by *necessarily,* most carefully, solicitously, cautiously, and skillfully taking advantage of every 'rift,' even the smallest, among the enemies, of every antagonism of interest among the bourgeoisie of various countries, between various groups or

Moscow's foreign policy tactics have also changed abruptly at times, as when the Soviet Union decided to join general disarmament talks in 1927 and became a member of the League of Nations in 1934 after having condemned both efforts for years. In 1955 a decision was taken to attempt a reconciliation with Communist Yugoslavia and Tito's regime after having denounced his leadership and his loyalty to communist ideology since 1948. The attitude towards socialist parties has varied; they have often been branded "social fascists," "social traitors," and "opportunists," and at other times have been sought as allies in a "popular front" tactic.

The variety and flexibility of such tactical undertakings lend a measure of credence to the contention that Soviet conduct is rational and is based on a "scientific" ideology. However, there is also an irrational component (or residue) in Soviet conduct, which is testified to by the fact that Soviet leaders have repeatedly expressed their commitment to grandiose goals; it is also evident in the Sino-Soviet dispute. Their view of the historical process is both utopian and at times megalomaniacal—at least in its verbal expression; the Party claims a monopoly on truth and wisdom. The distinctiveness of the lexicon of Soviet leaders makes it difficult to communicate with them. Their extensive preoccupation with enemies and their view of international relations as an extension of the class struggle and of ideological conflict can be viewed as reflecting a tendency to suffer from mass paranoia. There is also a fear of being "contaminated" by the part of the "bourgeois" world that is "evil" and "unclean." [8]

Despite the existence of certain disturbing syndromes in Soviet conduct as well as in their pronouncements, it is necessary to recognize the existence of an additional determinant of Soviet foreign

---

types of bourgeoisie within different countries, by taking advantage of every, even the smallest, opportunity of gaining a mass ally, even though this ally be only temporary, vacillating, unstable, unreliable and conditional. Those who have not understood this have not understood a particle of Marxism, or of scientific contemporary socialism *in general.*" V. I. Lenin, *Polnoe Sobranie Sochinenii,* 5th ed. (Moscow, 1963), XLI, 55 (italics in original).

[8] Various (Bolshevik) syndromes of this type are discussed in Nathan Leites, *A Study of Bolshevism* (Glencoe, Ill.: Free Press, 1953). Also see Leites' *Kremlin Moods* (Santa Monica, California: RAND Corporation Memorandum RM-3535-ISA, 1964).

policy. This is the ability of other powers to exercise some degree of influence on Soviet policy in particular situations. While it is recognized that the Soviet leadership will attempt to exercise initiative at advantageous times and places of its own choosing, it has on occasion been confronted with conditions, created by other powers, which have required revision of Soviet policy or even abandonment of a Soviet position that had been tenaciously held.

Among examples of such situations are the Soviet decision to recognize the Federal Republic of Germany in 1955 (after having ignored its existence for six years), the abandonment of the policy of ignoring the Japanese Peace Treaty of 1951, and the launching in 1956 of an attempt to influence Tokyo's foreign policy. Consistent and firm policies on the part of the states concerned led to modification in Soviet policy. Stalin's decision not to press the civil war in Greece in 1946–47 was another such instance, as was the Soviet withdrawal from Northern Iran in 1946 under pressure. Khrushchev retreated on Berlin after delivering to the Western powers in November, 1958, a six-month ultimatum demanding their withdrawal from West Berlin. Khrushchev also abandoned his efforts to emplace intermediate-range ballistic missiles in Cuba in October, 1962—again as a result of American firmness.

Retreats in the face of unanticipated obstacles or underestimated risks appear to be acceptable to the Soviet rulers whenever they do not involve vital interests. Yet the definition of "vital interests" has varied with the degree to which Soviet leaders have been able to employ credible threats and to persuade other powers that there is no room for compromise at Soviet expense or at the expense of countries, regimes, or movements that the Soviet Union regards as being within its sphere of influence. Thus, communist regimes were prevented from collapsing in North Korea in 1950 and in Hungary in 1956. Hungary's efforts to obtain neutral status, and to withdraw from the Warsaw Pact and revert to a coalition government (including socialists), were suppressed by Soviet troops in November, 1956; and Imre Nagy, who had voiced these demands, was executed along with other leaders. Yet at other times communist regimes have been sacrificed: that of Bela Kun in Hungary in 1919; that in Iranian Azerbaidjan in 1946 while the area was under Soviet occupation; the Finnish communist shadow regime established in December, 1939, behind Soviet military lines; and the Arbenz regime in Guatemala in 1954. In each instance various factors entered into the decision; these included an estimate of relative capabilities made by the Soviet leadership, the risks involved in intervening and the likelihood of a (nuclear) showdown, the consequences that would be likely to ensue in the event of nonintervention, and the immediacy of domestic concerns as opposed to further foreign involvement.

3. THE SOVIET VIEW OF INTERNATIONAL LAW

The use of international law has figured prominently in Soviet foreign policy pronouncements. Other states have been accused of violating international law while it is claimed that the Soviet Union always acts in accordance with such law. Soviet writers on the subject attempt to further the regime's interests and do not ignore political considerations. Initially, the Soviet regime rejected international law as a "bourgeois" instrument (in accordance with the Marxist notion of law as a tool of the ruling class), but soon recognized that it could be useful in furthering Soviet interests. As a result there is an abundant Soviet literature on international law, with textbooks, monographs, theoretical works, and collected documents. The subject is rather widely taught on the graduate level in the Soviet Union and is essential in the training of Soviet diplomats and foreign trade officials.

The Soviet Union views international law as subordinate to domestic law and regards states as the sole subjects of international law (excluding international organizations from this category). States are seen as sovereign entities, and the doctrine of sovereignty is utilized as a weapon against alleged "imperialist encroachments." However, with the granting of independent statehood to numerous colonies following World War II, Soviet ideologists devised the concept of neocolonialism to apply to selected new states regarded as economically (and politically) dependent upon capitalist states. Soviet spokesmen have advocated the right of national self-determination if its exercise has not been at Moscow's expense; in the latter case there is no advocacy. The Soviet Union has been an outspoken advocate of the primacy of states' domestic jurisdiction (especially its own) and has frequently objected to alleged encroachments by international bodies.

In the field of maritime law Soviet authorities recognize the open seas, although the regime has extended its territorial waters at their expense. It treats as interior maritime waters such bodies of water as the White Sea, the Gulf of Riga, the Sea of Azov, and certain Arctic waters (the Kara, Laptev, East Siberian, and Chukchi Seas). Non-Soviet vessels have generally been excluded from these waters except in accordance with conditions set down by Soviet authorities. The Barents Sea is placed in the category of open seas. The Soviet Union has led other states in extending territorial waters to the twelve-mile limit by a decree of May 24, 1921, and has exercised sovereignty in them as well as in the air space above them. The base line in determining the twelve-mile limit is the line of low tide or a line across the mouths of bays and inlets. In practice the Soviet Union has extended its waters well beyond the twelve-mile limit. For example, on July 21, 1957, the Soviet Foreign Ministry announced that henceforth the Bay of Peter the Great in the Sea of Japan would be considered as Soviet "interior waters." [9] Despite the protests of the United States, Great Britain, and Japan, Moscow in effect extended its territorial waters far out to a line passing through the Sea of Japan for a distance of 150 miles.

Another distinctive feature of Soviet policy is that regarding the legal status of the so-called closed seas. The Baltic and Black Seas, as well as the Sea of Okhotsk and the Sea of Japan, are placed in this category; it is contended that the regime for closed seas and that in the straits leading to them is to be determined by a treaty concluded between the littoral states. Although such seas are open to commercial vessels, it is the Soviet view that they are not international maritime routes and must be treated separately from the open seas.[10] The Soviet position has not gained general acceptance.

[9] G. L. Shmigel'skii and V. A. Iasinovskii, *Osnovy sovetskogo morskogo prava* (Moscow: izd. "Morskoi Transport," 1959), p. 29.

[10] *Ibid.*, p. 32.

The Soviet Union has adopted very different positions regarding Arctic and Antarctic waters. By a decree of April 15, 1926, it claimed all islands in the Arctic sector lying north of the Soviet landmass (excluding Spitzbergen and Bear Island). Although the Arctic Sea is not claimed, the Kara, Laptev, East Siberian, and Chukchi Seas are claimed as "historic bays" and are said to be under exclusive Soviet jurisdiction.[11] In the case of the Antarctic and its waters, a sector theory would not be to the Soviet Union's advantage; instead, the Soviet government has contended that it has an interest in the area based on whaling and on the explorations conducted by F. F. Bellingshausen and M. P. Lazarev in 1820–21. Thus, Moscow contests Norway's claim to Peter I and Alexander I Islands.[12] The Soviet position on the Antarctic received general recognition in the Antarctic Treaty of December 1, 1959, which was signed by twelve countries including the U.S.S.R. Although the treaty places territorial claims in abeyance, it provides for use of the Antarctic for peaceful and exclusively scientific purposes.

In the field of law dealing with air space the Soviet Union has been a staunch defender of its own sovereignty and has denied the right of innocent passage to foreign aircraft in the air space above its territorial waters. It has been Soviet policy to shoot down all such intruding military aircraft.[13] In recent years agreements have been concluded granting foreign commercial airlines flight routes into and across the Soviet Union on a reciprocal basis.

The Soviet position on the legal status of outer space has varied. Prior to the Soviet launching of the first artificial earth satellite on

[11] The U. S. Coast Guard icebreaker *Northwind* penetrated the eastern and central Soviet Arctic waters in 1963 (from Bering Strait to Cape Cheliuskin and Vil'kitskii Strait) and traversed the Kara Sea in 1965. Although Soviet naval vessels and military aircraft kept the *Northwind* under constant surveillance, it was not hindered in its scientific task of oceanographic surveying. However, two U. S. icebreakers were prevented from passing through the Vil'kitskii Strait in August, 1967, when the Soviet Foreign Ministry declared that the Strait is within Soviet territorial waters and such passage would be a violation of Soviet frontiers. The U. S. Department of State protested the Soviet assertion and declared the Vil'kitskii Strait to be international waters.

[12] Shmigel'skii and Iasinovskii, *op. cit.* (above, n. 9), pp. 35–36.

[13] See Oliver J. Lissitsyn, "The Treatment of Aerial Intruders in Recent Practice and International Law," *American Journal of International Law*, XLVII, No. 4 (October, 1953), pp. 559–589.

October 4, 1957, it claimed sovereignty into air space without limit. When this position proved to be embarrassing following Soviet success in space flight, it was modified to recognize the free use of outer space while also claiming a certain freedom of action, based on security considerations, in dealing with alleged violators and perpetrators of "space espionage." [14]

The Soviet desire to retain freedom of action and be judge in its own cause is evident in the position adopted on international arbitration and on participation in the International Court of Justice. Although tsarist Russia favored the principle of international arbitration, the Soviet government has not been willing to submit to an international arbitral body disputes in which it is a party; the U.S.S.R. is not a member of the Permanent Court of Arbitration at The Hague. Although the Soviet Union did join the League of Nations, it refused to recognize the Permanent Court of International Justice, which existed from 1920 to 1946, regarding it as an "instrument of the aggressive policies of the great imperialist powers." [15]

As a result of joining the United Nations, the Soviet Union became a signatory of the Statute of the International Court of Justice (ICJ). However, it has not seen fit to accept the jurisdiction of the ICJ in the adjudication of any disputes to which it has been a party. It is the Soviet contention that only disputes of a purely *legal* character should be submitted to the ICJ and that *political* questions should be taken up in the United Nations Security Council and General Assembly. A Soviet judge has always been elected to the ICJ, in accordance with the tenet that it should represent the principal legal systems and civilizations. However, during the Korean War (1950–53), the Soviet judge (Sergei B. Krylov and later Sergei A. Golunskii) did not participate in the work of the Court. Soviet judges have frequently dissented from the Court's findings. In general, the Soviet leadership views the judges of the ICJ as "representatives" of sovereign states and appears to doubt

[14] See Samuel Kucherov, "The USSR and Sovereignty in Outer Space," *Bulletin of the Institute for the Study of the USSR*, XII, No. 2 (February, 1965), 25–33.

[15] N. N. Polianskii, *Mezhdunarodnyi sud* (Moscow: izd. Akad. Nauk SSSR, 1951), p. 24.

that members of an international tribunal can be truly impartial in adjudicating disputes involving state interests.

4. THE SOVIET VIEW OF INTERNATIONAL ORGANIZATIONS

Soviet policy toward international bodies had its origins in hostility and contempt expressed toward the League of Nations because it was associated with the allegedly unjust Treaty of Versailles and was regarded as a tool of the "imperialist" states that were victorious in World War I. The Soviet decision to join the League in September, 1934, led to disappointment when Soviet membership did not prevent the collapse of the European security system. Nor was Moscow endeared to the defunct League when it became the sole member-state to be expelled—as an aggressor due to the Soviet attack on Finland in November, 1939.

The Soviet Union, the Ukrainian S.S.R., and the Belorussian S.S.R. became charter members of the United Nations in 1945. Although superficially the Soviet Union was regarded as having obtained "three votes" in the United Nations (as a result of a decision taken at the Yalta Conference), in reality three separate memberships were obtained, despite the fact that Ukraine and Belorussia joined the world organization while being union republics within the U.S.S.R.[16] Ukrainian and Belorussian memberships were also obtained in the international specialized agencies.

Soviet spokesmen in international organizations have championed state sovereignty and the equality of member states, while simultaneously defending the veto power exercised by any one of the five permanent members of the Security Council in deciding "substantive" issues as opposed to procedural matters. The doctrine of the sovereignty and the equality of states has been used to denounce alleged U. N. efforts to interfere in the domestic affairs of communist states—although Soviet spokesmen have not hesitated

[16] The motives, causes, and consequences of multiple Soviet membership in international bodies are discussed in Vernon V. Aspaturian, *The Union Republics in Soviet Diplomacy* (Geneva: No. 36 in the Publications of the Graduate Institute of International Studies, Librairie E. Droz, 1960); see especially Chaps. 4 and 8, and the appendices.

to advocate U. N. intervention in Angola, Mozambique, Southwest Africa, and Puerto Rico in the name of "anticolonialism." The U. N. was viewed initially as a security organization designed to maintain the military victory won in 1945; indeed, the successor to the League was named for the victorious World War II military alliance. The logical consequence was the principle of the unanimity of the "Big Five"—the permanent members of the Security Council—a synonym for the "veto." Thus, no decision could be binding and enforceable unless it had the support of the great powers. It was assumed erroneously that the foreign ministers of the great powers would first resolve an issue in closed negotiations and then present their decisions to the U. N.

In defending the veto, the Soviet Union has advocated a strict and "legalistic" interpretation of the U. N. Charter. It has insisted upon the soundness and legitimacy of the veto provision. Soviet judges in the ICJ and Soviet spokesmen in the U. N. have therefore repeatedly objected to the Court's interpreting the Charter and statutes of the specialized agencies in advisory opinions; they have insisted that Charter interpretation involves political and not legal questions. The generally rigid Soviet view of the Charter prompted Soviet spokesmen to object to efforts to resort to the General Assembly when action was prevented in the Security Council by a Soviet veto. However, as the number of African and Asian member-states increased, the communist states were less isolated; and Moscow in the mid-1950's lost its reluctance to utilize the Assembly.

The veto has not been a monopoly of the Soviet Union and is actually a symptom of tension rather than its cause. Many Soviet vetoes were employed in opposing membership applications, as on December 13, 1955, when the Soviet Union used it fifteen times in denying membership. By June, 1962, the Soviet Union had employed the veto one hundred times. If the other four permanent members of the Council have not employed the veto with the same frequency, it is because they have been able to rely on other devices to protect their interests. It is also significant that Moscow could veto any effort to expel it from the U. N. since such a proposal must be based on a Security Council recommendation and would be a substantive issue. Nor can the Charter be amended formally without the consent of the five permanent members.

The Soviet Union does not regard the U. N. as a "world government" in embryo and has frequently opposed modest efforts to enhance the U. N. Secretary-Generalship. It organized a campaign against Secretary General Trygve Lie in 1950, for instance, when he supported the U. N. effort to repel North Korean aggression against the Republic of Korea. In 1960–61 a Soviet effort to discredit Secretary General Dag Hammarskjöld resulted from his active role in the U. N. effort to restore order in the Congo. A Soviet attempt to reduce the influence of Western states in the Secretariat led to an unsuccessful proposal, advanced by Khrushchev in September, 1960, to replace the Secretary General with a three-man body representing Western, communist, and third-force states.[17]

Soviet presence in the U. N. Secretariat professional staff was limited to about one-tenth of its quota at the outset even though Moscow, Ukraine, and Belorussia have been contributing approximately 16 percent of the budget. The limited number of Soviet personnel resulted from Soviet policy and was due initially to a lack of qualified personnel and to Stalin's desire to limit official contacts with the non-Soviet world. Yet Soviet officials have usually held the key post of U. N. Under-Secretary of Political and Security Council Affairs, although their tenure has usually been rather brief. In 1959 Moscow demanded more professional Secretariat positions for Soviet citizens. However, a major difficulty has been the turnover in Soviet personnel as the result of a high rate of recall, usually after two or three years' service, as well as the fact that Moscow does not permit the Secretariat to recruit Soviet citizens directly but offers its own candidates. The Soviet Union has generally offered the U. N. the services of its own diplomats and other personnel, who are subsequently reassigned to its own service. In

[17] For a treatment of the campaign against Hammarskjöld, see Alexander Dallin, *The Soviet Union at the United Nations* (New York: Frederick A. Praeger, 1962), Chaps. 9, 10, and 11. Also see John G. Stoessinger, *The United Nations and the Superpowers* (New York: Random House, 1965), Chaps. 3, 5, and 6.

addition, Soviet officials in the U. N. Secretariat have repeatedly been accused by the United States of engaging in espionage activities and have been expelled from the country.

Increased Soviet interest in the Secretariat was preceded by a decision to join or rejoin a number of the specialized agencies. Originally the Soviet Union, Ukraine, and Belorussia had joined such bodies as the Universal Postal Union, the International Telecommunications Union, the World Health Organization, and the World Meteorological Union. In 1949 they withdrew from the World Health Organization because of dissatisfaction over the amount of financial aid received from it. The Soviet Union originally adopted a hostile attitude toward the International Labor Organization (ILO), the United Nations Educational Scientific and Cultural Organization (UNESCO), and the International Refugee Organization (which functioned from 1947 to 1951 resettling refugees whom the Soviet Union demanded be forcibly repatriated). It also refused to join the International Monetary Fund, the World Bank, and the Food and Agricultural Organization. However, in 1954 the three Soviet states joined UNESCO and ILO (the Soviet Union had joined ILO in 1935 but was expelled in 1940). The decision to end the boycott was probably motivated by a desire to obtain additional channels of contact with African, Asian, and Latin American countries. In UNESCO an effort was made to obtain recognition for communist viewpoints in cultural matters. The ILO had participated in an ad hoc committee that investigated forced labor (including Soviet concentration camps) during 1951–53; thus Moscow may have concluded that its absence from the ILO was disadvantageous.

The Soviet leadership is power conscious and has had no illusions regarding the U. N.; it has not relied upon the U. N. as more than an auxiliary instrument of Soviet policy. It does not desire a strong U. N., but neither does it wish to see the organization destroyed. Nor does the Soviet Union wish the U. N. to act in a manner contrary to Soviet interests; the organization's effectiveness is to be limited to areas in which Soviet interests are advanced. It does not wish to be bound by U. N. decisions of which it does not approve or have the organization resolve disputes between communist states. The Soviet Union has advocated a narrow construction of the Secretary General's powers on the assumption that they might be used to the Soviet Union's disadvantage. It refused to help finance U. N. peacekeeping forces in the Near East and the Congo despite an advisory opinion of the ICJ in July, 1962, that held the costs of such operations to be part of the expenses of the organization and an obligation of membership. In the Soviet view peacekeeping costs incurred by action of the Assembly and in the absence of a Security Council decision are "illegal" and contrary to the Charter. When a general financial crisis ensued (affecting the entire U. N. budget and causing the U. N. to issue bonds), an American effort in 1965 to deprive the three Soviet U. N. members of their right to vote failed to gain the support of a majority in the Assembly.

Soviet participation in the U. N. is advantageous in view of its permanent membership in the Security Council. The organization provides a forum in which Soviet doctrines, policies, and professions of support for peace can be expounded. The Soviet anticolonial resolution of 1960 was indicative of the attraction of such proposals for newer member-states, as well as of Soviet willingness and ability to utilize the Assembly to discredit the policies of other powers, especially the United States. The organization and the numerous delegations in attendance serve as sources of information of use to the Soviet Foreign Ministry. The U. N. has also provided an area of contact in which meaningful negotiations can occur, as when the Berlin Blockade was lifted in 1949.

5. THE COMMUNIST MOVEMENT AND SOVIET FOREIGN POLICY

From its very inception the Soviet regime anticipated the establishment of other communist regimes as proof that the Russian Revolution was the harbinger of a worldwide revolutionary movement. Indeed, it was Lenin's belief that such regimes were essential if the Soviet regime was to survive. However, efforts in 1919 to establish communist regimes in Hungary, Bavaria (Munich), Estonia, Latvia, and Lithuania were unsuccessful, just as an attempt to impose communism upon Finland had failed in 1918. However, Lenin's regime succeeded in surviving and even attempted to bring communist rule to Western Ukraine, Western Belorussia, and Poland in the summer of 1920, though without success.

The conviction that Moscow had become the capital of the world proletariat prompted Lenin to establish the Comintern or Third International in March, 1919. Since there were few communist parties in existence outside of Russia and most of the foreign "representatives" were prisoners of war who remained in Russia or foreign admirers of Bolshevism, the founding congress was more a tribute to Lenin's persistence and Russian staging than proof that Europe was about to be inundated by the tide of world revolution. Indeed, the German Party's delegate held that it was premature to found such an organization and abstained in the voting.[18]

As more communist parties were formed with the secession of the left wing of the socialist movement, the Comintern assumed organizational form. The 21 Conditions which parties had to accept to gain admission to the Comintern were adopted by the Second Congress in 1920. The requirements included commitment to the "dictatorship of the proletariat" and a revolutionary course; removal of "reformists" and "opportunists"; and establishment of a parallel illegal (covert) organization, even in bourgeois countries in which the Communist Party enjoyed legal status. Parties were to conduct agitation in the armed forces of "bourgeois" countries, and among the "rural proletariat and the poorest peasants"; and infiltration of trade unions, cooperatives and "other mass workers' organizations." Member-parties were obliged to purge their ranks of "petty-bourgeois elements" periodically, to give "unconditional support to any Soviet republic in its struggle against counterrevolutionary forces," and to accept all Comintern decisions as binding.

The fact that Comintern headquarters were in Moscow, that Russian communists or agents headed its Executive Committee, and that various commissions and Soviet funds were at its disposal to

[18] For an eyewitness account of the founding congress by the Comintern's First Secretary, see Angelica Balabanoff, *Impressions of Lenin* (Ann Arbor: University of Michigan Press, 1964), pp. 70–71. Also see Stanley Page, *Lenin and World Revolution* (New York: New York University Press, 1959).

subsidize the various parties meant that the Soviet Communist Party would exercise a dominant influence in the organization. The highly centralized character of the Comintern meant that there was no equality of parties. The CPSU actively intervened in the internal affairs of other communist parties—including the German Party—removing its leadership in 1921, 1923, and 1925. Non-Soviet communist parties were compelled by Stalin to become involved in the Soviet power struggle during the 1920's and those leaders who supported Stalin's rivals were removed. Efforts to seize power in Germany in March, 1921, and in October, 1923, failed as did attempts in Bulgaria in 1923 and in Estonia during December, 1924. Comintern policy in China failed in 1927, when Chiang Kai-shek moved to crush the Chinese Communist Party. The Comintern was further discredited by the contempt with which Stalin viewed it and by the fact that many foreign communists residing in the Soviet Union perished in the purges. Infiltration and espionage were practiced against the various parties in accordance with Russian secret police methods. The Kremlin also took the drastic step of dissolving the Polish and Korean communist parties in 1938, and the Yugoslav Party came close to being dissolved. Thus the interests of other parties were repeatedly subordinated to those of the Soviet regime. The Nazi-Soviet Non-Aggression Pact of August 23, 1939 (which communists throughout the world found difficult to explain because they had been denouncing Nazi Germany and calling for a "united front against fascism" during the preceding five years) resulted in the total disgrace of the Comintern.[19]

Stalin had the Comintern dissolved by its own Executive Committee in May, 1943, probably because of the wartime international situation and the desirability of fostering the impression that Moscow was abandoning the policy of world revolution. It is ironic that Soviet foreign policy and the communist movement should have enjoyed greater successes following the Comintern's dissolution. Despite numerous failures, the Comintern trained thousands

[19] The best general work on the Comintern is Günther Nollau, *International Communism and World Revolution, History and Methods* (New York: Frederick A. Praeger, 1961). Also see Franz Borkenau, *World Communism* (reprinting; Ann Arbor: University of Michigan Press, 1962).

of foreign communists in special schools in the Soviet Union. Its agents fought in civil wars in Spain, Greece, and elsewhere; conducted political strikes and agitational activities; fulfilled espionage assignments; and assisted Soviet intelligence in various ways.[20] Tested cadres were developed to promote Soviet domestic and foreign policies in the mass media of other countries. Although most of the approximately ninety communist parties in the world were small, the Kremlin could assume that in nearly every country it had some supporters upon whom it could rely.

The formal dissolution of the Comintern was useful because it lent some credence to the Soviet assertion that the various communist parties are independent and do not act on orders from Moscow. The Soviet military victory in 1945 led to the establishment of communist regimes in eight Eastern and Central European countries. This, together with the victory of the Chinese communists in 1949 and the creation of communist regimes in North Korea and North Vietnam, laid the groundwork for profound changes in the entire communist movement. Stalin endeavored to maintain Soviet control by founding the Cominform or Communist Information Bureau in September, 1947, at a meeting in Poland. Nine communist parties comprised the Cominform: the CPSU, and the Polish, Yugoslav, Rumanian, Czechoslovak, Hungarian, Bulgarian, French, and Italian parties. Asian communist parties were not represented, nor was the Socialist Unity (Communist) Party of East Germany (its presence would have divulged Soviet objectives in Germany prematurely). The Albanian Party of Labor did not join the Cominform because of its dependence upon the Yugoslav Communist Party at that time.

The fact that the Cominform encountered difficulties within less than a year after its founding has obscured somewhat the purposes that Stalin set for it. Although its strident anti-Americanism was much in evidence, the Cominform was not a successor to the Comintern. Its limited and predominantly East European membership indicated its role as a device for integrating and consolidating Soviet domination over the new regimes. The inclusion of the Italian

[20] The entire range of Comintern activities and controls is discussed in Nollau, *ibid.*, Chap. 4.

and French parties was probably related to the Soviet effort to obstruct the American Marshall Plan for Europe's economic recovery. In 1947 the Yugoslavs were given the task of criticizing the two West European parties for their ineffectiveness. The location of Cominform headquarters in Belgrade probably reflected Stalin's intention of using the organization to control the Yugoslav regime of Marshal Tito.[21] The Cominform had limited but important functions; its newspaper, *For a Lasting Peace, For a People's Democracy,* was controlled by the CPSU and was used to communicate directives and shifts in the line to various communist parties.

The Soviet decision to expel Yugoslavia from the Cominform in June, 1948, and to transfer the headquarters to Bucharest was to have far-reaching consequences which Stalin's subsequent sanctions to bring Tito to heel and which Khrushchev's effort to effect a reconciliation in May, 1955, could not undo. The Yugoslav Party had been accused of adopting a "nationalistic attitude"; and the evidence does indicate that Tito resisted Soviet controls, wished to establish a communist Balkan federation, and was utilizing the Greek "civil war" to that end. Alleged supporters of Tito in the various East European countries were brought to trial as Soviet controls tightened. The death of Stalin made possible the decision to attempt to attract Yugoslavia back into the communist fold, but the Soviet admission that Tito was "building socialism" also had the effect of rewarding heresy. Khrushchev's 1956 "secret speech" denigrating Stalin and his public proclamation that there were "various roads to socialism" led to disillusionment and confusion. Foreign communists asked what Khrushchev and his associates were doing while Stalin committed his crimes and were at a loss for a Marxist explanation of the "cult of personality." The speech also resulted in the Hungarian rebellion of October, 1956, and in the replacement of the Polish communist leadership (the restoration of the "Titoist" Wladyslaw Gomulka). Khrushchev's speech also elicited dissatisfaction from the Chinese communists, who ob-

[21] For a participant's account of the founding of the Cominform, see Eugenio Reale, "The Founding of the Cominform" in Milorad M. Drachkovitch and Branko Lazich, eds., *The Comintern: Historical Highlights* (New York: Frederick A. Praeger, 1966), pp. 253–268.

jected to the unilateral Soviet decision to criticize Stalin's excesses —a decision regarding the historical heritage of communism, affecting the entire movement but not the result of joint deliberations.

The Chinese had other grievances as well and resented the Soviet unwillingness to grant their party—the world's largest communist party—an effective veto over decisions. In return for such a veto Peking was willing to recognize the primacy of the CPSU. The limited nature of Soviet economic aid to China and the 1959 Soviet decision to terminate nuclear development aid were also causes of resentment. Basic to the rivalry was the question of which party would provide the most effective and relevant model and achieve purer Communism. Mao Tse-tung's contempt for Khrushchev as a theoretician and revolutionary and the fact that Mao had brought communist rule to the world's most populous country and oldest extant culture—accomplishing this with little Soviet aid and against Stalin's advice—contributed to Peking's combined sense of frustration and superiority. When Khrushchev failed to seize the initiative in the (Soviet-precipitated) Berlin crisis of 1959–61 and sought, instead, a limited détente with the United States, China's fears of betrayal were apparently confirmed. Peking became convinced that Moscow was not using its alleged military superiority in dealing with the United States. The deterioration of relations between the two largest communist parties was intensified by Khrushchev's unilateral decision to excommunicate Albania from the communist movement in October, 1961, which step the Chinese disapproved. The Albanian leadership, for its part, was embittered by the new conciliatory Soviet policy on Yugoslavia (a traditional Albanian enemy) and by the anti-Stalin campaign. Peking welcomed its new Balkan ally. Rumania utilized the Sino-Soviet dispute to adopt a "neutralist" stance within the communist world and to insist upon its right to rapid and diverse industrial development despite Soviet advocacy of a more specialized Rumanian economy. The Soviet occupation of Bessarabia also served as a source of grievance for Rumanian communists. China's sense of betrayal was confirmed by the nuclear Test Ban Treaty signed in Moscow in August, 1963. Peking became the second communist nuclear power in October, 1964.

No longer could Moscow demand and obtain the unqualified obedience of all of the world's communist parties. It had been an easy matter to cope with the Trotskyite deviation of the 1920's because the Trotskyites controlled no country, army, or state apparatus. Communist deviationists who led ruling parties and had their own bureaucracies and armed forces could not be disciplined easily and brought to heel by Moscow—especially if they had obtained power with little or no Soviet aid. The Soviet claim to a monopoly of Leninism while condemning those who disagree as "sectarians," "revisionists," or "dogmatists" lost its effectiveness. The variety of deviations and brands of communist doctrines ("Trotskyism," "Bukharinism," "Stalinism," "Titoism," "Khrushchevism," "Maoism," and Togliatti's "polycentism")—all descended from Leninism—undermined Moscow's authority and its claim to primacy.

By January, 1959, the CPSU had to claim that it recognized that communist parties were "equal and independent." However, the Sino-Soviet disagreement made it impossible to establish policy-making bodies and practices for the so-called Socialist Commonwealth that would be acceptable to all; nor was there agreement on voting (and veto) rights. The dissolution of the defunct Cominform in April, 1956, had eliminated the sole formal organizational expression of Soviet hegemony. The conferences of communist parties held in Moscow in November, 1957, and in November-December, 1960, were not effective and only served to conceal differences. More limited multilateral conferences have also been held. Under the circumstances the CPSU has had to rely upon a variety of devices in attempting to exercise leadership of other communist parties. These devices include the CPSU's Central Committee section dealing with other communist parties; Soviet officials responsible for this sector have included Mikhail Suslov, Boris N. Ponomarev, and Yuri Andropov. High Soviet leaders have attended the congresses of many other parties, and those parties regularly send nonvoting delegates to CPSU Congresses in Moscow. Such exchanges of representatives provide ample opportunity for efforts at persuasion.

Communists are expected to be ideologically schooled and to understand the need for tactical flexibility and sensitivity to new "cues" emanating from Moscow. Apart from official Soviet publications and secret circulars sent to other parties, the theoretical journal *Problems of Peace and Socialism* has been published since 1958 in numerous foreign languages in an effort to promote Moscow's influence.[22] Other channels of information and aid to foreign communist parties are provided by Soviet embassies, commercial missions, journalists, and special emissaries with appropriate cover. Small parties have been supported by Soviet subsidies and have usually remained loyal to Moscow.

The Soviet disputes with Yugoslavia, China, and Albania exposed the falsity of the oft-repeated claim that international communism was a monolithic movement. Nationalism has served as the principal eroding force and communist leaders have intrigued against each other. The Soviet Union has been confronted with economic, political, and ideological demands from its communist allies. Insofar as Moscow has retained an ability to attract the support of foreign communists, this has been due more to Soviet military capability, industrial might, and economic wealth than to ideological purity. If the claim to primacy has enabled Moscow to enjoy certain advantages, it has also imposed burdens.

6. THE FOREIGN MINISTRY

Soviet foreign policy is not exclusively the concern of the U.S.S.R. Ministry of Foreign Affairs. The Ministry is under the supervision of the Council of Ministers and the premier (or Chairman of the Council) plays an important role in Soviet diplomacy. However, all important foreign policy decisions emanate from the Central Committee's Politburo and are based on recommendations and studies made in the Central Committee department responsible for foreign affairs and in the Foreign Ministry. The Ministry

[22] The English language edition, *World Marxist Review*, is published in Toronto, although the editorial offices are in Prague.

has a special relationship with the Politburo and Party apparatus because of the highly important matters with which it is charged.

Although the Foreign Ministry does not bear final responsibility for the making of foreign policy, its political reporting and research are of inestimable value to the Party officials who make the ultimate decisions. The Ministry is organized along functional and geographic lines; the former include units concerned with protocol, the press, treaty and legal matters, and the like. The Minister is advised by his collegium of approximately twelve members, who are first deputy ministers, deputy ministers, or heads of important divisions within the Ministry. However, he bears full responsibility for the Ministry and cannot be overruled by the collegium, although it can appeal to the Council of Ministers or the Central Committee in the event that it disagrees with him.

The Soviet Union has had a limited number of foreign ministers, as several have held the post a decade or longer and have provided a remarkable degree of continuity. Trotsky, a revolutionary who had no taste for diplomacy, served as commissar of foreign affairs for several months. Georgii Chicherin, a gifted aristocrat and tsarist diplomat who had resigned from the Empire's foreign service in 1904 after seven years and had joined the Marxist movement, held the post from April, 1918, until 1930. He was succeeded by Maxim Litvinov, also an old revolutionary, who headed the foreign office from 1930 to 1939, when he was removed preliminary to the negotiation of the Nazi-Soviet Pact. Viacheslav Molotov served as Foreign Minister from 1939 to 1949, and again from 1953 to 1956. Andrei Vyshinsky, Stalin's chief prosecutor and former professor of law and rector of Moscow University, held the post from 1949 to 1953. The Minister with briefest tenure, next to that of Trotsky, was Dmitrii Shepilov, a Party official who served from June, 1956, to February, 1957, but broke with Khrushchev. Andrei Gromyko—a career diplomat and former Soviet ambassador to the United States, the United Kingdom, and the U. N.—was appointed to succeed Shepilov and survived Khrushchev when the latter was ousted in 1964.

Soviet Foreign Ministers have usually not risen above full membership in the Central Committee; and it appears that the Party leadership prefers a foreign minister who is a career diplomat and technician, and not a Party functionary or Politburo member. Only Trotsky and Molotov were in the Politburo as full members, while Vyshinsky and Shepilov were alternate members. Molotov enjoyed full Politburo membership because he was premier of the Soviet Union. Chicherin achieved Central Committee membership only in 1925 and Litvinov attained it in 1934—long after they became heads of the foreign office. Gromyko became a Central Committee member in 1956 as a first deputy foreign minister. The Foreign Minister who is not a Politburo member can probably avoid committing himself on many issues—especially those that concern domestic politics—and, unlike Shepilov, can avoid certain pitfalls. Not to be a Politburo member is advantageous because it probably makes him less vulnerable and assures him longer tenure; it also enables him to concentrate on foreign policy issues.

Soviet career diplomats must be Communist Party members and are trained in the Foreign Ministry's Higher Diplomatic School. All key diplomatic posts are filled only with the approval of the Central Committee apparatus. The Soviet diplomatic service's subordinate status was made especially evident when Stalin at the end of World War II ordered Foreign Ministry personnel to be put in uniform, complete with shoulder boards, rank insignia, and gold braid. The abandonment of the uniform and the restoration of the business suit in 1954 was followed by the infusion of Party and government functionaries into the diplomatic service. Although the service was severely purged in the late 1930's (and new personnel had to be drafted into it from other fields), the ouster of Molotov and Shepilov did not lead to the removal of career diplomats. However, career diplomats have usually not been entrusted with Soviet embassies in communist-ruled countries; these ambassadorships have usually gone to Party officials.

The role of Soviet diplomats is circumscribed and deals with the implementation of policy rather than with policy-making. Nor does the Soviet leadership rely exclusively upon diplomats for reporting on developments abroad. Although the ambassador reports to the Foreign Ministry, the military attachés report to the GRU (Chief Directorate of Intelligence) and the commercial counselor reports to the Ministry of Foreign Trade. The Party's representative, the secretary of the primary party organization within the embassy who uses a minor diplomatic post as a cover, reports directly to the Central Committee in Moscow. The KGB, the secret police, has its personnel in all Soviet embassies and also receives reports. The Central Committee apparatus sifts and evaluates all reports for use by the Politburo. In addition to providing multiple channels of communication, this system also facilitates the use of Soviet embassies for intelligence and espionage purposes, and encourages mutual surveillance. Although Soviet diplomats are spied upon and have had but a limited influence upon the Politburo, their status has been enhanced since Stalin's death because of Moscow's diplomatic offensive.

7. SOVIET DIPLOMATIC TECHNIQUE

The Soviet diplomat is trained to regard his work as part of a total strategy in which each of the skirmishes or encounters fought by him has its place. It undoubtedly was with this in mind that Stalin reminded his generals and marshals in June, 1945, following their military victory over Nazi Germany, that a shrewd foreign policy is worth several army corps. The Soviet diplomat is carefully instructed, his plenipotentiary powers are usually rigidly circumscribed, and he is backed by a powerful propaganda machine. He is not likely to mediate between the position of his government and that adopted by a foreign government. He does not readily reveal the areas in which he is permitted to negotiate and this makes it very difficult for his counterpart. His skill in engaging in delaying tactics and in repetitiousness is renowned. He can be abusive; rude and insulting; or pleasant, urbane, and polite as the situation or his instructions might demand. He is not troubled by inconsistencies. Thus, he thinks nothing of advocating the struggle against colonialism for Angola and Vietnam but not for Lithuania, Moldavia, Ukraine, or Uzbekistan.

Negotiations are employed not only to reach agreements. Soviet diplomacy frequently seeks to confuse and disarm its opponents by exploiting the "contradictions" said to exist between the various capitalist states, and between the imperialists and the colonies and semicolonial countries. The popular front tactic or the "anti-imperialist struggle" are cases in point. Soviet diplomacy attempts to exploit the greed and fears of particular countries. It attempts to utilize interest groups in other countries—as for example, appealing to businessmen to have their governments lift trade restrictions—and is not likely to be undercut by Soviet interest groups. Soviet foreign policy has taken full advantage of the mass media in pluralistic and democratic societies in an effort to pressure other governments into offering greater concessions.

Negotiations have frequently been employed to prevent agreement if the Soviet Union has been seeking to buy time. The peace talks conducted with the Central Powers by Trotsky at Brest-Litovsk early in 1918 provide a classic example of this tactic. Other examples are the negotiations for an Austrian State Treaty, in which Moscow stalled from 1947 to 1954 in more than 260 negotiating sessions; and the various disarmament meetings, the Korean truce talks (1951–53) as well as negotiations on German reunification since 1946. Extraneous issues are introduced and on occasion Soviet diplomats have simply walked out or absented themselves. Opponents are accused of engaging in obstructionist tactics and diplomatic conferences are used to "unmask" or discredit them and to impugn their motives. Repeatedly the Soviet Union has engaged in negotiations with no intention of offering a *quid pro quo;* it has treated as "negotiable" only concessions offered by others and has usually not offered genuine concessions in return. Thus, what is claimed as the Soviet Union's is not generally subject to negotiation.

Soviet diplomacy has frequently been related to propaganda considerations, and the use of the diplomatic conference as a propaganda sounding board can remain a side effect even when Moscow is pursuing negotiations seriously. The precedent of subordinating diplomacy to propaganda was set when Lenin's government, in one of its first acts, published the secret Anglo-Russian and Franco-Russian agreements of World War I regarding the planned division of spoils. Soviet spokesmen have frequently appealed directly to peoples over the heads of their governments in an effort to activate the forces of anticipated revolution. Soviet diplomatic notes have often told foreign governments what Moscow thinks their peoples to be thinking and what *their* national interests are. The notes are lengthy and often read like *Pravda* editorials; their purpose is not only to communicate with other governments but to influence public opinion. This objective has been especially evident when the Soviet government has published diplomatic communications before they have been translated and studied by the governments to which they are addressed.

Soviet leaders have employed a variety of diplomatic methods, ranging from summit meetings and state visits (including calls on the Pope by Foreign Minister Gromyko and chief of state Podgorny, despite the regime's hostility to the Catholic Church) to threats. The threat of Soviet "volunteers" and the vulnerability of London and Paris to H-bombs succeeded in October, 1956, in compelling Anglo-French and Israeli withdrawal from Egypt. Soviet threats regarding West German rearmament with nuclear weapons have been vague—i.e., the Soviet Union "will not tolerate" it. The use of a specific threat by Khrushchev in November, 1958, to sign a separate peace treaty with the East German Communist regime within six months backfired when Presidents Eisenhower and Kennedy called his bluff. Khrushchev then repeatedly extended the ultimatum and lost credibility by not transferring to East German authorities control of the access routes to West Berlin as he had threatened to do.

The various characteristics of Soviet diplomacy have made it difficult to negotiate with Moscow. The Soviet belief that persistence pays was evident when the Western Powers accepted the uninspected nuclear Test Ban Treaty in 1963 (although the Soviet Union offered a paper concession in agreeing to the exception for underground tests). Perseverance may also have been rewarded with the signing of the Soviet-West German Treaty of August 12, 1970, providing for renunciation of force and recognition of existing frontiers. The Soviet insistence upon a regime for the Antarctic was vindicated in the Antarctic Treaty of December, 1959, which embodied the provisions of a Soviet *aide memoire* of June 7, 1950, sent at a time when the Soviet Union was excluded from talks dealing with that subcontinent. The rewards of a persistent pursuit of policy objectives were evident in Soviet conduct at the Yalta and Potsdam conferences, which were very advantageous for Moscow. Soviet persistence has also obtained diplomatic immunity for its consular and foreign trade officials.

8. SOVIET FOREIGN TRADE POLICY

The system of central economic planning has as its logical consequence the state monopoly of Soviet foreign trade, although planners have tended to dislike such trade insofar as it requires them to deal with external factors that they cannot control. World trade involves too many variables to suit the communist economic planners. As a result, controls are maintained over all imports and exports, and foreign trade serves both as an instrument of Soviet foreign policy in the pursuit of political objectives and as a means of promoting internal economic development. If the Soviet Union has not in the past been a very important factor in world trade, this has been due to the regime's following a policy of autarky or economic self-sufficiency so as not to be permanently dependent upon other countries for essential items. Yet foreign trade has played a vital role in obtaining imports of entire factories from Western Europe and the United States to remedy shortcomings in the Soviet economy; the Soviet Union has furthermore sought from the West "strategic commodities"—goods that add appreciably to a country's capabilities. The state foreign trade monopoly has also sought to protect the Soviet Union from fluctuations of prices and output in the world's markets and to reduce the country's dependence for politico-military reasons.

The entire system of controls is administered by the U.S.S.R. Ministry of Foreign Trade and is based on fixed foreign exchange rates. The ruble is not freely convertible into other currencies and is exchanged only under controlled conditions; nor is the ruble backed by gold in practice, although it is said to have an official gold content. The need to manage the limited supply of foreign exchange and to exploit every possible means of earning foreign currency has led to the establishment of numerous specialized Soviet foreign trade organizations. Each has headquarters in Moscow, is known as an All-Union Combine (*Vsesoiuznoe Ob"edinenie*), and has an abbreviated special designation. Thus V/O "Vneshposyltorg" sells consumer goods, household appliances, automobiles, and vacation tours for delivery in the Soviet Union to persons purchasing such with foreign currency. The organization also operates special stores in the Soviet Union in which only hard currencies are accepted from Soviet citizens. Soviet trade organizations are often represented abroad by a single Soviet commercial agency as, for example, in the United States where the Amtorg Trading Corporation oversees Soviet imports and exports.

Soviet foreign trade has been complicated by the use of exchange rates and domestic prices that are arbitrary. Export prices are also manipulated; the use of bilateral trade agreements with other countries and the trade organizations' practice of selling at prices that differ from those charged domestically serve to keep the Soviet Union competitive in many areas. At the same time Soviet foreign trade is part of the economic plan, and it is conducted not on the basis of decisions made by numerous private individuals but by state agencies. Yet Soviet businessmen, despite the fact that they are government employees, have sought to buy cheaply and sell dearly—except where political considerations or bureaucratic interests might prompt them to do otherwise.[23]

The Soviet Union has not been eager to trade extensively with the Western industrial states except to obtain valuable equipment and items not readily manufactured by domestic producers. Most Soviet foreign trade has been with other communist states. Soviet exports include such items as petroleum, furs, caviar, machine tools, aircraft, merchant ships, hydroelectric equipment and raw materials (the latter exported to East European communist countries). Some of the most useful Soviet imports have been obtained from countries which have little need for Soviet export items. For example, beginning in 1963 the Soviet Union contracted to import

[23] The problems of Soviet foreign trade are discussed in Alan A. Brown and Egon Neuberger, eds., *Trade and Planning* (Berkeley and Los Angeles: University of California Press, 1967), and in Frederic L. Pryor, *The Communist Foreign Trade System* (Cambridge: MIT Press, 1963).

at great cost large shipments of grain from Australia, Canada, and the United States. Such purchases have resulted in balance of payments difficulties. The Soviet Union has attempted to cope with trade deficits by increasing its exports and foreign exchange earning activities wherever possible and also by selling gold for hard currencies that are used to purchase needed imports.

The Soviet Union is probably the world's second largest producer of gold (surpassed only by South Africa), although the size of its annual production is a state secret. This has made it possible for Moscow to remain aloof from the International Monetary Fund in dealing with balance of payment difficulties. The Soviet government sells gold through commercial banks that it controls in London, Paris, and Zurich; the London bank has a branch office in Beirut, Lebanon. The banks are also used to sell other precious metals, to finance trade credits, and to deal in foreign exchange.

The emergence of the Soviet Union as an international banker and as a creditor country was in marked contrast to its prior role as a debtor. In the mid-1950's Moscow began to offer credits to a limited number of neutralist states which included Afghanistan, Egypt, Syria, India, Indonesia, Burma, Iraq, and Yemen. The Soviet claim was that developing countries could obtain low-interest loans in Moscow without accepting the onerous conditions allegedly attached by international and capitalist lending agencies. The State Committee for Foreign Economic Relations was established to oversee the new loan program and to save African and Asian lands from the predatory grasp of neocolonialism—which allegedly sought to subvert their political independence by making them economically dependent upon Wall Street. Moscow also undertook to sell arms especially to neutralist states, beginning with Egypt and Afghanistan, as a means of countering Western military aid and alliance systems.

Soviet objectives in the foreign loan program are to reduce if not entirely eliminate the influence of the capitalist states in Asia, Africa, and Latin America. By depriving these states of their colonial territories and areas of investment, capitalism will be correspondingly weakened. In this way "contradictions" between the imperialist powers can be intensified as the competition for markets and investments increases. The Soviet Union is also interested in limiting the influence and membership of Western-sponsored defensive alliances like SEATO and CENTO. It hopes that the states receiving loans will support, or at least not obstruct, Soviet foreign policy undertakings and resolutions in the U. N. and in the international specialized agencies. Moscow also assumes that the export of Soviet capital and technology will promote the adoption of the Soviet model for modernization and rapid industrialization. While the Soviet Union is using the "nationalist bourgeoisie" of the borrowing countries in the struggle against imperialism, it also seeks to promote conditions that will lead to the emergence of communist parties and, ultimately, communist regimes. Although the Soviet financial investment in developing countries is more political than economic in nature, it serves to underscore Moscow's continuing interest in world trade and its ability to extend credits, to place on the market or withhold from it large quantities of goods and armaments as well as services.

9. CONDITIONS OF COEXISTENCE

The Soviet assertion that the ultimate triumph of communism is possible without resorting to cataclysmic thermonuclear warfare, has required a refurbishing of the concept of "peaceful coexistence." Although the term "coexistence" was employed by Lenin and Stalin, its more recent usage involves a redefinition of the means to be employed in the contest between the American and Soviet colossi. According to the new definition, economic competition and politico-ideological struggle are to be accompanied by a search for new allies and an effort to enlarge the ranks of the uncommitted countries. Although outright war is to be avoided in the relations between "states with different social systems," it has been said that there "can be no peaceful coexistence when it comes to internal processes of the class and national-liberation struggle in the capitalist countries or in the colonies." [24] The "peaceful coexist-

[24] From the Report of the Central Committee to the 23rd CPSU Congress as delivered by Brezhnev on March 29, 1966. See *XXIII S"ezd KPSS* (Moscow, 1966), I, 44.

ence" formula is designed to contribute to the immobilization of the Soviet Union's antagonists, while the communist cause is to be advanced by a variety of means that fall short of thermonuclear war. Thus "coexistence" cannot be based on a static condition but must reflect a changing international situation that is supposedly developing in the Soviet Union's favor.

If there remains much of the "two camps" doctrine in the "coexistence" concept, the Soviet Union can still be said to desire a modicum of stability in international relations. To this end it has maintained a limited dialogue with its various antagonists and has entered into limited agreements, such as the Test Ban Treaty of August, 1963; the Austrian State Treaty of May, 1955; the Antarctic Treaty of December 1, 1959; the Space Treaty of 1967; and the 1968 Treaty on the Non-Proliferation of Nuclear Weapons. Yet it has also utilized conflicts and rivalries between various countries, mounted diplomatic offensives, and has become involved in various regional international crises. It has maneuvered at the expense of unstable countries and has endeavored to split the bourgeoisie when there has been little chance of establishing a communist regime in a country. The Soviet leadership has also sought to capitalize upon divergent interpretations and analyses (in Western circles) concerning what Soviet policy actually is, thus contributing to confusion and indecision in the enemy camp.

Coexistence has also been complicated and even endangered by the various crises precipitated by direct action or by use of proxies. Thus the Berlin Blockade of 1948–49, the Korean War of 1950–53, the Berlin crises of 1958–61, the Cuban missile crisis of October, 1962, all threatened the international balance of forces and gave meaning to the Soviet definition of "coexistence." Subsequent Soviet decisions to arm the Vietcong guerrillas in their efforts to overthrow the Republic of (South) Vietnam and to become actively involved in the international politics of the Near East by arming certain Arab countries served to underline the fact that for Moscow coexistence has a dynamic that distinguishes it from a static balance of power. However, in such situations the Soviet decision-makers have at times encountered unanticipated reactions from the United States and from the anticipated victims of Soviet policies.

In the Soviet view, established communist regimes must be maintained in power even at great cost and in the face of open revolt as in Hungary in October-November, 1956, and in East Germany in June, 1953. This view was reaffirmed in the so-called Brezhnev doctrine of 1968, which asserted the claim of the Soviet Union to intervene militarily in a "fraternal" country in which there allegedly is a deviation from the "common laws governing socialist construction" or a "threat to the cause of socialism." If Soviet policy-makers vacillated initially in Poland and Hungary in 1956 and in the decision to occupy Czechoslovakia militarily in August, 1968, in the end they did not hesitate to employ military forces to preserve these regimes; and they were aided indirectly by the American decision not to intervene. The Soviet decisions to abandon a Finnish communist regime established behind Soviet military lines in 1940, and an Azerbaidjanian communist regime proclaimed in the Iranian city of Tabriz in 1945–46 under Soviet military occupation are rare exceptions to a policy that has sought to aid and protect even the weakest communist regime. However, there are more important considerations than the number of communist regimes in existence at a particular time.

The Soviet Union and the United States have sought to match each other's efforts to approximately the same degree in weapons systems, scientific research, technological ability, intelligence operations, and propaganda. Coexistence tends to promote the maintenance of countervailing power in the principal contenders, although parity in weaponry may also reduce Soviet awareness of risk in foreign policy ventures. Ideally coexistence should lead to greater discourse and it, in turn, might facilitate the resolution of the various contradictions that have characterized the Soviet Union's relations with noncommunist countries.

CHAPTER 10

THE SOVIET POLITY: PROBLEMS AND PROSPECTS

Attempts to predict the future development of the Soviet polity have not been especially successful in the past. Changes in the regime's policies have frequently been misinterpreted, as when the NEP was viewed as a restoration of capitalism or when Stalin's policy of industrialization and "socialism in one country" was erroneously regarded as a Russian species of isolationism. The 1936 Constitution was misunderstood by some as the harbinger of a new democracy. The military alliance of World War II was at the time mistakenly viewed by many as heralding a new era of international cooperation between the Soviet Union and the Western democracies. The impact of the various reforms undertaken by the post-Stalin regimes was frequently exaggerated. While each of these events was significant, the tendency was to anticipate consequences that did not ensue.

If the record of Soviet development is strewn with inaccurate predictions and dubious assumptions, such failures have been due principally to an apparent inability to understand the basic nature of the Soviet system. Although the system is subject to change, such change is limited by the system's parameters. However, if we are to understand the prospects for change it is necessary to define the characteristics of the Soviet polity. This can be done most readily by examining a number of models. Such a comparison of models also provides an overview of the Soviet polity, and also summarizes and categorizes our knowledge of the system.

A model is an effort to represent reality or important aspects of reality even though the complexity of reality cannot be captured and made static. Each model has a logic of its own and each simplifies to a degree in emphasizing a particular facet or set of traits that characterizes the system. Each model is based on a particular interpretation of the system and provides a different insight into the nature of the Soviet polity, but each must exclude certain variables while emphasizing others. Models facilitate inquiry and understanding, help to clarify controlling assumptions and hypotheses, and aid in the identification of traits. In addition to aiding cognition, models help to measure change in a system and aid in the development of expectations regarding the probable outcomes of its political process.

In this chapter six different models are examined: the totalitarian, the authoritarian, the bureaucratic, the oligarchic, the modernization, and the imperial. Each of these models raises fundamental questions. Each, taken alone, tends to project a single line of development, even though development usually proceeds on a number of planes and results from the interaction of many factors. No single model can be a faithful reproduction of an entire polity because no model fits the data completely and precisely.

It is preferable to have more rather than fewer models because there is always the likelihood that preoccupation with a single model will distort one's perception of the system under investigation. If an observer confines himself exclusively to a particular model he tends to replicate the error of the Marxists-Leninists in projecting a single line of development and adopting a deterministic approach. The validity and relevance of a particular model may vary over time and no single model provides *the* key to an understanding of the Soviet political system in its entirety. Indeed, models are most useful when they are juxtaposed and compared. Together they provide a multidimensional image or series of images that depict the Soviet polity with greater accuracy.

1. SIX MODELS

The Totalitarian Model. The totalitarian model of the Soviet polity derives from the fact that the Soviet Union emerged both as an original species of totalitarian dictatorship and as the quasi-prototype of the Italian Fascist regime of Mussolini and of Hitler's National Socialist movement. Totalitarian regimes constitute a special type of polity because of certain of their characteristics. The term "totalitarian" is derived from the desire of such regimes to bring under their control the totality of human existence and to equate the polity with the totality of society. Such a regime endeavors to claim as much of the whole person as it can. It seeks to maximize and monopolize political power for the sole ruling "party" while politicizing as many sectors of social, economic, and cultural activity as possible. In addition to maximizing political power, it must centralize the exercise of power so that it remains dictatorial. For if there is any significant devolution of such power it quickly ceases to be dictatorial.

The totalitarian model possesses at least *ten* unique but related characteristics apart from the general definition discussed above.[1] These may be summarized as follows:

(1) A mass "party" or movement—which remains a small minority of the population despite its numerically large membership—provides the principal means by which totalitarian rulers impose their will upon society and provide purposeful leadership. The "party" provides the means for recruiting persons into the political elite and has specialized courses and schools to train its members. It takes over the state, transforming the latter into its own instrument, usurping its sovereignty, and employing its authority in an arbitrary manner. The state is reduced to the role of fulfilling decisions adopted by the movement or in the latter's name. Thus the totalitarian movement extends beyond the state. The "party" renews itself and develops a following that has a stake in the system's perpetuation.

(2) An ideology provides an essential legitimizing and rationalizing device that gives the regime a quasi-intellectual basis. It enables totalitarian rulers to justify the most repressive measures in the name of professed millenarian goals that include

[1] All efforts to define and analyze totalitarianism owe a debt to the work of Carl J. Friedrich and Zbigniew Brzezinski, some of whose six traits of totalitarianism are incorporated into the ten characteristics presented here.

establishment of a totally new social order and the remaking of man.[2] The ideology rejects previous socio-political forms, and the rulers endeavor to predict and to make the future by appealing to "historical necessity." The doctrine's tenets are propagated through the mass media, educational institutions, and the arts.

(3) The totalitarian system also endeavors to justify itself and its methods in terms of ambitious undertakings, grandiose construction projects, and military power. It seeks to mobilize the population and exact sacrifices in the name of a revolutionary cause that claims moral justification on the basis of huge investments and concrete achievements, such as the construction of dams, canals and steel mills, space exploration, expansionism, and its ability to coerce. It often acts arbitrarily, recognizing no legal limitations on its rule.

(4) Organizations other than the "party" are controlled by the totalitarian movement, for the latter refuses to share power. No strictly voluntary or private organizations are permitted to function because the movement insists upon controlling all avenues of advancement in order to make the individual dependent and more willing to serve it. It denies autonomy to the individual and to groups, and persistently presses its claims. By preventing the development of a pluralistic society based on free and voluntary associations, the regime can extend itself into nearly all of society. Thus, it requires a high degree of involvement and commitment on the part of its subjects and does not permit them to choose between competing parties and leaders.

(5) The totalitarian movement retains ownership of the economy—or direct control over it—and endeavors to subordinate economic decision-making to its will through total or near-total planning. It limits the amounts and kinds of property that individuals can acquire. This gives it an ability to

[2] For a penetrating discussion of the professed totalitarian goals of the Nazis and communists and their effect on policies, see Ihor Kamenetsky, "Totalitarianism and Utopia." *Chicago Review*, XVI, No. 4 (1964), 114–159.

distribute or withhold material satisfactions in ways that reinforce its political power. By being the sole or ultimate employer, the totalitarian regime is in a position to enforce conformity. The purpose of economic policy is to enhance political power.

(6) The totalitarian system retains a monopoly on the media of mass communication (the press, radio, television and cinema), for the purpose of attempting to determine social beliefs and attitudes, and to condition or "program" the individual to repeat prepared answers to charged questions. It seeks to seal off the population from alien influences and certain kinds of news in order to prevent its being "contaminated" and permits relatively few of its subjects (and even of its officials) to travel abroad. To the extent that such measures are successful, it remains a closed society.

(7) If persuasion, exhortation, and indoctrination are inadequate, the totalitarian regime possesses a security police to terrorize its actual or potential opponents into submission. It maintains a large and costly coercive apparatus manned by specialists in the "technology of violence," whose task it is to eliminate or isolate the regime's most dangerous enemies and to break the will of lesser opponents. If necessary it maintains concentration or forced labor camps for political opponents. The security police apparatus and the "party" merge in the totalitarian movement.

(8) While endeavoring to homogenize social and political life, totalitarian rulers also seek to atomize society in order to render helpless the individual citizen. Through intimidation they limit the ability of individuals to create informal opposition groups. The individual is constantly reminded of his subordination to the collectivity. By employing psychological terror —and by resorting to outright coercion when necessary—the rulers induce fear and endeavor to impress upon their subjects the lack of any alternative system and the futility and danger

of opposition. Through networks of spies, agents, and informers who practice denunciation, the totalitarians seek to infiltrate everywhere, creating distrust and impotence among their subjects.

(9) The totalitarian movement tends to thrive on tension and is preoccupied with enemies—both internal and external as well as real and imagined. It preaches vigilance and espouses a "plot theory" of history that requires it to extirpate the "evil" personified by its enemies—whether foreign or domestic. Tension is sustained by means of periodic campaigns against "counterrevolutionaries," "reactionaries," and other enemies. The overly ambitious nature of the movement's goals requires reliance upon scapegoats, who are blamed for failures.

(10) To remain totalitarian the movement must retain its dynamic and expansionist quality. It must deliver self-proclaimed successes in order to justify its claim to rule. If it becomes quiescent and loses its revolutionary vision and zeal by resting on its laurels, it may retain power and preserve its viability as a political system, but will lose its totalitarian quality. It must retain the outward commitment and active involvement of a high percentage of its population in order to maximize the number of its active collaborators and passive supporters.

The above characteristics comprise a totalitarianism of an "ideal" type, and each of these characteristics will not be present in the same degree. It must be borne in mind that there are definite limits to totalitarianism and that it often possesses a synthetic quality that gives to its extravagant claims and pretences only the semblance of reality. Many of its goals are unrealizable and its performance often falls short of expectations. It endeavors to control too many aspects of life and undertakes more than it can accomplish. The regime's orders are not always carried out and it encounters resistance. It is unable to eradicate entirely the old society and the political culture that it sought to replace with a new social and political order. The totalitarian system tends to overburden its centralized decision-making apparatus, overcommits its resources, loses flexibility, and ultimately elicits apathy from many of its subjects.[3]

The applicability of the totalitarian model to the Soviet Union has been questioned, especially since Stalin's death. Although the model does not require that the movement be headed by a despotic charismatic leader, the dominant personalities of Stalin and Hitler made it appear that rule by one man was an essential attribute of totalitarianism. Thus the advent of rule by committee in the Soviet Union was interpreted by some observers as a sign of the erosion of its totalitarianism. Other developments that have been interpreted in a similar way are the persistence of religious belief and the growth of religious sectarianism; tourism and the failure of the regime to prevent foreign influences and radio broadcasts from penetrating the country; the "de-Stalinization" campaign and the limited criticism at times of some of Stalin's crimes; economic reorganization and greater reliance on the profit motive. Further evidence of the Soviet regime's inability to exercise total control is provided by the circulation of typed manuscripts of works that it will not publish, restiveness among youth, the persistence of the peasant's private plot and black market activities, and a greater tendency of courageous individuals and of oppressed groups like the Crimean Tatars to protest the regime's policies. The totalitarian regime's communications monopoly is not complete insofar as the official media do not always enjoy credibility, individuals tend to rely on word of mouth communication and foreign broadcasts, and rumors circulate with great rapidity. It has also become increasingly evident that the Communist Party is not monolithic (despite its claims to be such) because of factionalism, intraparty conflict, and shifting coalitions.

Yet there are many characteristics and policies of the Soviet

[3] See Karl W. Deutsch, "Cracks in the Monolith: Possibilities and Patterns of Disintegration in Totalitarian Systems," in Carl J. Friedrich, ed., *Totalitarianism* (Cambridge: Harvard University Press, 1954), pp. 308–333. Also see Hans Buchheim, *Totalitarian Rule: Its Nature and Characteristics* (Middletown, Conn.: Wesleyan University Press, 1968), especially Chap. 7, and Karl W. Deutsch, *The Nerves of Government* (New York: Free Press, 1966), Chap. 13.

regime that make the totalitarian model one of continuing relevance. The fact that the system readily survived Stalin's death, despite the overwhelming importance of the dictator's will, indicates that its totalitarian nature as a system has transcended the personal qualities of the individual dictator. If the Stalinist "cult of personality" was condemned in 1956 and in 1961, it found a counterpart in the cult of the Communist Party that depicts itself as the sole repository of truth and wisdom. Despite relaxation of controls in certain sectors at times, the Party has refused to share power and has persisted in imposing the official ideology. The search for enemies of various kinds and the manifestation of hostility and self-proclaimed destiny have survived Stalin. The efforts to combat religious belief persist. The Party still seeks to prescribe what writers and artists may create and to impose its aesthetic standards upon the public. It insists upon its right to define "truth" and to employ censorship. It employs severe repressive measures against any manifestation of politically deviant behavior and values. In foreign policy it has provoked or abetted international crises in Berlin, Korea, Cuba, Vietnam, and the Middle East. There persist too many instances of what George F. Kennan has termed the "congenital untruthfulness" of the Soviet regime.

The totalitarian model has been questioned by some on the grounds that the adjective "totalitarian" has been applied to different kinds of regimes; yet it has also been argued that, despite certain differences, such regimes are "basically alike." [4] The same criticism might be employed regarding the use of such adjectives as "democratic," "constitutional," and "parliamentary" in discussing types of political systems. If we were to abandon these terms on the grounds that "pure" types do not exist in practice, we would be impoverishing our vocabulary or be compelled to search for synonyms. The specific criteria used to define the totalitarian regime need not be present in each such regime in the same degree. It is even possible to define a regime as "semitotalitarian," "near-totalitarian," or "quasi-totalitarian" because of its unwillingness to aban-

[4] See Carl J. Friedrich and Zbigniew K. Brzezinski, *Totalitarian Dictatorship and Autocracy*, rev. ed. (Cambridge: Harvard University Press, 1965), especially Chap. 2.

don the claim to total power despite difficulties encountered in attempting to exercise that claim. If it is evident that a regime is becoming less totalitarian, the model is still useful because it can provide a standard against which to evaluate change.

The Authoritarian Model. A variety of dictatorships can be subsumed under the broad category provided by this model yet each stands apart from the totalitarian dictatorship. The authoritarian regimes have been more numerous than the totalitarian variety. The authoritarian model has been applied to Spain under Franco, to Turkey under Ataturk, to Haiti under Dr. Duvalier, and to a variety of tutelary regimes in developing countries.

The authoritarian regime includes conservative dictatorships and the single-party nationalist revolutionary post-colonial regimes in Asia and Africa, some of which have sought to effect radical social and economic transformations. It can be autocratic—with a single dictator, or oligarchic, or based on a military *junta.* If such a regime is based principally on the dictator's control of the police in the absence of a ruling party, it is most aptly called a "police state" in a very literal sense.

In the authoritarian regime, state authority is not effectively checked through institutions that exercise countervailing political power, but it frequently accepts self-limitation. The authoritarian dictatorship differs from the totalitarian species in numerous ways. Although the authoritarian regime usually operates under a one-party system, the ruling party sets limits to its role, pursuing reasonable or even modest goals and remaining within the framework of the nation-state. It does not ordinarily suffer from delusions of grandeur or seek to remake man and all of society. It does not regard itself as the embodiment of the will of history and as a model for other countries. The authoritarian regime may have an ideology, but it is usually vague and does not play a vital role. If there is no ruling party the regime may be based on the police, the army, or the bureaucracy.

An authoritarian regime does not endeavor to mobilize the entire population and penetrate all segments of society. A degree of pluralism is permitted, with some *de facto* subsystem autonomy for churches, trade unions, business corporations, and cultural bodies so long as they do not become directly involved in political matters. The press is controlled but can remain in private hands subject to self-censorship and the risk of the publisher's losing his license. The authoritarian regime may or may not operate a command economy (or can have a quasi-command economy), but usually permits a variety of entrepreneurship, including private ownership and state-operated enterprises. The authoritarian regime seeks to restrict freedom in the name of the national good but does not abolish it entirely. It does not rely extensively on indoctrination, for it is not committed to total revolutionary goals. Although authoritarian rulers can exercise power arbitrarily, they have been known to tolerate opposition in certain circumstances.

Authoritarian regimes have been far more numerous than the totalitarian species of dictatorship, which has been limited to such countries as Germany, the Soviet Union, Communist China, and Albania. It is possible that a communist regime need not be totalitarian, as has been demonstrated by the experience of some of the East European countries. Thus, a regime that does not collectivize agriculture or actively persecute religion, and that permits limited private entrepreneurship and a modest degree of freedom of expression, qualifies more as an authoritarian than as a totalitarian polity. The authoritarian model was applicable to the Soviet Union during the NEP period of the 1920's. Whether it will be applicable in the future cannot be stated with certainty. Some observers, impressed by certain developments since Stalin's death, have contended that the Soviet Union is in a post-totalitarian stage. Yet if such a judgment is premature, it is not inconceivable that the authoritarian model may again at some time be relevant to the Soviet polity.

The Bureaucratic Model. In this model the Soviet regime is viewed as a "bureaucracy writ large," sharing certain traits with such large bureaucratic organizations as the military, the modern giant corporation with its many subsidiaries, and the governmental agencies of the so-called democratic welfare-state.[5] Like any bureaucracy, that of the Soviet Union is based on specialization of

[5] This model has been expounded by Alfred G. Meyer in his *The Soviet Political System, An Interpretation* (New York: Random House, 1965), Chap. 8.

functions, expertise, hierarchy, and career service. The Soviet bureaucracy can be regarded as one of a species, all members of which suffer from a pathology. However, in the case of the Soviet Union the pathological aspects are more extensive and their consequences more evident. This is due to the fact that the scope of Soviet bureaucracy is unusually broad since all Soviet administration is public administration; it is also attributable to the general lack of extraadministrative restraints imposed on Soviet officialdom. The self-perpetuating nature of Communist Party rule makes the bureaucracy dependent upon the Party's leadership but it also often permits the bureaucrat to abuse his powers at the expense of the citizen.

Efforts to liken the Soviet bureaucracy to a modern giant corporation raise as many questions as they endeavor to answer. It has been suggested that the CPSU rank-and-file membership plays the role of stockholder—albeit in a more active capacity than that of shareholders of a capitalist corporation—and that the Central Committee, Politburo, and Secretariat together serve as a "board of directors" while the role of "corporate management" is fulfilled by the Soviet government (the Council of Ministers).[6] Although such analogies do serve to stimulate efforts at more precise role definition, they neglect certain differences between the Soviet bureaucracy and the corporation. Generally speaking, the corporation's board of directors is less influential than management, although the board can remove the managers should the corporation's condition require such action. A corporation's stockholders, should they become sufficiently aroused, can change the board of directors, while the Soviet counterpart in the analogy is a self-perpetuating "board" that is not removed at a Party Congress ("stockholders' meeting") but undergoes change as a result of internal power struggles and personnel shake-ups. The ethos of the Soviet "corporation" differs from that of the Western economic corporation;

[6] *Ibid.*, pp. 112–115, 134, 198, 467–68. Also see Alfred G. Meyer, "USSR, Incorporated," *Slavic Review*, XX, No. 3 (October, 1961), 369–376, as well as the article by Zbigniew Brzezinski on "The Nature of the Soviet System," pp. 351–368, which applies the totalitarian model, and the commentary of Robert C. Tucker, Reprinted in Donald W. Treadgold, ed., *The Development of the USSR: An Exchange of Views* (Seattle: University of Washington Press, 1964).

there is a basic difference between the Soviet political corporation and an American automobile or steel manufacturing concern both in ideology and in the objectives pursued by each.

The Soviet "corporate system" is unique in another respect. There are a number of bureaucracies in the Soviet Union: Communist Party, governmental, economic, military, security police, and the like. In place of a single unified bureaucracy there are parallel and, at times, competing and conflicting bureaucracies. Thus, the military intelligence (GRU) and the intelligence apparatus of the secret police (KGB) compete with each other. However, the dominant role of the CPSU bureaucracy and its leadership serves to relegate the other bureaucracies to the status of subsidiary "corporations," whose autonomy is usually tentative and conditional. For all responsible Soviet bureaucrats are Communist Party members and subject to Party discipline. Nor can the Soviet bureaucrat readily "sell out" within the system and transfer his loyalties and services to a competing corporate bureaucracy, as his Western counterpart can.

Despite such dissimilarities, there is utility in the bureaucratic model of Soviet political reality. The model serves to challenge the image of the Soviet system as a smoothly functioning monolith.[7] Like others of its species, the Soviet bureaucracy is obsessed with organizational matters and, because of the many demands made upon it, has experienced frequent reorganizations. Although it is based on rules and regulations (the criteria of bureaucracy known as precision and objectivity), these can and do become ends in themselves, and cease to be means for the fulfillment of organizational objectives. When rules must be evaded or violated in order to achieve the desired results, this has been tolerated by the Communist Party. If such practices do not produce the desired results, however, the responsible official is vulnerable to removal or a worse fate.

The frequent imposition of unreasonable goals and the periodic harassment of subordinates have necessitated their adopting surrep-

[7] The nature of the Soviet economic bureaucracy is discussed in John A. Armstrong, "Sources of Administrative Behavior: Some Soviet and Western European Comparisons," *American Political Science Review,* LIX, No. 3 (September, 1965), 643–655.

titious practices, especially in reporting on inventories, productive capacity, and actual production. Despite the preoccupation with formal organization, Soviet bureaucracy has fostered informal organization in order to cope with its tasks and to maintain necessary communication channels apart from the official lines. Yet it has also fostered evasion of responsibility, as well as resistance to innovation and the stifling of initiative, as established structures have sought to preserve their prerogatives and pursue settled routines. Soviet bureaucracy has not escaped conflict; this has taken the form of conflict within and between organizations, as well as between staff and line organizations and the center and the locale (or headquarters and the field). The Soviet principle of "dual subordination" means that many administrative organizations are responsible to the executive of the soviet in whose jurisdiction they function, as well as to superior bodies in the chain of command; this results in a certain degree of confusion in Soviet administration.

The bureaucratic model is useful insofar as it directs attention to the relationship between the various bureaucratic structures and the form that each is assuming in its development. It is important, moreover, to observe whether or not the Soviet bureaucratic behemoth will continue to attempt to influence all human activity and to equate itself with society. Will the Party bureaucracy grant greater autonomy to its subsidiary bureaucracies, creating a kind of political holding company of highly autonomous units, or will it retain a tight control? Will segments of the non-Party bureaucracy continue to serve as objects of criticism, performing the function of a lightning rod by directing the criticism away from the Communist Party apparatus and confining it to the *implementation* of policies, while leaving the Party's policies immune? While the various bureaucracies perform many vital functions and the regime relies heavily on specialists of various kinds, does this necessarily render the Party bureaucracy dependent? Will the Party retain the ability and the will to create new bureaucratic organizations that will compete with and undercut those on whom it may become too dependent? Will the Party bureaucracy itself become subject to checks of the kind that it has imposed on non-Party bodies? The usefulness of the bureaucratic model is that it promotes greater awareness of such questions.

The Oligarchic Model. Although "oligarchy" is a term of Greek origin and represents a form of classical political experience discussed by Aristotle in his *Politics,* it is a concept rarely employed by contemporary social scientists, who concern themselves with political elites. In its Greek meaning "oligarchy" is government by the few, who are usually wealthy and who rule in their own interests and form a plutocracy; oligarchy was regarded by Aristotle as a corruption of aristocracy (government by the best). In the twentieth century the concept of oligarchy received attention in the work of Roberto Michels dealing with political parties. Writing in 1911, Michels viewed all larger organizations as oligarchies "based upon the competence of the few" and having a professional leadership and a full-time staff of paid bureaucrats because of the sheer size of such organizations. Although Michels developed his so-called iron law of oligarchy prior to the emergence of communist parties as we know them, he applied it to democratic and socialist parties and even to anarchist organizations. Thus for Michels, all organizations tend to become oligarchic in practice—even those that profess democratic values.

The concept of oligarchy is relevant in two ways to an understanding of Soviet politics. It is relevant in Michels' sense and applicable to the Communist Party of the Soviet Union, in which the rank-and-file membership has no real voice in the selection of the organization's leaders and is not even presented with a choice in an electoral contest or in the Party Congress. The concept is also relevant in a broader sense in that, whenever it has not been ruled by an individual leader such as Lenin or Stalin, the Soviet polity can be defined as a dictatorship by a committee. Even a collegial dictatorship can be dominated by a single leader, who can be a *primus inter pares* or something more.

Some of the ground rules for the Soviet version of the game of oligarchical politics as practiced in the CPSU Politburo were discussed in Chapter 5, together with types of career patterns. Of course there is much that is not known about the relationships between the individual members of the Soviet oligarchy. Yet it is clear that that oligarchy is not monolithic and that cleavages frequently develop. Some members seek to replace or subordinate others in order to enhance their own role and status within the collegial dictatorship. Problems must be dealt with, and they become an integral part of power struggles. Improvisation, reorganization, and the search for more effective policies occur in spite of power struggles, but they also play a key role in such internal conflicts. Disagreements over specific policy issues can lead to open conflict within the ruling oligarchy, especially when accompanied by a confrontation of personal and/or group interests that can be cast in terms of what is ideologically "correct." The members of the Soviet oligarchy are not equal, and some members of the Politburo undoubtedly have greater influence than others.

Oligarchical rule tends to be unstable.[8] The lack of a clearly defined and constitutionally established line of succession and the absence of a formal order of ranking within the Politburo in accordance with offices held make for instability. Thus, oligarchy at worst can mean political crises, palace revolutions, and coups. At best, oligarchy can mean maneuvering between oligarchs for control over power bases represented by subsystem bureaucracies. It can mean jockeying for influence over key groups within the Central Committee membership, insofar as that body is recognized as an arbitral organ to which "appeals" are taken as a last resort when all other efforts to resolve conflict within the Politburo fail. Since oligarchies tend to be based on coalitions, there is a strong likelihood that such coalitions are temporary and reflect disparate interests but are held together by fear of potential rivals and opposition to alternative policies.[9]

It is obvious that membership in the Soviet oligarchy is not based on the acquisition or possession of wealth—a criterion that

[8] The oligarchic model is implicit in the published studies of Myron Rush, Sidney Ploss, Robert Conquest, Carl Linden, and Robert C. Tucker, although their works reflect different interpretations of data and events.

[9] William Riker, in his *The Theory of Political Coalitions* (New Haven: Yale University Press, 1962), offers the hypothesis that all coalitions tend to be only of such a minimal size as is needed to win in order to minimize the "price" paid for allies. Riker also contends that coalitions have a tendency to overspend for allies, and this leads to weakness and the ultimate decline of the coalition.

figures so prominently in the classical definition of the concept. Yet qualification for Politburo membership depends upon the manifestation of other skills. The question of whether or not the Soviet oligarchs rule for corrupt and selfish purposes—as classical oligarchs presumably did—does not make the model irrelevant. To the extent that the Soviet rulers are dedicated to the pursuit of communist goals and do not enjoy an excess of material satisfactions ostentatiously displayed, it might be argued that they do not qualify as "oligarchs" because they are not ruling in their own personal interests. However, it must be borne in mind that the Soviet oligarchy as such is ruling in its *collective* self-interest and engaging in *collective* self-aggrandizement. It is a self-perpetuating oligarchy, even though individual oligarchs may come and go. Although it may reorganize itself periodically, the Soviet oligarchy does not surrender the power of the CPSU, in whose name it rules.

Yet no modern oligarchy can rule exclusively in its own interest. The Soviet oligarchy must share perquisites and satisfactions with subgroups because it requires their support if its near-total mobilization efforts are to be effective. It depends not only upon the CPSU bureaucracy, but upon the governmental bureaucracy. While the latter is always represented in the inner ruling circle, it has not provided the Chairman of the Council of Ministers with an organizational power base that would enable him to dominate the oligarchy. Thus the careers of Rykov, Molotov, Malenkov, Bulganin, and Kosygin have indicated that the governmental bureaucracy has not been sufficiently homogeneous and interest-oriented to constitute a viable alternative to the Party-dominated oligarchy. Yet the possibility remains that the Soviet oligarchy may become increasingly diverse and more representative of the various social strata, ethnic groups, professional and economic interests, and of the society generally.

The Modernization Model. The concept of "modernization" implies a highly differentiated large-scale society based on industrialism and technology, literacy, a highly variegated division of labor and increasing urbanism. It assumes a steady rate of economic growth, with rising per capita consumption and adequate surpluses for investment. The modern society is highly stratified, is characterized by social mobility as well as by physical mobility, and is said to create a qualitatively different political system distinguished from traditional systems. The notion of "secularization" is also associated with modernization and is said to be synonymous with increasing rationality and an empirical and pragmatic approach to problem-solving. Presumably the "modernized" polity is one that is capable of dealing with change, and of adapting itself and achieving goals. It might be said to be in perpetual transformation as a result of its highly developed capacity for innovation.

Personalities are of less importance in modernized than in traditional political systems, and doctrinal considerations supposedly play a declining role in policy formulation. Attitudes are more dependent upon social class; the mass media and the educational system are important in the formulation of attitudes and beliefs. It is usually assumed that modernization, in addition to promoting the advent of more "rational" political norms, makes necessary a greater degree of popular involvement and participation in politics. Modernity is said to imply democracy and egalitarianism. The role of public opinion and of mass persuasion is enhanced. Demands made upon the system are said to be more effectively articulated. There supposedly is a desire to achieve and to enjoy greater personal freedom and the ability to make rational choices.[10] In its long-range impact, modernization supposedly leads to the emergence of new modal personality traits and behavior patterns, which in the case of the Soviet Union would differ from those outlined in Chapter 2.

The concept of "modernization" is sufficiently broad and vague to be applicable to a number of different systems. It includes not only a variety of mature industrial societies (the United States, Great Britain, Germany, and Japan), but also countries that are still pursuing that goal. The concept can be criticized on the grounds that it reflects a cultural bias and is derived largely from North American and West European experience. It can also be questioned whether all industrial urban societies are sufficiently alike to be subsumed under a single all-embracing concept. To

[10] See Edward Shils, *Political Development in the New States* (The Hague: Mouton, 1962).

equate all forms of industrialism—to the exclusion of differences between political cultures and their distinctive structures—may not be representative of scientific sophistication. Yet such a concept—one that is supposedly applicable to a variety of systems that are said to be becoming increasingly similar—possesses a certain appeal comparable to those qualities of Marxism that have attracted some intellectuals.

Whether or not all things are to be remade by the ubiquitous process of "modernization," it cannot be denied that the Soviet Union has been "modernized" in many respects and that the process is likely to continue. In support of this contention, one can cite the industrialism of the Soviet Union, its urbanism, its efforts to acquire a degree of affluence, its managerial bureaucracy, and its development of the mass communications media. The Soviet polity has also developed an impressive scientific establishment and has lavished resources on such scientific installations as those at Akademgorodok, the "science city" near Novosibirsk. The Soviet Union is also characterized by a substantial degree of physical and social mobility.

However, several serious reservations should be taken into account in any evaluation of the modernization model as the key to predicting the future of the Soviet polity. There is the basic question of whether many attributes of modernization may be only a veneer—especially when acquired in haste and adopted only by a part of the population. Do established institutional structures and practices that reflect attitudes and values acquired over generations readily yield to the new "superstructure" that reflects the modernized "base" of the society? Thus, the oligarchical crises and coups of June, 1957, and October, 1964, would appear to have been anomalies in a modernized Soviet polity, possessing the world's second largest industrial system. Yet they did occur, and the emergence of rational political norms and quasi-constitutional practices in the Soviet Union may require many years. Indeed, it might be more accurate to regard modernization as constituting part of a hybrid polity that also incorporates features of other models.

There is another disturbing aspect of the modernization model's simplicity and of the halcyon consequences that are supposed to ensue from it. The modernization model tends to rule out the possibility that totalitarianism of the kind imposed by Stalin and Hitler can emerge in a truly modernized society and polity. Yet the totalitarian dictators did promote technical innovation, grandiose construction projects, and modernization in addition to expending vast sums on their military establishments. Some proponents of the modernization model have endeavored to solve this problem by simply classifying Nazi Germany and Stalin's regime as "transitional" systems.[11] It is usually assumed that modernization, by definition, means a decline in totalitarianism. However, it can be questioned whether the problem of modern totalitarianism can be disposed of so neatly once and for all. There is also the fact that the instruments of science and technology—which are essential to modernization—are ideologically "neutral" and can be employed by a variety of regimes in pursuit of conflicting and mutually exclusive goals. It can be questioned whether the tools of modernization will actually produce the kind of stereotyped polity envisaged by some of the model's proponents.

Yet what is stressed in the modernization model is the ability to adapt and to adjust the system to enable it to cope with the constant growth and rapid change that the modernizers themselves initiated. Thus modernization is characterized by a *perpetuum mobile* of its own creation. However, ceaseless innovation can acquire a dysfunctional character unless there is a capacity for "systemic transformation" which makes it possible to satisfy changing demands made upon the system.[12] What is frequently neglected is the Soviet polity's substantial regulative capability that has enabled it to deflect, blunt, suppress, or modify the demands made upon it by its subjects. However, if urbanization and industrialism, in their Soviet variant, result in serious strains, mass frustration, and alienation with which the rulers cannot cope, then the system's ability to qualify as "modern" may be questioned.

[11] It has been argued that Hitler's and Stalin's regimes were incapable of genuine modernization and adaptation to change because of their reliance upon dogma and terror. For example, see Manfred Halpern, "The Revolution of Modernization in National and International Society," in Carl J. Friedrich, ed., *Nomos VIII, Revolution*, Yearbook of the American Society for Political and Legal Philosophy (New York: Atherton Press, 1966), especially pp. 192–193, 210.

[12] *Ibid.*, pp. 211–213.

The modernization model provides a rationale for two related hypotheses: (a) the "convergence" thesis, which represents the Soviet Union as becoming increasingly like other industrial societies and which foresees a substantial degree of convergence between the Soviet Union and the United States; and (b) the "technocracy" thesis, which foresees an increasingly "rational" Soviet leadership as a result of the emergence of a new class of elite members possessing technical training.

The convergence thesis has assumed several forms and has been based on different kinds of data as interpreted by its various proponents. The thesis has been advocated in differing degree by such observers as the late Pitirim Sorokin, W. W. Rostow, Raymond Aron, and John K. Galbraith. At least a partial convergence has been advocated by such prominent Soviet physicists as Andrei D. Sakharov and Piotr Kapitsa.[13]

Sorokin, a Russian émigré sociologist, was one of the first advocates of convergence—basing his thesis on the Soviet-American military alliance of World War II—and contended that Americans and Russians shared certain important traits and values. Thus, he seriously contended that there existed a "mutual mental, cultural and social congeniality" between Russians and Americans allegedly based on their occupying vast continents, on their ethnic diversity, and on the "essentially democratic structure of their basic sociocultural institutions."[14] When this alleged congeniality failed to prevent the advent of the cold war between the Soviet Union and the United States after 1945, Sorokin subsequently sought to

[13] Sakharov expressed his advocacy in an essay (not published in the Soviet Union) that is critical of the Soviet regime's policies. See Andrei D. Sakharov, *Progress, Coexistence, and Intellectual Freedom* (New York: W. W. Norton, 1968). Kapitsa endorsed Sakharov's thesis in an interview reported in the *New York Times* of October 9, 1969.

[14] Pitirim A. Sorokin, *Russia and the United States,* 2nd ed. (London: Stevens and Sons, 1950), pp. 4, 10–12, 34–35, and 41. Sorokin's controversial work, based on highly selective data and marred by special pleading, was first published in 1944. Sorokin was undoubtedly influenced by Stalin's reliance upon Russian nationalism during and after World War II and by the development of a more stratified Soviet society, with greater emphasis upon traditional values and norms as in family law, military rank, wartime concessions to the Russian Orthodox Church and the like. For a critique of Sorokin's views on Soviet-American relations, see the paper by Alex Inkeles in Philip J. Allen, ed., *Pitirim A. Sorokin in Review* (Durham, N. C.: Duke University Press, 1963), pp. 225–246, as well as Sorokin's reply on pp. 461–469.

explain events in terms of the "stupidity" and "blindness" of Soviet and American leaders.[15]

Another variant of the convergence thesis is based on the contention by J. K. Galbraith and others that the Western and Soviet economies and social systems are becoming more similar. It is argued that both systems share the same technology and management requirements, if not the same ideology, and will thus supposedly become more similar in spite of ideological differences. In support of the thesis it is contended that the nationalization (socialization) of parts of the economies of Western Europe as a result of state ownership of certain sectors, the emergence of the welfare state, and greater reliance on economic planning are moving Western economic and social systems closer to the Soviet model. It is also contended that the Soviet model is changing as a result of a decline of the command economy and the rise of a "socialist market economy" that is more consumer-oriented. The granting of somewhat greater initiative to the Soviet economic firm and greater reliance on the profit criterion are also cited in support of convergence, as is the doctrine of peaceful coexistence. Sorokin went as far as to argue that "liberties and rights" were increasing in Soviet Russia (after 1953) and declining in the United States as the two systems allegedly proceeded toward "mutual convergence."[16]

[15] Allen, *ibid.*, pp. 468–469. In the second edition of *Russia and the United States* (1950), Sorokin contended that the Soviet-American conflict was attributable, not to a lack of "congeniality," but to the fact that in 1945 the two countries emerged as the most powerful. In a somewhat Tolstoyan vein, he also attributed wars and international tensions to the "disintegrating sensate order" based on "sensory, material hedonistic values" rather than on "creative love or altruism" (pp. 169 and 174). Sorokin shifted the grounds for his thesis and insisted that lasting peace—and, by implication, convergence—could occur only in the event of "a fundamental reintegration and transvaluation of most of the contemporary cultural values" as well as "effective promulgation and inculcation among all states, nations, and social groups of a set of fundamental norms and values which shall be universally binding" (p. 201).

[16] In Philip J. Allen, ed., *op. cit.* (above, n. 14), p. 465. Sorokin's most extreme exposition of the convergence thesis is to be found in his article, "Mutual Convergence of the United States and the USSR to the Mixed Sociocultural Type," *International Journal of Comparative Sociology,* I, No. 2 (September, 1960), 143–176. There he argued that detotalitarianization was inevitable once the emergencies and crises that gave birth to it had subsided. He contended—on the basis of highly selective evidence and sheer imaginative

It is not difficult to observe in the Soviet Union many characteristics of a "modern" society apart from industrialism, science, and technology. Such phenomena as Western dance styles and popular music and dress, alcoholism, juvenile delinquency, the weakening of the family, the numerous tensions of urban living, and the search for affluence are generally evident. Indeed, at least some of the proponents of convergence see the Soviet Union experiencing an *embourgeoisement*, with its attendant corpulence, conformity, and accommodation and the gradual corruption of revolutionary ideals and goals. Thus, there are many features which, viewed superficially, would tend to lend credence to the convergence thesis.

In criticism of the thesis, one can cite the hostility to it on the part of *official* Soviet spokesmen, who have insisted that the socioeconomic and political superstructure of the Soviet system differs qualitatively from that of the "nonsocialist" systems. In their view state-ownership is the essential difference—however, the owning state must not be bourgeois but communist. Thus, it is claimed that the "relations of production" in the Soviet Union differ from those of the mixed (private and socialist) Western economies and that there is a qualitative difference between the two systems. In evaluating the official Soviet rejection of the convergence thesis, one can question its self-serving assumption that non-Soviet workers are employed by "exploiters" while Soviet workers work "for themselves" because "their" state owns the factories and farms. If the Soviet rulers continue to combat the idea of convergence to a mixed type of system on ideological grounds, this in itself is a significant input in the total interaction of factors. Communism's adherents hold that *it*—and not some synthesis of Soviet and Western industrialism—is the epitome of "modernization." Of course, doctrinaire communists have their own version of convergence, as represented in the old slogan "All roads lead to Communism."

The convergence thesis, as usually expounded in the West, reflects a form of economic determinism that regards the forces of

speculation—that convergence between the United States and the U.S.S.R. was rapidly occurring in such areas as science, philosophy, ethical and legal systems, education, sports and recreation, fine arts, religion, marriage and the family, the economic system, and the political system. His exposition probably ignored far more than it revealed.

production as the principal determinant of a political system. Some of its advocates may be engaging in projection—desiring that the Soviet system become more like Western systems—on the assumption that such a development will promote coexistence and aid the cause of international cooperation and world peace. Convergence is often a matter of belief rather than of scientific evidence; it is often expounded by those who want it to occur and who confuse the desirable with the inevitable in attempting to predict the Soviet future in terms relevant only to Western experience.

The concept of convergence can be criticized on a variety of grounds.[17] It can be questioned whether science, technology, and the factory system inevitably produce a single unified type of industrial system that results in a common political system. It might be argued, instead, that science and technology are neutral instruments that have served such diverse political systems as Nazism, communism, the American system, several French republics, Japanese militarism, and the British and other parliamentary systems. One is prompted to ask why Germany, Great Britain, the United States, and Japan—possessing essentially similar industrial systems and technologies during the period between the two world wars—did not "converge" and develop similar political structures but, instead, went to war. The notion of convergence in its extreme form ignores every quality and condition that causes a people to stand apart. It blithely ignores everything that is unique about a country's political system.

The convergence thesis can also be questioned on other grounds. Even if one assumes the existence of a number of highly similar industrial systems, this in itself does not guarantee that their interests will be identical or highly similar and that there will be an absence of conflict. Similar systems—whether "converged" industrial or totalitarian—can diverge when their vital interests conflict. There is no assurance that converged or converging systems will necessarily be more compatible.

[17] For a broad criticism, see Bertram D. Wolfe, "The Convergence Theory in Historical Perspective," *An Ideology in Power* (New York: Stein and Day, 1969), pp. 376–394. Also see Zbigniew Brzezinski and Samuel P. Huntington, *Political Power: USA/USSR* (New York: Viking Press, 1964).

Instead of positing a simple and inevitable process of convergence, it might be more realistic to distinguish between *limited* or *partial*, and *total* convergence, and between specific areas of convergence and divergence. Thus, full convergence would presumably require the Soviet Union to abolish censorship of the news media and literature, abandon the propagation of atheism, permit a wide variety of free entrepreneurial activity, and restore intellectual and artistic freedom.

Although two countries may have steel mills, computers, nuclear reactors and engineering institutes, comparable levels of electric power consumption and per capita income and the like, one can still ask whether the presence or absence of free labor unions is not a matter of vital significance. If one country has unions that are not controlled by the state, and such unions are able to coerce employers (including state-owned enterprises) into paying higher wages and offering greater fringe benefits, and the other country does not have such unions, is this not a vital difference? Is it not important to determine whether both converging systems have an independent press and other free media, more than one political party, and free elections? Is it not essential to ask whether ownership of all the means of production is in state hands and the government is, in effect, the sole employer? Thus two countries that are allegedly converging may be very similar in certain respects and significantly different in other respects. In knowledge of sociopolitical phenomena, as in all else, understanding comes as a result of the ability to discriminate—and through the recognition of distinctions rather than through the formulation of simple equations.

The other hypothesis derived from the modernization model regards the Soviet Union as increasingly governed by a new class of "technocrats" consisting of persons with scientific and technological training and including the members of the managerial elite. The technocracy thesis has its origins in James Burnham's *The Managerial Revolution* (1941), in which rule by a new elite of managers was foreseen. As applied to the Soviet Union the thesis foresees the displacement of the Party apparatus official and ideocrat by engineers, scientists, mathematicians, economic managers, and planners. Thus, rule by CPSU secretaries and *apparatchiki* is to be replaced by that of the new scientific, technical, and professional intelligentsia. These persons, it is argued, as a result of their specialized training—in which criteria of scientific objectivity and rationality predominate—will bring to Soviet politics an outlook totally different from that of the old-style Party bureaucrat. It is also contended that industrialism, in requiring large amounts of capital and careful calculation in determining how it is to be invested, promotes a rationality that will find an application in Soviet politics as well.[18]

In support of the thesis, it is contended that the Soviet regime must rely increasingly on the expertise possessed by the technical and scientific intelligentsia. It requires their services in administrative positions and as consultants; and therefore presumably their political influence can be expected to increase. Additional evidence cited in support of the thesis is the technical training of more recent Soviet leaders. Thus Khrushchev's successors—Brezhnev, Podgorny, and Kosygin—were graduates of various engineering institutes. Increasingly CPSU and Soviet governmental officials have been appointed from the ranks of graduates of technical and other specialized institutes.

The technocracy thesis can be criticized on the grounds that scientists, technicians, and managers—despite their grievances against CPSU bureaucrats and the Party's meddling in "their" work—do not constitute a homogeneous and cohesive group. The Party, it can be argued, will dominate so long as it can keep the technocrats divided and docile, and provide them with sufficient rewards. Although the technocrats can win concessions from a Party that seeks to keep them productive but politically impotent, it can be questioned whether they can succeed entirely in taking over the CPSU. It is quite possible that many in the technical and managerial elite are satisfied to be left alone to pursue their professional specialties and may not aspire to rule the country, being satisfied with having influence in certain policy matters. Many technocrats have a rather specialized competence and their narrow

[18] The technocracy thesis has found expression in W. W. Rostow's *The Dynamics of Soviet Society* (New York: W. W. Norton, 1952), p. 196. For a fuller exposition see Albert Parry, *The New Class Divided, Science and Technology versus Communism* (New York: Macmillan, 1966).

professional training does not prepare them to play the role of the generalist required of those who do aspire to rule. It can also be questioned whether the rational criteria and methods of objective inquiry emphasized in technical and scientific training necessarily carry over into the realm of political experience and practice. There is no assurance that engineers and scientists are more politically sophisticated or immune to being doctrinaire than other persons; they may be no less gullible and no more discriminating when dealing with matters that lie outside of their professional expertise.

While the Party has relied heavily on the managerial and technical intelligentsia, it has also insisted that those whom it promotes to responsible political and executive positions be politically schooled. To this end the CPSU maintains a network of special Party schools, whose graduates are deemed better qualified than other people for leadership posts. So long as acceptability to the Party apparatus in charge of personnel remains an important—though not the sole—criterion for advancement, it is not likely that the technocrats will take over completely. Yet even if the Party leadership and bureaucracy are increasingly staffed with persons trained originally as engineers or managers, it can be contended that they undergo a metamorphosis of sorts when they abandon engineering or business administration—as they do fairly early in their careers—and become professional Party officials. In any society the scientist who becomes a bureaucrat or the scholar who becomes an administrator often undergoes a change in attitudes, perspectives, and loyalties as a result of having changed roles. Professional Soviet politicians—irrespective of their background, training, and early career experiences—can reasonably be expected to preserve the system in its *basic* aspects rather than to subvert it.[19]

Thus, while it is likely that the technically skilled will hold im-

[19] George Fischer has argued that a Soviet system that is both "monist" and modern, rather than "pluralist," is a possible development. Such a system would reject the autonomy of subunits and groups and would be based on "public power" (not shared with private groups) and exercised by politicians ruling a highly centralized polity. See George Fischer, *The Soviet System and Modern Society* (New York: Atherton Press, 1968).

portant posts, in accordance with the technocracy thesis, it cannot be stated with certainty that a quasi-constitutional system will result. It cannot be assumed that technocrats are democrats, and that civil liberties and intellectual and artistic freedom will flourish because of their dominance. Yet there is value in the modernization model to the degree that it fosters a less static view of the Soviet polity and emphasizes adaptability and the system's developmental character.

The Imperial Model. The adjective "imperial" elicits a variety of responses because of its association with the historical bureaucratic and autocratic empires that have existed since ancient times. The term "imperial"—which is even employed in commercial advertising in certain countries—is often used to convey a sense of opulence, splendor, substance, quality, and permanence. In political parlance "imperial" often connotes the notion of pomp, ostentation, and military might. Despite the diverse meanings and connotations of the term, it is proposed to employ it here in a highly specific sense with reference to the Soviet polity.

The model of the imperial order is relevant to an understanding of the Soviet polity for a variety of reasons. The sheer extent and size of the Soviet Union's territory and the inclusion in it of a number of non-Russian nations subjugated by the Russian Empire would alone make the imperial model relevant. It is an irrefutable historical fact that the Russian nation has battened upon other nations as a result of its vast territorial acquisitions and assimilatory policies. Geographically and culturally the U.S.S.R. can be viewed not as a single country but as a group of countries comprising a multinational empire. An imperial polity aspires to universality, seeking to influence and, if possible, control other countries and to enjoy deference and "greatness" as a world leader while claiming to be acting in the interests of humanity. Thus it is significant that the state seal of the U.S.S.R. should include a globe with hammer and sickle superimposed upon all of Eurasia, Africa, the Near East, the Arctic and Greenland, and the North Atlantic and Indian Oceans. The record of Soviet foreign policy provides much evidence in support of the imperial model.

Because size of territory and population are essential criteria, very few modern polities can be said to qualify for the imperial model. The Soviet Union is one of the few because it is the world's largest territory under a single sovereignty and the third most populous country. However, there are other essential criteria. The imperial polity is highly centralized and is ruled from a single center wielding concentrated power. Internal order and unity are imposed, and diversity is suppressed in the effort to homogenize the population. A swollen imperial bureaucracy often acts irresponsibly and arbitrarily and ultimately becomes incompetent; its members are servile in dealing with superiors, harsh and condescending toward subordinates and the public. The dominant nationality takes full advantage of its preferred status, and the center flourishes at the expense of the dependencies and peripheries. It seeks to isolate its subjects and limits contacts with foreigners and with other cultures.

Although the imperial regime makes a fetish of bigness, regarding it as a virtue, the imperial polity need not be imperialistic in the sense of actively undertaking new ventures in pursuit of self-aggrandizement. It may simply seek to retain its gains. However, the burdens of the imperial polity are many for its size, and the hypertrophy of its state and bureaucracy results in certain consequences. The imperial polity is costly and wasteful. Heavy taxes are imposed, and substantial military and police establishments must be maintained in order to retain conquests and great-power status and inspire fear in the population. Bigness leads to the sacrifice of quality for quantity. Corruption and venality, peculation and pilfering contribute to the growth of cynicism. The imperial polity loses credibility and acquires a reputation for hypocrisy as its actions fail to correspond with its noble words, and its universal aims and grandiose pretensions are made hollow by its practices.

Imperial systems can acquire a grotesque character that is intensified as the ruling class becomes effete, commits more serious errors, and fails to solve problems. The imperial polity is unstable because it attempts to embrace too many and too much. The sheer size, diversity, and complexity of the imperial system ultimately make it unmanageable. In the end it overextends itself and its acquisitive capabilities exceed its digestive capacities. Its unity has a synthetic quality. Imperial polities are difficult to identify with because of their vastness and heterogenous nature; as loyalty becomes more formal, indifference grows, civic virtue declines, and the rulers are referred to as "they."

Imperial systems are vulnerable to decay and are mortal. They may disintegrate because (a) they attempt to govern too large an area from a single center and overextend themselves; (b) they fail to integrate disparate populations; or (c) the ruling element in the end suffers a failure of nerve in the face of crisis as a result of having become inflexible, corrupt, and ineffective. Yet the decline of an imperial regime may take a long time, and empires have been known to survive in debility for lengthy periods despite widespread internal decay and decomposition.

The imperial model does not find a ready reception among those observers who assume that the adjective "imperial" went out of use in World War I following the collapse of the Austro-Hungarian and Russian Empires. The model is also resisted by those who look approvingly upon any large political system, and who favor centralism and the integration or even the homogenization of peoples and cultures in the name of humanistic universalism and "progress." Other critics of the imperial model regard the Soviet Union as a modernizing system not to be equated with the depravities and despotism of the corrupted historical universal empires, despite Stalin's excesses. Still others see the model as a threat to "eternal Russia." Those who may be overwhelmed by the outwardly impressive panoply of Soviet power cannot imagine its degeneration and, instead, view it as stable, permanent, and invincible.

Nevertheless there are weighty reasons for not discarding the imperial model.[20] Numerous large polities have suffered breakdown and dissolution in the past. The Russian Empire experienced total collapse in 1917–19 and was resurrected as the Soviet Union only in the name of the "new legitimacy" provided by its newly

[20] The imperial model is evident in implicit or explicit form in the works of such scholars as Richard Pipes, Robert Conquest, Hugh Seton-Watson, the late Walter Kolarz, and the late Georgii Fedotov. On the historical empires, see Robert G. Wesson, *The Imperial Order* (Berkeley and Los Angeles: University of California Press, 1967).

adopted creed of Marxism-Leninism. Of course, if the Russian S.F.S.R. were to exercise its constitutional right and were to secede from the Soviet Union, the model would lose much of its relevance. However, such a development is unlikely, and the Russians by denying their subject peoples the right to national self-determination pay the high price of subjecting themselves to a dictatorship that preserves the imperial patrimony. As the eminent historian Hugh Seton-Watson has observed:

> Under Communist rule, Russia has remained an empire. . . . The evidence shows that the Soviet leaders are afraid of anti-Russian nationalism among their own subjects. Relaxation of the dictatorship might lead to dangerous separatist movements. It would thus seem that the multi-national nature of the Soviet Union is an important obstacle to the extension of liberties. The Russian citizen is in the predicament from which the citizens of other empires have suffered. By depriving Ukrainians, Letts, Tatars or other peoples of their liberty, the Russian substantially reduces his own chances of winning liberty.[21]

The Soviet polity reflects many of the characteristics of the imperial mentality. It glorifies itself and its might, and claims to be the embodiment of a new order. Its demands on its subjects for loyalty and obedience have exceeded those of most other polities. However, the principal value of the imperial model lies in its promoting a greater awareness of the concealed fissures in the Soviet polity which may result in the system's fragmentation under appropriate conditions.

2. THE DYNAMICS OF CHANGE

Each of the six models discussed in the preceding section is based on a body of empirical data and each represents a distinctive theory of the Soviet polity. Of course there is always the Procrustean danger of cutting or stretching data to fit a particular

[21] Hugh Seton-Watson, "The Evolution of Communist Dictatorship," *Modern World, Annual Review of International Relations,* VI (Düsseldorf and Vienna: Econ-Verlag, 1968), 63. Georgii Fedotov also noted that Muscovy's autocratic order was the price that Russia paid for its expansion and that the "imperial way of life" based on force was incompatible with liberty. See Georgii P. Fedotov, *Novyi grad, sbornik statei,* ed. Iu. P. Ivask (New York: izd-vo im. Chekhova, 1952), pp. 198 and 244.

model. Yet a model need not be entirely compatible with reality in order to be of use. It is therefore useful to juxtapose models and to be confronted with more than one model, because it would be simplistic to insist that only one model has validity and that all others be discarded as irrelevant.[22] Thus, a rigid totalitarian model, taken alone, can be as misleading as a modernization model that depicts a democratic, peace-loving, humanistic, and reasonable Soviet Russia of the future. Political reality is far too complex to be understood in terms of a single theoretical model.

Each of the models is relevant and taken together they need not be mutually exclusive. Thus, a totalitarian regime is bureaucratic, and can be oligarchic as well as imperial. An oligarchic regime can be based on a bureaucracy, and can be totalitarian or authoritarian as well as modernizing and imperial. At a given point in time, then, the Soviet polity may be defined as a hybrid or amalgam of several models.

Efforts to predict the future development of the Soviet polity are, like all predictions, conditional and depend upon the outcome of important events and fortuitous occurrences that have yet to take place. It is safe enough to predict change, but predicting the quality and extent of change is another matter. While no particular line of development, however remote or unlikely, should be excluded, it is probably safe to assume that the Soviet regime will not develop along a smooth evolutionary course free of crises.

The numerous changes that have occurred since the mid-1950's probably portend greater change. Among these changes are the greater, if not always effective, articulation of group interests, usually of an institutional rather than of an associational nature. Group interests that lack a formal organization are expressed through the limited circulation of petitions, some of which have been signed by persons of distinction. Appeals and protests have

[22] For a discussion of various typologies and problems of method in the study of Soviet politics, see Frederic J. Fleron, Jr., ed., *Communist Studies and the Social Sciences* (Chicago: Rand McNally, 1969), especially the papers by Fleron and by H. Gordon Skilling, T. H. Rigby, Robert S. Sharlet, Erik P. Hoffmann, and William A. Welsh. Also see Zbigniew Brzezinski, ed., *Dilemmas of Change in Soviet Politics* (New York: Columbia University Press, 1969).

also been presented to officials by courageous individuals who seek changes in specific policies. While it is presumably safe to protest water pollution, the postal service, and the destruction of certain historical and architectural monuments, criticism of the regime's policies in the sensitive areas of censorship, nationality policy, and the powers of the union republics has involved considerable personal risk and even arrest. If acts of open resistance can be dealt with by the KGB, acts of passive resistance by the many are a problem of a different order. Thus, a restive population confronts a conservative oligarchy that desires to retain power and grants the bare minimum of concessions.

The Soviet polity can be viewed as a system that seeks to mobilize and direct human effort and material resources in pursuit of certain ends. Like any system it generates outputs in the form of decisions, priorities, programs, policies, propaganda, rewards, and deprivations. It must also reckon with inputs in the form of interests, demands, values, and expectations, while at the same time seeking to create support for the system through the generation of more effective outputs. The effort to control or modify such inputs as increased demands is necessary if the system is not to be subjected to excessive stress. If the system is to survive it must possess a capacity to restructure itself and to innovate.

Thus, maintenance of the system requires an increased learning and adaptive capacity on the part of the leadership. The maintenance of a Stalinist system could be based on support generated through terror, isolation, and indoctrination. However, as the environmental context of the polity begins to change as a result of modified outputs, this affects the quantity and nature of the demands with which it is confronted. In seeking self-maintenance, a system that adopts enough new policies and reforms actually may undergo a qualitative change so that in "maintaining" itself it actually becomes a different system. Whether or not the Soviet polity undergoes such a qualitative change will depend ultimately upon the problem-solving abilities of its leaders.

The problems that confront the Soviet leadership are many and varied. By taking responsibility for the entire economy, it must also assume ultimate blame for failures. Antiquated retailing practices inspire little confidence. The chronic inadequacy of Soviet agriculture, the lack of adequate incentives, reliance on extensive farming rather than increased yields, the livestock shortage, and the waste of manpower all testify to the need to reevaluate the entire system. The shortage of adequate recreational facilities, quality eating establishments, variety in housing and styles, and the absence of the numerous other physical amenities that make life more tolerable, result in popular dissatisfaction. Yet more important than per capita consumption levels is the quality of life. A polity that claims to have created a "new man" and that preaches a boundless optimism inevitably raises expectations that cannot be fulfilled. The persistence of many social ills testifies to the regime's inability to mobilize the population fully.

The system also faces problems of a political nature. Apathy and alienation have grown as a result of the tiresome nature of political indoctrination, the irrelevance of much of the rhetoric for solving the country's problems, and the prying into matters of a personal nature. Many Soviet citizens seek *pokoi*—to be left alone—and desire to withdraw by cultivating personal interests, enjoying leisure, and acquiring material possessions. An excessively bureaucratized youth movement elicits waning enthusiasm at best and utter indifference at worst. The attempts to muzzle critics and domestic opponents prompted the well known writer Anatolii Kuznetsov to despair: "My God, to what has the unfortunate country come if even the elementary demand 'Observe the Constitution' or 'Do not imprison innocent persons in the camps' is the height of political struggle, courage and heroism." [23] However, in the long run the failure to observe constitutional norms can only result in a loss of confidence.

Yet the problem of establishing and observing meaningful norms also plagues the Soviet ruling elite itself. It is undoubtedly an improvement to have the members of the elite cease executing each other for political errors and ideological deviations, but the price exacted from the defeated is humiliating silence, in return for

[23] In a letter of September 6, 1969, addressed to the playwright Arthur Miller in his capacity as International President of the P.E.N. Reproduced in *Po Sovetskomu Soiuzu* (Radio Liberty), No. 312, October 17, 1969, pp. 1–6.

which they receive a pension. However, so long as basic procedures and relationships within the Soviet inner ruling circle remain vague and unstructured, there is the likelihood of intrigue and new political crises and instability. The Soviet polity has no clearly defined and undisputed chief executive, and the relationship between the CPSU General Secretaryship and the Chairmanship of the Council of Ministers is not defined. The powers of the General Secretary are not specified in the Party Statutes and his term of office is not fixed. Nor are the powers of the Politburo and the Central Committee delineated in relationship to the Secretariat. There is no legally defined line of succession in either the Party or government leadership.

Despite various palliatives and efforts at partial reforms by a lackluster leadership, significant aspects of the Soviet polity remain essentially unchanged. Thus, the leadership is not truly responsible in the sense that it must give a complete accounting and have its policies fully debated at specified intervals in terms of alternative policies. It remains a self-perpetuating elite and party bureaucracy that rejects the notion of a loyal opposition. The internal passport system, introduced by Stalin, restricts the movement of Soviet citizens within the country. Few citizens are permitted to visit communist countries and even fewer can visit noncommunist countries; only in rare instances are they permitted to emigrate. The line between the expression of dissent and "treason" remains ill-defined.

The maintenance of the Soviet polity is complicated by certain fundamental internal contradictions. The polity is confronted by the need to reform and restructure itself, and by demands for restoration and recrimination. It is faced with the task of attempting to satisfy the growing individual needs of its subjects, while tempted to pursue costly and chimeric foreign and domestic goals. The CPSU seeks to remain an elite while confronted with the practical need to renew itself by absorbing more of the ruled and identifying with their aspirations. It seeks to profess "internationalism" while employing practices that deny the equality of nations and peoples. It is torn between the need for (and the fear of) decisive and dynamic individual leadership, and the recourse to a dull and faceless "collective" rule of colorless functionaries. Thus, the CPSU is caught between the desire to prevent the abuse of political power and the continuing need to base itself on the centralization of power. It is confronted with growing demands for autonomy and the inertia of its commitment to centralism.

The presence of profound contradictions within the Soviet polity imposes serious limitations upon its development. The problem-solving abilities and farsightedness of Russian political leaders—whether tsars or their successors—have never been very impressive, and there is no assurance that the Soviet leadership will not continue to offer its subjects a patchwork of improvised policies and partial solutions. No political system can escape the ultimate consequences of its excesses and extravagance and of the quality of its leadership. The Soviet polity is no exception.

SELECTED BIBLIOGRAPHY

The annotated titles listed below for the various chapters of this book represent but a fraction of the voluminous literature on the Soviet polity now available in English. Detailed bibliographical works that can profitably be consulted include the following:

The American Bibliography of Slavic and East European Studies (Bloomington, Ind.: Indiana University Publications, Russian and East European Series) published annually.

Foreign Affairs Bibliography, 1932–1962, 3 vols. (New York: Bowker, 1945, 1955, 1964).

Hammond, Thomas T., ed., *Soviet Foreign Relations and World Communism, A Selected, Annotated Bibliography of 7,000 Books in 30 Languages* (Princeton, N.J.: Princeton University Press, 1965).

Horak, Stephan M., ed., *Junior Slavica; A Selected Annotated Bibliography of Books in English on Russia and Eastern Europe* (Rochester, N.Y.: Libraries Unlimited, Inc., 1968).

Horecky, Paul L., ed., *Russia and the Soviet Union: A Bibliographic Guide to Western-Language Publications* (Chicago: University of Chicago Press, 1965).

Kolarz, Walter, ed., *Books on Communism: A Bibliography,* 2nd ed. (New York: Oxford University Press, 1964). The first edition (1959) was prepared by R. N. Carew Hunt and was a continuation of Philip Grierson's *Books on Soviet Russia* (1943).

Lachs, John, ed., *Marxist Philosophy, A Bibliographic Guide* (Chapel Hill: University of North Carolina Press, 1967).

Shapiro, David, ed., *A Select Bibliography of Works in English on Russian History, 1801–1917* (Oxford: Basil Blackwell, 1962).

Important collections of documents and reference sources are:

Berman, Harold J. and Quigley, John B., Jr., eds., *Basic Laws on the Structure of the Soviet State* (Cambridge: Harvard University Press, 1969).

Current Soviet Policies, ed. Leo Gruliow, 4 vols. (New York: 1953, 1957, 1960, 1962). Documentary records of the 19th, 20th, 21st, and 22nd CPSU Congresses.

Daniels, Robert V., ed., *A Documentary History of Communism* (New York: Random House, 1960).

Prominent Personalities in the USSR (Metuchen, N.J.: Scarecrow Press, 1968). Previous volumes were entitled *Who's Who in the USSR* (1962 and 1966 editions) and *Biographic Directory of the USSR* (1958).

Soviet Law and Government (a quarterly published since 1962 by International Arts and Sciences Press).

Soviet Statutes and Decisions (a quarterly published since 1964 by International Arts and Sciences Press).

Triska, Jan F., ed., *Soviet Communism: Programs and Rules* (San Francisco: Chandler, 1962).

Yearbook on International Communist Affairs (Stanford: The Hoover Institution), published annually beginning in 1967.

The following periodicals publish significant articles in the form of analysis or documentation of Soviet developments:

Bulletin of the Institute for the Study of the USSR (Munich)
Canadian Slavonic Papers
Canadian Slavic Studies
Current Digest of the Soviet Press
Digest of the Soviet Ukrainian Press
Foreign Affairs
Problems of Communism (United States Information Agency)
Russian Review
Slavic Review (formerly *American Slavic and East European Review*)
Soviet Studies (Glasgow)
Studies in Comparative Communism (School of Politics and International Relations, University of Southern California)
Studies in Soviet Thought (Institute of East-European Studies, Uni-

versity of Fribourg, Switzerland, and the Russian Philosophical Studies Program at Boston College)

Studies on the Soviet Union (Institute for the Study of the USSR, Munich)

Survey: A Journal of Soviet and East European Studies (London)

Among the various general histories of Imperial Russia and the Soviet Union that merit attention are those by Jesse D. Clarkson, Herbert Ellison, Michael T. Florinsky, Sidney Harcave, Anatole Mazour, Ivar Spector, B. H. Sumner, George Vernadsky, and Warren B. Walsh. The works of the Polish historians Henryk Paszkiewicz and Jan Kucharzewski, and of the Ukrainian historian Mykhailo Hrushevsky, that challenge basic tenets in Russian national historiography, also merit attention.

The several books of readings on the Soviet political system vary considerably in emphasis and scope. Samuel Hendel, ed., *The Soviet Crucible,* 3rd ed. (Princeton, N.J.: Van Nostrand, 1967) includes Soviet materials and a variety of analyses and commentaries. William G. Andrews, ed., *Soviet Institutions and Policies, Inside Views* (Princeton, N.J.: Van Nostrand, 1966) consists exclusively of Soviet documents and official statements. Randolph L. Braham, ed., *Soviet Politics and Government* (New York: Alfred A. Knopf, 1965) juxtaposes Soviet statements with selections from the writings of various Western scholars. Harry G. Shaffer, ed., *The Soviet System in Theory and Practice* (New York: Appleton-Century-Crofts, 1965) presents Soviet and Western (Marxist and non-Marxist) views on a wide variety of issues. Richard Cornell, ed., *The Soviet Political System* (Englewood Cliffs, N.J.: Prentice-Hall, 1970) consists of selections from the writings of various Western analysts.

CHAPTER 1. THE USSR: A MULTINATIONAL EMPIRE

Armstrong, John A., *Ideology, Politics and Government in the Soviet Union,* rev. ed. (New York: Frederick A. Praeger, 1967) provides a very succinct and competent introduction to the Soviet political system.

Black, Cyril E., ed., *The Transformation of Russian Society: Aspects of Social Change since 1861* (Cambridge: Harvard University Press, 1960). Thirty-eight contributors provide analyses of a century of Russian development.

Campbell, Robert W., *Soviet Economic Power,* 2nd ed. (Boston: Houghton Mifflin, 1966) is a concise survey of Soviet economic performance.

Dmytryshyn, Basil, *USSR; A Concise History* (New York: Charles Scribner's Sons, 1965). A readable and thorough text that also contains documentary appendices.

Fitzsimmons, Thomas et al., *USSR: Its People, Its Society, Its Culture* (New Haven: HRAF Press, 1960) is a survey prepared by the Human Relations Area Files, useful as a handbook.

Hopkins, Mark W., *Mass Media in the Soviet Union* (New York: Pegasus, 1970) is a thorough work that also offers useful comparisons.

Kolarz, Walter, *Russia and Her Colonies* (New York: Frederick A. Praeger, 1953) provides general background on the major non-Russian peoples.

Kulski, W. W., *The Soviet Regime: Communism in Practice*, 4th ed. (Syracuse: Syracuse University Press, 1963) is a highly useful work that deals with policies.

Lang, David Marshall, *A Modern History of Georgia* (New York: Frederick A. Praeger, 1962) is an important work that provides necessary background but concentrates on Georgia under the tsars and Soviets, offering a very competent account.

Lensen, George Alexander, ed., *Russia's Eastward Expansion* (Englewood Cliffs, N.J.: Prentice-Hall, 1964) is a compendium of brief selections.

Nutter, Warren G. et al., *Growth of Industrial Production in the Soviet Union* (Princeton, N.J.: Princeton University Press, 1962) is a massive study that places Soviet economic growth in perspective.

Pierce, Richard A., *Russian Central Asia, 1867–1917; A Study in Colonial Rule* (Berkeley: University of California Press, 1960) provides a scholarly treatment of Russian rule in Turkestan.

Pipes, Richard, *The Formation of the Soviet Union: Communism and Nationalism, 1917–1923*, rev. ed. (Cambridge: Harvard University Press, 1964), is a basic work of great value.

Seton-Watson, Hugh, *The New Imperialism* (New York: Capricorn Books, 1967) is a provocative essay on Russian and Soviet expansion by a noted historian.

——, *The Russian Empire, 1801–1917* (New York: Oxford University Press, 1967) is a significant study that conveys clearly and in detail the diverse nature of the Empire.

Shabad, Theodore, *Basic Industrial Resources of the USSR* (New York: Columbia University Press, 1969) is a detailed survey of regions and types of resources.

Treadgold, Donald W., ed., *The Development of the USSR; An Exchange of Views* (Seattle: University of Washington Press, 1964) is a collection of provocative discussions on fundamental topics that were originally published in the *Slavic Review*.

——, *Twentieth Century Russia*, rev. ed. (Chicago: Rand McNally, 1964) provides a good general survey, including treatment of cultural developments and foreign policy.

Ukraine: A Concise Encyclopaedia, ed. Volodymyr Kubijovyč, 2 vols. (Toronto: University of Toronto Press, 1963 and 1971) is a valuable reference work.

Wheeler, Geoffrey, *The Modern History of Soviet Central Asia* (New York: Frederick A. Praeger, 1964) provides a general historical treatment that emphasizes the impact of Soviet rule.

Whiting, Kenneth R., *The Soviet Union Today, A Concise Handbook,* rev. ed. (New York: Frederick A. Praeger, 1966) provides a convenient, if brief, introduction.

CHAPTER 2. SOVIET POLITICAL CULTURE AND THE RUSSIAN POLITICAL TRADITION

Anderson, Thornton, *Russian Political Thought: An Introduction* (Ithaca, N.Y.: Cornell University Press, 1967) provides a very competent treatment.

Avrich, Paul, *The Russian Anarchists* (Princeton, N.J.: Princeton University Press, 1967) is an important work that deals with the origins of the anarchist movement and its role in the 1905 and 1917 Revolutions.

Billington, James H., *The Icon and the Axe: An Interpretive History of Russian Culture* (New York: Alfred A. Knopf, 1966) is a highly significant and provocative work.

Cherniavsky, Michael, *Tsar and People: Studies in Russian Myths* (New Haven: Yale University Press, 1961) is an imaginative historical treatment of an important but neglected subject.

Gaucher, Roland, *Opposition in the USSR, 1917–1967* (New York: Funk and Wagnalls, 1969) provides an excessively popular but still useful synthesis of the various opposition movements, ranging from the White Guards and Trotskyites to Ukrainian nationalism and literary protest.

Gorer, Geoffrey and Rickman, John, *The People of Great Russia, A Psychological Study* (New York: W. W. Norton, 1962) discusses the Russian character and sets forth the controversial swaddling hypothesis.

Kline, George L., *Religious and Anti-Religious Thought in Russia* (Chicago: University of Chicago Press, 1969) deals concisely and very ably with an important aspect of Russian thought.

Lampert, Evgenii, *Sons against Fathers: Studies in Russian Radicalism and Revolution* (New York: Oxford University Press, 1965) is a readable treatment of such radicals as Chernyshevsky, Dobroliubov, and Pisarev, that places them in the broad context of Russian development.

——, *Studies in Rebellion: Belinsky, Bakunin and Herzen* (New York: Frederick A. Praeger, 1957) discusses three types of revolutionaries and relates them to their time.

Mead, Margaret, *Soviet Attitudes toward Authority* (New York: McGraw-Hill, 1951) complements the anthropological work of Geoffrey Gorer.

Miller, Wright, *Russians as People* (New York: E. P. Dutton, 1961) is a perceptive interpretation of the Russian character and way of life by a knowledgeable observer.

Pipes, Richard, ed., *The Russian Intelligentsia* (New York: Columbia University Press, 1961) contains diverse essays, some of which are very penetrating.

Pyziur, Eugene, *The Doctrine of Anarchism of Michael A. Bakunin* (Chicago: Regnery, 1968) provides an incisive discussion of the origins and components of Bakunin's anarchism.

Utechin, S. V., *Russian Political Thought* (New York: Frederick A. Praeger, 1964) offers a concise introduction to the subject.

Venturi, Franco, *Roots of Revolution: A History of the Populist and Socialist Movements in Nineteenth Century Russia* (New York: Alfred A. Knopf, 1960) is an important work on Russian radicalism prior to 1881.

Von Laue, Theodore H., *Why Lenin? Why Stalin? A Reappraisal of the Russian Revolution, 1900–1930* (Philadelphia: J. B. Lippincott, 1964), apart from the historical narrative, provides a provocative and original interpretation of the revolution and modernization in terms of Russian conditions.

CHAPTER 3. THE IDEOLOGICAL HERITAGE

Acton, H. B., *What Marx Really Said* (New York: Schocken Books, 1967) offers a penetrating analysis of Marxism.

Anderson, Thornton, ed., *Masters of Russian Marxism* (New York: Appleton-Century-Crofts, 1963) offers appropriate selections from the writings of Lenin, Stalin, Plekhanov, Bukharin, Kollontai, and others.

Baron, Samuel H., *Plekhanov: The Father of Russian Marxism* (Stanford: Stanford University Press, 1963) is a thorough biography that discusses Plekhanov's relations with Lenin.

Berdyaev, Nicolas, *The Origin of Russian Communism* (Ann Arbor: University of Michigan Press, 1960) is an important work that stresses the Russian origins of the Soviet regime.

DeGeorge, Richard T., *Patterns of Soviet Thought; The Origins and Development of Dialectical and Historical Materialism* (Ann Arbor: University of Michigan Press, 1966) is a valuable introductory survey.

——, *Soviet Ethics and Morality* (Ann Arbor: University of Michigan Press, 1969) discusses the basic issues and questions in communist moral philosophy.

Drachkovitch, Milorad M., ed., *Marxist Ideology in the Contemporary World: Its Appeal and Paradoxes* (New York: Frederick A. Praeger, 1966) offers some highly thoughtful papers by prominent scholars.

Feuer, Lewis S., *Marx and the Intellectuals* (Garden City, N.Y.: Doubleday, 1969) is a stimulating collection of the author's thoughtful essays.

Gregor, A. James, *A Survey of Marxism* (New York: Random House, 1965) provides a concise and thoughtful introduction that also discusses Leninism.

Haimson, Leopold H., *The Russian Marxists and the Origins of Bolshevism* (Cambridge: Harvard University Press, 1955) deals with Lenin's Marxist precursors in the Russian Empire.

Hammond, Thomas T., *Lenin on Trade Unions and Revolution, 1893–1917* (New York: Columbia University Press, 1957) is a useful monograph for understanding Lenin's tactics.

Hunt, R. N. Carew, *The Theory and Practice of Communism,* 5th ed. (New York: Macmillan, 1958) remains one of the very best introductions to communist thought.

Jaworskyj, Michael, ed., *Soviet Political Thought: An Anthology* (Baltimore: Johns Hopkins Press, 1968) deals largely with lesser known Soviet writers on the theory of the state and law.

Kuusinen, Otto V., ed., *Fundamentals of Marxism-Leninism,* 2nd ed. (Moscow: Foreign Languages Publishing House, 1963) is the official CPSU statement of communist doctrine.

Leites, Nathan, *A Study of Bolshevism* (Glencoe, Ill.: Free Press, 1953) provides a massive novel analysis of "classical" Bolshevik doctrinal pronouncements.

Medvedev, Zhores A., *The Rise and Fall of T. D. Lysenko* (New York: Columbia University Press, 1969) is a Soviet scientist's account, unpublished in the U.S.S.R., concerning the high cost of Lysenko's doctrines in Soviet biology, dictated at the time by ideological considerations as understood by Stalin and Khrushchev.

Meyer, Alfred G., *Leninism* (Cambridge: Harvard University Press, 1957) provides an able survey of Lenin's more important political ideas.

Wetter, Gustav A., *Dialectical Materialism,* rev. ed. (New York: Frederick A. Praeger, 1958) is a basic work.

——, *Soviet Ideology Today* (New York: Frederick A. Praeger, 1966) provides an incisive critique of Soviet philosophical doctrines.

Wolfe, Bertram D., *Marxism: One Hundred Years in the Life of a Doctrine* (New York, Dial Press, 1965) is a penetrating historical work that deals with the various efforts to apply Marxism in the world of action.

CHAPTER 4. THE COMMUNIST PARTY OF THE SOVIET UNION: DEVELOPMENT AND ORGANIZATION

Armstrong, John A., *The Politics of Totalitarianism* (New York: Random House, 1961) is a carefully documented history of the CPSU from 1934 to 1960.

Balabanoff, Angelica, *Impressions of Lenin* (Ann Arbor: University of Michigan Press, 1964) is the valuable memoir of the first secretary of the Comintern and a close associate of Lenin's who broke with him.

Carr, Edward Hallett, *A History of Soviet Russia, The Bolshevik Revolution, 1917–1923,* 3 vols. (New York: Macmillan, 1950, 1951, 1953); *The Interregnum, 1923–1924* (New York: Macmillan, 1954); *Socialism in One Country, 1924–1926,* 3 vols. (New York: Macmillan, 1958, 1959, 1964) is a massive and highly detailed work, dealing with domestic and foreign policies, that is not likely to be equaled.

Chamberlin, William Henry, *The Russian Revolution, 1917–1921,* 2 vols. (New York: Macmillan, 1952) is a standard work on the subject first published in 1935.

Daniels, Robert V., *The Conscience of the Revolution* (Cambridge: Harvard University Press, 1960) is a thorough study of oppositionist movements in the CPSU through the 1920's.

Deutscher, Isaac, *The Prophet Armed: Trotsky, 1879–1921; The Prophet Unarmed: Trotsky, 1921–1929; The Prophet Outcast: Trotsky, 1929–1940* (New York: Oxford University Press, 1954, 1959, 1963) is a definitive though highly sympathetic 3-volume biography.

——, *Stalin, A Political Biography,* 2nd ed. (New York: Oxford University Press, 1967) remains a standard work.

Orlov, Alexander, *The Secret History of Stalin's Crimes* (New York: Random House, 1953) consists of revelations by a former NKVD officer who defected when ordered home while on duty in the Spanish Civil War.

Pipes, Richard, ed., *Revolutionary Russia* (Cambridge: Harvard University Press, 1968) is a valuable symposium on the 1917 Revolution.

Rabinowich, Alexander, *Prelude to Revolution: The Petrograd Bolsheviks and the July 1917 Uprising* (Bloomington, Ind.: Indiana University Press, 1968) discusses Lenin's role and the divisions among Bolsheviks over tactics in the summer of 1917.

Randall, Francis B., *Stalin's Russia: An Historical Reconsideration* (New York: Free Press, 1965) is a sprightly analytical history that emphasizes Stalin's willful and paranoid personality and his ideological convictions.

Reshetar, John S. Jr., *A Concise History of the Communist Party of the Soviet Union*, rev. ed. (New York: Frederick A. Praeger, 1964) provides a general survey of the Party's development.

Rigby, Thomas H., ed., *Stalin* (Englewood Cliffs, N.J.: Prentice-Hall, 1966) is an excellent compilation of diverse and well-chosen selections.

Schapiro, Leonard, *The Communist Party of the Soviet Union* (New York: Random House, 1960) is an able historical treatment.

——, *The Origin of the Communist Autocracy: Political Opposition in the Soviet State—First Phase, 1917–1922* (Cambridge: Harvard University Press, 1955) is an important monograph.

——, and Reddaway, Peter, eds., *Lenin: the Man, the Theorist, the Leader* (New York: Frederick A. Praeger, 1967) contains papers by twelve specialists who discuss Lenin's thought and activities.

Smith, Edward Ellis, *The Young Stalin: The Early Years of an Elusive Revolutionary* (New York: Farrar, Straus and Giroux, 1967) is a detailed and well-written biographical study dealing with the first thirty-seven years of Stalin's life and presenting the purely circumstantial evidence for the controversial hypothesis that Stalin was a tsarist secret police agent.

Sukhanov, N. N., *The Russian Revolution 1917, A Personal Record*, ed. Joel Carmichael (New York: Oxford University Press, 1955), is the most competent eyewitness account of the Revolution.

Treadgold, Donald W., *Lenin and His Rivals* (New York: Frederick A. Praeger, 1955) deals with Lenin's attitudes toward the non-Bolshevik parties prior to 1906.

Ulam, Adam B., *The Bolsheviks: The Intellectual and Political History of the Triumph of Communism in Russia* (New York: Macmillan, 1965) is a significant historical work that is primarily a biographical study of Lenin.

Wolfe, Bertram D., *Khrushchev and Stalin's Ghost* (New York: Frederick A. Praeger, 1956) includes the text of Khrushchev's "secret speech" with an incisive commentary.

——, *Three Who Made a Revolution* (New York: Dial Press, 1948) is a standard work, a triple biography of Lenin, Stalin, and Trotsky.

The functioning of the CPSU is dealt with in the following works:

Armstrong, John A., *The Soviet Bureaucratic Elite* (New York: Frederick A. Praeger, 1959) is a pioneer analysis of the Ukrainian Party apparatus.

Avtorkhanov, Abdurakhman, *The Communist Party Apparatus* (Chicago: Henry Regnery, 1966) is a detailed study by a former CPSU official.

Fainsod, Merle, *How Russia Is Ruled,* rev. ed. (Cambridge: Harvard University Press, 1963), is a basic work.

——, *Smolensk under Soviet Rule* (Cambridge: Harvard University Press, 1958) is an important study based on the captured files of the Smolensk *obkom* of the CPSU.

Hough, Jerry F., *The Soviet Prefects: The Local Party Organs in Industrial Decision-Making* (Cambridge: Harvard University Press, 1969) is a detailed study of relationships between *raikom, gorkom,* and *obkom* secretaries and industrial managers that also involves consideration of administrative theory.

Stewart, Philip D., *Political Power in the Soviet Union: A Study of Decision-Making in Stalingrad* (Indianapolis: Bobbs-Merrill, 1968) is a pioneer study of the Stalingrad (Volgograd) *obkom* from 1954 to 1960.

CHAPTER 5. THE COMMUNIST PARTY AND THE STRUCTURE OF POWER

Barghoorn, Frederick C., *Politics in the USSR* (Boston: Little, Brown, 1968) is an effort to apply to Soviet politics the structural-functional scheme of analysis developed by G. Almond.

Conquest, Robert, *Power and Policy in the U.S.S.R.* (New York: St. Martin's Press, 1961) is an outstanding example of detailed "Kremlinological" analysis.

Crankshaw, Edward, *Khrushchev: A Career* (New York: Viking Press, 1966) is a readable biography by a veteran journalist that stresses Khrushchev's personality and political style.

Dallin, Alexander and Larson, Thomas B., eds., *Soviet Politics since Khrushchev* (Englewood Cliffs, N.J.: Prentice-Hall, 1968) is a collection of essays by specialists on various areas of policy.

—— and Westin, Alan F., eds., *Politics in the Soviet Union: 7 Cases* (New York: Harcourt, Brace and World, 1966) is a collection of diverse studies, some of which are purely historical and others more analytical in nature.

Farrell, R. Barry, ed., *Political Leadership in Eastern Europe and the Soviet Union* (Chicago: Aldine, 1970) contains incisive essays and comments by a diverse group of scholars.

Frankland, Mark, *Khrushchev* (New York: Stein and Day, 1967) is a brief but well written essay in biography.

Gehlen, Michael P., *The Communist Party of the Soviet Union, A Functional Analysis* (Bloomington, Ind.: Indiana University Press, 1969) is a useful analysis, especially of the composition of central Party bodies for the 1956–66 period.

Juviler, Peter H. and Morton, Henry W., eds., *Soviet Policy-Making:*

Studies of Communism in Transition (New York: Frederick A. Praeger, 1967) offers various case studies ranging from family law to literature and foreign policy.

Leonhard, Wolfgang, *The Kremlin since Stalin* (New York: Frederick A. Praeger, 1962) provides a competent account of the Khrushchev era.

Linden, Carl A., *Khrushchev and the Soviet Leadership, 1957–1964* (Baltimore: Johns Hopkins Press, 1966) is a useful monograph that emphasizes the opposition to Khrushchev's leadership within the CPSU.

Pistrak, Lazar, *The Grand Tactician: Khrushchev's Rise to Power* (New York: Frederick A. Praeger, 1961) is an able and well-documented study especially valuable for its treatment of Khrushchev's early career.

Ploss, Sidney I., *Conflict and Decision-Making in Soviet Russia: A Case Study of Agricultural Policy, 1953–1963* (Princeton, N.J.: Princeton University Press, 1965) is a pioneer study of internal conflict within the Soviet leadership, although often relying on circumstantial evidence.

Rigby, Thomas H., *Communist Party Membership in the U.S.S.R., 1917–1967* (Princeton, N.J.: Princeton University Press, 1968) is a significant detailed compilation and analysis of all relevant statistics regarding Party membership.

Rush, Myron, *The Rise of Khrushchev* (Washington, D.C.: Public Affairs Press, 1958) is a brief monograph of special interest because of its reliance on minute "clues" in Kremlinological analysis.

Schueller, George K., *The Politburo* (Stanford: Stanford University Press, 1951) provides data on careers of Politburo members from 1917 to 1951; reprinted in Harold D. Lasswell and Daniel Lerner, eds., *World Revolutionary Elites* (Cambridge: M.I.T. Press, 1965).

Simmonds, George W., ed., *Soviet Leaders* (New York: Thomas Y. Crowell, 1967) contains extensive biographical sketches of forty-two prominent figures, including political leaders.

Swearer, Howard R. with Myron Rush, *The Politics of Succession in the USSR* (Boston: Little, Brown, 1964) offers an amalgam of analysis and documentary materials on Khrushchev's rise between 1953 and 1958.

Tatu, Michel, *Power in the Kremlin: From Khrushchev to Kosygin* (New York: Viking Press, 1968) is an admirably thorough reportorial work and thoughtful analysis of Soviet politics in the 1960's by an able journalist.

On the Komsomol see:

Fisher, Ralph T., Jr., *Pattern for Soviet Youth* (New York: Columbia University Press, 1959) is a historical study of the Komsomol Congresses from 1918 to 1954.

Kassof, Allen, *The Soviet Youth Program: Regimentation and Rebel-*

lion (Cambridge: Harvard University Press, 1965) is a brief but incisive sociological study that describes and critically appraises the Komsomol organization and its activities.

The activities of the Soviet secret police are discussed in:

Conquest, Robert, *The Great Terror: Stalin's Purges of the Thirties* (New York: Macmillan, 1968) is the definitive work on a grisly subject, essential to an understanding of Stalinism.

Deriabin, Peter and Gibney, Frank, *The Secret World* (Garden City, N.Y.: Doubleday, 1959) is a study of the Soviet secret police; Deriabin is a former MVD officer who defected.

Poretsky, Elisabeth K., *Our Own People* (Ann Arbor: University of Michigan Press, 1970). Soviet intelligence operations and the NKVD are discussed by the widow of the agent "Ignace Reiss," who defected in 1937 and was subsequently murdered.

Wolin, Simon and Slusser, Robert M., eds., *The Soviet Secret Police* (New York: Frederick A. Praeger, 1957) is especially valuable for its historical treatment of the subject and for its chapters written by former Soviet citizens with personal knowledge of the police.

Among the more important works on the Soviet military are:

Armstrong, John A., ed., *Soviet Partisans in World War II* (Madison: University of Wisconsin Press, 1964) is a valuable detailed study of Soviet guerrilla operations in papers by seven authors.

Bialer, Seweryn, ed., *Stalin and His Generals: Soviet Military Memoirs of World War II* (New York: Pegasus, 1969) contains revealing selections from memoirs of Soviet generals regarding political aspects of military affairs.

Erickson, John, *The Soviet High Command: A Military-Political History, 1918–1941* (New York: St. Martin's Press, 1962) is a thorough and well-documented work on Party-military relations.

Garthoff, Raymond L., *Soviet Military Policy, An Historical Analysis* (New York: Frederick A. Praeger, 1966) succinctly relates the Soviet military establishment to foreign policy.

Gouré, Leon, *The Siege of Leningrad* (Stanford: Stanford University Press, 1962) is a significant scholarly account of the twenty-eight-month siege in World War II that took one million lives.

Kolkowicz, Roman, *The Soviet Military and the Communist Party* (Princeton, N.J.: Princeton University Press, 1967) is a basic work.

Penkovskiy, Oleg, *The Penkovskiy Papers* (Garden City, N.Y.: Doubleday, 1965) contains the highly revealing observations of a colonel in Soviet military intelligence who became a spy for the West.

CHAPTER 6. THE CENTRAL GOVERNMENT

Carson, George Barr, Jr., *Electoral Practices in the USSR* (New York: Frederick A. Praeger, 1955) provides a thorough treatment of the subject, including its historical background.

Churchward, L. G., *Contemporary Soviet Government* (New York: American Elsevier Publishing Co., 1968) is a rather uncritical account written essentially from a Marxist-Leninist point of view.

Crowley, Edward L. et al., eds., *Party and Government Officials of the Soviet Union, 1917–1967* (Metuchen, N.J.: Scarecrow Press, 1969) is valuable for its listings of organizational changes and officeholders, compiled by the Institute for the Study of the USSR (Munich).

Denisov, A. and Kirichenko, M., *Soviet State Law* (Moscow: Foreign Languages Publishing House, 1960) is a typical Soviet textbook which omits much of significance.

Gripp, Richard C., *Patterns of Soviet Politics,* rev. ed. (Homewood, Ill.: Dorsey Press, 1967) provides a concise but broad introduction.

Hazard, John N., *The Soviet System of Government,* 4th ed. (Chicago: University of Chicago Press, 1968) offers a broad but brief introduction that relates Soviet government to some broader issues.

Mote, Max E., *Soviet Local and Republic Elections* (Stanford, Calif.: The Hoover Institution, 1965) is an important pioneer field study of the 1963 elections in Leningrad.

Schuman, Frederick L., *Government in the Soviet Union,* 2nd ed. (New York: Thomas Y. Crowell, 1967) provides a brief but stimulating introduction.

Scott, Derek J. R., *Russian Political Institutions,* 3rd ed. (New York: Frederick A. Praeger, 1966) is a brief but able work that stresses management and administration.

Towster, Julian, *Political Power in the USSR, 1917–1947* (New York: Oxford University Press, 1948) remains useful as a reference work.

CHAPTER 7. ADMINISTRATION: CENTRAL AND LOCAL

Azrael, Jeremy R., *Managerial Power and Soviet Politics* (Cambridge: Harvard University Press, 1966) discusses the development of economic management and its relationship to the CPSU.

Berliner, Joseph, *Factory and Manager in the USSR* (Cambridge: Harvard University Press, 1957) is a pioneer study of Soviet economic management based in part on interviews with former managers.

Davies, Robert W., *The Development of the Soviet Budgetary System* (New York: Cambridge University Press, 1958) provides a detailed historical account to 1941.

Granick, David, *The Red Executive* (Garden City, N.Y.: Doubleday, 1960) is an informative and readable study of Soviet industrial managers.

The Soviet legal system is discussed in the following works:

Berman, Harold J., *Justice in the USSR*, rev. ed. (New York: Random House, 1963) is a concise but broad treatment of the Soviet legal system.

——, ed., *Soviet Criminal Law and Procedure: The RSFSR Codes* (Cambridge: Harvard University Press, 1966) has an extensive introduction in addition to the texts of the RSFSR Criminal Code and Code of Criminal Procedure.

Gray, Whitmore, ed., *Soviet Civil Legislation* (Ann Arbor: University of Michigan School of Law, 1965) has a translation of the RSFSR Civil Code and is in a loose-leaf edition.

Grzybowski, Kazimierz, *Soviet Legal Institutions: Doctrines and Social Functions* (Ann Arbor: University of Michigan Press, 1962) endeavors to place the Soviet legal system in the civil law tradition and compares it with Western European systems.

Hazard, John N., *Law and Social Change in the USSR* (London: Stevens, 1953) has essays on various aspects of Soviet law, relating it to broader issues and including much valuable historical data.

——, *Settling Disputes in Soviet Society: The Formative Years of Legal Institutions* (New York: Columbia University Press, 1960) deals with the emergence of a structured judicial and legal system between 1917 and 1926.

——, Shapiro, Isaac and Maggs, Peter B., *The Soviet Legal System*, 2nd ed. (Dobbs Ferry, N.Y.: Oceana Publications, 1969) is a significant compilation of essays, documents, and commentary.

La Fave, Wayne R., ed., *Law in Soviet Society* (Urbana: University of Illinois Press, 1965) is a useful symposium of seven essays, some of which go beyond purely legal matters.

Morgan, Glenn G., *Soviet Administrative Legality: The Role of the Attorney General's Office* (Stanford: Stanford University Press, 1962) is a standard monograph on the Soviet Procuracy and its powers of "supervision."

Romashkin, P. S., ed., *Fundamentals of Soviet Law* (Moscow: Foreign Languages Publishing House, ca. 1961) provides a Soviet interpretation of the various fields of law.

On Soviet local government see:

Cattell, David T., *Leningrad: A Case Study of Soviet Urban Government* (New York: Frederick A. Praeger, 1968) is an important pioneer monograph based on limited field study.

CHAPTER 8. THE SOVIET POLITY: FUNCTIONS AND POLICIES

Ames, Edward, *Soviet Economic Processes* (Homewood, Ill.: Richard D. Irwin, 1965) offers a useful if somewhat technical analysis.

Feiwel, George R., *The Soviet Quest for Economic Efficiency: Issues, Controversies and Reforms* (New York: Frederick A. Praeger, 1967) provides a thorough account of various economic and management reform efforts.

Holzman, Franklyn D., *Soviet Taxation; the Fiscal and Monetary Problems of a Planned Economy* (Cambridge: Harvard University Press, 1955) provides a thorough discussion of the bases of the Soviet system of taxation.

Laird, Roy D. and Crowley, Edward L., eds., *Soviet Agriculture: The Permanent Crisis* (New York: Frederick A. Praeger, 1965) is a collection of papers on the agricultural policies and problems of the Khrushchev era.

—— and Laird, Betty A., *Soviet Communism and Agrarian Revolution* (Baltimore: Penguin Books, 1970) is a thoughtful evaluation of the entire collective farm system.

Nove, Alec, *The Soviet Economy, An Introduction,* rev. ed. (New York: Frederick A. Praeger, 1965) provides a substantial introductory treatment.

Schwartz, Harry, *An Introduction to the Soviet Economy* (Columbus, Ohio: Charles E. Merrill, 1968) provides a very succinct treatment.

Sherman, Howard J., *The Soviet Economy* (Boston: Little, Brown, 1969) provides a very good introduction to the economic system and its problems.

Among the works on educational and social policy, the following are important:

Bereday, George Z. F. and Pennar, Jaan, *The Politics of Soviet Education* (New York: Frederick A. Praeger, 1960) is a collection of brief but informative papers.

Bronfenbrenner, Urie, with the assistance of Condry, John C., Jr., *Two Worlds of Childhood, U.S. and U.S.S.R.* (New York: Russell Sage Foundation and Basic Books, 1970) is a significant comparative study.

Field, Mark G., *Soviet Socialized Medicine: An Introduction* (New

York: Free Press, 1967) is a very useful survey of the Soviet system of medical care.

Madison, Bernice Q., *Social Welfare in the Soviet Union* (Stanford: Stanford University Press, 1968) is an important work that stresses achievements and shortcomings of the Soviet welfare system.

McAuley, Mary, *Labor Disputes in Soviet Russia, 1957–1965* (New York: Oxford University Press, 1969) is a useful account of the kinds of labor disputes that can be aired in the Soviet Union.

Osborn, Robert J., *Soviet Social Policies: Welfare, Equality, and Community* (Homewood, Ill.: Dorsey Press, 1970) is a very useful survey dealing largely with educational opportunity, employment, and urban conditions.

Sorenson, Jay B., *The Life and Death of Soviet Trade Unionism, 1917–1928* (New York: Atherton Press, 1969) is a very readable historical account.

Among the works on Soviet nationalities and nationality policy, the following merit attention:

Allworth, Edward, ed., *Central Asia: A Century of Russian Rule* (New York: Columbia University Press, 1967) is an impressive collection of essays.

Armstrong, John A., *Ukrainian Nationalism*, 2nd ed. (New York: Columbia University Press, 1963) is an important study that relates Ukrainian nationalism to Soviet policies and to conditions during and after World War II.

Bacon, Elizabeth E., *Central Asians under Russian Rule, A Study in Cultural Change* (Ithaca, N.Y.: Cornell University Press, 1966) is a useful study of the impact of Russian rule on the Turkic peoples.

Barghoorn, Frederick C., *Soviet Russian Nationalism* (New York: Oxford University Press, 1956) explores the Soviet regime's reliance upon Russian nationalism as a source of support.

Bilinsky, Yaroslav, *The Second Soviet Republic: The Ukraine after World War II* (New Brunswick, N.J.: Rutgers University Press, 1964) is an important study offering extensive documentation and analysis.

Borys, Jurij, *The Russian Communist Party and the Sovietization of Ukraine, A Study in the Communist Doctrine of Self-Determination of Nations* (Stockholm, 1960) is a detailed and exhaustively documented work on the development and application of Leninist nationality policy.

Caroe, Sir Olaf, *Soviet Empire, The Turks of Central Asia and Stalinism*, 2nd ed. (New York: St. Martin's Press, 1967) is a historical account of Soviet policy in Turkestan.

Chornovil, Vyacheslav, ed. and compiler, *The Chornovil Papers* (New York: McGraw-Hill, 1969) contains very revealing materials and documents compiled by a Soviet Ukrainian journalist on the arrests and trials of numerous Ukrainian intellectuals in 1965–66 for protesting the violation of constitutional rights of Ukrainians by the Soviet regime.

Conquest, Robert, *Soviet Deportation of Nationalities* (New York: St. Martin's Press, 1960) is a carefully documented account of the deportation of Chechens, Crimean Tatars, and others during World War II. A revised edition was published in London by Macmillan in 1970 under the title, *The Nation Killers; The Soviet Deportation of Nationalities.*

Dmytryshyn, Basil, *Moscow and the Ukraine, 1918–1953* (New York: Bookman Associates, 1956) provides a very competent historical survey.

Dzyuba, Ivan, *Internationalism or Russification? A Study in the Soviet Nationalities Problem* (London: Weidenfeld and Nicolson, 1968) is a carefully documented—even scholarly—appeal by a prominent Soviet Ukrainian literary critic who has laid bare the essence of Soviet nationality policy, skillfully basing his case on the writings of Lenin and on official CPSU statements.

Goldhagen, Erich, ed., *Ethnic Minorities in the Soviet Union* (New York: Frederick A. Praeger, 1968) is a valuable symposium which includes general analytical papers as well as separate papers on the major non-Russian nationalities.

Kochan, Lionel, ed., *The Jews in Soviet Russia since 1917* (New York: Oxford University Press, 1970) surveys the changing status of the Soviet Jews in a series of papers.

Kolasky, John, *Education in Soviet Ukraine, A Study in Discrimination and Russification* (Toronto: Peter Martin Associates, 1968) is a documented study based on two years of residence and personal observation in Soviet Ukraine.

Kostiuk, Hryhory, *Stalinist Rule in the Ukraine; A Study of the Decade of Mass Terror, 1929–1939* (New York: Frederick A. Praeger, 1960) analyzes very closely a tragic period.

Low, Alfred D., *Lenin on the Question of Nationality* (New York: Bookman Associates, 1958) is a very useful monograph.

Matossian, Mary Kilbourne, *The Impact of Soviet Policies in Armenia* (Leiden: E. J. Brill, 1962) provides a historical treatment of Soviet policies in Armenia in the 1920's and 1930's.

Mazlakh, Serhii and Shakhrai, Vasyl', *On the Current Situation in the Ukraine*, ed. Peter J. Potichnyj, intro. Michael M. Luther (Ann Arbor: University of Michigan Press, 1970), is an annotated translation of *Do Khvyli*, the first statement of national communism critical of Lenin, published in Ukrainian in Saratov in 1919.

Rakowska-Harmstone, Teresa, *Russia and Nationalism in Central Asia; The Case of Tadzhikistan* (Baltimore: Johns Hopkins Press, 1970) is a valuable case study.

Schwarz, Solomon M., *The Jews in the Soviet Union* (Syracuse, N.Y.: Syracuse University Press, 1951) provides useful historical background.

Sullivant, Robert S., *Soviet Politics and the Ukraine, 1917–1957* (New York: Columbia University Press, 1962) ably traces the development of nationality policy as applied to the Ukrainian S.S.R.

Tillett, Lowell R., *The Great Friendship; Soviet Historians on the Non-Russian Nationalities* (Chapel Hill: University of North Carolina Press, 1969) is a valuable study of Soviet historiography as it has affected the interpretation of Russian colonialism and ethnic relations.

Vakar, Nicholas P., *Belorussia, The Making of a Nation* (Cambridge: Harvard University Press, 1956) is a substantial work.

Vardys, V. Stanley, ed., *Lithuania under the Soviets: Portrait of a Nation, 1940–1965* (New York: Frederick A. Praeger, 1965) is a useful collection of papers written principally by Lithuanian émigrés.

The following works relating to Soviet policy in the areas of religion and the arts are important:

Curtiss, John S., *The Russian Church and the Soviet State, 1917–1950* (Boston: Little, Brown, 1953) is a scholarly historical treatment.

Fletcher, William C., *Nikolai: Portrait of a Dilemma* (New York: Macmillan, 1968) is a study of the late Metropolitan, who attempted to resist the assault on religion.

——, and Strover, Anthony J., eds., *Religion and the Search for New Ideals in the USSR* (New York: Frederick A. Praeger, 1967) offers informative papers by eleven authors.

Kolarz, Walter, *Religion in the Soviet Union* (New York: St. Martin's Press, 1962) is a very thorough survey that includes treatment of smaller sects, encyclopedic in scope.

Blake, Patricia and Hayward, Max, eds., *Dissonant Voices in Soviet Literature* (New York: Pantheon, 1962) is a convenient if incomplete anthology of writers who have challenged the canons of "socialist realism."

Ehrenburg, Ilya, *Memoirs: 1921–1941, The War: 1941–1945, Post-War Years: 1945–1954* (Cleveland: World Publishing Company, 1964, 1965, 1967) are the valuable recollections of a prominent Soviet writer and journalist who saw much and who managed to survive the various purges.

Hayward, Max, ed., *On Trial: The Soviet State versus "Abram Tertz" and "Nikolai Arzhak"* (New York: Harper and Row, 1966) is an unofficial but undoubtedly authentic transcript of the 1966 trial of the writers Andrei Siniavsky and Iuli Daniel.

Swayze, Harold, *Political Control of Literature in the USSR, 1946–1959* (Cambridge: Harvard University Press, 1962) is a detailed study of the various CPSU decrees, speeches, activities of the Writers' Union and of literary critics and their impact on literature.

CHAPTER 9. SOVIET FOREIGN POLICY

Allen, Robert L., *Soviet Economic Warfare* (Washington, D.C.: Public Affairs Press, 1960) relates Soviet foreign trade policy and practices exclusively to political objectives.

Aspaturian, Vernon V., *The Union Republics in Soviet Diplomacy* (Geneva: Droz, 1960) is a very useful pioneer monograph on a neglected subject.

Barghoorn, Frederick C., *The Soviet Cultural Offensive* (Princeton, N.J.: Princeton University Press, 1960) is a study of Soviet cultural diplomacy and the use of exchanges.

——, *Soviet Foreign Propaganda* (Princeton, N.J.: Princeton University Press, 1964) is a useful survey and analysis of the targets, themes, and techniques of the Soviet propaganda organization.

Beloff, Max, *The Foreign Policy of Soviet Russia, 1929–1941,* 2 vols. (London: Oxford University Press, 1947–1949) provides a sequel to the 2-volume study by Louis Fischer.

Bishop, Donald, *The Roosevelt-Litvinov Agreements: The American View* (Syracuse, N.Y.: Syracuse University Press, 1965) is an important study on the establishment of diplomatic relations in 1933 in terms of the tactics employed by Moscow and the worth of the agreements.

Brzezinski, Zbigniew K., *The Soviet Bloc: Unity and Conflict,* rev. ed. (Cambridge: Harvard University Press, 1967) is an important study of the contradictory relations between communist states.

Cornell, Richard, *Youth and Communism: An Historical Analysis of International Communist Youth Movements* (New York: Walker, 1965) provides a brief but reliable survey.

Dallin, Alexander et al., *The Soviet Union and Disarmament* (New York: Frederick A. Praeger, 1964) surveys the background of Soviet policy.

Dallin, Alexander, *The Soviet Union at the United Nations* (New York: Frederick A. Praeger, 1962) is a standard work.

Dallin, David J., *Soviet Espionage* (New Haven: Yale University Press, 1955) provides much data on a difficult subject.

——, *Soviet Foreign Policy after Stalin* (Philadelphia: Lippincott, 1961) remains an important study of the reorientation of Soviet policy in the 1950's.

Degras, Jane, ed., *The Communist International, 1919–1943,* 3 vols. (New York: Oxford University Press, 1956, 1960, 1965) presents the history of the Third International in documents.

——, *Soviet Documents on Foreign Policy, 1917–1941,* 3 vols. (New York: Oxford University Press, 1951–1953) is an important source.

Eudin, Xenia J. and Fisher, Harold H., eds., *Soviet Russia and the West, 1920–1927, A Documentary Survey* (Stanford: Stanford University Press, 1957) and Eudin, Xenia J. and North, Robert C., eds., *Soviet Russia and the East, 1920–1927, A Documentary Survey* (Stanford: Stanford University Press, 1957) are significant compilations.

Eudin, Xenia J. and Slusser, Robert M., eds., *Soviet Foreign Policy, 1928–1934; Documents and Materials,* 2 vols. (University Park, Pa.: Pennsylvania State University Press, 1967) is a Hoover Institution publication that provides lengthy analyses along with significant documents.

Fischer, Louis, *The Soviets in World Affairs,* 2 vols. (1929; reprinting by Princeton University Press, 1951) remains an original work because of the author's access to rare data.

Gehlen, Michael P., *The Politics of Coexistence: Soviet Methods and Motives* (Bloomington: Indiana University Press, 1967) provides a useful introduction in terms of doctrinal, strategic, and tactical considerations.

Goodman, Elliot R., *The Soviet Design for a World State* (New York: Columbia University Press, 1960) is a well-documented study.

Gouré, Leon, *Civil Defense in the Soviet Union* (Berkeley: University of California Press, 1962) demonstrates that the Soviet leadership has made preparations for civil defense.

Griffith, William E., *Albania and the Sino-Soviet Rift* (Cambridge: M.I.T. Press, 1963) is a carefully detailed account of the deterioration of Soviet-Albanian relations prior to 1961.

——, *The Sino-Soviet Rift, Analyzed and Documented* (Cambridge: M.I.T. Press, 1964) concentrates on the intensification of the rift in 1963–64.

Grzybowski, Kazimierz, *Soviet Public International Law, Doctrines and Diplomatic Practice* (Durham, N.C.: Rule of Law Press, 1970) is a detailed and thorough study.

Horelick, Arnold L. and Rush, Myron, *Strategic Power and Soviet Foreign Policy* (Chicago: University of Chicago Press, 1966) is an incisive analysis of the relationship of Soviet military capabilities and foreign policy objectives and tactics.

Jacobson, Harold K., *The USSR and the UN's Economic and Social Activities* (Notre Dame, Ind.: University of Notre Dame Press, 1963) explores in considerable detail Soviet policy regarding the nonpolitical activities of the U.N.

Kaznacheev, Aleksandr, *Inside a Soviet Embassy: Experiences of a Russian Diplomat in Burma* (Philadelphia: J. B. Lippincott, 1962) is a revealing account by an attaché who defected from the Soviet embassy in Rangoon in 1959.

Kennan, George F., *Russia and the West under Lenin and Stalin* (Boston: Little, Brown, 1961), although somewhat uneven in coverage, is the author's principal work of a general nature on Soviet foreign policy.

Kulski, Wladyslaw W., *Peaceful Co-existence: An Analysis of Soviet Foreign Policy* (Chicago: Henry Regnery, 1959) provides a very detailed and critical study of Soviet objectives.

Lederer, Ivo J., ed., *Russian Foreign Policy: Essays in Historical Perspective* (New Haven: Yale University Press, 1962) is an excellent collection of papers emphasizing continuity and differences between tsarist and Soviet policy.

Mayer, Peter, *Cohesion and Conflict in International Communism* (The Hague: Martinus Nijhoff, 1968) is a well-documented study emphasizing doctrinal factors.

McKenzie, Kermit E., *Comintern and World Revolution, 1928–1943: The Shaping of Doctrine* (New York: Columbia University Press, 1964) is a detailed examination of the problems of world revolution as related to the development of communist theory and Comintern practice.

McLane, Charles B., *Soviet Strategies in Southeast Asia* (Princeton, N.J.: Princeton University Press, 1966) is a substantial study confined to the Lenin and Stalin periods.

McNeal, Robert H., *International Relations among Communists* (Englewood Cliffs, N.J.: Prentice-Hall, 1967) is a brief documentary study.

Mosely, Philip E., *The Kremlin and World Politics* (New York: Random House, 1960) is a collection of incisive essays and papers by a veteran scholar and diplomat.

Nogee, Joseph L., *Soviet Policy towards International Control of Atomic Energy* (Notre Dame, Ind.: University of Notre Dame Press, 1961) traces negotiations on atomic energy from 1945 to 1960 in terms of Soviet "gamesmanship."

Ra'anan, Uri, *The USSR Arms the Third World* (Cambridge: M.I.T. Press, 1969) concentrates in detail on Soviet military aid to Egypt and Indonesia.

Rosser, Richard F., *An Introduction to Soviet Foreign Policy* (Englewood Cliffs, N.J.: Prentice-Hall, 1969) provides a convenient, largely chronological, brief account.

Rubinstein, Alvin Z., *The Soviets in International Organizations* (Princeton, N.J.: Princeton University Press, 1964) is an important study of Soviet policy in certain of the U.N.'s specialized agencies.

Rush, Myron, ed., *The International Situation and Soviet Foreign Policy: Reports of Soviet Leaders* (Columbus, Ohio: Charles E. Merrill, 1969) is a compilation of important official statements from 1918 to 1969.

Seton-Watson, Hugh, *From Lenin to Khrushchev*, 2nd ed. (New York:

Frederick A. Praeger, 1960) is a broad but detailed study of world communism and its relationship to Soviet domestic developments.

Shulman, Marshall D., *Stalin's Foreign Policy Reappraised* (Cambridge: Harvard University Press, 1963) advances the thesis that the post-Stalin foreign policy began in the last years of the dictator's regime.

Triska, Jan F. and Finley, David D., *Soviet Foreign Policy* (New York: Macmillan, 1968), in addition to providing a general analytical treatment of the subject, endeavors to employ quantitative methods and has an extensive bibliography.

Triska, Jan F. and Slusser, Robert M., *The Theory, Law and Policy of Soviet Treaties* (Stanford: Stanford University Press, 1962) is a valuable analysis of Soviet practice regarding observance of treaties over four decades.

Ulam, Adam B., *Expansion and Coexistence; The History of Soviet Foreign Policy, 1917–1967* (New York: Frederick A. Praeger, 1968) offers a lengthy but lively and thoughtful treatment of the subject.

Warth, Robert D., *Soviet Russia in World Politics* (New York: Twayne, 1963) provides a useful historical introduction and has an extensive bibliography.

Wesson, Robert G., *Soviet Foreign Policy in Perspective* (Homewood, Ill.: Dorsey Press, 1969) offers a thoughtful appraisal along with a general survey.

Zagoria, Donald S., *The Sino-Soviet Conflict, 1956–1961* (Princeton, N.J.: Princeton University Press, 1962) discusses the immediate origins of the rift.

Zimmerman, William, *Soviet Perspectives on International Relations, 1956–1967* (Princeton, N.J.: Princeton University Press, 1969) examines the changing appraisal of international politics by Soviet writers and includes much bibliographical data.

CHAPTER 10. THE SOVIET POLITY: PROBLEMS AND PROSPECTS

Amalrik, Andrei, *Will the Soviet Union Survive until 1984?* (New York: Harper and Row, 1970) is a Soviet writer's penetrating appraisal of the regime's future prospects.

Brumberg, Abraham, ed., *In Quest of Justice; Protest and Dissent in the Soviet Union Today* (New York: Frederick A. Praeger, 1970) is a valuable compilation of documents and materials.

Brzezinski, Zbigniew and Huntington, Samuel P., *Political Power: USA/USSR* (New York: Viking Press, 1963) is an imaginative study that compares leadership, political ideas, policy-making, and problems in the two countries and explores the question of convergence.

Conquest, Robert, *Russia after Khrushchev* (New York: Frederick A. Praeger, 1965) stresses the threat of instability and the problems facing the Soviet leadership.

Fleron, Frederic J., ed., *Communist Studies and the Social Sciences* (Chicago: Rand McNally, 1969) is a very useful collection of methodological essays.

Hollander, Paul, ed., *American and Soviet Society: A Reader in Comparative Sociology and Perception* (Englewood Cliffs, N.J.: Prentice-Hall, 1969) is a compilation of selections from the writings of sociologists of the two countries organized in terms of population, social stratification, social problems, values, and the like.

Inkeles, Alex and Bauer, Raymond A., *The Soviet Citizen: Daily Life in a Totalitarian Society* (Cambridge: Harvard University Press, 1959) is an important sociological analysis based on data from Soviet refugees.

Johnson, Chalmers, ed., *Change in Communist Systems* (Stanford: Stanford University Press, 1970) is a collection of perceptive essays by twelve specialists.

Kanet, Roger E., ed., *The Behavioral Revolution and Communist Studies* (New York: Free Press, 1970) is a compendium of selections that stresses empirical and new theoretical approaches.

Kassof, Allen, ed., *Prospects for Soviet Society* (New York: Frederick A. Praeger, 1968) is a useful collection of papers by eighteen specialists on various sectors and problems of Soviet society.

Rush, Myron, *Political Succession in the USSR*, rev. ed. (New York: Columbia University Press, 1965) is a brief but thoughtful work on the significant problem in Soviet politics.

Schapiro, Leonard, ed., and Boiter, Albert, assoc. ed., *The U.S.S.R. and the Future* (New York: Frederick A. Praeger, 1963) contains seventeen critical essays on various aspects of the 1961 CPSU Program.

Sharlet, Robert, *Soviet Modernization, Building a Communist System in the U.S.S.R.* (New York: Pegasus, 1970) explores the problems attendant upon urbanization and industrialization and their relationship to system maintenance and Party control.

Simirenko, Alex, ed., *Soviet Sociology, Historical Antecedents and Current Appraisals* (Chicago: Quadrangle Books, 1966) defines the limits of sociological research and writing in the U.S.S.R.

——, *Social Thought in the Soviet Union* (Chicago: Quadrangle Books, 1969) contains twelve essays by specialists on developments in the various social sciences and related fields in the U.S.S.R.

POLITICAL NOVELS

The novels listed here are of varying literary quality, convey different degrees of information regarding life in the Soviet Union, and emphasize particular aspects of the system or a historical period. A political novel is obviously not significant as a source of empirical data, for it may deviate from historical fact and may exaggerate or minimize an event or development. Yet the novel can in its own way be more "true" for certain purposes than a body of empirical data. Fiction can serve as a means of perceiving and interpreting reality more accurately. If novels do not provide *the* key to an understanding of the Soviet polity, they can lay bare a problem, scrutinize a facet of the structure, capture the temper of a period, and convey something of the ethos of the system. Few works are literary classics or near-classics, but even literature that is not great can still be read with profit. Unfortunately something can be muted or even lost in translation. Yet, despite all such caveats the political novel can serve as an important collateral source that offers many insights.

Abramov, Fyodor, *One Day in the "New Life"* (New York: Frederick A. Praeger, 1963), originally entitled *Round and About,* deals with the frustrations and disillusionment of a communist chairman of a collective farm and offers a realistic depiction of Soviet rural life.

Bulgakov, Mikhail, *Heart of a Dog* (New York: Grove Press and Harcourt, Brace, 1968) is a biting satire at the expense of Soviet officialdom, written in 1925 and not published in the Soviet Union.

Chukovskaya, Lydia, *The Deserted House* (New York: E. P. Dutton, 1967) conveys the tribulations of a courageous Leningrad widow during the nightmare of the Stalin terror.

Dudintsev, Vladimir, *Not by Bread Alone* (New York: E. P. Dutton, 1957) tells of an impractical inventor who does battle with the Soviet bureaucracy, which is depicted in all its grossness.

Ehrenburg, Ilya, *The Thaw* (Chicago: Henry Regnery, 1955) is important chiefly for its depicting conditions in the immediate post-Stalin period and daring to deal with such forbidden themes as official art versus nonconformist free art and individuals seeking to regain a measure of spontaneity following the Stalinist "freeze."

Gouzenko, Igor, *The Fall of a Titan* (New York: W. W. Norton, 1954) is a large-scale novel dealing with the demise of Maxim Gorky and was written by a famous defector who uncovered a Soviet spy ring in Canada in 1945.

Koestler, Arthur, *The Age of Longing* (New York: Macmillan, 1951), which depicts the pessimistic temper of Western Europe in the early 1950's and the politics of the European intelligentsia, also provides a characterization of a certain type of Soviet official and of the communist mentality.

——, *Darkness at Noon* (New York: Macmillan, 1940) is a near-classic based on the Moscow purge trials and the ritual of confession as performed by an old revolutionary.

Nekrasov, Victor, *Kira Georgievna* (New York: Pantheon Books, 1962) is a not entirely successful novella about the life story of a sculptress and the three men in her life, and the return of her first husband from twenty years of imprisonment and Siberian exile; it conveys the passivity and fatalism of much of Soviet life.

Pasternak, Boris, *Doctor Zhivago* (New York: Pantheon Books, 1958) is a historical novel that depicts the Russian Revolution in terms of personal life-histories against a broad canvas and offers a harsh judgment on revolution and civil war.

Salisbury, Harrison E., *The Northern Palmyra Affair* (New York: Harper, 1962) deals with Leningrad in Stalin's time under siege and in the postwar period—depicting the Soviet bureaucracy, the purges, and day-to-day life.

Serge, Victor, *The Case of Comrade Tulayev* (Garden City, N.Y.: Doubleday, 1950) offers a grim and dramatic account of the excesses of the Stalinist dictatorship in the 1930's by an old revolutionary and Trotskyite who left the Soviet Union in 1936.

Sholokhov, Mikhail, *And Quiet Flows the Don* (New York: Alfred A. Knopf, 1941). *The Don Flows to the Sea* (New York: Alfred A. Knopf, 1941). *Seeds of Tomorrow* (New York: Alfred A. Knopf, 1935). Also published as *Virgin Soil Upturned. Harvest on the Don* (New York: Alfred A. Knopf, 1961). These novels all deal in an earthy manner with the revolution and civil war in the Don River region and with the realities of collectivization and opposition to it; the author, the CPSU's leading writer-member, has been awarded the Nobel Prize, has served the regime and remained in its good graces.

Solzhenitsyn, Aleksandr, *Cancer Ward* (New York: Dial Press, 1968) offers vivid contrasts of freely speaking characters brought together in a hospital in 1955 and depicts the injustices inflicted upon the hero, Kostoglotov, a victim of Stalinism deprived of nearly everything at the age of thirty-four.

——, *The First Circle* (New York: Harper, 1968) is a story of imprisoned scientists and intellectuals conducting research in 1949 while incarcerated, and stresses the deception and irony of Stalinism.

——, *One Day in the Life of Ivan Denisovich* (New York: E. P. Dutton, 1963; Frederick A. Praeger, 1963) depicts the relentless struggle of an ordinary man for physical and spiritual survival in a concentration camp, as seen through the eyes of the prisoner; the novel created great controversy after Khrushchev permitted its publication; the two English translations differ markedly.

Tarsis, Valerii, *The Bluebottle* (New York: Alfred A. Knopf, 1963) contains this and another novella, *Red and Black,* by a bitterly satirical anticommunist writer who became completely alienated and was permitted to leave the Soviet Union in 1966.

——, *Ward 7; An Autobiographical Novel* (New York: E. P. Dutton, 1965) deals with the practice of incarcerating political dissenters in mental hospitals.

Wilson, Mitchell, *Meeting at a Far Meridian* (Garden City, N.Y.: Doubleday, 1961) deals with an American physicist in Moscow and with the Soviet scientific establishment; the author is one of the most popular American novelists in the Soviet Union.

Yurasov, Vladimir, *Parallax* (New York: W. W. Norton, 1966) is a partly autobiographical novel by a former Soviet army officer who defected and who depicts postwar Stalinism in the U.S.S.R. and in Germany in terms of the careers of an officer who defects and another who returns home.

Zamiatin, Eugene, *We* (New York: E. P. Dutton, 1924, 1952). A Russian precursor of George Orwell depicts the hypertrophy of totalitarianism in a famous utopian novel.

Zoshchenko, Mikhail, *Nervous People and Other Satires* (New York: Pantheon, 1963).

——, *Scenes from the Bathhouse and Other Stories of Communist Russia* (Ann Arbor: University of Michigan Press, 1961). These are difficult to translate novellas and humorous stories by the boldest of Soviet satirists, who stressed the ironic and absurd in Soviet life and was attacked by the Politburo member Andrei Zhdanov in 1946.

GLOSSARY

advokat member of a group of lawyers engaged in the practice of law.

Agitprop Department of Propaganda and Agitation of the CPSU Central Committee.

agitpunkt (*agitatsionnyi punkt*) a propaganda station or agitation center used in elections or other campaigns.

aktiv the leading cadres and most active members of an organization or society including the CPSU.

apparat the administrative apparatus of the Soviet state or of the CPSU.

artel' a voluntary association of persons engaged in production, as in agriculture, manufacturing, or fishing and having a claim to a share of its income.

blat an illicit or questionable economic transaction often entered into in order to fulfill production quotas; in conversational usage, "pull" or protection.

Cheka the original Soviet secret police organization.

Chekist a member of the Cheka or of any of its successor organizations.
chistka literally "cleansing" or purging of personnel.
dekret decree, a term used prior to 1936 when it was replaced by *ukaz.*
domkom (*domovyi komitet*) house committee, a voluntary but elected body that organizes activities in housing developments.
DOSAAF (*Dobrovol'noe obshchestvo sodeistviia armii, aviatsii i flotu*) The Voluntary Society for Assistance to the Army, Air Force, and Navy—the Soviet civil defense organization.
druzhiny volunteer semiofficial organizations of aides to the police.
edinonachalie single command or one-man control and responsibility in management and administration.
General'nyi Prokuror SSSR the Procurator (Attorney) General of the U.S.S.R.
Glavlit (*Glavnoe upravlenie po delam literatury i izdatel'stv*) Chief Administration of Literary and Publishing Affairs. The term is still employed to refer to the successor organization responsible for censorship, the Chief Administration for the Protection of State Secrets in the Press.
glavnoe upravlenie chief administration.
gorispolkom (*gorodskoi ispolnitel'nyi komitet*) the executive committee of a city soviet.
gorkom (*gorodskoi komitet*) committee of a city CPSU organization.
gorod city.
Gosarbitrazh the system of state arbitration bodies that resolve disputes involving property and fulfillment of contracts between enterprises.
Gosbank (*Gosudarstvennyi Bank*) the State Bank of the U.S.S.R.
Gosplan SSSR (*Gosudarstvennyi Planovyi Komitet*) State Planning Committee of the U.S.S.R.
ispolkom (*ispolnitel'nyi komitet*) executive committee.
iuriskonsul't · legal counsel in the permanent employ of an enterprise or institution.
izbiratel'nyi okrug constituency or election district.
KGB (*Komitet Gosudarstvennoi Bezopasnosti*) Committee of State Security, the secret police.
khoziain boss, master, "owner"—used to refer to Stalin but not applied exclusively to him.
khuliganstvo activity that grossly violates social order, indicating a lack of respect for society; rowdyism, ruffianism.
kolkhoz (*kollektivnoe khoziaistvo*) collective farm.
kollegiia a board of officials summoned for consultation; also used to refer to a group of lawyers engaged in legal practice.

Komsomol (*Kommunisticheskii soiuz molodezhi*) Young Communist League.

KPSS (*Kommunisticheskaia partiia Sovetskogo Soiuza*) Communist Party of the Soviet Union (CPSU).

krai territory.

kraiispolkom (*kraevoi ispolnitel'nyi komitet*) executive committee of a territory soviet.

kraikom (*kraevoi komitet*) committee of a territory CPSU organization.

kulak literally "fist," used to refer to a "wealthy" peasant who allegedly exploited hired labor.

kul't lichnosti the cult of personality, based on an exaggerated emphasis on the role of an individual in history; a euphemism usually employed to refer to the less attractive features of Stalin's regime.

mestnichestvo localism, placing the interests of one's locale ahead of those of the state.

militsiia the ordinary Soviet police.

ministerstvo ministry of the U.S.S.R., a union republic, or an autonomous republic.

MVD (*Ministerstvo Vnutrennikh Del*) Ministry of Internal Affairs.

narodnyi sud people's court.

narodnyi zasedatel' people's assessor, a lay person who serves as a temporary member of all Soviet courts hearing civil and criminal cases but who does not participate in appellate proceedings.

natsional'nyi okrug an ethnically distinctive part of an *oblast'* or *krai* constituting a separate administrative and territorial subdivision such as that of the Chukchi.

NEP (*Novaia Ekonomicheskaia Politika*) New Economic Policy initiated by Lenin in 1921.

notariat the system of state-operated notarial offices.

obkom (*oblastnoi komitet*) committee of a CPSU province organization.

oblast' province.

oblispolkom (*oblastnoi ispolnitel'nyi komitet*) executive committee of a province soviet.

Oktiabriata Little Octobrists, Communist children's organization for those in the seven to nine age group.

okrug area (either electoral or ethnic).

otdel department (or section), usually of the CPSU Secretariat or of a ministry.

partiinost' party-mindedness in terms of acts and teachings that promote the CPSU's objectives.

pervichnaia partiinaia organizatsiia primary party organization.

piatiletka five-year plan, usually for economic development.

Pionery the Young Pioneers, Communist children's organization for ages nine to fourteen.

plenum plenary session of a body as, for example, the Central Committee, one attended by all members.

politruk (*politicheskii rukovoditel'*) political instructor.

poselok settlement, often referred to as a *rabochii poselok* (workers' settlement) or a *dachnyi poselok* (settlement of suburban homes).

postanovlenie an ordinance or act issued by the Supreme Soviet or its Presidium or by a council of ministers in fulfillment of a law; also refers to acts adopted by a plenary session of the U.S.S.R. Supreme Court.

predsedatel' chairman.

prezidium presidium or presiding council.

profsoiuz (*professional'nyi soiuz*) trade union.

prokuratura the unified system of state attorneys.

protektsiia patronage, influence, wire-pulling.

rasporiazhenie a regulation of an operational character issued by a council of ministers or by a local soviet, usually directing an agency to undertake certain actions.

raiispolkom (*raionnyi ispolnitel'nyi komitet*) executive committee of a district soviet.

raikom (*raionnyi komitet*) committee of a district CPSU organization.

raion district, either rural or an urban borough.

reshenie the decision of a soviet or its executive body.

samokritika self-criticism.

seksot (*sekretnyi sotrudnik*) secret collaborator of or informer for the secret police.

selo village.

sel'sovet (*sel'skii sovet*) village soviet.

semeistvennost' family relations or "nepotism," denoting collusion and a closeness between officials designed for mutual protection.

sledovatel' investigating official, interrogator conducting preliminary investigation in criminal cases.

soveshchatel'nyi golos "consultative vote" giving a candidate-member or delegate the right to speak but not to cast a vote.

Sovet Ministrov Council of Ministers.

Sovet Natsional'nostei Soviet (Council) of Nationalities, a chamber of the U.S.S.R. Supreme Soviet.

Sovet Soiuza Soviet (Council) of the Union, a chamber of the U.S.S.R. Supreme Soviet.

Sovet Stareishin Council of Elders.

sovkhoz (*sovetskoe khoziaistvo*) state farm.

sovnarkhoz (*sovet narodnogo khoziaistva*) economic council.

sovnarkom (*sovet narodnykh komissarov*) executive and administrative body that was renamed the Council of Ministers in 1946.

tekhnikum vocational or technical school.

tolkach a "pusher," one who expedites business transactions and serves as a factory representative.

tovarishcheskii sud comradely court.

Ts K Central Committee of the CPSU or of a union republic.

uchastok election precinct or polling place.

ukaz decree issued by Presidium of Supreme Soviet.

Verkhovnyi Sovet Supreme Soviet of the U.S.S.R., a union republic, or an autonomous republic.

Verkhovnyi Sud Supreme Court.

vuz (*vysshee uchebnoe zavedenie*) higher educational institution.

zakon statute.

zampolit (*zamestitel' komandira po politicheskim voprosam*) deputy military commander for political affairs.

zveno smallest unit of Young Pioneers, also a small work unit ("link") on a collective farm.

INDEX

Printed in USA